Natural Resources and the Green Economy

Queen Mary Studies in International Law

Edited by

Malgosia Fitzmaurice
Panos Merkouris
Phoebe Okowa

VOLUME 10

The titles published in this series are listed at brill.com/qmil

Natural Resources and the Green Economy

Redefining the Challenges for People, States and Corporations

Edited by

Elena Blanco and Jona Razzaque

MARTINUS
NIJHOFF
PUBLISHERS

LEIDEN · BOSTON
2012

Library of Congress Cataloging-in-Publication Data

Natural resources and the green economy : redefining the challenges for people, states and corporations / edited by Elena Blanco and Jona Razzaque.
p. cm. -- (Queen Mary studies in international law ; v. 10)
Includes bibliographical references and index.
ISBN 978-90-04-22706-4 (hardback : alk. paper)
1. Conservation of natural resources--Law and legislation. 2. Sustainable development--Law and legislation. I. Merino-Blanco, Elena. II. Razzaque, Jona.
K3478.N38 2012
333.7--dc23

2012027987

This publication has been typeset in the multilingual "Brill" typeface. With over 5,100 characters covering Latin, IPA, Greek, and Cyrillic, this typeface is especially suitable for use in the humanities. For more information, please see www.brill.com/brill-typeface.

ISSN 1877-4822
ISBN 978 90 04 22706 4 (hardback)
ISBN 978 90 04 22707 1 (e-book)

This book is printed on acid-free paper.

FSC www.fsc.org MIX Paper from responsible sources FSC® C109576

Printed by Printforce, the Netherlands

CONTENTS

LIST OF CONTRIBUTORS

Elena Blanco is an Associate Professor of Economic Law at the Department of Law, University of the West of England (UWE Bristol, UK) where she is in charge of the LL.M. in International Trade Law and Knowledge Exchange in the areas of trade and globalization. She holds a degree in law from the Universidad Complutense de Madrid, an LL.M. in International Environmental Law from the University of London and postgraduate qualifications from the Universities of Madrid and Belgrade. She has written widely on Spanish and private international law, including two books on Spanish law and legal system and recently published a book on Globalization and Natural Resources Law (Edward Elgar, 2011).

Dr Indira Carr is Professor of Law at the University of Surrey. Her research areas are international trade law and information technology law. Her interest in international trade law led her to examine, in detail, the frameworks to combat corruption. Professor Carr has received funding from the British Academy and the Arts & Humanities Research Council for research projects on corruption.

Nathan Cooper is a doctoral student and university teacher in the School of Law, University of Sheffield. His research focuses on the right to water in South Africa, for which he has undertaken qualitative research. He has numerous publications and has presented his work at various international conferences. Nathan also teaches International Law, European Law and Contract.

Dr Lorenzo Cotula is a senior researcher in 'law and sustainable development' at the International Institute for Environment and Development (IIED), a policy research institute based in the UK. Lorenzo carries out research, capacity building and policy work on the role of law in sustainable development, focusing on natural resource investments in lower-income countries. He has published numerous journal articles and UN and think-tank reports, as well as the book 'Human Rights, Natural Resource and Investment Law in a Globalised World: Shades of Grey in the Shadow of the Law'. Lorenzo holds a Law Degree (cum laude) from the University "La Sapienza" of Rome, an MSc in Development Studies

(Distinction) from the London School of Economics, and a PhD in Law from the University of Edinburgh.

Professor Malgosia Fitzmaurice LLM PhD (Warsaw) holds a chair of public international law at the Department of Law, Queen Mary, University of London. She specialises in international environmental law, the law of treaties, international water law and indigenous peoples. She has published widely on these subjects. In July 2001, she was invited to deliver keynote lectures on 'International Protection of the Environment' at the Hague Academy of International Law. In 1996, Professor Fitzmaurice delivered a paper at the 50th anniversary of the International Court of Justice in The Hague. She lectured widely in the United Kingdom and abroad at various universities, including several US Law Schools, such as University of Berkeley Law School. She also participated in many international conferences. She is the Editor in Chief of the International Community Law Review and a former Co-Rapporteur of the International Law Association Committee on Non-State Actors. Professor Fitzmaurice's previous teaching positions include Readership in international law at the Department of Law, University of Amsterdam. She also worked at the Iran-United States Claims Tribunal in The Hague. Professor Fitzmaurice teaches undergraduate and graduate international law courses, including international environmental law and the law of treaties. Professor Fitzmaurice is the Nippon Foundation Professor of Marine Environmental Protection at the International Maritime Law Institute in Malta of the International Maritime Organisation.

Duncan French is Professor of International Law at the University of Lincoln where he is the Head of the Law School. Duncan is also co-rapporteur of the International Law Association Committee on International Law on Sustainable Development and has published widely on international environmental law and development law. Recent publications are the edited collection 'Global Justice and Sustainable Development' (Martinus Nijhoff, 2010), which was nominated for the International Studies Association Harold and Margaret Sprout Prize for Environmental Studies, and papers on a diverse array of topics including EU-Caribbean investment law, the Antarctic Treaty System and the role of complaint and grievance mechanisms in international law.

Carmen G. Gonzalez is a Professor of Law at Seattle University School of Law in the United States. She holds a B.A. from Yale University and a J.D. from Harvard Law School. Her research interests include environmental justice, food security, international environmental law, and trade and the environment. In 2011–2012, Professor Gonzalez served as chair of the Environmental Law Section of the Association of American Law Schools. She is currently a member of the Research Committee of the International Union for the Conservation of Nature (IUCN) Academy of Environmental Law, a member of the Board of Trustees of Earthjustice, and a member scholar of the Center for Progressive Reform, a non-profit research and educational organization that seeks to inform policy debates regarding environmental regulation. Professor Gonzalez has served as member and vice chair of the International Subcommittee of the National Environmental Justice Advisory Council (an advisory committee to the U.S. Environmental Protection Agency on environmental justice matters) and has represented non-governmental organizations in multilateral environmental treaty negotiations. Professor Gonzalez has taught and/or worked on environmental law projects in Latin America, the former Soviet Union, and China. She was a U.S. Supreme Court Fellow in 2004–2005 and a Visiting Fellow at the Lauterpacht Centre for International Law at the University of Cambridge in 2006. She is currently working on a three-year environmental law capacity-building project in Central America funded by the U.S. Agency for International Development.

Elina Konstantinidou is a PhD researcher, Law School, University of Surrey. She is working on corruption in the extractive industries sector with special reference to Extractive Industries Transparency Initiative (EITI).

Shanta Martin is an Australian lawyer in Leigh Day & Co's international and group claims department. Prior to joining Leigh Day, Shanta led Amnesty International's business and human rights work at AI's International Secretariat in London. Previously, she was Oxfam Australia's Mining Ombudsman and Extractive Industries Advocacy Coordinator. Shanta has 10 years' experience in cases relating to corporate human rights abuses, with particular expertise in the impacts of extractive industry operations. She has also lived in Argentina and Guatemala working on corporate accountability in the textile and agricultural sectors and as a legal adviser on international human rights law. Prior to this, Shanta practised as a commercial litigation solicitor for four years with Mallesons Stephen Jaques in Melbourne. Shanta is a barrister and solicitor of the Supreme Court of Victoria and is entered on the Register of Practitioners of the High Court of Australia. She holds a Master of Laws, a Bachelor of

Laws with Honours, a Bachelor of Science majoring in Pharmacology and Toxicology, and a Postgraduate Diploma in Arts.

Jona Razzaque is an Associate Professor of Environmental Law at the Department of Law, University of the West of England (UWE, Bristol). Jona is a barrister and holds a PhD in law from the University of London. Prior to joining the UWE, she worked as a staff lawyer with the Foundation for International Environmental Law and Development (FIELD). She previously taught at the University College London, School of Oriental and African Studies and Queen Mary University of London. She has researched widely on access to justice and participatory rights in environmental matters and her publications include Public Interest Environmental Litigation in India, Pakistan and Bangladesh (Kluwer, 2004) and Globalisation and Natural Resources Law (Edward Elgar, 2011).

Thomas West recently graduated with distinction from the University of the West of England studying Environmental Law and Sustainable Development. He studied law at the University of Plymouth and then gained his first Masters in European Legal Studies from the University of Exeter. After working under a Robert Schuman Scholarship with the European Parliament, where he worked on maritime employment issues, he pursued doctoral research and expertise in international migration and development at the University of Exeter and the University of Leicester. His expertise is now focused on sustainable use of natural resources and the move towards green economics.

INTRODUCTION

Elena Blanco and Jona Razzaque

There is finally a 'growing recognition that achieving sustainability rests almost entirely on getting the economy right' and as such the paradigm of a 'green economy'[1] is one set to dominate the policy and research agenda in the next decade.[2] Chosen as one of the main themes of Rio +20,[3] major UN agencies, think-tanks and policy makers worldwide have concentrated their efforts in signalling the changes that are needed in order to ensure sustainable trade and investment that will lead to growth worldwide. This will require considerable changes in the legal structures underpinning trade, investment and, more generally, a new understanding of the drivers of globalisation.

The green economy is set to be 'one that results in improved human well-being and social equity, while significantly reducing environmental risks and ecological scarcities'.[4] In its simplest expression, a green economy can be thought of as one which is low carbon, resource efficient and socially inclusive. For many, the term 'green economy' is embedded in the broader sustainable development concept described as 'an economy in which economic growth and environmental sustainability work together

---

[1] Although there is no consensus on what the 'green economy' is as recognized by the UN See Para. 60, at p.18 of the Synthesis report of the United Nations Conference on Sustainable Development, (A/CONF.216/PC/6) UNEP has developed a working definition of a green economy 'as one that results in improved human well-being and social equity, while significantly reducing environmental risks and ecological scarcities. In its simplest expression, a green economy can be thought of as one which is low carbon, resource efficient and socially inclusive' www.unep.org/greeneconomy/about GEI/what is GEI/ See, in general: *Towards a Green Economy: Pathways to Sustainable Development and Poverty Eradication*, UNEP, 2011. Available at: www.unep.org/greeneconomy (accessed on 14 March 2012).

[2] Literature on 'greening' the economy is not new. See, among others, Brian Milani, *Designing the Green Economy: The Post-industrial Alternative to Corporate Globalization* (Rowman & Littlefield Publishers, Lanham, MD, 2000) Chapter 11 generally, and especially at 186–193. Current literature on the 'Green Economy' includes R. Hahnel, *Green Economics: Confronting the Ecological Crisis* (New York: M.E. Sharpe, 2010).

[3] The UN Conference on Sustainable Development (4–6 June 2012), available at: http://www.uncsd2012.org/rio20/index.html (accessed on 14 March 2012).

[4] UNEP 'What is the Green Economy? Working definition' www.unep.org/greeneconomy/about GEI/what is GEI/.

in a mutually reinforcing fashion while supporting progress on social development'.[5]

Thus, we have an institutional endorsement of a proposition that aims to translate the 'environment vs. development' dichotomy into a so called 'win-win' solution. A solution where business and industry will play a crucial and willing role in delivering the economically viable products, processes, technologies, services, and solutions required for the transition to a 'green economy'.[6] But before we all embrace this solution, it is important to look at the conceptual underpinnings of this idea and its institutional and practical ramifications.

Natural resources or green capital are the drivers of globalisation.[7] Despite the current age of technological innovation, it is natural capital which constitutes the physical basis for wealth. This little explored relationship between green capital and globalisation rest upon complex legal principles of sovereignty over resources, access and benefit sharing and cooperative solutions sought by principles such as common but differentiated responsibility. Global problems and concerns[8] and national and sectoral interests need to be articulated in forums where the typical power structures do not get replicated and the *status quo* can be challenged. Globalisation has contributed to this new understanding of regulatory powers and responsibilities and has, largely, facilitated new initiatives where business and civil society via organised non-governmental organisations mostly, voice their interests and work alongside the traditional governmental structures to propose regulatory solutions for sectors, groups or industries.[9] It is also argued that, in today's world, globalisation acts both as an amplifier and a limit for the regulatory choices of states. Regulatory choices no longer have only state or regional effects but can have extraterritorial effects alongside industry self-regulation affecting

---

5 ICC comments on Harnessing Freedom of Investment for Green Growth, 11 March 2011. Available at www.iccwbo.org (accessed on 14 March 2012).

6 Un Confrence on Sustainable Development, The Future we want: outcome document adopted at Rio+20 (19 June 2012, Rio de Janeiro, Brazil), UN Doc A/CONF.216/L.1*. Available at: http://www.uncsd2012.org/content/documents/727The%20Future%20We%20Want%2019%20June%201230pm.pdf.

7 We have studied and analysed the complex relationship between globalisation and natural resources in E. Blanco and J. Razzaque, *Globalisation and Natural Resources Law: Perspectives, Themes and Key Issues* (Cheltenham: Edward Elgar, 2011).

8 Such as climate change or the destruction of biodiversity.

9 See Blanco and Razzaque, n 7, pp 111–114. Examples of multi-stakeholder initiatives include the Kimberley Process, the Extractives Industries Transparency Initiate (EITI) discussed by Carr and Konstantinidou in this book, and the Ruggie Principles on Business and Human Rights 2011.

trade and market actors' behaviour well beyond the territorial scope originally intended.[10] This provides an opportunity for greater sustainability as states can regulate the behaviour of economic actors beyond their borders and create a 'race to the top' driving environmental or social standards up. But it has already been denounced as a dangerous and potentially covert form of protectionism that risks alienating developing countries further from a level playing field in world trade markets.[11]

The much trumpeted 'green economy' needs an institutional framework that understands the shifting paradigms of world economic forces and the multiple actors that interact in the legal sphere is certainly required in one form or another. In the discussions and preparatory works that fed into Rio+20, a large number of non-state actors have consolidated their strategic strength in the debate and foster the belief and readiness to take the lead in the deployment of this new economic era.[12]

The importance of this edited collection cannot be overstated as the new patterns of economic growth currently emerging in countries such as China, India, Brazil or South Africa with large natural resource reserves and growing populations impatient to join into the consumption patterns of the developed world may conflict with the now proposed 'green economy' and sustainable development model favoured by developed countries. How should we – the international, trade and environmental legal community – react to this green economic transformation and strategic repositioning of sustainable development? Are we just witnessing an economic transition that can be accommodated within our current regulatory agenda or do we need a new legal structure that reduces the current power imbalances?

While it is important to reformulate economic theories that put exclusive emphasis on growth and industrial development, it is also crucial

---

[10] A good example of this is the Bribery Act 2010 that came into force in July 2011 and have significant extra-territorial effects as a foreign company which carries on any 'part of a business' in the UK could be prosecuted under the Bribery Act for failing to prevent bribery committed by any of its employees, agents or other representatives, even if the bribery takes place outside the UK and involves non-UK citizens. This issue of bribery is explored further in Carr and Konstantinidou's chapter in this book. Also see Razzaque's chapter in this book.

[11] Especially by M Khor. See: Jose Antonio Ocampo, Aaron Crosby and Martin Khor, 'The Transition to a Green Economy: Benefits, Challenges and Risks from a Sustainable Development Perspective. Report by a Panel of Experts' to Second Preparatory Committee Meeting for United Nations Conference on Sustainable Development UN-DESA, UNEP, UNCTAD (2011). Available at: http://www.uncsd2012.org/rio20/content/documents/Green%20Economy_full%20report%20final%20for%20posting%20clean.pdf.

[12] See, for example, the ICC Initial Comments on UNEP draft report of the Green Economy. Document No. 213-18/4, 6 May 2011.

to address social inequality and participation in order to ensure that communities engage with and benefit from current technological development and are able to reap the benefits of carefully planned sustainable investment and trade regimes. At the same time interdependence of countries requires cooperative solutions for governance that incorporate the multiplicity of actors and define power and control in the inter-related economic and natural resource management spheres.

Issues and Themes

In this edited collection, we explore several issues. The first one is that of the drivers of sustainable investment. We have witnessed over the last decades the progressive greening or 'sustainabilisation' of the economic discourse mostly advanced within the corporate social responsibility (CSR) agendas of major multinational corporations. The much criticised CSR agenda[13] has permeated not only to traditional industries but moved into portfolio investors, banks[14] and pretty much every economic actor playing in the global markets.[15] Yet, many would argue that very little has improved. Indeed, companies with perfect green CSR agendas are still among the worst polluters[16] and many of the instruments adopted lack not only enforcement mechanisms but even the most basic level of monitoring that would make them effective. This takes us to the second of our issues that of the regulatory potential of the different actors, especially state regulation vs self-regulation. The third one considers the related issue of whether corporate control over natural resources creates conflicts between access and sustainability or has the potential to facilitate this.

There are three inter-related themes that are crystallised in this edited collection: the link between investment, trade and natural resource

---

[13] For survey and critical discussion of the main positions on the Corporate Social Responsibility debate see B. Horrigan, *Corporate Social Responsibility in the 21st Century* (Cheltenham: Edward Elgar, 2010). N. Boeger, R. Murray, C. Villiers (eds) *Perspectives on Corporate Social Responsibility* (Cheltenham: Edward Elgar, 2008).

[14] A good example is provided by The Equator Principles (EPs) now adopted by 73 financial institutions and which provide the framework by which banks can manage environmental and social issues in project financing. Available at: www. Equator-principles .com (Accessed on 12 March 2012).

[15] B. Richardson, *Socially Responsible Investmnet. Regulating the Unseen Polluters.* (Oxford: OUP, 2008).

[16] For example: BP, one of the worst polluters in the world, endorses principles of human rights and sustainable and green development in its corporate social responsibility page.

management in the context of the growing economic inequalities between states; the environmental and social conflicts arising out of economic globalisation; and the response of regulatory and institutional mechanisms to the challenges of rapid resource depletion.

The first theme of corporate control over natural resources brings us to the important questions of whether sustainability is really informing market and government decisions, or are we instead witnessing a process where market forces are driving the 'sustainability' agenda. If so, one may ask, what is needed for 'sustainability' to drive the market? Cotula's contribution looks at investment contracts and their potential to contribute towards, or undermine, an overall objective of sustainable development. Within a conceptual framework that looks not only at the extent to which a balance between social, economic and environmental considerations has been struck but also at the contracting process where public voices and accountability are often missing. Economic liberalisation, improved transport and communication systems, and the global demand for energy, minerals and agricultural commodities have fostered natural resource investment in many lower- and middle-income countries. Undoubtedly, increased investment may create opportunities to improve living standards – but it also creates risks such as environmental damage and loss of key livelihood assets like land, water and grazing. For host countries, attracting investment is not an end in itself, but a means to an end. The ultimate goal is to improve living conditions and enable people to have greater control over their lives, whilst protecting the environment. This goal can be described as sustainable development – the careful and evolving balancing of social, environmental and economic considerations. Investment contracts define the terms of an investment project, and the way risks, costs and benefits are distributed. They are therefore crucial in determining the extent to which the investment advances – or undermines – sustainable development goals.

Gonzalez's contribution topically looks at China's involvement in Latin America's natural resource sector investment and attempts to bridge the contentious debate over China's role in Latin America by interrogating the dominant narratives that portray China as either a menace to Latin America's development or as a model worthy of emulation. China's growing economic ties with Latin America have sparked both optimism and alarm. With titles such as "The Coming China Wars" and "The Dragon in the Backyard," recent books and articles depict China as a rising imperial power scouring the globe for natural resources and as a competitive threat to Latin America. According to Gonzalez, other studies applaud China's pragmatic, unorthodox development strategies and portray China as a successful model for developing countries. The competing narratives about China's rise do agree on one thing: China has become a formidable force in the developing world whose influence merits careful evaluation. Seeking raw materials for its industries and markets for its finished products, China is importing primary commodities from Latin America (such as petroleum, iron ore, soybeans, and copper) and is exporting manufactured goods. Chinese companies are also investing in the Latin American mining and petroleum sector in order to secure long-term access to energy and minerals. In addition to trade and investment, China is vying with the World Bank and the Inter-American Development Bank to become a major lender in Latin America in order to cultivate good will, to secure long-term contracts for natural resources at favourable rates, and to help finance imports from China. China has also strengthened diplomatic and cultural ties to Latin America, and has forged an alliance with Brazil, India, and Russia to demand a greater voice for developing countries in international economic and political affairs. Indeed, China has successfully appealed to developing countries by emphasizing "peaceful development," "strategic partnerships," and "win-win solutions" as alternatives to western economic and political hegemony. The chapter provokes several questions: will China's engagement with Latin America produce alternative paradigms of economic development that improve the quality of life while respecting ecological limits? Or will China replicate the trade and investment regimes that reinforced the economic and political subordination of developing countries, facilitated the exploitation of their natural resources, and brought the planet's ecosystems to the brink of collapse? The chapter examines the claim that China's economic rise should be regarded as a model for Latin America and discusses the implications of China's rise for international economic law and for sustainable development.

The second theme of environmental and social conflicts arising out of economic globalisation is explored by Razzaque, Cooper and French, and West. With enormous corporate control over natural resources, the discussion in these three chapters focuses on the dynamics of relationship between individuals and the state, and the power allocation within the state. As resource dependent communities struggle to benefit from national regulatory frameworks, these chapters assess the external factors impacting on resource governance, market priorities and the cost of development from developing country perspectives. As the 'green economy' casts its upcoming shadow over existing resource conflicts, it is important to evaluate its potential for sustainable change and development. If we fail to do that, the implementation of yet another economic driven shift will be translated into new global arrangements and structures that will further marginalise the needs of developing countries.[17]

Razzaque's chapter assesses the level of influence external bodies have on the environmental policy making and resource governance of a state. While states have sovereign rights to explore and develop their natural resources, quite how sovereignty is interpreted in the environmental legal regime remains less than straightforward. At the national level, there has been a growth in the number of environmental regulations over the last decade. Some of these regulations are the outcome of the international environmental development and some are the direct result of the obligations created under multilateral environmental agreements. A number of external factors have an impact on the national environmental law-making processes. These factors include the influence of international agreements, export market requirements in trade, pressure from the civil society, and requirements of multilateral lending agencies. The non-absolute form of sovereignty suggests that states, by entering into international agreements and agreeing to abide by the rules of international institutions, have imposed restrictions on its resource sovereignty. This chapter analyses these external factors, and moves on to assess the level of influence external bodies including non state actors have on the national and local environmental policy-making. Faced with increased activities of multinational corporations in developing countries, the discussion in this chapter focuses on the dynamics of relationship between individuals and state, and the power allocation within and between states.

Cooper and French's chapter focuses on commercialisation of water services in South Africa. In the general discussion on foreign direct investment (FDI) and natural resources, views of polar extreme are often taken – either FDI is inherently neglectful of local priorities or that FDI is the most effective way of promoting local development. Even where a more nuanced approach is taken, which includes contextual insights from

[17] Alarm has already been raised pointing ath the potential dangers that the 'green economy' once it is translated into policy and legal frameworks can have for developing countries in terms of trade restrictions, new protectionism and the facilitation of business for developed countries. See, Jose Antonio Ocampo, Aaron Crosby and Martin Khor,' The Transition to a Green Economy: Benefits, Challenges and Risks from a Sustainable Development Perspective. Report by a Panel of Experts'to Second Preparatory Committee Meeting for United Nations Conference on Sustainable Development UN-DESA, UNEP, UNCTAD (2011).

the host country's governance, political and legal systems, it invariably is premised upon a formal top-down approach to such questions. This chapter, using the right to water in the South African Constitution as its case study, seeks to engage with the issue of FDI and natural resources. Though the level of FDI in the South African water sector is currently relatively low, there has been a marked increase in the commercialisation of the sector more generally, reflecting market choices and priorities. This discussion of South Africa introduces two new elements into the debate, which whilst far from complementary, must both be included if the debate is to be a more realistic representation of the contribution of law to private-sector involvement and natural resources. The first is the apparent formalism of a domestic constitutional framework which whilst talking in the terms of norms actually functions on the basis that embedded rights, however guaranteed, are politically acceptable only to the extent that they are inherently malleable within a broad judicial policy discretion. The second is the informality of the priorities and public discourse of end-users and the extent that formal questions of control, ownership and sustainability matter less than access and price, especially to a poor majority. The authors argued that the inclusion of such elements within the debate can thus begin to provide a closer (though still far from complete) layer of social reality to an increasingly sterile debate as to the overall value of market principles – which inherently incorporates FDI – to the sustainable development of natural resources.

Establishing a green economy is going to require a shift in economic and political ideology and motivations. West's chapter shows that the achievement of food security is a matter of political and economic decision and is intertwined in the predominantly neoliberal ideology of our political and economic elites and the international institutions. This ideology is at the heart of why the right to food is realised progressively and is ineffectual against the regressive nature of economic competition and the intertwined relationship between the economic market and political interests. Lack of corporate responsibility is a major contributing factor not only in denying individual rights to food but also in driving an illusion of global food security. The corporate food regime needs to shift to an integrated approach that is rather coordinated and established in green economics. An impossible trinity of feeding ever increasing populations, producing biofuel and the necessity for sustainable and efficient use of land has to be resolved by prioritising food security and controlling government and corporate behaviour regarding land acquisitions and the market for biofuels. This chapter highlights that the present food and energy regimes cannot work sustainably without economic and political desire for corporate sustainability and the establishment of a green economy.

The third theme of regulatory and non regulatory response is addressed by Martin in her chapter on CSR and human rights and Fitzmaurice when she explores the regulatory frameworks to sustainably manage the fishery regime. Moreover, Carr and Konstantinidou's chapter focuses upon that of contrasting the effectiveness of state regulation and mixed or voluntary initiatives in the natural resource sector in respect of the growing problem of corruption. These chapters by Martin, Fitzmaurice, Carr and Konstantinidou explore the following question: does corporate control over natural resources create a conflict between access and sustainability? Business may seek to implement some solutions that are environmentally sound and improve sustainability and profit but in doing so important human rights aspects may be overlooked and poor communities worldwide risk further alienation from access to resources central to their basic needs and the productive process in general. Non regulatory options such as the CSR policies of many multinational companies that commit to high and uniform standards of behaviour raise the level of social and environmental well-being in the countries where they operate. Similarly, instruments such as the Global Compact seek to encourage the world-wide adherence to a minimum standard of universally agreed principles of human rights, environmental protection and labour conditions among others. Moreover, there has been a recent trend to see natural capital as a critical asset[18] to advocate for a proliferation of market based-instruments for natural resource management.

Martin's chapter examines the themes of state regulation and voluntary approaches in the context of CSR policies and the respect for human rights. During the consultations by the UN Secretary General's Special Representative (Professor John Ruggie) on Business and Human Rights, respect for human rights was often discussed within the CSR discourse, almost to the point of being used interchangeably. Indeed, analysis of the basis for the Respect pillar of the Framework reveals that the Special Representative founded it on societal expectation, not on law.[19] Society

---

[18] World Resources Institute, Millennium Ecosystem Assessment, 2005 (Washington DC: Island Press, 2005). Available at: http://www.maweb.org/en/index.aspx (accessed on 15 March 2012).

[19] UN Human Rights Council, Protect, Respect and Remedy: a Framework for Business and Human Rights: Report of the Special Representative of the Secretary-General on the issue of human rights and transnational corporations and other business enterprises, April 2008, A/HRC/8/5, para 9.

wants business to respect human rights and, we are told, business is responding. How are the companies responding? More often than not, through the adoption of CSR initiatives, some of which specifically mention human rights. Throughout the Special Representative's consultations, non-governmental organizations (NGOs) continued to document corporate-related human rights abuses, but the companies involved almost always espoused a commitment to CSR. According to Martin, almost all companies who are thrown into the spotlight by NGO reports on human rights abuses either deny them or respond to them as 'lapses' in an otherwise steady commitment to social responsibility. States followed suit, espousing a commitment to implementing the Framework while, for example, appointing a CSR Counsellor in Canada, or introducing mandatory CSR reporting in Denmark. But questions must be asked as to whether this adoption of CSR actually results in greater corporate respect for human rights, and whether it assists rights-holders to defend their rights. The chapter challenges the predominance of voluntary approaches and CSR policies as a conceptual model within which to discuss the role of companies in respecting human rights while considering why law and state enforcement are central to the ability of individuals and communities to defend their human rights, and must play a central role in ensuring corporate respect for those rights.

Fitzmaurice's chapter explores fisheries regulation as this natural resource requires urgent protection. The world marine catch has increased more than four times between 1950s and 1992, from 18.5 million to 82.5 million. This increase resulted in overfishing. Another worrying trend is a by-catch of marine mammals and other animals during fishing operations. The problem derives from 20 fishing countries which fleets land 80 percent of the total marine catch worldwide. It may be said that fishing in most of these countries is very poorly managed. Therefore the effective legal framework regulating fisheries is absolutely indispensible for saving the world's fish stocks. The law regulating fisheries is very complicated and consist of a nexus of norms which are international (such as the 1982 Law of the Sea Convention, the 1995 UN Agreement for the Implementation of the Provisions of the UN Convention on the Law of the Sea of 10 December 1982 relating to the Conservation and Management of Straddling Fish Stocks and Highly Migratory Fish Stocks, decisions of various fisheries commissions, the FAO codes), national and that of the European Union. The chapter highlights that the freedom of the high seas is limited to a certain extent due international and national regulations (the case of so-called creeping jurisdiction). However, the existing law is not fully effective as there are growing problems of illegal, unregulated and unreported fishing. The way ahead regarding the regulation of fisheries in the 21st Century appears to be eco-system based fisheries management.

Carr and Konstantinidou's chapter on extractive industries highlights that the natural resources sector, be it oil, gas, forestry or minerals is prone to corruption on a grand scale. The international community has tried to address the problem through regional and international conventions, the United Nations Convention against Corruption 2003 (UNCAC) being the most widely known. The regulation-oriented measures have not made much of an impact in the behaviour of companies who are the major 'suppliers' of corruption. Self regulatory measures are seen as an important tool in the fight against corruption both by inter-governmental organisations such as the UN and OECD, and by NGOs such as Transparency International. This chapter focuses on problems related to the extractive industries sector and examines the Extractive Industries Transparency Initiative (EITI) with a view to seeing whether it is capable of delivering.

Throughout the collection, the role of state and public initiatives and of private actors is re-cast by asking: what type of policies , programmes, government intervention and civil society and business interventions work towards ensuring that sustainability and the green economy agenda are not just the latest ingredients of corporate growth plans? The answer to this question is rather nuanced but vigorous arguments for public control of the monitoring and enforcement processes of existing and emerging standards and rules coupled with increased public participation in decision marking have been put forward in different chapters.

RETHINKING INVESTMENT CONTRACTS THROUGH A SUSTAINABLE DEVELOPMENT LENS

Lorenzo Cotula

1. Why Contracts Matter

In recent years, economic liberalisation, improved transport and communication systems, and the global demand for food, energy, minerals and agricultural commodities have fostered investment in agriculture, mining and petroleum projects in some previously marginal lower and middle-income countries. Increased natural resource investment may create opportunities to improve living standards in recipient countries, for example via economic growth and higher government revenues. For poorer countries with relatively abundant natural resources, incoming investors may bring capital, technology, infrastructure, know-how and market access, which may play an important role in catalysing economic development. And in some of the poorest countries, natural resources may constitute one of the few sectors that can be of interest to outside investors.

However, many past natural resource investments have delivered disap pointing contributions to sustainable development, or have even undermined its pursuit. Desired economic opportunities may not be realised if investment plans are not properly implemented, dealings with local businesses are limited, employment is mainly temporary or seasonal, and government revenues are reduced by tax breaks and other financial incentives that host governments grant to investors. If public revenues generated by extractive industry investments are misused, they contribute little to sustainable development. And ill-designed investments can cause economic harm to host countries and communities, for instance where local farmers are marginalised by new large-scale plantations, or where an investor acquires land for an investment which it then does not implement, thereby creating significant opportunity costs for the host country. In addition, economics is only one aspect of sustainable development. To achieve goals like poverty reduction and environmental sustainability, economic factors need to be balanced with social and environmental considerations. In this regard, natural resource investments raise significant challenges, especially where local people depend on natural resources for their livelihood. If governments make resources available to prospecting investors, people may lose access to key livelihood assets like land, water, wood and grazing. And while foreign investors may sometimes be associated with higher environmental standards than those applied by domestic operators, many natural resource investments have resulted in environmental damage, with lasting effects on the resource base and public health.

Given these major risks and opportunities, the extent to which natural resource investments advance or undermine sustainable development goals depends to a large extent on their governance – on how decisions are taken and by whom, and on the terms and conditions regulating individual investment projects and the wider industry they fit in. Together with applicable national and international law, contracts between investors and host governments ('investment contracts') define the terms of an investment project, and the way risks, costs and benefits linked to that project are distributed. Who has the authority to sign the contract and through what process greatly influences the extent to which people can have their voices heard. Therefore, investment contracts are an important tool for public policy. And interrogating these contracts is an important mechanism to ground-test competing claims about natural resource investment, to assess the extent to which opportunities are maximised and risks minimised, and to increase accountability in public decision-making.

Focusing on best-practice contractual experience from lower-income countries, this chapter discusses investment contracts from the perspective of maximising the contribution of natural resource investment to sustainable development goals like poverty reduction and environmental sustainability.[1] This approach is in line with recent developments in the business literature, where attention has shifted away from conventional corporate social responsibility programmes and towards integrating sustainability and inclusiveness in the core business model.[2] Contracts are at the heart of the core business model, as they set the rights and

---

[1] For a more detailed analysis of the topic discussed in this chapter, see Lorenzo Cotula and Kyla Tienhaara, 2012, 'Reconfiguring Investment Contracts to Promote Sustainable Development', *Yearbook on International Investment Law & Policy*.

[2] See for example the concept of 'shared value' discussed by M.E. Porter and M.R. Kramer, 2011, 'Creating Shared Value', *Harvard Business Review*, January-February, pp. 62–77.

obligations of the parties. In recent years, investment contracts have formed the object of much attention from non-commercial perspectives, particularly human rights: international non-governmental organisations (NGOs) have published challenging reports,[3] academics have produced insightful analyses,[4] legal practitioners have engaged with the topic[5] and the UN Special Representative to the Secretary-General on Business and Human Rights (Professor John Ruggie) commissioned an important study[6] and produced a set of 'Principles on Responsible Contracting'.[7]

Three important caveats are in order. First, interrogating the contracts is only part of the story. By definition, a contract means that a deal has been concluded, and that an investment project will go ahead. Public debate, scrutiny and accountability are also needed 'upstream', with regard to strategic policy decisions as to whether investment in a given sector should be promoted in the first place and, if so, what models of investment are in the country's best interest. Second, contract analysis is no replacement for empirical assessments of social, environmental and economic impacts: well negotiated contracts may be poorly implemented and produce disappointing results; conversely, an investment may improve livelihoods even if the contract is lacking, though a weak contract means that

---

[3] Amnesty International UK, 2005, *Contracting out of Human Rights: The Chad-Cameroon Pipeline Project*, London, Amnesty International UK, http://www.amnesty.org/en/library/info/POL34/012/2005. Amnesty International UK, 2003, *Human Rights on the Line: The Baku-Tbilisi-Ceyhan Pipeline Project*, London, Amnesty International UK, http://www.amnesty.org.uk/uploads/documents/doc_14538.pdf. Global Witness, 2006, *Heavy Mittal? A State within a State: The Inequitable Mineral Development Agreement between the Government of Liberia and Mittal Steel Holdings NV*, London, Global Witness.

[4] See for instance, O. De Schutter, O., 2005, 'Transnational Corporations as Instruments of Human Development', in P. Alston and M. Robinson (Eds), *Human Rights and Development: Towards Mutual Reinforcement*, 403 Oxford, Oxford University Press. S. Leader, 2006, 'Human Rights, Risks, and New Strategies for Global Investment', *Journal of International Economic Law*, 9: 657.

[5] A. Sheppard and A. Crockett, 2010, 'Stabilisation Clauses: A Threat to Sustainable Development?', in Cordonier-Segger, M.C., Gehring, M., and Newcombe, A. (Eds), *Sustainable Development in World Investment Law*, The Hague: Kluwer Law International, pp. 333–350.

[6] A. Shemberg, 2009, *Stabilization Clauses and Human Rights*, A research project conducted for IFC and the United Nations Special Representative to the Secretary General on Business and Human Rights, 27 May. Online. Available at: http://www.ifc.org/ifcext/sustainability.nsf/AttachmentsByTitle/p_StabilizationClausesandHumanRights/$FILE/Stabilization+Paper.pdf.

[7] Addendum to the Report of the Special Representative of the Secretary-General on the Issue of Human Rights and Transnational Corporations and Other Business Enterprises, John Ruggie – 'Principles for Responsible Contracts: Integrating the Management of Human Rights Risks into State-Investor Contract Negotiations: Guidance for Negotiators', 25 May 2011, UN Doc. A/HRC/17/31/Add.3.

mechanisms to hold the investor to account are less effective. And third, while each investment project typically involves a complex web of contracts with a wide range of stakeholders (including for instance lenders, insurers, contractors and suppliers), the focus here is on contracts between investors and host states.

The next section develops a conceptual framework for interrogating contracts through a sustainable development lens. The subsequent sections discuss examples for each of the four constituent parts of that framework. A short concluding section develops some final remarks.

2. Contracts through a Sustainable Development Lens: Conceptual Framework

From a sustainable development perspective, promoting investment is not an end in itself, but a means to an end. The ultimate goal is to improve local livelihoods whilst protecting the environment. While many governments have made efforts to attract more investment, not all investment is good – the quality of the investment is as important as its quantity. Quality is to be assessed based on core characteristics of the investment, rather than corporate social responsibility programmes at the fringes. This involves a thorough scrutiny of the social, environmental and economic considerations at stake.

Different people define sustainable development in different ways. Here, sustainable development is defined as the policy imperative to balance economic, environmental and social considerations so as to meet 'the needs of the present without compromising the ability of future generations to meet their own needs'.[8] While the concept of sustainable development has been criticised by some for being too vague, it does have important implications for key aspects of investment contracts. These implications can be clustered in four groups:

- The ***contracting process*** – from negotiation through to contract management. A critical issue is the extent to which affected people have voice in decision making, and the public at large can hold governments and investors to account through transparency and public scrutiny. These aspects are linked to Principles 1 and 10 of the 1992 Rio Declaration on

[8] *Our Common Future: Report of the World Commission on Environment and Development* ("Brundtland Report"), Annex to UN doc A/42/427, 4 August 1987, available at www.un-documents.net/wced-ocf.htm (last accessed on 5 October 2011), para. 27.

Environment and Development, which state that sustainable development entails putting people at the centre of the development process, and that sustainable development issues are best handled with the participation of all concerned citizens.[9]

- The ***economic deal*** between the investor and the host country. This aspect involves maximising economic benefits and minimising economic harm in the host country and communities, including for instance through public revenues, capital contributions, positive linkages with the local economy (for instance, via employment and business opportunities), technology transfer or infrastructure development.
- ***Addressing social and environmental issues.*** This aspect involves minimising negative impacts on the environment and on people's lives, for instance linked to land takings, water abstraction or resource degradation; ensuring that economic benefits are distributed equitably and used for poverty reduction and broad-based development; and supporting environmentally friendly activities, such as investment in low-carbon technologies.
- The ***extent to which the balance between economic, social and environmental considerations can evolve*** over often long contract durations, for example by ensuring that stabilisation clauses protecting the 'economic equilibrium' of the contract do not make it more difficult for host states to take action to improve social or environmental standards.

Sustainable development issues vary across different sectors. This is partly due to sectoral specificities. For example, while petroleum operations necessarily involve large-scale investment, in agriculture family farmers have proved competitive in many parts of the world, and it should not be assumed that large-scale investment is the way to go. Diversity across sectors is also linked to differences in contractual practice. For example, revenues are typically crucial in extractive industry contracts, but some agriculture contracts involve no or little land fees – employment and infrastructure are seen as the main benefits, so the content and specificity of clauses regulating these issues is particularly important. 'Infrastructure for resources' deals have also been used in extractive industries, however, particularly by some Asian operators. In addition to differences across sectors, there is also huge diversity of contractual practice and sustainable development issues within sectors. In agriculture, for instance, some

[9] The full text of the Rio Declaration is available at http://www.unep.org/Documents .Multilingual/Default.asp?documentid=78&articleid=1163, last accessed on 5 October 2011.

government-to-government deals for large-scale land acquisitions appear to be mainly political documents, though the legal obligations they create are binding; contracts for different crops may raise different legal issues;[10] and the economics of projects involving the construction of processing plants are different to projects only involving plantations.[11]

The next few sections discuss selected contractual issues to illustrate the four aspects identified above. Given the great diversity and complexity of contractual arrangements for natural resource investments, it is impossible to cover all the contractual issues that deserve discussion, and the next few sections are meant to be for illustrative purposes only.

3. The Contracting Process: Transparency and Public Accountability

Key sustainable development issues concerning the contracting process include local voice and public accountability in decision making. Local voice raises questions about who has the authority to conclude the contract, who takes decisions and through what process, and who can participate, how and with what redress. Public accountability refers to the mechanisms that enable affected people and the public at large to hold decision-makers to account for their actions. The focus here is on a key issue affecting public accountability – contract transparency. Most investment contracts are negotiated confidentially. Some aspects of contracting may be public – for instance, where public tendering is used. In other cases, the very existence of the negotiation process may not be publicly known. There may be good reasons to keep parts of the negotiation confidential. Putting aside the investor's concern about commercially valuable information, some confidentiality may also better enable the parties to make mutual concessions without losing face, and thus make it easier to reach a compromise. But, given the important public interests at stake, it is important to establish effective mechanisms to ensure transparency in the contractual relationship.

---

[10] For example, in a tree farm where tree ownership at contract expiry is transferred to the host government, arrangements are needed to ensure that towards the end of the lease the investor has continued incentives to manage the farm sustainably, including through ongoing replanting. This issue would not arise in a rice project, for instance.

[11] For an analysis of a sample of agricultural investment contracts, see Lorenzo Cotula (2011). *Land Deals in Africa – What is in the Contracts?*, London, International Institute for Environment and Development (IIED), http://pubs.iied.org/12568IIED.html.

It is often argued that investment contracts typically deal with highly sensitive commercial issues, which would justify protecting the confidentiality of the negotiation, of key project information and of the contract itself. Investors may be concerned that access to sensitive information may give competitors a commercial advantage. Equally, host governments may be concerned that future investors might invoke favourable treatment granted in earlier contracts in order to extract better terms than the government may be prepared to offer in the present.[12] However, contracts signed with host governments are not just commercial transactions – they are also tools for public policy: they set the terms and conditions of investments that may affect the livelihoods and environments of many. Lack of transparency and public scrutiny in contract negotiation and management creates the breeding ground for corruption and, more generally, for deals that do not maximise the public interest. Arguably, citizens have a right to know how their government is managing the natural resources it owns on behalf of the nation.[13] Access to information and public participation in decision-making are key pillars in the concept of sustainable development (under principle 10 of the 1992 Rio Declaration on Environment and Development). In addition to being a good in itself, greater transparency may promote better contractual terms. Firstly, transparency may increase pressure for more balanced contracts because the parties may be held more easily accountable for the deals they sign up to. Secondly, a pool of publicly available contracts can be a powerful way of strengthening the negotiating capacity of host governments, for instance by highlighting the diverse contractual options that might be available in different circumstances.

There are a number of ways to increase transparency and accountability. The first relates to accountability in strategic policy choices. Even before starting the negotiation of individual contracts, it is possible to facilitate public debate on the development of policy orientations, laws and model contracts. These documents represent strategic policy decisions (for instance, about whether and how efforts should be made to attract foreign investment in particular sectors) and provide the framework for the subsequent negotiations of individual contracts.

---

[12] P. Rosenblum and S. Maples, 2009, *Contracts Confidential: Ending Secret Deals in the Extractive Industries*. Revenue Watch Institute, Washington DC. www.revenuewatch.org/news/publications/RWI-Contracts-Confidential.pdf.

[13] Ibid.

The host government may also seek input from the public during the negotiation of individual contracts, particularly in the early stages of contracting (e.g. public tendering, evaluation or award process). This may involve time-limited and focused consultations. In these cases, disclosure of the main points of the project is key to enable an informed public response. The design of these consultation systems may also be the object of consultation.[14]

For major investment projects, parliamentary approval of deals negotiated by the government can increase public scrutiny. Parliamentary approval is already a legal requirement for natural resource contract in some jurisdictions (in Liberia and Ghana, for instance). However, some conditions need to be in place for this mechanism to enable genuine scrutiny. In order to make well informed decisions, parliamentarians need adequate time and information, as well as technical assistance from experts in the field. Politicians may also consider using parliamentary processes as a forum for public debate, for instance by inviting civil society organisations to express their views on proposed contracts. Finally, for parliamentary scrutiny to be robust, parliamentarians should be able to propose amendments to the contract, rather than making a 'take-it-or-leave-it' decision.

Procedural rights may provide an additional way to gain greater public scrutiny not only of contract negotiation but also of contract management. Procedural rights are legal entitlements that enable the public to have a say in government decisions. They concern access to information, public participation in decision making, and the ability to seek judicial review of adverse decisions. Procedural rights may be established by international law – for instance, under the 1998 Aarhus Convention on Access to Information, Public Participation in Decision-Making and Access to Justice in Environmental Matters, which specifically deals with environmental information.[15] For states parties to it (mainly in Europe and Central Asia), the 1998 Aarhus Convention recognises:

- The public's right to obtain access to environmental information, with exceptions granted on several grounds (e.g. confidentiality of

---

[14] R. Kaul and A. Heuty with A. Norman, 2009, *Getting a Better Deal from the Extractive Sector – Concession Negotiation in Liberia, 2006-2008*, Washington DC, Revenue Watch Institute, http://www.revenuewatch.org/news/publications/getting-better-dealextractive-sector-concessions-negotiation-liberia-2006-2008.

[15] Open for signature at Aarhus on 25 June 1998, and entered into force on 30 October 2001.

commercial and industrial information) that are to be interpreted in a restrictive way (article 4);

- The right of 'the public concerned' (i.e. those likely to be affected by a decision) to be informed about proposed projects that are likely to have a significant effect on the environment; and to be able to participate in decision making 'when all options are open', and expect decision-makers to take these views into 'due account' (article 6); and
- The right of 'the public concerned' with a 'sufficient interest' (which explicitly includes NGOs) to access judicial review procedures to challenge the legality of decisions, acts or omissions (article 9).

National law may also establish procedural rights, for instance under Freedom of Information legislation that allows the public to request access to information held by public bodies. Freedom of Information legislation usually contains exceptions, which commonly include trade and commercial secrets. In other words, the public body holding the information can refuse disclosure if it can show that disclosure would damage trade and commercial secrets. However, depending on the national legal system, for this exception to be applicable it must be shown that the information is not already in the public domain. This is an important caveat because information not available to civil society may be known in industry circles and as such deemed to be in the public domain.[16]

Investment contracts typically contain provisions protecting confidentiality of information. These provisions are often drafted in very open terms to include the contract itself, negotiations or action taken under it, any related documentation (e.g. reports, compilations, data, studies and other materials) and key project information. Contracts may restrict the ability of the parties to disclose this information, unless both parties mutually agree to it. In some cases, confidentiality clauses feature some narrowly defined exceptions, concerning for instance disclosure required by stock exchange regulations, negotiation of financing arrangements, international arbitrations and other aspects. Confidentiality clauses that are too strict may undermine the ability of the public to scrutinise the investment project, and of people adversely affected by the project to claim their rights. When regulating confidentiality in contracts, genuine commercial concerns need to be balanced with the public interest. There are some ways to do this including:

[16] P. Rosenblum and S. Maples, 2009, *supra* note 12.

- As a public policy tool, it is good practice for the contract itself not to be confidential; if specific aspects of the contract constitute genuinely confidential information, they may be redacted before publication.
- If the contractual relationship involves sharing genuinely sensitive commercial information (for instance, concerning the investor's cost structures in exploration and development), a confidentiality clause may be included to protect these specific aspects. In these cases, it is necessary to clearly define what type of information is confidential and therefore protected, and for the parties to have to prove on a case-by-case basis that a particular piece of information falls within that category.
- Clauses prohibiting the disclosure of confidential information without the consent of both parties can be qualified by language requiring that such consent cannot be unreasonably withheld or delayed. They can also clarify that if the public interest outweighs commercial considerations, information should be made public.
- Protection of confidential information can also be subject to exceptions concerning disclosure required by law (including not only stock exchange regulations, as is frequently done, but also freedom of information legislation), or for the purpose of protecting health, safety and the environment, particularly in emergency situations.
- Separate, more stringent clauses may be used to protect from disclosure proprietary information, particularly in contracts involving technology transfers.

4. The Economic Deal: Maximising Positive Economic Linkages

The economic deal embodied in natural resource contracts raises numerous and highly complex issues – from public revenues to capital contributions, income generation via employment and business links, technology transfer, through to infrastructure development. Space constraints make it impossible to discuss such a wide range of contractual issues. A recurring issue in natural resource investments, especially extractive industry projects, is that they tend to create economic enclaves with limited links with the local economy. Job creation is often limited because of the capital-intensive nature of the industry. Opportunities for local businesses are also often limited. As a result, natural resource investments may contribute to the national economy at macro level (economic growth, export promotion, foreign reserves), yet have limited impacts on poverty reduction. Developing ways to maximise positive linkages with the local economy is therefore critical. Investment contracts can play an important role in promoting these linkages through provisions on employment creation, upward and downward business links, and infrastructure development.

Local content provisions illustrate these issues. These clauses typically require the investor to employ and train local staff and contractors, and/or to procure local goods and services during the implementation of the investment project. These provisions may be included in the investment contract, or in national legislation. In this context, 'local' usually refers to employees and suppliers that are nationals of the host state, even if they have no direct link with the locality where the investment project is implemented. Often, employment opportunities created by an investment project may be taken by groups from other parts of the country. Local content requirements are a means by which governments seek to ensure that investment projects generate employment and business opportunities for the national economy. They may also be a way to promote investment in strengthening local business capacity, for instance through on-the-job learning, formal training opportunities and transfer of know-how. These potential benefits make local content requirements an additional way of maximising the economic benefits of an investment project to the host country. From the investor's perspective, local content requirements may strengthen the investor's 'social licence to operate', by creating greater support for the investment in the host country.

Local content provisions do have significant limitations and may require trade-offs in other parts of the contract. If sourcing local labour, goods and services increases project costs, the investor will probably want to compensate this by paying lower public revenues. Thus, there may be a trade-off between local content and public revenues. There may be further trade-offs when maximising local content along with promoting higher safety, social and environmental standards, particularly in countries with limited local business capacity. In these cases, the rigorous enforcement of international standards, such as requirements for certification to ISO 14001 (environmental management systems) and ISO/OHSAS 18008 (health and safety) may create barriers for local businesses. At the same time, waiving these standards to help local companies access the contracting chain may weaken compliance with international standards.[17]

[17] For a study of social and environmental issues in oil and gas contracting chains, see E. Wilson and J. Kuszewski (2011). Shared Value, Shared Responsibility – A New Approach to Managing Contracting Chains in the Oil and Gas Sector, London, IIED, http://pubs.iied.org/12026IIED.html.

Finally and quite importantly, local content requirements can distort trade and may be viewed with suspicion due to their inherently protectionist nature. If inappropriately designed and managed, these requirements may result in high levels of inefficiency and may be exploited for patronage purposes by national elites in government and business. For example, investors and their contractors or suppliers may come under pressure from government and local authorities to hire favoured contractors. The host government's ability to include local content requirements may also be affected by international obligations that the government may be committed to, for example through free trade or investment treaties. This is particularly relevant to the supply of goods and services, as opposed to clauses promoting local employment. The World Trade Organisation (WTO) Agreement on Trade-Related Investment Measures (TRIMS) prohibits measures that are inconsistent with state commitments not to discriminate against non-nationals ('national treatment') and to remove quantitative restrictions. These commitments are embodied in articles III and XI of the General Agreement on Tariffs and Trade, which is also part of the WTO. The TRIMS agreement lists examples of prohibited measures and local content requirements concerning trade in goods are prohibited under these norms (local content provisions on employment and services are outside the scope of the TRIMS agreement). Some investment treaties also contain provisions restricting local content requirements. This is the case, for example, of the bilateral investment treaty (BIT) between Japan and Lao PDR (Japan-Lao PDR BIT 2008). Article 7.1 of this BIT prohibits parties from according preference to nationally produced goods in key aspects of investment processes.

If local content requirements are an option, careful contract drafting and effective implementation are key to make them work in practice. As investment projects often involve long chains of contractors and subcontractors, it is useful to clarify that local content requirements apply to economic activities run by subcontractors and to extend reporting requirements to these players.

Effective local content provisions to maximise local employment opportunities would require that priority for unskilled positions be given to local nationals or even, more specifically, to people adversely affected by the project. In addition, contracts may require that, all else being equal, local nationals be prioritised in recruitment, training opportunities and promotions for skilled positions. They may also set specific percentage skilled labour targets for local nationals, and establish sliding scales, whereby the local employment percentage targets for skilled positions increase during the duration of the project. In the early stages of the project local workers may be predominantly in unskilled positions, but ambitious sliding scales coupled with capacity-building requirements can increase the numbers of local employees in technical and managerial positions. For these sliding scales to work, contracts should also include robust on-the-job training requirements, including minimum annual financial commitments, to open up professional development opportunities for the local workforce. Some Liberian contracts for agricultural and mining projects feature provisions along these lines. While investors may resist binding commitments on job quantity and quality, it may be possible to include in the contract a provision whereby the investor 'declares' that it expects to create a given number of jobs, as was done in the contract for a sugarcane plantation and processing facility in Mali. Regulating labour conditions is also key, for instance with regard to wages, health and safety or service provision to employees and their dependants (e.g. medical care, housing or education). In addition to compliance with national law and applicable International Labour Organization conventions, contracts may require compliance with international standards, such as International Finance Corporation Performance Standard 2 on Labour and Working Conditions. This Performance Standard sets basic requirements like compliance with national law, fair treatment and non-discrimination in labour relations, health and safety, and prohibition of use of forced labour.

In local content clauses concerning supply chain relations, the investor will probably want to ensure that using local content does not result in lower quality or higher costs. But it is possible to frame local content provisions that require the investor to give priority to local goods and services if the cost, quality and/or time of delivery are comparable internationally. It is also possible to require that priority be given to local suppliers even if this increases project costs to some extent. For example, the contract may require the investor to give preference to national suppliers if their costs are within a certain percentage of alternative suppliers available internationally (for instance, no more than 10 per cent above the cost of comparable, internationally available suppliers). This percentage can be higher in the initial phase, when local business capacity may be limited, and be reduced over project duration. Depending on the local business capacity, it is also possible to include specific percentage targets for local goods and services that the project must meet. For example, the agreement regulating a large gas pipeline in West Africa states that 'not less than 15% (by value) of the goods and services used in the construction of the Pipeline System will be sourced from Local Businesses'. Proper thinking is needed where sourcing goods and supplies locally has implications for project costs. Given the trade-offs that may arise between local content requirements on the one hand and public revenues and other project benefits on the other, it is important to have a clear understanding of what cost the host country is prepared to pay to promote stronger links with the local economy.

Investment contracts may also promote economic linkages downstream. Requirements that at least part of the processing be done locally can help the host country progressively move up the value chain – from the low value added, primary sector to the secondary sector. An agricultural concession from Liberia requires the investor to assess the feasibility of local processing and conditions contract renewal to meeting key performance indicators, including on local value addition. Finally, linkages may be created not only upstream or downstream the value chain, but also by creating opportunities in other sectors. Local energy access clauses in oil and gas contracts, or requirements that transport or other infrastructure developed by the project be publicly accessible are examples of this.

To successfully implement these various provisions it is vital to have clear reporting requirements for the investor (and its subcontractors) so they can demonstrate compliance with contractual provisions. This may involve periodic reporting of progress made. Other factors can also make a difference, including: a properly staffed and clearly mandated government agency responsible for monitoring compliance; established channels that enable dialogue between the investor, the government and other stakeholders; credible financial and other penalties in case of investor non-compliance; as well as contract termination for material breaches of particularly important obligations.

5. Social and Environmental Safeguards: Protecting Local Land Rights

Even a deal that is economically beneficial to the country as a whole (in terms of gross domestic product or public revenues, for instance) is bad news if social and environmental interests are not properly taken into account – if local people are arbitrarily dispossessed of their land and do not benefit from the deal, or if irreversible damage is done to precious ecosystems, for example. Arrangements to address social and environmental concerns are therefore crucial. Key issues include environmental and social impact assessment and management systems, legal liability for environmental pollution, water abstraction, local food security or regulating the conduct of security forces. This is an area where linking the contract to national and international law is particularly important to fully understand the implications of the contracts. This section briefly discusses land acquisition issues, which are often one of the primary sources of conflict in natural resource investments.

Contracts may commit the government to make land available to the investor 'free of any encumbrances'. Such provisions must be read in conjunction with applicable national law. In many developing countries, the state claims ownership not only of subsoil resources like oil and minerals, but also of land and surface resources; local people may formally only have use rights on state owned land. In these contexts, the gap between legality (whereby the government may formally own the land and allocate it to investors) and legitimacy (whereby local people feel the land they have used for generations is theirs) exposes local groups to the risk of dispossession and investors to that of contestation. In many African jurisdictions, for example, protection of local rights is often weakened by a number of factors:

- Most people do not have certificates for their land – only 2-10% of land in Africa is estimated to be held under formal tenure.[18]
- National legislation may grant states extensive powers of eminent domain, for instance through unspecific 'public purpose' requirements that allow governments to expropriate local land users to pave the way to commercial investments.
- Legal protection is often subject to visible productive use[19] and some forms of local resource use (fallow, pastoralism, hunting and gathering) may not be considered to meet this requirement despite their importance to local livelihoods.
- There is usually no legal requirement to obtain free, prior and informed consent of local landholders before land is allocated to an investor; local consultation requirements, where they exist, rarely require conclusion

[18] World Bank, 2003, *Land Policies for Growth and Poverty Reduction*, Washington DC, World Bank.

[19] See e.g. article 15 of Senegal's Law No. 64–46 of 1964; and articles 15 and 17 of Cameroon's Ordinance No. 74–1 of 1974.

of binding agreements and their implementation may fall short of expectations.[20]

- Compensation is often paid for loss of visible improvements, not for loss of land,[21] with the consequence that payments may be inadequate to restore livelihoods and that no compensation may be paid for rangelands or for lands set aside for future generations. Loss of resources other than land, such as water and forest resources, is rarely compensable.[22]

From a sustainable development perspective, addressing these issues requires rethinking national law as much as contractual practice. Fundamental human rights may be at stake, including the right to food,[23] the rights of indigenous peoples over their ancestral territories,[24] and the right to property.[25] Local landholders must have greater voice in contracting processes affecting their lives. They must also have stronger land rights – for instance through protecting rights irrespective of formal registration or productive use, and through granting 'customary' rights the same legal status available to land rights issued by the state. Safeguards can also be strengthened, including through robust impact assessments, tighter

[20] K. Deininger, and D. Byerlee with J. Lindsay, A. Norton, H. Selod and M. Stickler, 2011, *Rising Global Interest in Farmland: Can it Yield Sustainable and Equitable Benefits?*, Washington DC, World Bank, http://econ.worldbank.org/external/default/main?pagePK=64165259&theSitePK=469382&piPK=64165421&menuPK=64166322&entityID=000334955_20110208033706.

[21] For instance, Cameroon's Law No. 85–09 of 1985 requires compensation for loss of land but does not apply to takings of land use rights.

[22] For a more extensive discussion of these issues, see L. Cotula, 2011, *Land Deals in Africa – What is in the Contracts?*, London, International Institute for Environment and Development (IIED), http://pubs.iied.org/12568IIED.html. L. Cotula, 2012, *Human Rights, Natural Resource and Investment Law in a Globalised World: Shades of Grey in the Shadow of the Law*, London and New York, Routledge.

[23] Article 25 of the Universal Declaration of Human Rights, adopted by the UN General Assembly on 10 December 1948, *at* http://www.un.org/en/documents/udhr/; and article 11 of the International Covenant on Economic, Social and Cultural Rights, adopted in New York on 16 December 1966, entered into force on 3 January 1976, *at* http://www2.ohchr.org/english/law/cescr.htm. See also O. De Schutter, Report of the Special Rapporteur on the Right to Food, 11 August 2010, UN Doc. A/65/281.

[24] Articles 13–19 of the Convention Concerning Indigenous and Tribal Peoples in Independent Countries, adopted on 27 June 1989, entered into force on 5 September 1991, *at* http://www2.ohchr.org/english/law/indigenous.htm.

[25] Article 17 of the Universal Declaration of Human Rights, *supra* note 18; article 14 of the African Charter on Human and Peoples' Rights, adopted by the Assembly of Heads of State and Government of the Organization of African Unity in Nairobi on 27 June 1981, entered into force on 21 October 1986, http://www.achpr.org/english/_info/charter_en.html; article 21 of the American Convention on Human Rights, adopted in San José on 22 November 1969, entered into force on 18 July 1978, *at* http://www.oas.org/juridico/English/treaties/b-32.html; and article 1 of Protocol No. 1 of 1952 to the European

public-purpose requirements, and compensation tied to restoration of local livelihoods. International best practice increasingly points to the notion of free, prior and informed consent (FPIC) – whereby local landholders have a right to say 'yes' or 'no' to proposed development projects. The notion of FPIC is better established for indigenous and tribal peoples. In relation to these groups, FPIC is enshrined in the Convention Concerning Indigenous and Tribal Peoples in Independent Countries,[26] and in progressive international jurisprudence.[27] In recent years, FPIC has been also applied beyond the context of indigenous and tribal peoples, to protect all people that may be adversely affected by large development projects. For example, the 2009 Mining Directive adopted by the Economic Community of West African States (ECOWAS) requires companies to obtain the free, prior and informed consent of 'local communities' before initiating mining operations.[28]

Where national law falls short, contracts can refer to international standards like those developed by the International Finance Corporation (IFC) or by industry-based bodies like the Roundtable on Sustainable Biofuels (RSB), irrespective of whether these lenders or industry bodies are involved in the project. The Principles on Responsible Contracting developed by the UN Special Representative of the Secretary-General on Human Rights and Transnational Corporations and Other Business Enterprises explicitly mention the possibility of referring to international standards to complement national law where needed to prevent, mitigate or remediate negative human rights impacts.[29] Therefore, governments can feel confident insisting that contracts refer to the performance standards outlined in the institutional policies of multilateral lenders, and civil society organisations can feel comfortable to put pressure on their government to do so.

Convention for the Protection of Human Rights and Fundamental Freedoms, adopted in Paris on 20 March 1952, entered into force on 18 May 1954, *at* www.echr.coe.int/nr/rdonlyres/d5cc24a7-dc13-4318.../englishanglais.pdf.

[26] Convention No. 169, adopted on 27 June 1989, entered into force on 5 September 1991, *at* http://www2.ohchr.org/english/law/indigenous.htm, Articles 6, 15 and 16.

[27] For example, in *Saramaka People v. Suriname,* 28 November 2007, Inter-American Court on Human Rights, http://www.corteidh.or.cr/docs/casos/articulos/seriec_172_ing.pdf, para. 134; and in *Centre for Minority Rights Development and Minority Rights Group International on behalf of Endorois Welfare Council v. Kenya,* Communication No. 276/2003, African Commission on Human and Peoples' Rights, para. 226.

[28] Directive C/DIR.3/05/09 on the Harmonization of Guiding Prinplies and Policies in the Mining Sector, Economic Community of West African States, Sixty Second Ordinary Session of the Council of Ministers, Abuja 26–27 May 2009, Article 16(3).

[29] Under the 'Key implications' of Principle 3. For these principles full reference, see footnote 7 above.

For reference to international standards to be effective, however, it is important to give proper thought to resourcing the host government's capacity to monitor compliance with those standards, as well as to create effective grievance mechanisms for affected people.

In addition to ensuring application of international standards, contracts can also provide for specified project benefits to flow to adversely affected people, including those that lost land to the project. It is relatively common for contracts to provide for the establishment of a community development fund, to be financed through a share of project revenues. Community development funds may also be established on the basis of a Community Development Agreement concluded directly between the investor and affected communities. The investment contract may require negotiation of a Community Development Agreement, and tie investor material non-compliance with the Community Development Agreement to sanctions and grounds of termination under the investor-state contract. Where FPIC is required, the Community Development Agreement may constitute the instrument for manifestation of local consent, provided it is concluded before negotiation of the investor-state contract. For example, a Memorandum of Understanding authorizing the investor to carry out a feasibility study may also require the investor to secure free and informed consent.

6. An Evolving Balance: Stabilisation Clauses and Sustainable Development

The balancing of economic, social and environmental considerations that is at the heart of the concept of sustainable development is not a static one. Rather, it evolves as a result of changing circumstances – for example, as new hazards are discovered, as new technologies are developed that more effectively mitigate social and environmental risks, or as changing social needs and sensitivities require changes in national law. This issue is particularly important given that many investment contracts have very long durations, and that national law on social and environmental matters is currently not well developed in many lower income countries. On the other hand, investors may be concerned that arbitrary regulatory changes may adversely affect the investment, particularly as the balance of negotiating power shifts in favour of the host state during project implementation. Lenders may also be concerned about regulatory risk insofar as this can affect the project's ability to generate revenues and repay loans, and thus the project's 'bankability'. Indeed, once most of the investment is made – for example, after an oil pipeline is constructed – the investor becomes vulnerable to arbitrary changes in applicable rules that may undermine the project. These concerns are particularly pressing in countries where political risk is high.

To manage this regulatory risk, stabilisation clauses are often included in the investment contract to stabilise applicable law. Broadly speaking, stabilisation clauses involve a commitment by the host state not to alter the regulatory framework governing the project outside specified circumstances – such as consent of the other contracting party, restoration of the economic equilibrium and/or payment of compensation. That said, stabilisation clauses come in all shapes and forms. Under 'freezing clauses', for example, the applicable national law is the one in force at a time specified in the contract, to the exclusion of subsequent legislation; while under 'consistency clauses' national law only applies if consistent with the investment contract.[30] On the other hand, 'economic equilibrium clauses' link alterations of the terms of the contract to a renegotiation of the contract to restore its original economic equilibrium or, in absence, to the payment of compensation. In other words, differently to freezing clauses, economic equilibrium clauses effectively aim to stabilise the economic equilibrium of the contract rather than the regulatory framework itself.[31] In recent years, use of economic equilibrium clauses has increased,[32] mainly because of their greater flexibility and versatility. Despite their relative decline, however, freezing clauses are still used. A survey of stabilisation clauses found that freezing clauses are particularly common in sub-Saharan Africa, especially in extractive industries.[33] This may be due to the higher perceived regulatory risk, but also, arguably, to the usually weaker negotiating power of African countries compared to capital-exporting nations.

---

30 P.D. Cameron, 2010, *International Energy Investment Law – The Pursuit of Stability*, Oxford: Oxford University Press.

31 Ibid. K.P. Berger, 2003, 'Renegotiation and Adaptation of International Investment Contracts: The Role of Contract Drafters and Arbitrators', *Vanderbilt Journal of Transnational Law*, 36(3): 1347–1380.

32 P.D. Cameron, 2007, 'Stabilization in Investment Contracts and Change of Rules by Host Countries: Tools for O & G Investors', Association of International Petroleum Negotiators. Available at: http://www.aipn.org/modelagreements/research.asp (accessed 14 November 2010).

33 A. Shemberg, 2009, *supra* note 6.

The broad stabilisation clauses used in some large oil projects in the Caspian region and in Africa have attracted much NGO interest, for instance.[34] The problem is that, if not properly formulated, clauses that stabilise applicable law may restrict the ability of the host state to take action in the public interest. Indeed, bona fide action to improve social and environmental safeguards can adversely affect the economic equilibrium of an investment project, for instance by increasing project costs or delaying project implementation, and may therefore fall within the scope of a stabilisation clause. Examples may include the introduction or tightening of carbon taxation to tackle global climate change, stricter environmental regulations that ban certain chemicals, or more stringent requirements for the taking of local land rights or the consultation of affected people. Where a stabilisation clause applies, the host government would have to either exempt the project from complying with the new standards, or compensate the investor for losses suffered. Where public finances are a concern, the obligation to compensate investors may make it more difficult for host governments to take action needed to protect people or the environment.

Concerns that stabilisation clauses may cause a 'regulatory chill' on measures that pursue human rights goals have recently received much public attention. In 2009, the UN Special Representative of the Secretary-General on Human Rights and Transnational Corporations and Other Business Enterprises and the International Finance Corporation published a study on the matter.[35] The study drew on a large sample of stabilisation clauses, and concluded: '[I]t is clear that in a number of cases the stabilization clauses are in fact drafted in a way that may allow the investor to avoid compliance with, or seek compensation for compliance with, laws designed to promote environmental, social, or human rights goals. Assuming the validity of using social and environmental laws as a surrogate for human rights, it is possible to infer further that some stabilization clauses in modern contracts may negatively impact the host state's implementation of its human rights obligations'.[36]

Of course, stabilisation clauses would not prevent host states from adopting new measures if these states exclude ongoing investment projects from the application of these measures. However, this approach

---

[34] Amnesty International UK, 2005, *supra* note 3. Amnesty International UK, 2003, *Human Rights on the Line: The Baku-Tbilisi-Ceyhan Pipeline Project, supra* note 3.

[35] A. Shemberg, 2009, *supra* note 7.

[36] Ibid. Para. 135.

would raise issues for the coherence of the overall legal framework, as similar investment projects may be governed by different rules, and is problematic in light of two factors. Firstly, investment projects involving wide-ranging stabilisation clauses can be of very considerable size, both in economic terms relative to the host state's national economy and in terms of social and environmental impacts, including for example land takings. Large oil and gas projects in very poor countries illustrate this. Secondly, the contracts may have very long durations, possibly spanning several decades. As a result of these two factors, applying new regulatory measures only to future investment projects may delay the application of those measures to a major share of economic activity for a very long time. This is particularly problematic in lower-income countries where the national legal framework setting social and environmental standards at project inception may be not well developed. From a human rights perspective, a selective application of new measures would also raise issues of consistency with the non-discrimination principle enshrined in human rights treaties, as citizens more directly affected by an ongoing investment project would be granted a lower level of protection than others.[37]

If a stabilisation clause is included in the contract, best contractual practice clearly defines its scope to ensure that social and environmental matters are not stabilised. This can be done not only by wording the clause around arbitrary, discriminatory or similar treatment, but also by explicitly stating that public-purpose measures are outside the scope of the clause. If tax, exchange rates, tariff structures or other similarly specific issues are the real investor's concern, then any stabilisation commitments may be tailored to these needs. If lending and the project's bankability is the issue, a stabilisation clause may have sufficient duration to ensure debt repayment, which may be shorter than the full contract term. For example, a mining contract from Ghana has a duration of 50 years but its freezing clause applies for 15 years only.

In addition, freezing clauses tend to leave no room for regulatory change. Freezing clauses are also quite inflexible: faced with a breach, the investor can either put up with it or go to arbitration, which risks undermining the entire project. Given their greater flexibility, choosing economic equilibrium over freezing clauses makes good business sense from the investor's perspective. Economic equilibrium clauses are also

37 Amnesty International UK, 2003, *supra* note 3.

restrictive because they require the restoration of the economic equilibrium including through compensation – but they do not actually freeze applicable law. Economic equilibrium clauses lend themselves to placing emphasis on fair procedures to deal with regulatory change, rather than on predefined outcomes. For example, the contract may require the parties to negotiate 'in good faith' to restore the economic equilibrium and establish a defined procedure to deal with irreconcilable disagreements (such as determination by an independent expert). These directions are broadly reflected in guidance provided under Principle 4 of the 'Principles on Responsible Contracting' developed by the UN Special Representative of the Secretary-General on Human Rights and Transnational Corporations and Other Business Enterprises.

7. Conclusion

Good contracts are no replacement for a well thought-out strategic development vision or for robust national laws. But ensuring that investment promotes sustainable development requires rethinking aspects of the legal frameworks that regulate investment, including investment contracts. And for sustainable development to matter, it must be fully reflected in those legal frameworks. Conversely, interrogating contracts through a sustainable development lens can help improve accountability and social, economic and environmenal outcomes. This refers not just to contract content – process is also crucial, ranging from inclusive decision-making to skillful negotiation through to effective contract management.

This requires rethinking contractual practice, and also aspects of national law, as illustrated by the examples discussed in this chapter. The great diversity of contractual practice provides opportunities to build on better practice – within a country as well as internationally. Cross-fertilisation across sectors can also be beneficial. Transparency of contracting and public disclosure of contracts is key – as a good in itself, as a way to promote better contracts, and as a signal to attract the more responsible investors.

Getting the contract right also requires strong capacity among negotiators, implementers and scrutinisers to translate new concepts into real change. Recent experience of the renegotiation of mining and agricultural concessions in Liberia shows the difference that investing in the government's capacity to negotiate can make. An independent evaluation of this renegotiation noted significant improvements, namely, an increase in public revenues, requirements to source labour, goods and services locally, and the relocation of certain processing activities to the host country. Determined political will at the highest level, a clear negotiating strategy, a strong negotiating team within an influential government institution and world-class external legal and other advice were all crucial to this outcome.[38] So strengthening the capacity of host governments to negotiate contracts and manage investment can make a real difference.

In addition, vigorous scrutiny of contract negotiation and management by parliament, civil society and the media is key to promoting sustainable development. Greater capacity for independent scrutiny of contracts is essential for host countries to get a better deal from natural resource investment. In the agricultural sector, farmer organisations must be central to debates about the future of the agricultural sector, the roles of agribusiness and family farming within it, and the implications of these for the types of agricultural investments to be promoted – including through well thought-out contractual arrangements. Greater capacity for civil society and producer organisations to play these roles is also critical. Finally, with growing awareness of the business case for responsible practice, it is also important for investors to have a good understanding of how contracts can be negotiated to maximise sustainable development outcomes.

[38] R. Kaul, and A. Heuty with A. Norman, 2009, *supra* note 14.

CHINA'S ENGAGEMENT WITH LATIN AMERICA: PARTNERSHIP OR PLUNDER?

*Carmen G. Gonzalez**

The emergence of China as a significant economic force in Latin America has sparked debate among scholars, pundits, and policymakers.[1] Recent books, articles, and reports portray China as a rising imperial power scouring the globe for natural resources and as a competitive threat to Latin America.[2] Other studies praise China's pragmatic, unorthodox development strategies and depict China as a successful model for developing countries.[3] The conflicting narratives about China's rise do agree on one

* A version of this chapter was originally published in the *Environmental Law Reporter* 40 (2010): 10171–10184.

[1] *See* World Bank, *Latin America and the Caribbean's Long-Term Growth: Made in China?* (Washington, DC: World Bank, 2011), accessed January 16, 2012, http://siteresources.worldbank.org/LACEXT/Resources/Annual_Meetings_Report_LCRCE_English_Sep17F2.pdf; Rhys Jenkins and Enrique Dussel Peters, eds., *China and Latin America: Economic Relations in the Twenty-First Century* (Bonn: German Development Institute, 2009), accessed January 10, 2012, http://www.die-gdi.de/CMS-Homepage/openwebcms3.nsf/(ynDK_contentByKey)/ANES-7Y5EQU/$FILE/Studies%2049.pdf; Tyler Bridges, 'China Makes Big Moves in Latin America,' *The Miami Herald*, August 10, 2009; Arturo Oropeza García, coord., *China-Latinoamérica: Una visión sobre el nuevo papel de China en la región* (Mexico City: Universidad Nacional Autónoma de México/Instituto de Investigaciones Jurídicas, 2008); Javier Santiso, ed., *The Visible Hand of China in Latin America*, (Paris: Organization for Economic Co-operation and Development Publishing, 2006); Robert Devlin et al., eds., *The Emergence of China: Opportunities and Challenges for Latin America and the Caribbean*, (Washington, DC: Inter-American Development Bank, 2006).

[2] Peter Navarro, *The Coming China Wars: Where They Will be Fought and How They Can be Won* (Upper Saddle River, New Jersey: Financial Times Press, 2007), 87–107; 'The Dragon in the Backyard,' *The Economist*, Aug. 13, 2009; Minqi Li, *The Rise of China and the Demise of the Capitalist World Order* (New York: Monthly Review Press, 2008); Nicola Phillips, *Consequences of an Emerging China: Is Development Space Disappearing for Latin America and the Caribbean?* (Waterloo, Canada: Center for International Governance Innovation, Working Paper No. 14, 2007), accessed January 10, 2010, http://www.cigionline.org/sites/default/files/Paper14_Nicola_Phillips.pdf; Mauricio Mesquita Moreira, 'Fear of China: Is There a Future for Manufacturing in Latin America?' *World Development* 35 (2007): 355–376; Roldan Muradian, 'Is China a Threat to Mesoamerica's Development?' *Seattle Journal for Social Justice* 5 (2007): 797–819; Sanjaya Lall & John Weiss, 'China's Competitive Threat to Latin America: An Analysis for 1990–2002.' *Oxford Development Studies* 33(2005): 163–194.

[3] Gracia Abad, *The Beijing Consensus in the Shadow of the Global Financial Crisis*, UNISCI Discussion Paper No. 24 (Madrid: Research Unit on International Security and Cooperation, Complutense University of Madrid, 2010) accessed January 10, 2012, http://www.ucm.es/BUCM/revistas/cps/16962206/articulos/UNIS1010330045A.PDF; Randall Peerenboom,

thing: China has become a formidable force in the developing world whose influence merits careful evaluation.

China is currently Latin America's second largest trading partner after the United States.[4] Seeking raw materials for its industries and markets for its finished products, China is importing primary commodities from Latin America (such as petroleum, iron ore, soybeans, and copper) and is exporting manufactured goods.[5] Chinese companies are also investing in the Latin American mining sector in order to secure long-term access to energy and minerals.[6]

In addition to trade and investment, China is vying with the World Bank and the Inter-American Development Bank to become a major lender in Latin America.[7] Between 2009 and 2011, China announced loans of $10 billion to Brazil's national oil company, $10 billion to Argentina, $24 billion to Venezuela, $4.7 billion to Ecuador, and $138 million to Jamaica.[8] The ostensible purpose of these loans is to cultivate good will, to secure long-term contracts for natural resources at favorable rates, and to help finance imports from China.[9]

China's economic influence has been accompanied by deepening diplomatic and cultural ties. China has expanded embassies, promoted tourism to Latin America, sent high-level trade delegations to the region, financed educational opportunities in China for foreign students, and opened up Confucius Institutes to teach Chinese language and culture.[10] China has also forged an alliance with Brazil, India, and Russia to demand

---

China Modernizes: Threat to the West or Model for the Rest? (Oxford: Oxford University Press, 2007), 26–81 (2007); James Angresano, 'China's Development Strategy: A Game of Chess That Countered Orthodox Development Advice.' *Journal of Socio-Economics* 34(2005): 471–498.

[4] Simon Romero & Alexei Barrionuevo, 'Deals Help China Expand Sway in Latin America,' *New York Times*, April 16, 2009.

[5] Bridges, 'China Makes Big Moves'; 'The Dragon in the Backyard.'

[6] 'The Dragon in the Backyard'; Naomi Mapstone, 'Cash Flows Into Peru Mine Bring Rights Fear.' *Financial Times,* Jan. 19, 2011.

[7] Bridges, 'China Makes Big Moves.'

[8] Ibid; Romero & Barrionuevo, 'Deals Help China Expand'; 'The Dragon in the Backyard'; Michael Sainsbury, 'Venezuela the Latest Destination on China's World Tour,' *The Australian*, April 27, 2010; Mercedes Alvaro, 'Ecuador, China Development Bank Sign $2B Loan – Government,' *Wall Street Journal*, June 27, 2011; Ezequiel Minaya, 'Venezuela Finalizing New Loans Totaling $8B With China, Russia,' *Wall Street Journal*, August 11, 2011.

[9] Romero & Barrionuevo, 'Deals Help China Expand'; Bridges, 'China Makes Big Moves.'

[10] Bridges, 'China Makes Big Moves'; C. Fred Bergsten et. al., *China's Rise: Challenges and Opportunities* (Washington D.C.: Peterson Institute for International Economics & Center for Strategic and International Studies, 2008), 214.

a greater voice for developing countries in international economic and political affairs.[11] Indeed, China has successfully appealed to developing countries by emphasizing "peaceful development," "strategic partnerships," and "win-win solutions" as alternatives to western economic and political hegemony.[12]

This chapter attempts to bridge the contentious debate over China's role in Latin America by interrogating the dominant narratives that portray China as either a menace to Latin America's development or as a model worthy of emulation. The chapter proceeds in five parts. Part I places China's engagement with Latin America in historical context by providing an introduction to the economic history of Latin America. Part II examines the claim that China's economic rise should be regarded as a model for Latin America. Part III evaluates the claim that China poses a threat to Latin America's development. Parts IV and V discuss the implications of China's rise for international economic law and for sustainable development.

The chapter concludes that the emerging patterns of trade and investment between China and Latin America pose both challenges and opportunities. While China's economic rise provides short-term benefits to countries that export natural resources, it ultimately threatens to reinforce Latin America's economically disadvantageous and ecologically unsustainable specialization in the production of primary commodities (such as minerals and agricultural products) and to retard the evolution of more dynamic economic sectors that promise higher wages and revenues. At the same time, China's unorthodox approach to economic development and the growing international recognition of the staggering environmental costs of its growth-at-any-cost economic model may lay the foundation for the emergence of an alternative to the discredited Washington Consensus – an alternative that is both environmentally sustainable and economically just. In particular, China and Latin America have the opportunity to work collaboratively towards a Southern agenda on international trade and investment that recognizes the importance of integrating economic development, poverty alleviation, and environmental protection.

---

11 Bridges, 'China Makes Big Moves.'

12 Bergsten, *China's Rise*, 214.

1. A Brief Economic History of Latin America

In order to evaluate the developmental impact of China's growing influence in Latin America, it is important to place this relationship in the context of Latin American economic history. Latin America's post-independence development strategies can be divided into three distinct but overlapping phases: primary product specialization (prior to the Great Depression), import substitution industrialization (beginning in the late nineteenth century but peaking between 1930 and 1970), and free market economic reforms (dominant after the debt crisis of the 1980s).[13]

From the 19th century through the Great Depression, Latin America was incorporated into the world economy as an exporter of primary products and an importer of manufactured goods.[14] This pattern of trade and production had been imposed several hundred years earlier by Spain and Portugal, but persisted in the aftermath of political independence due, in part, to the power wielded by the existing system of international trade and finance.[15] As industry expanded in Britain, the United States, Germany, and France, manufacturers closely aligned with the major banks offered credit to the newly independent Latin American nations to encourage them to purchase U.S. and European manufactured goods.[16] In addition, the rapid pace of industrialization in Europe and the United States generated a voracious demand for raw materials from the former colonies.[17] Seeking to capitalize on this demand, Latin American governments borrowed heavily to construct the ports, railways, and roads necessary to bring these commodities to market.[18] In theory, Latin America's growing debt would be repaid from the revenues generated by the increased output of primary commodities.[19] In practice, reliance on primary product exports proved to be a serious economic bane.

Specialization in primary commodity production rendered Latin American economies dangerously vulnerable to market fluctuations and to the declining terms of trade for primary products relative to

---

13 Victor Bulmer-Thomas, *The Economic History of Latin America Since Independence*, 2nd ed. (Cambridge: Cambridge University Press, 2003) 17, 393.

14 Ibid., 14–18, 78.

15 James M. Cypher and James L. Dietz. *The Process of Economic Development* (London & New York: Routledge, 1997), 86.

16 Ibid.

17 Ibid., 86–88.

18 Ibid.

19 Ibid., 88.

manufactured goods.[20] Using data from the late 19th century to the late 1930s, Argentine economist Raul Prebisch demonstrated that the export prices of primary commodities declined significantly over time relative to the price of manufactured goods.[21] As a result, developing countries that specialized in primary commodity production were required to sell increasing amounts of their output on world markets in order to purchase the same amount of manufactured goods.[22]

Known as the Singer-Prebisch hypothesis, this analysis suggests that it is economically disadvantageous to specialize in the export of natural resources and that countries should instead promote industrialization so as to develop a comparative advantage in much more dynamic economic sectors.[23] The Singer-Prebisch hypothesis has been confirmed by subsequent studies and has been cited to explain the economic decline and increasing debt burdens experienced by many developing countries.[24]

Following the collapse of commodity prices during the Great Depression, many Latin American countries embarked upon a new phase of economic development known as import substitution industrialization (ISI).[25] ISI began as an emergency effort by Latin American countries to produce manufactured goods that could no longer be purchased abroad because the crisis in commodity markets had deprived these countries of hard currency.[26] Over time, ISI became an economic strategy designed to jump start industrialization by substituting imported manufactured goods with domestically produced equivalents.[27] ISI came about through state intervention in the economy in the form of tariffs and quotas designed to protect infant domestic industries from foreign competition.[28] Far from being a Latin American innovation, virtually all industrialized countries utilized elements of ISI to promote the development of a domestic industrial base.[29]

---

20 Ibid., 171–74.

21 Ibid., 73.

22 Ibid., 172.

23 Ibid., 174, 177–79.

24 Ibid., 87 (Box 3.5), 177–80; Raphael Kaplinsky, 'Revisiting the Revisited Terms of Trade: Will China Make A Difference?' *World Development* 34 (2006): 982; United Nations Food & Agriculture Organization (FAO), *The State of Agricultural Commodity Markets 2004* (Rome: FAO, 2004), 10–13, 20–21 (2004), accessed January 16, 2012, ftp://ftp.fao.org/docrep/fao/007/y5419e/y5419e00.pdf.

25 Bulmer-Thomas, *Economic History,* 17; Duncan Green, *Silent Revolution: The Rise and Crisis of Market Economics in Latin America* (New York: Monthly Review Press, 2003), 22.

26 Green, *Silent Revolution,* 22.

27 Ibid., 22–23; Cypher & Dietz, *Economic Development,* 271–72.

28 Cypher & Dietz, *Economic Development,* 276–80.

29 Ibid., 271.

In Latin America, ISI produced a dramatic increase in industrial output, high levels of economic growth, and improved standards of living, but did not fundamentally alter the region's specialization in primary product exports.[30] Because ISI depended on the importation of inputs and machinery, Latin American countries continued to rely on the export of minerals and agricultural commodities to earn the foreign exchange necessary to keep the ISI industries operating.[31] Beginning in the 1960s, some Latin American countries (particularly Brazil and Mexico) prioritized the development of export-oriented industry in order to diversify exports and generate additional foreign exchange.[32] While Latin American manufactured exports did increase substantially between 1967 and 1980, the bulk of industrial production continued to be oriented to the domestic market, and the region's dependence on primary commodity exports persisted.[33]

Some scholars attribute Latin America's failure to alter its productive structure in favor of efficient, internationally competitive industries to the so-called "natural resource curse."[34] According to these scholars, countries with abundant natural resources will be tempted to simply increase the volume of primary commodity exports to maintain growth rates and avoid balance of payments crises rather than undertake more difficult economic restructuring.[35] Indeed, efforts to promote other industries will often provoke resistance from the agricultural and mineral elites who profit from primary product production.[36]

The demise of ISI was precipitated by the debt crisis of the 1980s. In response to significant petroleum price increases by the Organization of Petroleum Exporting Countries (OPEC) in the early 1970s, many developing countries borrowed money from the major commercial banks to finance the importation of petroleum, machinery, and other products necessary for industrialization.[37] The commercial banks eagerly encouraged massive borrowing by these countries in order to earn interest on the "petrodollars" deposited in their coffers by OPEC nations.[38] Regrettably, in

30 Green, *Silent Revolution,* 23–24; Cypher & Dietz, *Economic Development* 319.

31 Green, *Silent Revolution,* 25; Cypher & Dietz, *Economic Development,* 302.

32 Green, *Silent Revolution,* 27; Cypher & Dietz, *Economic Development,* 319.

33 Green, *Silent Revolution,* 27; Cypher & Dietz, *Economic Development,* 319.

34 Cypher & Dietz, *Economic Development,* 312, 319.

35 Ibid., 312–13.

36 Ibid., 312, 319.

37 Susan George, *A Fate Worse Than Debt: The World Financial Crisis and the Poor* (New York: Grove Weidenfeld Press, 1990) 28–29; Richard Peet, *Unholy Trinity: The IMF, The World Bank, and the WTO* (London: Zed Books, 2003), 71.

38 Peet, *Unholy Trinity,* 71–72; George, *A Fate Worse Than Debt,* 29.

many Latin American countries, the loan proceeds were misappropriated by corrupt officials or were used by authoritarian government to purchase weapons.[39]

When additional oil price rises in 1979-80 caused interest rates to skyrocket just as world market prices for primary commodities plummeted, many developing countries were unable to meet their debt repayment obligations.[40] The debt crisis forced Latin American nations into constant rounds of negotiation with the International Monetary Fund (IMF) and the World Bank for the restructuring of loans to facilitate repayment.[41] By the mid-1980s, almost three quarters of Latin American countries were operating under IMF and World Bank-supervised loan repayment programs.[42]

As a condition of IMF and World Bank assistance, developing countries were required to adopt structural adjustment programs consisting of a standard recipe of neoliberal economic reforms designed to reduce the role of government in the economy and to give greater power and resources to the private sector.[43] Known as the "Washington Consensus," these reforms included deregulation and privatization of industry and public services, trade liberalization, curtailment of government expenditures, elimination of barriers to direct foreign investment, and financial liberalization.[44]

With its emphasis on export-led growth and specialization based on comparative advantage, the Washington Consensus reinforced Latin America's historic reliance on the export of primary commodities rather than promoting investment in new, dynamic economic sectors.[45] Latin American countries were encouraged to export traditional primary commodities (such as soy and copper), new "nontraditional" agricultural products (such as strawberries and flowers), and low-tech manufactured goods (such as shoes and textiles) produced in low-wage assembly plants known as *maquiladoras*.[46] In addition, by requiring Latin American countries to open up their markets to cheap, imported manufactured goods,

---

39 Green, *Silent Revolution*, 29.
40 Peet, *Unholy Trinity*, 72, 74–75.
41 Green, *Silent Revolution*, 30.
42 Peet, *Unholy Trinity*, 75.
43 Green, *Silent Revolution*, 50–56.
44 John Williamson, ed., *Latin American Adjustment: How Much Has Happened?* (Washington D.C.: Peterson Institute for International Economics, 1990), 18.
45 Green, *Silent Revolution*, 136.
46 Ibid., 119–20; 124–31.

the Washington Consensus bankrupted local firms and jeopardized the region's industrial future.[47]

Adherence to the Washington Consensus resulted in significant slowdown in economic growth relative to the 1960s and 1970s, mounting indebtedness, sharp increases in poverty and inequality, and growing social and political unrest.[48] Indeed, Latin American cities were periodically rocked by "IMF riots" that left hundreds dead and wounded and produced property damage totaling millions of dollars.[49] Beginning in the early 1990s, grassroots social movements engaged in mass mobilizations, strikes, and popular insurrections to bring down regimes closely identified with the IMF, the World Bank, and major transnational corporations.[50]

The devastation wrought by the Washington Consensus produced a resurgence of the left and center left in Latin American electoral politics. The electoral victories of Michele Bachelet in Chile, Hugo Chavez in Venezuela, Nestor Kirchner (and subsequently Cristina Fernandez Kirchner) in Argentina, Luiz Inacio Lula da Silva (and subsequently Dilma Rousseff) in Brazil, Tabare Vazquez in Uruguay, Daniel Ortega in Nicaragua, Evo Morales in Bolivia, Rafael Correa in Ecuador, Mauricio Funes in El Salvador, Fernando Lugo in Paraguay, Alvaro Colom in Guatemala, and Ollanta Humala in Peru indicate a significant leftward shift in Latin American politics.[51]

The Washington Consensus, as its name implies, was largely engineered and supported by the United States, and was regarded by its critics as a new form of colonial domination.[52] Structural adjustment opened up the

---

[47] Ibid., 120, 136.

[48] Joseph Stiglitz, *Globalization and its Discontents* (New York: W.W. Norton & Co., 2002), 18–20; Jean Grugel and Pia Riggirozzi, 'The End of the Embrace? Neoliberalism and Alternatives to Neoliberalism in Latin America,' in *Governance after Neoliberalism in Latin America*, ed. Jean Grugel and Pia Riggirozzi (New York: Palgrave Macmillan Publishers, 2009), 15; William Finnegan, 'The Economics of Empire: Notes on the Washington Consensus.' *Harper's*, May 1, 2003, 45–50.

[49] Green, *Silent Revolution*, 39.

[50] Gerardo Renique, 'Strategic Challenges for Latin America's Anti-Neoliberal Insurgency,' in *Dispatches from Latin America: On the Frontlines Against Neoliberalism*, ed. Vijay Prashad and Teo Ballvé (Cambridge, MA: South End Press, 2006), 35–38.

[51] Tom Phillips, 'Dilma Rousseff Wins Brazil's Presidential Election.' *The Guardian*, October 31, 2010; Juan Forero, 'Nationalist Humala Edges Out Rival, Unnerving Investors,' *Washington Post*, June 6, 2011; Grugel & Riggirozzi, 'The End of the Embrace?,' 16; Blake Schmidt and Elisabeth Malkin, 'Leftist Party Wins Salvadoran Vote,' *New York Times*, March 17, 2009; Hector Tobar, 'Guatemala's New Leader Inherits Woes,' *Los Angeles Times*, November 6, 2007; 'Daniel Ortega: Return of the Sandinista,' *The Independent*, Nov. 8, 2006.

[52] Paul Drake, 'The Hegemony of U.S. Economic Doctrines in Latin America,' in *Latin America After Neoliberalism: Turning the Tide in the 21st Century?*, ed. Eric Hershberg and Fred Rosen (New York: The New Press, 2006), 33; Green, *Silent Revolution*, 68–71.

economies of Latin America to U.S. and European traders and investors.[53] The mass privatizations of the 1990s enabled transnational corporations to purchase Latin American banks, airlines, and telecommunications companies and to invest in the oil sector.[54] By emphasizing export-led growth, structural adjustment increased the supply and lowered the price of raw materials for the benefit of the global North while locking the global South into its traditional role as exporter of primary commodities.[55] It is against this background that China emerged as a major player on the Latin American economic scene.

2. Is China a Model for Latin America?

China is engaging with Latin America at the very moment that center and center-left Latin American governments are searching for alternatives to the Washington Consensus. Some scholars contend that China represents an alternative model of successful economic growth and development or, at the very least, a source of insights that can be adapted to the Latin American context.[56] This Part critically evaluates this claim.

China has undergone one of the most remarkable economic transformations in modern history. While Latin America stagnated under the Washington Consensus, China achieved average annual growth rates of at least 8–10%.[57] China currently ranks as the world's second largest national economy and second largest exporter.[58] Since 1980, more than 400 million Chinese citizens have risen from abject poverty,[59] and China is generally on track to meet the Millennium Development Goals by 2015.[60]

---

53 Green, *Silent Revolution,* 68; Ross P. Buckley, 'The Economic Policies of China and India, and of the Washington Consensus: An Enlightening Comparison,' *Wisconsin International Law Journal* 27 (2010): 725–726.

54 Green, *Silent Revolution,* 68.

55 Ibid.

56 Robert Devlin, 'China's Economic Rise,' in *China's Expansion into the Western Hemisphere: Implications for Latin America and the United States*, ed. Riordan Roett and Guadalupe Paz, 111–147. (Washington D.C.: Brookings Institution Press, 2008), 138; Joshua Kurlantzick, 'China's Growing Influence in Southeast Asia,' in *China's Expansion into the Western Hemisphere: Implications for Latin America and the United States*, ed. Riordan Roett and Guadalupe Paz (Washington D.C.: Brookings Institution Press, 2008), 198.

57 Devlin, et. al., *The Emergence of China,* 3; Bergsten et al., *China's Rise,* 9.

58 Bergsten et al., *China's Rise,* 9.

59 Dani Rodrik, *One Economics, Many Recipes: Globalization, Institutions, and Economic Growth* (Princeton: Princeton University Press, 2007), 2.

60 Peerenboom, *China Modernizes,* 129, 132.

China achieved its economic success by disregarding many of the policy prescriptions associated with the Washington Consensus.[61] Instead of liberalizing its trade regime, China imposed high tariffs and quotas on imports to protect domestic industries and to boost foreign exchange reserves.[62] China did not relax these restrictions until very late in its economic development process.[63] Instead of opening its markets to foreign investment, China steered foreign companies into joint ventures, imposed onerous technology transfer requirements in order to develop domestic technological capacity, and required foreign companies to purchase a certain proportion of their inputs from local firms.[64] These restrictions were not lifted until China joined the World Trade Organization (WTO).[65] Instead of engaging in large-scale deregulation and privatization of industry, China continued to regulate private companies and to hold the majority share in many enterprises while encouraging the expansion of the private sector.[66] Instead of minimizing state intervention in the economy, the Chinese government has maintained a strong and proactive presence designed to achieve long-term development goals.[67] In the mid-1990s, for example, the Chinese government intervened in the economy to favor capital-intensive industries such as automobiles, electronics, machinery, and petrochemicals.[68] In the late 1990s, the government's industrial policy shifted toward support of technologically advanced enterprises, particularly in the software, integrated circuits, and automobile industries.[69]

Dubbed the "Beijing Consensus,"[70] China's alternative path to economic development is not a one-size-fits-all economic recipe.[71] On the contrary, the Beijing Consensus represents an unorthodox approach to economic development that rests on two key pillars: pragmatism and state intervention in the economy.[72]

---

[61] Rodrik, *One Economics, Many Recipes,* 239; Angresano, 'China's Development Strategy,' 472.

[62] Peerenboom, *China Modernizes*, 73.

[63] Ibid.

[64] Ibid., 74; Devlin, et. al., *The Emergence of China,* 28; Ha-Joon Chang, *Bad Samaritans: The Myth of Free Trade and the Secret History of Capitalism* (New York: Bloomsbury Press, 2008), 29–30.

[65] Peerenboom, *China Modernizes*, 74.

[66] Ibid.; Angresano, 'China's Development Strategy,' 481.

[67] Devlin, et. al., *The Emergence of China*, 27–29.

[68] Ibid., 32.

[69] Ibid.

[70] Joshua Cooper Ramo, *The Beijing Consensus* (London: The Foreign Policy Center, 2004); Peerenboom, *China Modernizes,* 5–7, 73–77, 80–81.

[71] Ching Cheong, 'The Rise of the Beijing Consensus?' *China Daily*, October 28, 2008, 9.

[72] Peerenboom, *China Modernizes,* 5.

The hallmark of the Beijing Consensus is pragmatism.[73] Rather than following a pre-determined recipe for economic reform such as that set out in the Washington Consensus, China adopted policies, institutions, and legal norms uniquely suited to local conditions.[74] China also implemented its economic reforms gradually and incrementally–with small-scale pilot experiments typically preceding general application of new policies.[75]

The second key feature of the Beijing Consensus is the central role of the state in the process of economic development.[76] The Chinese government actively intervened in the economy in order to guide economic development, regulate foreign trade and investment, and mitigate the negative impact of globalization on disadvantaged economic actors.[77] Indeed, China's spectacular economic rise confirms the pivotal role of the state in the process of economic diversification and industrialization.[78] China's rise is a reminder that nearly all industrialized countries (including the United States, Great Britain, France, Germany, Japan, Taiwan, and South Korea) achieved economic prosperity through the use of protectionist instruments, including tariffs, subsidies, quotas, and other measures designed to promote those industries and sectors most likely to contribute to long-term economic growth.[79]

Latin America is the region where the free-market reforms associated with the Washington Consensus were most diligently implemented and where the corresponding results have been most disappointing.[80] As left-of-center governments reevaluate national economic policy, China's use of long-term strategic planning and proactive state intervention to achieve national development goals can serve as a source of inspiration and as an antidote to the rigid prescriptions of the Washington Consensus.[81]

---

73 Ibid.; Angresano, 'China's Development Strategy,' 479–80.
74 Peerenboom, *China Modernizes*, 5.
75 Devlin, et. al., *The Emergence of China* 31, 35–36.
76 Peerenboom, *China Modernizes*, 5.
77 Ibid.
78 *See generally*, Ha-Joon Chang, *Globalization, Economic Development and the Role of the State* (London: Zed Books, 2003); Stiglitz, *Globalization and its Discontents;* Meredith Woo-Cumings, ed., *The Developmental State* (Ithaca & London: Cornell University Press, 1999); Peter B. Evans, *Embedded Autonomy: States and Industrial Transformation* (Princeton: Princeton University Press, 1995); Peter B. Evans, et. al., eds, *Bringing the State Back In,* (Cambridge: Cambridge University Press, 1985).
79 Ha-Joon Chang, *Kicking Away the Ladder: Development Strategy in Historical Perspective* (London: Anthem Press, 2002), 19–51, 59–66.
80 Rodrik, *One Economics, Many Recipes*, 99.
81 Devlin, 'China's Economic Rise,' 137–40.

Following China's lead, Latin American nations would do well to pursue a pragmatic approach to economic development that studies the experiences of other successful countries, adapts insights from other countries to local circumstances, implements reforms gradually and incrementally, and adjusts and expands reforms according to the observed results.[82]

However, it is important to acknowledge the enormous costs of China's economic rise and the numerous challenges that the country faces, including rapid urbanization, growing unemployment and inequality, rising social protest, and serious environmental degradation.[83] One of the most important lessons that Latin America can derive from China's experience is the importance of integrating environmental protection into economic planning rather than adopting the "grow first, clean up later" approach.

China is facing an environmental crisis of staggering proportions. Water pollution, water scarcity, desertification, air pollution, deforestation, loss of biodiversity, waste accumulation, depletion of fisheries, soil erosion, and contamination of crop land impose enormous costs on the Chinese economy, and jeopardize the health of millions of its citizens.[84] According to the World Bank, China experiences 750,000 premature deaths per year as a consequence of air and water pollution.[85] Of the world's 20 most polluted cities, 16 are located in China.[86] Only 1% of China's 560 million urban dwellers breathes air considered safe by European Union (EU) standards.[87]

---

[82] For example, drawing lessons from the recent experiences of New Zealand, Ireland, and Finland, Latin American countries might forge strategic alliances between the private sector, the public sector, and academia to promote innovation and investment in new, dynamic export-oriented industries. Drawing inspiration from China, Latin America's countries might place renewed emphasis on education, research and development, infrastructure investment, and access to domestic credit. Devlin, 'China's Economic Rise,' 126–43 (describing how the Chinese government, guided by a long-term strategic vision, cautiously and gradually introduced market-based reforms and discussing innovative approaches to economic development in other countries).

[83] Barbara Stallings, 'The U.S.-China-Latin America Triangle: Implications for the Future,' in *China's Expansion into the Western Hemisphere: Implications for Latin America and the United States*, ed. Riordan Roett and Guadalupe Paz (Washington D.C.: Brookings Institution Press, 2008), 255.

[84] Elizabeth Economy, 'The Great Leap Backward? The Costs of China's Environmental Crisis.' *Foreign Affairs* 86 (2007): 38–59; Barry Naughton, *The Chinese Economy: Transitions and Growth* (Cambridge: Massachusetts Institute of Technology Press, 2007), 487–503; Jianguo Liu and Jared Diamond, 'China's Environment in a Globalizing World.' *Nature* 435 (2005): 1179–1186.

[85] Richard McGregor, 'Environmental Damage Stirs Public Anger.' *Financial Times* (London), July 3, 2007, 6; David Barboza, 'China Reportedly Urged Omitting Pollution Death Estimates.' *New York Times*, July 5, 2007.

[86] Economy, 'The Great Leap Backward?,' 40.

[87] Joseph Kahn and Jim Yardley, 'As China Roars, Pollution Reaches Deadly Extremes.' *New York Times*, August 26, 2007.

Pollution and natural resource degradation cost the Chinese government between 8–12% of the country's annual gross domestic product (GDP).[88] These costs include hospital and emergency room visits, workplace absenteeism, damage to fisheries and agriculture, the incapacitating effects of chronic illness, and the long-term consequences of childhood lead exposure.[89] China has also become one of the leading contributors to major global environmental problems, including climate change, the illegal timber trade, transboundary air pollution, and marine pollution.[90]

While rejecting the Washington Consensus, the Chinese government has adopted the unsustainable, resource-intensive, growth-at-any-cost economic model pioneered by the United States and other wealthy countries.[91] This economic model equates progress with economic growth as measured by GDP.[92] GDP growth is achieved by consuming ever-increasing amounts of natural resources and by discharging ever-growing amounts of pollution.[93]

Regrettably, China is replicating this resource-intensive path at a time when the world's ecological systems are severely stressed and increasingly

[88] Economy, 'The Great Leap Backward?,'46; Naughton, *The Chinese Economy,* 493.

[89] Naughton, *The Chinese Economy,* 493–94.

[90] Economy, 'The Great Leap Backward?,'44–46; Jacques Leslie, 'The Last Empire: Can the World Survive China's Headlong Rush to Emulate the American Way of Life?' *Mother Jones*, January/February 2008, 34–39.

[91] Leslie, 'The Last Empire,' 83; Bergsten, et. al., *China's Rise,* 78; Caitlin Morray, 'Ill Wind: Air Pollution in the Pearl River Delta.' *Pacific Rim Law and Policy Journal* 19 (2010): 223–24 (describing the adverse environmental consequences of China's growth-at-any-cost economic model).

[92] James Gustave Speth, *The Bridge at the Edge of the World: Capitalism, the Environment, and Crossing from Crisis to Sustainability* (New Haven: Yale University Press, 2008), 46–50.

[93] Ibid., 49–51. Although China has passed hundreds of environmental statutes since 1983, economic development has traditionally taken priority over environmental protection, and local officials are evaluated and promoted based upon their success in promoting economic growth. Nevertheless, the Chinese government embarked upon an ambitious and unprecedented effort to quantify the costs of pollution by calculating 'Green GDP.' Released in 2006, China's first Green GDP report subtracted the costs associated with environmental degradation from traditional GDP in order to provide a more realistic assessment of the health of the Chinese economy. The report revealed that pollution cost the country the equivalent of three percent of GDP in 2004–a conservative assessment that did not take into account groundwater or soil contamination or the over-exploitation and depletion of resources. Under fierce pressure from local officials, China's innovative efforts to quantify Green GDP were scuttled in 2007–reportedly because the second Green GDP report indicated an increase in the amount of economic loss due to environmental pollution. Jane Qiu, 'China's Green Accounting System on Shaky Ground.' *Nature* 448 (2007): 518–519; Jane Spencer, 'Why Beijing is Trying to Tally the Hidden Costs of Pollution as China's Economy Booms.' *Wall Street Journal*, October 2, 2006, A2.

unable to support the growing global economy.[94] According to the United Nations (UN) Millennium Ecosystem Assessment Synthesis Report, human economic activity over the past 50 years has produced more rapid and severe ecosystem degradation than in any comparable period in human history.[95] Approximately 60% of the valuable ecosystem services examined in the UN report have deteriorated, including flood control, water filtration, air purification, erosion control, waste treatment and detoxification, and regulation of regional and local climate.[96] An economic development strategy that exacerbates this environmental degradation is likely to be catastrophic for China and for the rest of the world.[97]

Ecological economists have long warned that the scale of the global economy is rapidly exceeding the capacity of the planet's ecological systems to supply essential resources and to assimilate wastes.[98] Given these ecological constraints, unlimited economic growth is a physical impossibility.[99] Sustainability will only be achieved by maintaining the scale of the economy within the regenerative and assimilative capacities of the planet's ecosystems.[100]

Instead of embracing an outdated economic model based upon the fallacy of unlimited economic growth, Latin American governments should recognize that growing numbers of Chinese officials, scholars, and grassroots environmentalists are calling for an alternative path to industrialization that respects ecological limits and seeks to minimize resource consumption and waste generation.[101] The Chinese government has

---

94 Christopher Flavin and Gary Gardner, 'China, India, and the New World Order,' in Worldwatch Institute, *State of the World 2006* (New York & London: W.W. Norton & Company, 2006), 15, 21.

95 Millennium Ecosystem Assessment, *Ecosystems and Human Well-Being: Synthesis* (Washington, DC: Island Press, 2005), 1–5, accessed January 10, 2012. http://www.millenniumassessment.org/documents/document.356.aspx.pdf.

96 Ibid., 6–7.

97 Flavin & Gardner, 'China, India, and the New World Order,' 7, 15–18.

98 Robert Costanza, et. al., *An Introduction to Ecological Economics* (Boca Raton, FL: CRC Press LLC, 1997), 1–18; Kristen Sheeran, 'Ecological Economics: A Progressive Paradigm?' *Berkeley La Raza Law Journal* 17 (2006): 26–28; Flavin & Gardner, 'China, India, and the New World Order,' 15–18.

99 Costanza et. al., *Ecological Economics,* 7.

100 Ibid., 15.

101 Flavin & Gardner, 'China, India, and the New World Order,' 94, at 18–19, 23; Mark Leonard, *What Does China Think?* (New York: Public Affairs, 2008), 41–44; James Fallows, 'China's Silver Lining: Why Smoggy Skies Over Beijing Represent the World's Greatest Environmental Opportunity.' *The Atlantic,* June 2008, 43–47; Alex Wang, 'The Role of Law in Environmental Protection in China: Recent Development.' *Vermont Journal of Environmental Law* 8 (2007): 200–201; Jesse L. Moorman and Zhang Ge, 'Promoting and Strengthening Public Participation in China's Environmental Impact Assessment Process:

articulated environmental protection as a national priority and announced numerous initiatives to advance it.[102] Nevertheless, China's environment continues to deteriorate, and government reports confirm worsening air and water pollution and a rapidly rising death rate due to cancer.[103] Latin American governments might well draw inspiration from China's economic success, but should avoid replicating China's disastrous growth-at-any-cost economic model.

3. Is China a Threat to Latin America's Development?

Far from serving as model for Latin America, China has emerged in the writings of some scholars as a threat to Latin America's economic development.[104] For example, three recent books on China's growing ties with Latin America conclude that China's rise may reinforce Latin America's economically disadvantageous integration into the global economy as a producer of primary products and an importer of manufactured goods.[105]

China's trade with Latin America is motivated by China's quest for raw materials to fuel its rapid industrialization and to feed its population and by China's pursuit of new markets to sustain its export-driven economic growth.[106] China is importing petroleum, copper, iron, steel, soy,

---

Comparing China's EIA Law and U.S. NEPA.' *Vermont Journal of Environmental Law* 8 (2007):283; Sholto Byrnes, 'The Man Making China Green.' *New Statesman*, December 18, 2006-January 4, 2007, 60.

102 Cynthia W. Cann, Michael C. Cann, and Gao Shangquan, 'China's Road to Sustainable Development,' in *China's Environment and the Challenge of Sustainable Development*, ed. Kristen A. Day (Armonk, New York: East Gate Books, 2005), 11–25 (describing some of the Chinese government's efforts to promote sustainable development).

103 Andrew Jacobs, 'In China, Pollution Worsens Despite New Efforts.' *New York Times*, July 28, 2010; Lee Liu, 'Made in China: Cancer Villages.' *Environment Magazine*, March/April 2010. Accessed January 10, 2012. http://www.environmentmagazine.org/Archives/Back%20 Issues/March-April%202010/made-in-china-full.html.

104 Rhys Jenkins, 'China's Global Expansion and Latin America.' *Journal of Latin American Studies* 42 (2010): 834–35. For additional books and articles portraying China as a menace to Latin America's development, please see footnote 2, *supra*.

105 Kevin P. Gallagher and Roberto Porzecanski, *The Dragon in the Room: China and the Future of Latin American Industrialization* (Stanford: Stanford University Press, 2010), 136–39; R. Evan Ellis, *China in Latin America, The Whats and Wherefores* (Boulder, Colorado: Lynne Rienner Publishers, 2009), 3–4, 286–87; Stallings, 'The U.S.-Latin America Triangle,' 249, 253; Francisco E. Gonzalez, 'Latin America in the Economic Equation – Winners and Losers: What Can Losers Do?' in *China's Expansion into the Western Hemisphere: Implications for Latin America and the United States*, ed, Riordan Roett and Guadalupe Paz (Washington D.C.: Brookings Institution Press, 2008), 151–55.

106 Ellis, *China in Latin America*, 9–13; Xiang Lanxin, 'An Alternative Chinese View,' in *China's Expansion into the Western Hemisphere: Implications for Latin America and the*

wood/wood pulp, fishmeal, and various other primary commodities from Latin America.[107] At the same time, it is exporting a variety of manufactured goods, including textiles, footwear, motorcycles, computers, appliances, and automobiles.[108] Like the imperial powers of an earlier period, China is also financing infrastructure projects in Latin America in order to improve the flow of commerce and is investing in petroleum and mining operations in order to secure access to these valuable commodities.[109] Despite official Chinese government pronouncements about South-South cooperation, China's engagement with Latin America bears a striking resemblance to the colonial model described in Part I of this chapter.

In order to develop a more nuanced understanding of the impact of China's presence in Latin America, it is useful to classify the region into three parts: the Southern Cone (Argentina, Brazil, Chile, Paraguay, and Uruguay); the Andean region (Bolivia, Colombia, Ecuador, Peru, and Venezuela); and Mexico, Central America, and the Caribbean.[110]

The Southern Cone and Andean nations have benefited in the short-term from the spike in commodity prices caused by China's voracious demand for energy and raw materials.[111] These nations rely on natural resources to generate the bulk of export revenues, and their export structures are thus complementary to those of China.[112]

However, some Southern Cone nations have suffered losses as a consequence of competition from China in manufactured goods. Chief among these is Brazil. While Brazil does export raw materials to China and cooperates with China in information technology, space satellites, biotechnology, and medicine, Brazil's domestic manufacturing industry faces intense competition from China in both the Brazilian market and abroad (including the United States, Japan, the EU, and Mercosur countries).[113]

United States, ed. Riordan Roett and Guadalupe Paz (Washington D.C.: Brookings Institution Press, 2008), 54–57. Latin America's interest in China is driven by the lucrative opportunity to export commodities to the world's most populous nation, by the attractiveness of China as a potential investor, and by the hope that growing ties with China will help mitigate the political and economic influence of the United States. Ellis, *China in Latin America*, 24–28.

107 Ellis, *China in Latin America*, 12, 50–53, 273–74.

108 Ibid., 204.

109 Ibid., 278–281, 288, 110–115, 126–28, 151–52.

110 Ibid., 7.

111 Phillips, *Consequences of an Emerging China*, 9.

112 Ibid.; Gonzalez, 'Winners and Losers,' 152.

113 Gonzalez, 'Winners and Losers,' 153; Monica Hirst, 'A South-South Perspective,' in *China's Expansion into the Western Hemisphere: Implications for Latin America and the*

Even Chile, Colombia, and Argentina, whose exports generally complement those of China, have suffered losses as a consequence of competition from Chinese manufactured goods; these countries, along with Brazil, have imposed numerous anti-dumping and safeguard measures on Chinese manufactured products.[114]

In sharp contrast to the natural resource exporting countries, Mexico, Central America, and the Caribbean have faced direct competition from China in the export of textiles and apparel.[115] Mexico also competes with China in the electronics, computer, appliance, automobile, and motorcycle markets.[116] As Chinese manufactured exports have penetrated the U.S. market, Mexico and Central America have experienced a steep decline in their share of that market.[117] In 2003, China overtook Mexico as the largest exporter of goods to the United States.[118] China also competes with Mexico and Central America for foreign investment.[119] Between 2000 and 2006, Mexico lost over half a million manufacturing jobs as a consequence, among other things, of low-wage competition from China.[120] The enormous losses suffered by Mexico due to China's economic rise have resulted in frequent calls for protection of Mexican industry.[121]

Finally, Chinese companies have invested in the petroleum and mining sectors of certain Andean countries (Venezuela, Ecuador, and Peru) in order to secure access to valuable resources, but their presence has generated controversy and social unrest.[122] In Ecuador, Chinese firms took over certain petroleum exploration contracts formerly held by Occidental Petroleum, were awarded additional oil exploration and development contracts, and later purchased the oil field and pipeline assets of a Canadian firm.[123] In Peru, a Chinese company owns and operates the

---

United States, ed. Riordan Roett and Guadalupe Paz (Washington D.C.: Brookings Institution Press, 2008), 99–100.

114 Gonzalez, 'Winners and Losers,' 152–53; Ellis, *China in Latin America*, 163.

115 Gonzalez, 'Winners and Losers,' 157–60; Phillips, *Consequences of an Emerging China*, 8–9.

116 Gonzalez, 'Winners and Losers,' 160–61; Ellis, *China in Latin America*, 204.

117 Muradian, 'Is China a Threat to Mesoamerica's Development?,' 809, 816; Phillips, *Consequences of an Emerging China*, 21; Jenkins, 'China's Global Expansion,' 820–21.

118 Ellis, *China in Latin America*, 205.

119 Muradian, 'Is China a Threat to Mesoamerica's Development?,' 811.

120 Ellis, *China in Latin America*, 205–06; Muradian, 'Is China a Threat to Mesoamerica's Development?,' 811.

121 Ellis, *China in Latin America*, 206.

122 Ibid., 110–15, 126–28, 150–51.

123 Ibid., 126–27, 274.

nation's largest iron mine.[124] In Venezuela, Chinese firms operate several oilfields.[125] In both Peru and Ecuador, Chinese firms have been embroiled in labor disputes with workers, conflicts with indigenous peoples, tax disputes with local authorities, and numerous conflicts with government officials over environmental law violations.[126] Regrettably, the limited but troubling record of Chinese resource extractive companies in Latin America appears to mimic the behavior of their western transnational counterparts.[127]

In sum, China's engagement with Latin America has produced winners and losers. Latin American countries that export primary commodities have benefited in the short term from China's demand for raw materials. Those countries that produce manufactured goods have encountered stiff competition from China, and have suffered mounting losses. In addition, China's limited direct investment in Latin American resource extractive industries has exacerbated social and environmental conflicts.

Notwithstanding the short-terms gains of natural resource exporters, China's engagement with Latin America threatens to impoverish rather than enrich that region in the long term. China's demand for natural resources is likely to lock Latin America into primary product specialization that produces neither technological innovation nor demand

124 Ibid., 150.

125 Ibid., 111.

126 Ibid., 104, at 150–51, 275–76 (describing conflicts between Chinese mining enterprises and local people in Ecuador and Peru); Simon Romero, 'Tensions Over Chinese Mining Ventures in Peru,' *New York Times,* August 14, 2010; Milagros Salazar, 'Peru-China: Social Responsibility Missing Growing Trade Ties,' IPS Inter Press Service, Feb. 3, 2010, accessed January 10, 2012, http://ipsnews.net/print.asp?idnews=50206. Indeed, according to diplomatic cables released by Wikileaks, neighboring Colombia, which is eager to attract Chinese investment in infrastructure, automobile plants, consumer electronics, and chemicals, is wary of investment in mining and petroleum because it is "suspicious of China's environmental and labor practices and unwilling to make concessions on those fronts." Hannah Aronowitz, 'Colombia Wary of Chinese Investment: Wikileaks.' *Colombia Reports,* January 19, 2011.

127 The literature on the abuses of Western transnational corporations in Latin America is voluminous. *See, e.g.,* Soren Hvalkof, 'Outrage in Rubber and Oil: Extractivism, Indigenous Peoples, and Justice in the Upper Amazon,' in *People, Plants & Justice: The Politics of Nature Conservation,* ed. Charles Zerner (New York: Columbia University Press, 2000), 83–116; Scott Holwick, 'Transnational Corporate Behavior and Its Disparate and Unjust Effects on the Indigenous Cultures and the Environment of Developing Countries: Jota v. Texaco, a Case Study,' *Colorado Journal of International Environmental Law and Policy* 11 (2000): 183–221; Richard L. Herz, 'Litigating Environmental Abuses under the Alien Tort Claims Act: A Practical Assessment,' *Virginia Journal of International Law* 40 (2000): 545–638; Judith Kimerling, 'Disregarding Environmental Law: Petroleum Development in Protected Natural Areas and Indigenous Homelands in the Ecuadoran Amazon,' *Hastings International and Comparative Law Review* 14 (1991): 849–903.

for skilled labor and that has long been associated with economic stagnation.[128] Indeed, commodity booms in Latin America have historically frustrated economic development by shifting resources away from manufacturing and by producing economic busts when commodity prices subsequently collapsed.[129] Furthermore, Latin American countries seeking to diversify into more dynamic, technology-intensive manufactured products will find themselves constrained by formidable competition from China and may even experience de-industrialization.[130] It is hardly surprising that "Latin American countries, if taken together, initiate more [anti-dumping] investigations and adopt more final measures against China than any other jurisdiction in the world."[131]

Finally, China's trade and investment presence in Latin America poses significant risks to the region's environment. Agro-export specialization in the developing world has generally led to erosion of genetic diversity, unsustainable levels of pesticide use, agrochemical contamination of lakes, rivers, and groundwater, increased human exposure to toxic pesticides, depletion of aquifers, and deforestation (due to the conversion of forests to crop land).[132] Mining and petroleum extraction are among the

---

128 Gallagher & Porzecanski, *The Dragon in the Room*, 29–32; Phillips, *Consequences of an Emerging China*, 11; Roldan Muradian and Joan Martinez-Alier, 'Trade and the Environment from a 'Southern' Perspective.' *Ecological Economics* 36 (2001): 286. For a discussion of the relationship between specialization in natural resource exportation and economic stagnation, see Macartan Humphreys et al., 'What is the Problem with Natural Resource Wealth?' in *Escaping the Natural Resource Curse*, ed. Macartan Humphreys et al. (New York: Columbia University Press, 2007), 1–20; Tobias Kronenberg, 'The Curse of Natural Resources in Transition Economies,' *Economics of Transition* 12 (2004): 400–401; Edward B. Barbier, 'Agricultural Expansion, Resource Booms and Growth in Latin America: Implications for Long-Run Economic Development,' *World Development* 32 (2004): 145–47; Sanjaya Lall, 'The Technological Structure and Performance of Developing Country Manufactured Exports 1985–1998,' *Oxford Development Studies* 28 (2000): 340–41.

129 Bulmer-Thomas, *Economic History*, 69–72; Barbier, 'Agricultural Expansion,' 146–47; Mamerto Perez, et al., *The Promise and Perils of Agricultural Trade Liberalization: Lessons from Latin America* (Washington, DC and Medford, MA: Washington Office on Latin America and Global Development and Environment Institute, 2008), 4–5, accessed January 16, 2012, http://ase.tufts.edu/gdae/Pubs/rp/AgricWGReportJuly08.pdf.

130 Gallagher & Porzecanski, *The Dragon in the Room*, 39–97; 137–38; Mesquita Moreira, 'Fear of China,' 372–73; Ellis, *China in Latin America*, 287.

131 International Bar Association Divisions Project Team, *Anti-Dumping Investigations Against China in Latin America* (London: International Bar Association, 2010) 5, accessed January 10, 2010, http://papers.ssrn.com/sol3/papers.cfm?abstract_id=1555619.

132 Carmen G. Gonzalez, 'Trade Liberalization, Food Security, and the Environment: The Neoliberal Threat to Sustainable Rural Development.' *Transnational Law and Contemporary Problems* 14 (2004): 469–70; Barbier, 'Agricultural Expansion,' 139; Perez et al., *The Promise and Perils of Agricultural Trade Liberalization*, 13–14; Working Group on Development and Environment in the Americas, *Globalization and the Environment:*

most polluting sectors of the economy,[133] and typically result in toxic discharges to air, water, and land as well as conflict with local and indigenous communities.[134] In the absence of effective environmental stewardship by Latin American governments, the region's growing commercial ties with China will likely accelerate environmental degradation by increasing pollution, depleting non-renewable resources, and promoting the unsustainable use of renewable resources.

As one Chinese analyst candidly observes:

> The fact remains that Chinese trade and investment in the region cannot escape the stigma of a neocolonial pattern, especially given China's very narrow commodity needs. The historical precedent of success in this framework is, ironically, not the United States, but Great Britain. From the sixteenth century to the early twentieth century, Britain invested heavily in South America to extract primary materials and agricultural goods to sustain its enormous manufacturing capacity.... Whether this trade pattern is sustainable and for how long remains a key question.[135]

In order to grapple with the challenges posed by China's rise, Latin America needs to upgrade its industrial capabilities, to invest in technology and education, and to integrate sustainability into development planning. While the current patterns of trade and investment between China and Latin America may not bode well for sustainable development in Latin America, it is important to recognize that China is not the root cause of Latin America's predicament. Instead of demonizing China (as a threat) or idealizing it (as a model), it would be more productive to consider ways in which China and Latin America might collaborate to make the legal regimes governing trade and investment more environmentally sustainable and development-friendly.

Lessons from the Americas (Washington, DC: Heinrich Boll Foundation, 2004), 16–19, 34, accessed January 12, 2012, http://ase.tufts.edu/gdae/Pubs/rp/WorkingGroupReportJuly04.pdf.

133 *See* Roldan Muradian and Joan Martinez-Alier, *Globalization and Poverty: An Ecological Perspective* (Berlin: Heinrich Boll Foundation, 2001), 14, accessed January 10, 2012, http://www.worldsummit2002.org/publications/WSP7.pdf.

134 Joan Martinez-Alier, *The Environmentalism of the Poor: A Study of Ecological Conflicts and Valuation* (Cheltenham, UK & Northampton, MA: Edward Elgar Publishing, 2002), 54–67, 100–108.

135 *See* Lanxin, 'An Alternative Chinese View,' 55. *See also* Lall & Weiss, 'China's Competitive Threat,' 184 (describing the pattern of trade between China and Latin America as "almost a classic illustration of colonial trade between developing and industrialized regions.").

4. Towards a More Just Economic Order

China's growing economic clout will undoubtedly influence the evolution of international trade law and international investment law. This section examines the implications for economic development in Latin America of China's role in the international trade and investment regimes.

4.1. *China and the WTO*

The need for South-South cooperation to transform the rules governing international trade has been recognized since the post-World War II period. The majority of developing countries were under colonial rule at the 1947 inception of the General Agreement on Tariffs and Trade (GATT).[136] Developing countries quickly realized that political independence was not tantamount to economic independence given the economic stagnation that had occurred under colonial domination and given an international economic system that seemed to favor industrialized countries.[137] The GATT, for example, advanced the interests of industrialized countries at the expense of those less developed. While industrialized countries benefited from the GATT's reduction of tariffs on manufactured goods, various GATT exceptions enabled industrialized countries to limit or exclude textiles, clothing, and agricultural products from their less developed counterparts.[138]

By the mid-1950s, developing countries had organized to demand a variety of measures to overcome the colonial legacy, stimulate economic development, and address persistent inequities in the international trading system.[139] These measures included the removal of industrialized country trade barriers and subsidies on primary products; preferential market access and non-reciprocal tariff concessions for the benefit of

---

[136] Faizel Ismail, 'Rediscovering the Role of Developing Countries in GATT before the Doha Round,' *The Law and Development Review* 1 (2008):50, 55.

[137] Philippe Cullet, *Differential Treatment in International Environmental Law* (Burlington, VT: Ashgate Publishing Company, 2003), 60.

[138] Ismail, 'Rediscovering the Role of Developing Countries,' 58–59; Carmen G. Gonzalez, 'Institutionalizing Inequality: The WTO Agreement on Agriculture, Food Security, and Developing Countries.' *Columbia Journal of Environmental Law* 27 (2002): 441–45; Yong-Shik Lee, *Reclaiming Development in the World Trading System* (Cambridge: Cambridge University Press, 2006), 107–110.

[139] *See* Ismail, 'Rediscovering the Role of Developing Countries,' 59; Peter Lichtenbaum, 'Reflections on the WTO Doha Ministerial: 'Special Treatment' vs. 'Equal Participation': Striking a Balance in the Doha Negotiations,' *American University International Law Review* 17 (2002): 1009.

developing countries; and the right of developing countries to promote industrialization through the imposition of tariffs and quotas to protect infant industries.[140]

In 1964, the United Nations Conference on Trade and Development (UNCTAD) entered into operation as an organ of the UN General Assembly to promote trade-related initiatives that would accelerate economic development.[141] That same year, developing countries came together as the Group of Seventy-Seven (G-77) to build solidarity and cooperation among developing countries in the area of trade and development and to demand a more just international economic order.[142]

As a consequence of sustained pressure from developing countries, the GATT was amended several times to make its provisions more development-friendly.[143] The amendments included provisions permitting developing countries to engage in infant industry protection and encouraging industrialized countries to provide greater market access opportunities for developing country products.[144]

Regrettably, the amendments fell far short of expectations. Their language was often non-binding and frequently excluded the very products of greatest interest to developing countries (clothing, textiles and agricultural products).[145] The benefits of preferential market access declined over time as overall tariff levels decreased.[146] The infant industry protection provisions proved unworkable because they required developing countries to negotiate compensatory measures with affected trading partners.[147]

The WTO, which succeeded the 1947 GATT, did not improve matters. In exchange for enhanced market access for developing country textiles and agricultural products, developing countries agreed to undertake new obligations in a variety of areas that were of particular interest to industrialized countries (including intellectual property, services, and investment).[148]

---

140 Ismail, 'Rediscovering the Role of Developing Countries,' 59–67.
141 Cullet, *Differential Treatment,* 61.
142 Hirst, 'A South-South Perspective,' 91.
143 Ismail, 'Rediscovering the Role of Developing Countries,' 65–67.
144 Ibid.
145 Lee, *Reclaiming Development,* 37–38.
146 Ibid., 37.
147 Ibid., 29–30.
148 Frank J. Garcia, 'Beyond Special and Differential Treatment.' *Boston College International and Comparative Law Review* 27 (2004): 297.

Lamentably, the WTO did not succeed in dismantling the trade barriers that excluded developing country products from industrialized country markets.[149] With respect to agricultural products, for example, industrialized countries maintained import barriers and actually *increased* subsidies in the years following the WTO's entry into force.[150] As a consequence of these subsidies and import barriers, developing countries lost an estimated $35 billion a year.[151] While the United States and EU continued to subsidize domestic agribusiness and to utilize tariffs to exclude developing country agricultural products, the structural adjustment programs mandated by the IMF and the World Bank typically required developing countries to open up their markets to ruinous foreign competition.[152] In addition, the WTO restricted the ability of developing countries to use tariffs and subsidies to strategically promote potentially dynamic industries; dismantled the import barriers that had been used by developing countries to protect domestic industries from more technologically advanced foreign competitors; and imposed a host of new and costly obligations on developing countries in the areas of intellectual property, services, and investment.[153]

In recognition of developing countries' dissatisfaction with the WTO legal framework, the ministerial declaration launching the Doha Round of WTO negotiations promised a review of the development-friendly provisions of the WTO in order to make them "more precise, effective and operational."[154] Developing countries organized themselves into coalitions in order to exert their collective influence on the trade negotiations.[155] However, little progress had been made on the issues of most concern to developing countries by the time of the 2003 Fifth Ministerial Conference in Cancun, Mexico.[156] Frustrated by the unwillingness of the

---

149 Ibid., 298.

150 Gonzalez, 'Institutionalizing Inequality,' 468.

151 'World Trade Talks Near Collapse Over Farm Subsidies Row,' *Financial Times*, October. 19, 1990, 1.

152 Gonzalez, 'Trade Liberalization, Food Security, and the Environment,' 457–60; 463–464; Oxfam, *Rigged Rules and Double Standards: Trade, Globalisation and the Fight Against Poverty* (London: Oxfam Publishing, 2002), 95–106; Gonzalez, 'Institutionalizing Inequality,' 446–49, 459–68.

153 Garcia, 'Beyond Special and Differential Treatment,' 147, at 298; Lee, *Reclaiming Development*, 41–42.

154 *See* World Trade Organization, Ministerial Declaration of 14 November 2001, ¶ 44, WT/MIN(01)/DEC/1, 41 I.L.M. 746 (2002).

155 Sonia E. Rolland, 'Developing Country Coalitions at the WTO: In Search of Legal Support,' *Harvard International Law Journal* 48 (2007):492–499.

156 Eugenia McGill, 'Poverty and Social Analysis of Trade Agreements: A More Coherent Approach?' *Boston College International and Comparative Law Review* 27 (2004): 376.

United States and the EU to reduce their agricultural subsidies, delegates from Asia, Africa, and Latin America walked out of the negotiations.[157] The Doha Round of trade negotiations collapsed again in 2008 and 2011 as a consequence of ongoing disputes between developed and developing countries over agricultural trade and over U.S. and EU demands that developing countries drastically reduce tariffs on industrial goods.[158]

In light of the dependence of so many developing countries on agricultural production, the Doha Round of WTO negotiations must, at a minimum, require developed countries to reduce agricultural subsidies and open their markets to developing country agricultural products and allow developing countries to protect the livelihoods of poor and subsistence farmers.[159] However, this is only the first step. As China's economic rise demonstrates, successful industrialization has historically required state intervention in the economy to subsidize and protect key industries until they were strong enough to compete in world markets. In order to advance rather than frustrate economic development, any reforms emerging from the Doha Round of WTO negotiations must give developing countries the permission to deploy subsidies, tariffs, quotas, local content requirements, technology transfer obligations, and other trade-restrictive measures to promote those industries most likely to contribute to long-term national well-being.[160]

China, at least rhetorically, has emphasized that it shares a common history of colonial domination, poverty and struggle for independence with Latin America.[161] China's official pronouncements support developing country efforts to transform the current WTO legal framework and recognize the importance of development.[162]

---

[157] Elizabeth Becker, 'Poorer Countries Pull Out of Talks Over World Trade,' New York Times, September 15, 2003, A1; Gretchen Peters, 'In Cancun, a Blow to World Trade,' *Christian Science Monitor*, September 16, 2003, 6.

[158] Heather Stewart, 'Tariffs: WTO Talks Collapse after India and China Clash with America over Farm Products,' *The Guardian*, July 30, 2008; Martin Khor, 'The Blame Game Still Stalling Doha Round of WTO Talks,' *The China Post*, March 1, 2011; John W. Miller, 'Trade Talk Impasse Prompts a Plan B,' *Wall Street Journal*, April 28, 2011.

[159] Carmen G. Gonzalez, 'Deconstructing the Mythology of Free Trade: Critical Reflections on Comparative Advantage.' *Berkeley La Raza Law Journal* 17 (2006): 69.

[160] Ibid.; Lee, *Reclaiming Development*, 62–68. *See generally*, Kevin Gallagher, ed. *Putting Development First: The Importance of Policy Space in the WTO and International Financial Institutions* (London: Zed Books, 2005).

[161] Lanxin, 'An Alternative Chinese View,' 45.

[162] Marcia Don Harpaz, 'China and the WTO: New Kid in the Developing Bloc?' *International Law Forum of the Hebrew University of Jerusalem Law Faculty, Research Paper No. 2–07* (Feb. 2007), 48–49, accessed January 10, 2012. http://papers.ssrn.com/sol3/papers.cfm?abstract_id=961768.

However, countries that arrive at the pinnacle of economic success through protectionism have a disconcerting tendency to advocate free trade in order to prevent other countries from catching up.[163] Professor Ha-Joon Chang underscores this historic tendency by quoting the observations of 19th century German economist Friedrich List regarding British industrial development:

> It is a very common clever trick that when anyone has attained the summit of greatness, he *kicks away the ladder* by which he climbed up, in order to deprive others of the means of climbing up after him.... Any nation which by means of protective duties and restrictions on navigation has raised her manufacturing power and her navigation to such a degree of development that no other nation can sustain free competition with her, can do nothing wiser than *to throw away these ladders* of her greatness, to preach to other nations the benefits of free trade, and to declare in penitent tones that she has hitherto wandered in the paths of error, and has now for the first time succeeded in discovering the truth.[164]

Like Great Britain, the United States achieved its economic might through protectionist means, but became an ardent proponent of free trade once it achieved industrial supremacy after World War II.[165] By imposing free market reforms on developing countries through aid and trade policy and through the World Bank, the IMF, and the WTO, industrialized countries are, in effect, consigning developing countries to poverty.

It is unclear whether China, having achieved economic success, will kick away the development ladder or will work with other developing countries to promote a more just international economic order.

Notwithstanding its pro-development rhetoric, China has refused to assume a leadership role among developing countries and has asserted that it seeks to serve as a bridge between developed and developing countries.[166] For example, prior to the Cancun Ministerial Conference, China joined the alliance of approximately 20 developing countries that sought to reform agricultural policy in the United States and the EU.[167] However, China maintained a low profile in the agriculture debate and allowed other developing countries, particularly India and Brazil, to lead the struggle against U.S. and EU agricultural protectionism.[168]

---

163 Chang, *Kicking Away the Ladder*, 4–5.
164 Ibid. (quoting Friedrich List).
165 Ibid., 5.
166 Harpaz, 'China and the WTO,' 50.
167 Ibid., 51.
168 Ibid., 51–52.

China's positions in the Doha Round of WTO negotiations have been motivated largely by its national self-interest rather than the collective interests of developing countries. With respect to market access for non-agricultural commodities, for example, China proposed more flexible commitments (e.g., longer compliance timeframes and/or lower tariff reductions) for newly acceded WTO members than for other developing countries despite developing country objections.[169] In connection with the review of the dispute settlement mechanism, China proposed that developed country WTO members be prohibited from bringing more than two cases per year against a particular developing country member and that the time-frame for WTO disputes over safeguards and anti-dumping measures be shortened.[170] These proposals advance China's self-interest in two distinct respects. First, in light of growing trade frictions between China and the United States,[171] China's proposal must be regarded as an effort to limit the number of WTO complaints that the United States may bring against China.[172] Second, because China is the world's leading target of anti-dumping investigations, China appears to be laying the groundwork for rapid, offensive WTO action whenever WTO members impose anti-dumping measures on Chinese exports.[173] To its credit, China did advocate a dispute resolution reform proposal that does enjoy substantial developing country support. China proposed that in cases brought by developed country WTO members against developing country WTO members, if the developing country respondent is found not to have violated its WTO obligations, the developed country complainant should bear the developing country's legal costs.[174]

Finally, China has taken positions directly contrary to the interests of other developing countries in order to advance its economic interests. For example, when the WTO Agreement on Textiles and Clothing required the elimination of textile quotas by 2005, it soon became apparent that China and India would wind up dominating textile imports to the detriment of other developing countries.[175] China blocked a proposal calling for

---

169 Ibid., 53–56.

170 Chan Kar Keung, 'The Reform of the WTO Dispute Settlement Mechanism and the Participation of China.' *Journal of Chinese and Comparative Law* 6 (2003): 224–226.

171 *See generally,* Chad P. Brown, 'U.S.-China Trade Conflicts and the Future of the WTO.' *Fletcher Forum of World Affairs* 33 (2009): 27– 48.

172 Harpaz, 'China and the WTO,' 59–60.

173 Ibid., 60.

174 Chan Kar Keung, 'The Reform of the WTO Dispute Settlement Mechanism,' 225.

175 Harpaz, 'China and the WTO,' 63–64.

a formal work group to study the impact of the elimination of the textile quotas, and opposed a proposal to enable developing countries to maintain their market share once quotas ended.[176] Indeed, China even opposed the WTO's proposed technical assistance program to help developing countries adjust to the new regime out of concern that this program would instruct developing countries on the textile agreement's safeguard provisions.[177]

China is a relative newcomer to the WTO, and its role in the organization is still evolving. By virtue of its economic power and participation in the so-called BRIC group (Brazil, Russia, India, and China) of developing countries, China will undoubtedly exert significant influence in the evolution of international trade law. Indeed, China flexed its muscles during the Doha Round of WTO negotiations by joining forces with India and Brazil to reject trade liberalization commitments demanded by wealthy countries that were perceived as unfair and one-sided by most developing countries.[178] Nevertheless, the impact of China on the rules governing international trade remains uncertain. While the limited evidence available to date suggests that China is likely to advance its own interests rather than struggle to create a more just economic order, it is too early to make a definitive assessment.

4.2. *China and International Investment Law*

Although the academic literature on globalization has focused largely on the WTO, foreign direct investment (FDI) is regarded by many scholars as the primary engine of economic development.[179] The capital flows produced by FDI vastly exceed those generated by the international trade in goods, and the BRIC countries are quickly joining the United States and Europe as the world's leading capital exporters.[180]

Global investment flows are governed by over 2800 bilateral investment treaties (BITs) and over 300 regional free trade agreements (FTAs) that contain investment provisions.[181] These agreements arguably induce

[176] Ibid.
[177] Ibid., 64–65.
[178] Khor, 'The Blame Game,' 157.
[179] Jose E. Alvarez, 'An 'Empire of Law' or the 'Law of Empire'?' *Alabama Law Review* 60 (2009): 956.
[180] Ibid.
[181] United Nations Conference on Trade and Development (UNCTAD), *World Investment Report 2011: Non-Equity Modes of International Production and Development* (New York & Geneva: United Nations, 2011), 100, accessed January 16, 2012. http://www.unctad-docs.org/files/UNCTAD-WIR2011-Full-en.pdf.

greater compliance than the WTO because they authorize foreign investors to initiate binding arbitration of investor-state disputes, whereas the WTO relies on governments to bring claims against one another.[182] With roughly 80,000 enterprises engaged in FDI, investment disputes vastly outnumber WTO claims, and have produced a burgeoning body of international investment jurisprudence.[183]

While BITs and FTA investment chapters are by no means uniform, they typically provide that the host state will give the foreign investor: (1) no less favorable treatment than it gives its own investors (national treatment); (2) no less favorable treatment than it gives other foreign investors (most favored nation, or MFN, treatment); (3) "fair and equitable treatment"; (4) prompt, adequate, and effective compensation in the event of direct or indirect expropriation; and (5) the ability to repatriate profits without undue restrictions.[184] In addition, these agreements generally permit foreign investors to bypass the host state's legal system by submitting disputes to international binding arbitration, usually under rules established by the World Bank's International Centre for the Settlement of Investment Disputes (ICSID).[185]

International investment law has its origins in the global expansion of European trade and investment between the seventeenth and early twentieth centuries.[186] "Unequal" or capitulation treaties opened China and other non-European territories to Western trade and investment, and granted Western consular officials exclusive jurisdiction over Western nationals and their property in lieu of the local legal system.[187] Based on the construction of non-European legal systems as "uncivilized" or

---

182 Alvarez, 'An Empire of Law,' 961.

183 Ibid., 959.

184 Ibid., 957–58.

185 Ibid., 958.

186 Kate Miles, 'International Investment Law: Origins, Imperialism and Conceptualizing the Environment.' *Colorado Journal of International Environmental Law and Policy* 21 (2010): 1–2.

187 Ibid., 6–7; Alvarez, 'An Empire of Law,' 957. One of the most famous of the unequal treaties was the Treaty of Nanjing, which was signed in 1842 after China's defeat by the British in the Opium War. The Opium War was triggered by the Chinese Emperor's refusal to permit British traders to sell opium in China. Under the Treaty of Nanjing, China ceded Hong Kong to Great Britain, opened five Chinese ports for trade, and paid the British government $21 million in reparations. Soon thereafter, the United States and France concluded their own unequal treaties with China, which provided, among other things, for consular jurisdiction over disputes involving U.S. and French nationals. Because the British had inserted a most favored nations clause in a supplement to the Treaty of Nanjing, this additional concession applied to the British as well. Jonathan Spence, *The Search for Modern China* (New York: W.W. Norton & Company, 1990), 158–162.

inferior, direct consular control over trade and investment disputes enabled Western powers to impose their own conception of property rights on non-European territories and peoples for the economic benefit of European traders and investors.[188] This tradition arguably continues under modern BITs, with international arbitrators taking the place of Western consular officials.[189]

By the nineteenth century, international investment law had evolved into a series of international minimum standards for the treatment of the persons and property of aliens, the breach of which triggered state responsibility and permitted the home state to intervene diplomatically and/or militarily in defense of the interests of its citizens.[190] In Latin America, disputes over the persons and property of aliens often served as pretexts for naval blockades and military invasions.[191] For example, England intervened in Latin America at least 40 times between 1820 and 1914.[192] Napoleon III invaded Mexico in 1862 ostensibly in response to Mexico's default on bonds purchased by French citizens.[193] In order to forestall further European intervention, the United States announced that it would "begin preemptive landings and seizures of customs houses in defaulting Central American and Caribbean nations."[194] Between 1798 and 1945, the United States intervened in Latin America at least 68 times, including all instances of territorial incursions.[195]

In response to these violations of national sovereignty, Latin American countries promoted the inclusion in constitutions, domestic legislation, and treaties of a set of principles known as the Calvo Doctrine.[196] Named after the Argentine diplomat and scholar Carlos Calvo, the Calvo Doctrine consisted of three distinct elements: (1) state sovereignty and freedom from interference by other states; (2) equal treatment for foreigners and nationals (no special privileges for foreigners); and (3) the use of local tribunals and local laws in resolving disputes with foreigners.[197]

188 Miles, 'International Investment Law,' 6–7.
189 Alvarez, 'An Empire of Law,' 960.
190 Ibid., 14–15.
191 Frank Griffith Dawson, 'Contributions of Lesser Developed Nations to International Law: The Latin American Experience.' Case Western Reserve Journal of International Law 13 (1981): 46–48.
192 Ibid., 48.
193 Ibid., 49.
194 Ibid., 53.
195 Richard F. Grimmett, *Instances of Use of United States Armed Forces Abroad, 1798–2010* (Washington, DC: Congressional Research Service, 2011), 2–11.
196 Dawson, 'Contributions of Lesser Developed Nations to International Law,' 51.
197 Ibid., 49.

The Calvo doctrine was embraced by Latin American governments, and endorsed in the post-World War II period by the newly independent states in Asia and Africa because it enhanced national sovereignty by requiring foreign investors to settle all disputes in accordance with national law and to refrain from seeking the assistance of their homes states.[198] The Calvo doctrine reached its apogee of popularity as developing countries banded together to demand a New International Economic Order favorable to Third World economic interests.[199]

However, when the debt crisis of the 1980s forced Latin American countries to turn to FDI rather than commercial loans to finance development, many countries abandoned the Calvo Doctrine and adopted legislation designed to attract foreign capital, including special preferences for foreign investors, international minimum standards of treatment, and compulsory arbitration of investment disputes.[200] Indeed, the Calvo Doctrine gave way in the 1990s to an unprecedented worldwide wave of BIT ratifications and changes in domestic legislation that favored foreign investment.[201]

The model investment agreements developed by Europe and the United States have been adopted as the template for thousands of BITs and FTA investment chapters currently in existence.[202] Countries that once endorsed the Calvo Doctrine are now parties to investment agreements that provide high levels of protection for foreign investors, constrain the regulatory discretion of the host state, and require the submission of disputes to international arbitration in lieu of recourse to host state tribunals.[203] These international investment agreements give foreign investors a wide panoply of rights without any corresponding duties and responsibilities (such as the obligation to comply with local laws, including labor, environmental, and anti-corruption standards) and without any

---

[198] Wenhua Shan, 'Is Calvo Dead?,' *American Journal of Comparative Law* 55 (2007): 129; Anthony Anghie, *Imperialism, Sovereignty and the Making of International Law* (Cambridge: Cambridge University Press, 2004), 209.

[199] *See* Dawson, 'Contributions of Lesser Developed Nations to International Law,' 75–76.

[200] Shan, 'Is Calvo Dead?,' 131–132.

[201] Jose E. Alvarez, 'A Special Tribute to Andreas Lowenfeld: A Bit on Custom,' *New York University Journal of International Law and Policy* 42 (2009): 49–55.

[202] Ibid., 49–50.

[203] Ibid., 50–55.

legal remedy for local communities or host states harmed by the foreign investor's activities.[204]

China, which once supported the New International Economic Order and rejected investor protection norms that interfered with its national sovereignty, has adopted BITs inspired by U.S. models that typically include national treatment, fair and equitable treatment, protections against direct and indirect expropriations, liberal capital transfer provisions, and compulsory investor-state arbitration.[205] Indeed, China has become one of the world's largest BIT signatories, and its BITs with both developed and developing countries are generally comparable to those of traditional capital-exporting countries.[206]

The BITs and FTA investment chapters inspired by U.S. and European models restrict the policy space available to capital-importing nations to dictate their own development paths in numerous ways, four of which are highlighted below.

First, BIT provisions requiring states to accord foreign investors fair and equitable treatment have been interpreted by arbitration tribunals "as requiring the host state to inform the investor of all rules and regulations that will govern the investment for its duration and requiring the host state to maintain a stable legal and business framework throughout the term of the investment."[207] This extraordinarily investor-protective standard demands an extremely well-run administrative apparatus that would present challenges even in nations with highly developed legal systems.[208] Due to its breadth and ambiguity, this standard has generated an avalanche of claims against host states by foreign investors, and has deterred states from reforming obsolete regulatory policies.[209]

---

[204] Wenhua Shan, 'From 'North-South Divide' to 'Private-Public Debate': Revival of the Calvo Doctrine and the Changing Landscape in International Investment Law,' *Northwestern Journal of International Law and Business* 27 (2007): 655–659.

[205] Alvarez, 'A Bit on Custom,' 50; *see generally*, Stephan W. Schill, 'Tearing Down the Great Wall: The New Generation Investment Treaties of the People's Republic of China,' *Cardozo Journal of International and Comparative Law* 15 (2007): 73–118 (describing the evolution of China's BITs).

[206] Schill, 'Tearing Down the Great Wall,' 82; *see generally*, Nora Gallagher and Wenhua Shan, *Chinese Investment Treaties: Policy and Practice* (Oxford: Oxford University Press, 2009) (explaining the gradual convergence of China's BITs toward the European model).

[207] Miles, 'International Investment Law,' 42.

[208] Alvarez, 'An Empire of Law,' 964–65.

[209] Marie-Claire Cordonier Segger and Avidan Kent, 'Promoting Sustainable Development through International Law,' in *Sustainable Development in World Investment*

Second, arbitration tribunals have adopted an expansive interpretation of the duty to compensate investors for government action that constitutes an indirect expropriation. Originally intended to shield investors from arbitrary takings of property, this provision has enabled foreign investors to challenge host state health and environmental regulations, thereby permitting the foreign investor to exploit the natural resources of the host state without regard to the impact on the host state, its people, or its environment.[210]

Third, arbitration tribunals have construed the national treatment clause in BITs to preclude almost any difference in the treatment of foreign and domestic investors. As a result, "the State is left with little room to implement measures to promote national economic sectors which are in need of governmental aid to be able to compete with foreign companies."[211]

Fourth, the investor-state arbitration mechanism bypasses local courts, lacks transparency, excludes communities affected by the investment from the dispute resolution process, and emphasizes investor protection to the exclusion of competing regulatory priorities, including developmental, environmental, and human rights considerations.[212] For example, arbitration tribunals have generally refused to consider the human rights implications of their decisions,[213] and have denied states the opportunity to bring counterclaims based on the conduct of the foreign investor.[214]

In short, international investment law has evolved from the practices of European investors, traders and colonizers into a regime designed to protect only the foreign investor – often at the expense of the interests of the state, the environment, and the local communities affected by the investment.[215] Notwithstanding its imperial origins, the one-sided BIT model favored by capital-exporting countries has been "normalized," depoliticized, and universalized.

Law, ed. Marie-Claire Cordonier Segger, et al. (The Netherlands: Kluwer Law International, 2011), 772–773, 779.

210 *See* Miles, 'International Investment Law,' 40–42.

211 Ximena Fuentes, 'The Impact of International Foreign Investment Rules on Domestic Law,' in *Global Justice and Sustainable Development,* ed. Duncan French (Leiden: Martinius Nijhoff Publishers, 2010), 198–199.

212 Miles, 'International Investment Law,' 19–20; Jorge Daniel Taillant & Jonathan Bonnitcha, 'International Investment Law and Human Rights,' in *Sustainable Development in World Investment Law,* ed. Marie-Claire Cordonier Segger, et al. (The Netherlands: Kluwer Law International, 2011), 68–69.

213 Taillant & Bonnitcha, 'International Investment Law and Human Rights,' 77–80.

214 Fuentes, 'The Impact of International Foreign Investment Rules,' 200.

215 Miles, 'International Investment Law,' 44–47.

However, the tide is beginning to turn against the existing BITs and in favor of a more balanced and equitable approach to foreign investment law.[216] Alarmed by the mounting investor-state arbitration claims, several Latin American countries have begun to re-evaluate their approach to investment liberalization and to adopt mechanisms to limit investor-state arbitration.[217] As affluent countries find themselves on the receiving end of investor-state complaints, the pressure is growing to develop an investment regime that takes better account of the rights and interests of the host state.[218] Even the United States has modified its original Model BIT to narrow the scope of compensable indirect takings, restrict fair and equitable treatment guarantees, and enhance governmental regulatory authority.[219]

China has long distinguished itself from the United States and Europe by emphasizing in its foreign relations the principles of national sovereignty, self-determination, and non-interference in the internal affairs of other countries.[220] However, by adopting BITs and FTA investment chapters comparable to U.S. and European models, China is replicating the West's single-minded emphasis on investor protection at the expense of capital-importing nations.

Instead of reproducing economic imperialism, China has an opportunity to work collaboratively with Latin American nations to develop more balanced and socially responsible BITs and FTA investment chapters that protect investors' interests while also recognizing the social, environmental, and developmental needs of the host state. One excellent starting point for South-South negotiations is the Model International Agreement on Investment for Sustainable Development developed by the International Institute for Sustainable Development (IISD), which is discussed more fully in the next section.[221] This model investment agreement attempts to adopt a more equitable approach to FDI by spelling out the rights and obligations of the host state, the home state, and the

216 Shan, 'North-South Divide,' 655–656.
217 Ibid., 634–35.
218 Miles, 'International Investment Law,' 47.
219 Alvarez, 'An Empire of Law,' 966–70.
220 Peter K. Yu, 'Lost in Translation?: Sinic Trade Agreements.' *U.C. Davis Law Review* 44 (2011): 1003.
221 Howard Mann, et al., *IISD Model International Agreement on Investment for Sustainable Development* (Winnipeg: International Institute for Sustainable Development, 2005), accessed January 10, 20102, http://www.iisd.org/pdf/2005/investment_model_int_agreement.pdf.

foreign investor and linking these obligations to the goal of sustainable development.[222]

5. The Challenge of Sustainable Development

In sharp contrast to China's uncertain role in the evolution of international trade and investment law, the impact of China's rise on sustainable development is becoming increasingly clear.

In its influential 1987 report, the World Commission on Environment and Development defined sustainable development as "development that meets the needs of the present without compromising the ability of future generations to meet their own needs."[223] Another widely accepted definition of sustainability is "improving the quality of life while living within the carrying capacity of supporting ecosystems."[224] Despite its vagueness, sustainable development is a useful concept because it underscores the indivisibility of social and economic development and environmental protection.[225]

The greatest long-term threat to sustainable development is the resource-intensive, growth-at-any-cost economic model pioneered and promoted by the United States and other wealthy countries. Until now, this chapter has considered the threat posed by this economic model to the domestic environment in China and in Latin America. This Part discusses the implications of this model for the global environment.

Mahatma Gandhi observed long ago that the planet does not have the ecological capacity to permit every citizen of the world to enjoy the wasteful, consumption-driven lifestyle of the West.[226] The industrialization of England, he noted, had required the enslavement and exploitation of large

---

[222] Mahnaz Malik, 'The IISD Model International Agreement on Investment for Sustainable Development,' in *Sustainable Development in World Investment Law,* ed. Marie-Claire Cordonier Segger, et al. (The Netherlands: Kluwer Law International, 2011), 565–584.

[223] World Commission on Environment and Development. *Our Common Future* (Oxford: Oxford University Press, 1987), 43.

[224] Andrew Dobson, *Fairness and Futurity: Essays on Environmental Sustainability and Social Justice* (Oxford: Oxford University Press, 1999), 23.

[225] David Hunter, et al., *International Environmental Law and Policy* (New York: Foundation Press, 2007), 200.

[226] Ramachandra Guha, *How Much Should a Person Consume? Environmentalism in India and the United States* (Berkeley & Los Angeles: University of California Press, 2006), 231–232.

parts of the world.[227] If India were to adopt a similar development path, he warned, "it would strip the world bare like locusts."[228]

The world's wealthiest countries and its rising economic powers (India and China) are currently consuming a disproportionate share of the world's natural resources by importing primary products and exporting wastes (to other countries or to the global commons) in addition to drawing upon their domestic natural resource endowments.[229] The United States, China, Japan, India, and the EU are currently using 75% of the planet's biocapacity–the amount of biologically productive land required to supply resources and absorb wastes.[230] This situation is sustainable only if poor countries freeze their economic development and continue to use only a fraction of their biocapacity.[231] If all countries of the world were to pursue growth at any cost, they would quickly exceed the carrying capacity of the world's ecosystems and would provoke global environmental catastrophe.[232]

Climate change is perhaps the most well-known example of human activity exceeding the ecological limits of the planet. After decades of debate, the reality of climate change is now indisputable. As the Intergovernmental Panel on Climate Change (IPCC) explained in a recent report, "warming of the climate system is unequivocal, as is now evident from observation of increases in global average air and ocean temperatures, widespread melting of snow and ice, and rising global average sea level."[233]

Developed countries are the major contributors to global warming. While the United States and China are the world's largest *current* emitters of carbon dioxide (CO_2),[234] developed countries account for 86% of the world's *cumulative historic* carbon dioxide emissions; developing

227 Ibid., 231.

228 Ibid.

229 Flavin & Gardner, 'China, India, and the New World Order,' 16; Carmen G. Gonzalez, 'Beyond Eco-Imperialism: An Environmental Justice Critique of Free Trade.' *Denver University Law Review* 78 (2001): 1001–1003.

230 Flavin & Gardner, 'China, India, and the New World Order,' 16.

231 Ibid.

232 Ibid., 18; Gonzalez, 'Beyond Eco-Imperialism,' 1003.

233 Intergovernmental Panel on Climate Change (IPCC), 'Summary for Policy-Makers,' in Climate Change 2007: The Physical Science Basis, Contribution of Working Group I to the Fourth Assessment Report of the Intergovernmental Panel on Climate Change (Cambridge: Cambridge University Press, 2007), 5, accessed January 10, 2012. http://www.ipcc.ch/pdf/assessment-report/ar4/wg1/ar4-wg1-spm.pdf.

234 'Gas Exchange: CO_2 Emissions 1990–2006,' *Nature* 447 (2007): 1038.

countries (including China) represent only 14%.[235] Moreover, the per capita CO_2 emissions of the United States are approximately six times greater than those of China.[236]

Notwithstanding their limited responsibility for producing climate change, developing countries will be disproportionately harmed by climate change due to their economic dependence on agricultural production, their vulnerable geographic locations, and their limited resources for adaptation and response to disasters such as floods and hurricanes.[237] Within each country, the communities most directly affected will likely be members of marginalized or subordinated populations, including the poor, women, and members of racial, ethnic and religious minorities.[238] As Hurricane Katrina in the United States demonstrated, even in wealthy countries, racial minorities and the poor are often inadequately protected against environmental hazards and forced to resort to self-help when environmental disasters strike.[239]

One of the central dilemmas for the international community is how to create incentives for China, the United States, and other countries to accept and enforce binding commitments to reduce greenhouse gas (GHG) emissions.[240] As China and the United States continue to blame each other for the international stalemate on climate change,[241] the planet teeters on the brink of catastrophe, with the world's most vulnerable people bearing the greatest risk.[242]

Some scholars contend that China has become a modern day imperial power–scouring the globe for natural resources, exploiting less powerful nations, and rejecting international environmental agreements that would curb its profligate consumption of the world's natural resources.[243] Others point out that China has become a popular offshore destination for the

---

235 Ruchi Anand, *International Environmental Justice: A North-South Dimension* (Burlington, VT: Ashgate Publishing, 2004), 30.

236 Michael Vandenbergh, 'Climate Change: The China Problem.' *Southern California Law Review* 81 (2008): 988.

237 Anand, *International Environmental Justice*, 35–41.

238 Ibid.

239 Center for Progressive Reform, *An Unnatural Disaster: The Aftermath of Hurricane Katrina* (Center for Progressive Reform White Paper, 2005), 23–40, http://www.progressivereform.org/articles/Unnatural_Disaster_512.pdf.

240 Vandenbergh, 'Climate Change: The China Problem,' 907.

241 Ibid., 908–911, 923–928.

242 Ruth Gordon, 'Climate Change and the Poorest Nations: Further Reflections on Global Inequality.' *University of Colorado Law Review* 78 (2007): 1589–1599.

243 Guha, *How Much Should a Person Consume?*, 238–239.

industrialized world's most polluting industries.[244] In other words, industrialized countries have achieved domestic environmental improvements (such as clean air and, in some cases, lower GHG emissions) while maintaining unsustainable levels of natural resource consumption by shifting their dirtiest industries to China and to other developing countries.[245] Indeed, recent studies confirm that the United States has out-sourced many of its GHG-emitting industries to developing countries[246] and that at least 30% of China's GHG emissions are attributable to the production of manufactured goods consumed primarily in developed countries.[247] Furthermore, when one takes into account the energy embodied in traded goods, China emerges as a net exporter of energy–in sharp contrast to its popular image as an insatiable energy consumer.[248]

These studies suggest that a post-Kyoto climate change agreement must continue to allocate the lion's share of responsibility for financing GHG abatement to the United States, the EU, and other developed countries based on production of GHGs (current and historic) and on consumption of products whose manufacture elsewhere in the world resulted in GHG emissions. While estimating GHG emissions based on consumption rather than production significantly lowers China's contribution to global warming, it does not absolve China from responsibility. China's projected increases in GHG emissions are so huge that China's emissions, when added to the GHGs already in the atmosphere, are likely to trigger catastrophic climate disruptions even if all other countries achieve near-zero emissions.[249]

Climate change is both an environmental issue and a development issue because its disproportionate impact on poor countries and vulnerable populations poses a direct threat to global efforts to alleviate poverty and improve economic and social well-being. Climate change is also a

---

[244] Jiahua Pan, et al., 'China's Balance of Emissions Embodied in Trade: Approaches to Measurement and Allocating International Responsibility.' *Oxford Review of Economic Policy* 24 (2008): 374.

[245] Muradian and Martinez-Alier, 'Trade and the Environment from a 'Southern' Perspective,' 286; Muradian & Martinez-Alier, *Globalisation and Poverty*, 15.

[246] Rhitu Chatterjee, 'Outsourcing U.S. Greenhouse-Gas Emissions.' *Environmental Science & Technology*, July 15, 2007, 4834–4835. Curiously, even stalwart environmentalists such as Lester Brown have applauded the United States' recent drop in carbon emissions (after a century of ever-increasing emissions) without mentioning the outsourcing of these emissions to China and other developing countries. Lester Brown, 'On Energy, We're Finally Walking the Walk.' *Washington Post*, September 20, 2009.

[247] Pan, et al., 'China's Balance of Emissions Embodied in Trade,' 373–74.

[248] Ibid., 374.

[249] Vandenbergh, 'Climate Change: The China Problem', 908.

development issue because the greatest future increases in GHG emissions are predicted to come from developing countries and because the problem cannot be solved without the participation of developing countries.[250]

Climate change is only one example of the myriad ways that human economic activities are exceeding ecosystem limits and producing a variety of harmful consequences, including unprecedented extinction of species; widespread chemical contamination of land, air, water, and human bodies; grave shortages of freshwater; and rapid degradation and desertification of agricultural lands.[251] If we are to achieve social and economic development without exceeding the limits of the planet's seriously degraded ecosystems, it is important to acknowledge that the resource-intensive, growth-at-any-cost economic model is no longer viable. Instead of demonizing China as an imperial power or depicting it as victim of an unjust international division of labor, we must devise a radically different paradigm of economic development that places human well-being, including the right to a healthy environment, at its core rather than relying on GDP as a proxy for human flourishing.

One of the benefits of the growing economic ties between China and Latin America is the opportunity to formulate a Southern agenda on trade and environment under the framework of sustainable development that integrates economic development, environmental protection, and poverty alleviation. Such an agenda would steer the trade and environment debate toward developing country concerns and away from efforts to impose Northern labor and environmental standards on developing countries in a manner reminiscent of the IMF's imposition of the Washington Consensus on debtor nations.[252]

The 1992 United Nations Conference on Environment and Development (UNCED) produced a series of guiding principles (the Rio Declaration) as well as an 800 page "blueprint" (Agenda 21) to achieve sustainable

[250] Matthew Clarke, 'The Climate and Development Nexus', *ICFAI Journal of Environmental Economics* 4 (2006): 33.

[251] Speth, *The Bridge at the Edge of the World*, 1–9.

[252] Magda Shahin, 'To What Extent Should Labor and Environmental Standards Be Linked to Trade?' *Law and Development Review* 2 (2009): 35–36 (describing the reasons that developing countries have generally opposed the incorporation of labor and environmental standards into trade agreements); Gonzalez, 'Beyond Eco-Imperialism,' 1004–09 (explaining why developing countries have regarded the use of unilateral trade restrictions, eco-duties, and upward harmonization of environmental standards to improve the environmental performance of the Global South as manifestations of imperialism).

development.[253] Agenda 21 acknowledges that "[i]nvestment is critical to the ability of developing countries to achieve needed economic growth to improve the welfare of their populations and to meet their basic needs in a sustainable manner, without deteriorating or depleting the resource base that underpins development."[254]

Energy is essential to sustainable development, and China is a pioneer in the field of renewable energy. China is the world's leading producer of wind turbines and solar panels, and it surpassed the United States in 2009 as the country with the highest installed renewable energy capacity.[255] Chinese innovations, if shared with Latin America through investment and technology transfer, could steer a path toward a more green economy.

Regrettably, China's investments in Latin America have been quite limited to date – in sharp contrast with its burgeoning trade with the region. China's investments have been concentrated in primary industries, and have thus far reinforced Latin America's commodity dependence rather than fostering technology diffusion, green production, renewable energy, or integration into lucrative global production chains.[256]

Moreover, the BITs and FTA investment chapters that have proliferated in recent decades to facilitate foreign direct investment focus almost exclusively on protecting the interests of foreign investors, and rarely mention sustainable development, investment in clean technology, or integration of social, environmental, and economic considerations.[257] China has entered into free trade agreements with Costa Rica, Chile, and Peru, and has signed bilateral investment treaties with over a dozen nations in Latin America.[258] While all three FTAs include sustainable

---

253 Rio Declaration on Environment and Development, in *Report of the U.N. Conference on Environment and Development,* 13 June 1992, U.N. Doc. A/CONF.151/26 (vol. I)(1992), reprinted in 31 I.L.M. 874 (1992); Agenda 21, in *Report of the U.N. Conference on Environment and Development,* 13 June 1992, U.N. Doc. A/CONF.151/26 (vols. I, II & III)(1992).

254 Agenda 21, at 2.23.

255 Pew Charitable Trusts, *Who's Winning the Clean Energy Race? – 2010,* (Philadelphia & Washington, DC: The Pew Charitable Trusts), 2–3, 34, accessed January 17, 2012, http://www.pewenvironment.org/uploadedFiles/PEG/Publications/Report/G-20Report - LOWRes-FINAL.pdf.

256 World Bank, *Latin America and the Caribbean's Long-Term Growth,* 135–36.

257 Marie-Claire Cordonier Segger & Andrew Newcombe, 'An Integrated Agenda for Sustainable Development in International Investment Law' in *Sustainable Development in World Investment Law,* ed. Marie-Claire Cordonier Segger, et al. (The Netherlands: Kluwer Law International, 2011), 124.

258 For a complete list of trade agreements in force for Latin American nations, see Organization of American States, Foreign Trade Information System, accessed January 10, 2012, http://www.sice.oas.org/agreements_e.asp. For a complete list of BITs signed by

development as one of the objectives in the preamble and two of the FTAs provide for cooperation on environmental, labor, and social security matters, China's BITs with Latin American nations tend to focus exclusively on protecting the rights of the investor by guaranteeing fair and equitable treatment, national treatment, most favored nation treatment, and fair and prompt compensation in the event of direct or indirect expropriation.[259] Only two of these bilateral investment treaties (with Guyana and Trinidad & Tobago) contain preambular language recognizing that BIT objectives can be achieved "without relaxing health, safety, and environmental measures of general application."[260]

In response to these one-sided investment agreements, the International Institute for Sustainable Development (IISD) has drafted a model investment agreement and accompanying negotiators' handbook with numerous suggestions on ways to balance investor rights and host country policy space.[261] Several scholars have advanced additional proposals to combine high levels of investment protection with greater concern for environmental protection and human flourishing.[262]

China as of June 1, 2011, see UNCTAD Investment Instruments Online, Total Number of Bilateral Treaties Concluded, accessed January 10, 2012, http://www.unctad.org/sections/dite_pcbb/docs/bits_china.pdf.

[259] Free Trade Agreement Between the Government of the Republic of Peru and the Government of the People's Republic of China, Art. 161 (2009) (entered into force March 1, 2010), accessed January 10, 2012, http://www.sice.oas.org/TPD/PER_CHN/Texts_28042009_e/FullText_20090422_e.pdf; Free Trade Agreement Between the Government of the People's Republic of China and the Government of Chile, Art. 108 (2005) (entered into force October 1, 2006), accessed January 10, 2012, http://www.sice.oas.org/Trade/CHL_CHN/CHL_CHN_e/chilechinind_e.asp. *See also* Free Trade Agreement Between the Government of the People's Republic of China and the Government of Costa Rica, (2010)(entered into force August 1, 2011), accessed January 10, 2012, http://www.sice.oas.org/Trade/CRI_CHN_FTA/Texts_Apr2010_e/CRI_CHN_Core_text_en.pdf.

[260] Agreement between the Government of the People's Republic of China and the Government of the Republic of Guyana on the Promotion and Protection of Investments, accessed January 10, 2012, http://www.sice.oas.org/Investment/BITSbyCountry/BITs/GUY_China.pdf (entered into force Oct. 26, 2004); Agreement between the Government of the Republic of Trinidad and Tobago and the Government of the People's Republic of China on the Reciprocal Promotion and Protection of Investments (entered into force May 24, 2004), accessed January 10, 2012, http://www.sice.oas.org/Investment/BITSbyCountry/BITs/TRI_China.pdf.

[261] Mann et al., *Model International Agreement on Investment for Sustainable Development*; Howard Mann, et al., *IISD Model International Agreement on Investment for Sustainable Development: Negotiators' Handbook 2nd ed.* (Winnipeg: International Institute for Sustainable Development, 2006), accessed January 10, 2012, http://www.iisd.org/pdf/2005/investment_model_int_handbook.pdf.

[262] Graham Mayeda, 'Sustainable International Investment Agreements: Challenges and Solutions for Developing Countries' in *Sustainable Development in World Investment*

With the Doha Round of WTO negotiations at an impasse, China and Latin America should use bilateral trade and investment agreements as an opportunity to innovate and experiment rather than merely replicating the models developed by the United States and other wealthy nations. If Sino-Latin American economic relations are to embrace sustainable development and to reject the North-South colonial model, it is vitally important that any future agreements contain additional measures to reconcile economic, social, and environmental objectives. China and Latin America have the opportunity to develop a new BIT template that breaks the investor protection-centered BIT paradigm by adopting the suggestions contained in the IISD model investment agreement and related scholarly literature. For example, China and Latin America might reform the current BIT model as follows: (1) insert language in the preamble and objectives clause making sustainable development the objective of the agreement and reaffirming the host state's right to regulate in the public interest; (2) require foreign investors to contribute to the development of green industries, including renewable energy; (3) redraft the substantive obligations of the host state to explicitly preserve regulatory flexibility; (4) include exceptions and reservations that authorize host state measures to promote sustainable development; (5) require foreign investors to comply with domestic and international norms with respect to environmental protection, the rights of indigenous peoples, labor rights, and the prevention of corruption; (6) require the host state to adopt high levels of environmental protection and protection of the aformentioned rights in its national legislation; (7) establish civil liability in the investor's home state for breach of these domestic and international norms; and (8) modify the dispute resolution clause to permit the host state to make counterclaims against the investor for failure to comply with the obligations set forth in the investment agreement.[263] This approach imposes standards of conduct on transnational corporations, requires the home country of the foreign investor to more closely monitor and regulate the extraterritorial activities of its companies, and expands the rights of

---

Law, ed. Marie-Claire Cordonier Segger, et al. (The Netherlands: Kluwer Law International, 2011), 539; Malik, 'The IISD Model International Agreement', 565.

[263] Mann et al., *Model International Agreement on Investment for Sustainable Development*; Mayeda, 'Sustainable International Investment Agreements,' 544–54; Aaron Cosbey et al., *Investment and Sustainable Development: A Guide to the Use and Potential of International Investment Agreements* (Winnipeg: International Institute for Sustainable Development, 2004), accessed January 10, 2012, http://www.iisd.org/pdf/2004/investment_invest_and_sd.pdf; Malik, 'The IISD Model International Agreement,' 566–73.

victims of environmental, labor and other abuses.[264] Furthermore, trade and investment agreements between China and Latin America might provide that environmental, labor, and human rights obligations will prevail in the event of conflict with the provisions of trade and investment agreements. Finally, China and Latin America should mandate social and environmental impact assessments of both current and proposed trade and investment agreements, and should provide for public participation and consultation during the impact evaluation and treaty negotiation process.[265] These suggestions are illustrative rather than exhaustive, and are intended to emphasize the opportunities for bilateral and regional South-South innovation in the area of trade and investment so as to foster rather than frustrate social, economic, and environmental goals and to create a template for broader South-South cooperation.

6. Conclusion

The demise of the Washington Consensus and the rise of China as a major economic power have created challenges and opportunities for Latin America. While China's rise has discredited neoliberal orthodoxy, China's economic development has been based upon the resource-intensive, consumption-driven, growth-at-any-cost economic model pioneered by the United States and other affluent countries. This economic strategy has produced widespread environmental degradation, threatens to produce irreversible harm to the ecological systems necessary to support human life and human economic activity, and may reinforce resource-extractive models of trade and investment in Latin America.

China's contribution to the evolving international regimes governing trade and investment remains uncertain. It is too early to determine whether China will ally itself with developing countries at the WTO to create greater policy space for development or will simply "kick away the ladder" and reinforce the status quo. With respect to bilateral trade and

[264] Cosbey, et al., *Investment and Sustainable Development,* 29–35; Howard Mann, *International Investment Agreements, Business and Human Rights: Key Issues and Opportunities* (Winnipeg: International Institute for Sustainable Development 2008), 13–15, accessed January 10, 2012, http://www.iisd.org/pdf/2008/iia_business_human_rights.pdf.

[265] Markus W. Gehring, 'Impact Assessment of Investment Treaties,' in *Sustainable Development in World Investment Law,* ed. Marie-Claire Cordonier Segger, et al. (The Netherlands: Kluwer Law International, 2011), 149–173.

investment agreements, it appears that China has thus far replicated the dominant models rather than adopted innovative approaches designed to promote sustainable development.

However, China shares with Latin America a history of colonial domination that should inspire critical reflection on the ways that international economic law has facilitated the subordination of the Third World and the exploitation of its natural resources. Rather than portraying China as a threat to Latin America's development or idealizing it as an economic model, this chapter proposes that China and Latin America work collaboratively with other nations to develop alternative paradigms of economic development and alternative models of environmental and economic governance that improve the quality of life while respecting ecological limits.

RESOURCE SOVEREIGNTY IN THE GLOBAL ENVIRONMENTAL ORDER

Jona Razzaque

1. Introduction

Over the last two decades, the growth in the number of environmental regulations is influenced partly as a direct result of the obligations created under multilateral agreements. While a large number of regulations may be the outcome of the government priorities at the national and local level – not all of these laws represent national priorities. As the following discussion shows, other external factors certainly have an impact on the national environmental law making processes, effecting sustainable resource management. Noting that states are the primary actors in any investment contracts dealing with resource sectors (e.g. water, energy, biodiversity), the focus of this chapter is to identify and discuss these external factors rather than the internal factors such as political manifestos, economic agenda or emergency prevention. It assesses the level of influence external bodies have on the environmental policy making at the national and local level. While the chapter acknowledges that states play a central role in managing their resources, it attempts to highlight the influence of international law and non-state actors in managing resources at the national level.

This paper focuses on two aspects of resource sovereignty. First, intra-state sovereignty that is evidenced in the dynamics of relationship between state sovereignty and individual sovereignty (part 2). This vertical nature of sovereignty deals with the power allocation between nationals (e.g. indigenous people, communities) and the state (e.g. national or local government) and the ownership of natural resources. Especially in environmental matters, there are many instances where the national judiciary steps into law making as well as interpreting the law to protect the right of the community to access and use natural resources.

Secondly, the discussion focuses on external factors influencing the sovereign rights over natural resources. Some of the factors influencing the environmental law making processes under discussion here include: the influence of multilateral agreements, export market requirements in trade, pressure from the civil society, and requirements of multilateral lending agencies. This is linked to power allocation (i.e. who has the power to decide and whether international institutions or national governments have the right to decide on a specific issue) – it means the international treaties (e.g. investment or environmental) or institutions may take a decision on a certain issue, and the state needs to consent before to implement the decision, standard or rule at the national level (discussion in parts 3 and 4).

The non-absolute form of sovereignty suggests that states by accepting the authority of international law, entering into international agreements and agreeing to abide by the rules of international institutions have imposed restrictions on their resource sovereignty. As the discussion shows, first, this positive limitation on sovereignty includes ratification of international treaties, membership of regional organisations (e.g. European Union, ASEAN, NAFTA) and international institutions. The European Union (EU) provides a unique example because the membership of this regional body limits the power of the member states to adopt decisions in certain areas. Second, several acts of sovereign states may also limit sovereign rights over natural resources, e.g. by allowing market access to foreign investors (e.g. under Bilateral Investment Treaties), sharing benefits of genetic resources (e.g. Biodiversity Convention), settling disputes with other states or multinational corporations (e.g. ICSID, ITLOS), or implementing international standards for export products. Third, in both developed and developing countries, a large number of domestic laws are enacted to meet obligations created under international agreements. The states may also limit their sovereign rights by allowing the human rights bodies to determine the quality of life of citizens and to ascertain property and ownership rights of indigenous people.[1] Examples can be drawn from human rights arena where fundamental civil and political rights are included either in the national constitution or in the Bill of Rights.[2] In the environmental field, constitutional provisions as well as domestic regulations integrate environmental rights.[3] Many developing countries also have 'model law' to frame their national legislation. Lastly, the following

---

[1] Jona Razzaque, 'Right to a healthy environment in Human Rights Law' in Mashood Baderin and Manisuli Ssenyonjo (eds.) *International Human Rights Law: 60 Years after the UDHR* (Aldershot: Ashgate, 2011) 115–135.

[2] For example, Universal Declaration of Human Rights, adopted 10 December 1948, UNGA Res. 217 (AIII),U.N. GAOR, 3rd Session, pt 1, at 71, U.N. Doc A/810 (1948).

[3] Earthjustice, Environmental Rights Report: Human Rights and the Environment (2008). Available at: http://earthjustice.org/sites/default/files/library/reports/2008-environmental-rights-report.pdf (accessed 12 March 2012).

discussion shows that many legal mandates related to conservation and sustainable development stem from the requirements imposed by foreign aid programmes, international development banks, and UN agencies as prerequisites for grants, loans, technology transfers, or various alternative forms of economic assistance.

2. Changing Face of Sovereignty in a Globalised World

The state with its sovereignty over natural resources remains central to the well-being of its citizens and is responsible for adopting legal policies which are conducive to greater economic integration and sustainable development. Sovereignty[4] includes the power to impose authority over the population, freely use or dispose of territory under the jurisdiction – known as internal sovereignty, and no other state can intrude the state's territory (i.e. external sovereignty).[5] Permanent sovereignty over natural resources is a legal concept and closely linked to political and economic aspects of sovereignty.[6] Sovereignty over natural resources also includes a bundle of rights – e.g. the right to possess, the right to use, and the right to manage.[7] With the exclusive control and use of the natural resources within the territory, state has the right to profits gained from the resources, and conserve, explore and exploit these resources.[8]

To ensure that states respect the public goods,[9] there are certain limitations imposed on their sovereignty over natural resources. First, 'permanent sovereignty over natural resources has to be exercised for national development and the well being of the people.'[10] With the wide discretion to interpret, states' exercise of this duty may not always be beneficial to

4 Sovereignty of a state is an integral part of its existence along with three other elements – a permanent population, a defined territory and government. Malcolm Shaw, *International Law* (Cambridge: Cambridge University Press, 2008) 197–204.

5 Antonio Cassese, *International Law* (Oxford: Oxford University Press, 2001) 88–89.

6 Nico Schrijver, *Sovereignty Over Natural Resources: Balancing Rights and Duties* (Cambridge: Cambridge University Press, 1997) Chapter 2 and 3.

7 Richard Barnes, *Property Rights and Natural Resources* (Oxford: Hart, 2009) 228–230.

8 Ibid.

9 Public goods are non-rivalrous (available for all to consume) and non-excludable (no-one can be effectively excluded from using the good). Frank Wijen, Kees Zoetman and Jan Pieters (eds.), *A Handbook of Globalisation and Environmental Policy: National Government Intervention in A Global Arena* (Cheltenham: Edward Elgar, 2005) 89–91.

10 Para 1 of GA Res 1803 (XVII), 17 UN GAOR Supp (no 17) 15, UN Doc A/5217 (1962), Article 1(2) of the International Covenant on Civil and Political Rights, 1966, 999 UNTS 171. Schrijver (1997), *supra*, 168.

the people or natural resources. However, the application of public trust doctrine confirms the role of state as the custodian of natural resources (e.g. watercourses, air, ecosystems) for the benefit of present and future generations.[11] In addition, states have a 'responsibility to ensure that activities within their jurisdiction or control do not cause damage to the environment of other States or of areas beyond the limits of national jurisdiction.'[12] Second, the duty of a state to compensate foreign investors whose property has been expropriated and provide due legal process.[13] States should enter into foreign investment agreements in good faith and respect the 'sovereignty of peoples and nations over their natural wealth and resources'.[14] Third, the state has a duty to protect the interest of indigenous peoples.[15] Fourth, the state has a duty to cooperate in respect of shared natural resources[16] and notify and consult people in activities linked to resource use.[17]

Several actions of the state have reshaped the conventional definition of sovereignty. First, states by ratifying international agreements (e.g. UN Charter, human rights and environmental treaties) and agreeing to abide by the rules of international institutions (e.g. World Trade Organisation) have imposed restrictions on their resource sovereignty. An associated and integrated risk of such restriction is the promotion of market access of goods and services into markets of countries with weak regulatory frameworks to defend their resource sectors. The ongoing negotiation on the definition of environmental goods and services, and broadening the ambit of 'environmental goods and services' to include some of the sensitive resource sectors and public utilities are examples of integrated risks in

11 David Takacs, 'The Public Trust Doctrine, environmental human rights and the future of private property', NYU Environmental Law Journal, 16 (2008):711.

12 Declaration of the United Nations Conference on the Human Environment (Stockholm Declaration), Stockholm, 16 June 1972; UN Doc. A/Conf. 48/14, 11 ILM 1461 (1972), Chapter I.

13 Schrijver (1997), *supra*, 339-364. Several conditions have to be fulfilled in order to exercise the right to expropriation or nationalisation: it has to be for public purpose, non-discriminatory, payment of compensation, due process and right to appeal.

14 Paragraphs 4 and 8 of General Assembly Resolution 1803 (XVII), 14 December 1962.

15 United Nations, UN Declaration on the Rights of Indigenous Peoples (2007). UN Resolution 61/295 (13 September 2007). Available at: http://www.un.org/esa/socdev/unpfii/documents/DRIPS_en.pdf (accessed 12 March 2012).

16 UN General Assembly Resolution on Environmental Cooperation Concerning Natural Resources Shared by States (1974) 13 International Legal Materials 232.

17 Lac Lanoux Arbitration (France v Spain) 24 ILR 101 (1957), Fisheries Jurisdiction (UK v Iceland) Merits (1974) ICJ reports 3; (Federal Republic of Germany v Iceland) Merits (1974) ICJ Reports 174. Argentina v Uruguay (Case concerning Pulp Mills on the River Uruguay), 20 April 2010.

opening up of policy space to external influence.[18] By accepting funds from international financial institutions (e.g. World Bank, International Monetary Fund), the states accept conditions that may have adverse social and environmental impact (e.g. structural adjustment funds). This acceptance of funds can lead to national level law reform[19] or impact assessment legislation (e.g. in South Asia).[20]

An example could be the EU where the surrender of absolute sovereignty by the member states means the supremacy of the EU law.[21] The EU jurisprudence and legislation apply between the supranational level and the member states, and at the level of Union citizens.[22] However, the EU should only act where 'the objectives of the proposed action cannot be achieved sufficiently by the Member States' and 'by reason of the scale or effects of the proposed action', the EU could achieve better result.[23] Applying the principle of subsidiarity, the EU has the power to adopt measures in order to achieve its environmental objectives protecting habitats, migratory species or water.[24] Thus, the Aarhus Convention has considerably influenced law-making at the EU level.[25] Apart from taking necessary measures to apply the provisions of the Aarhus Convention to EU's own institutions,[26] the EU has adopted and amended several

18 Gaëlle Balineau and Jaime de Melo, 'Stalemate at the Negotiations on Environmental Goods and Services at the Doha Round', working paper, FERDI, October 2011. Available at: http://www.ferdi.fr/uploads/sfCmsContent/html/112/P28.pdf (accessed 12 March 2012).

19 E.g. *Bolivian Government passed Law 2029 (the Drinking Water and Sanitation) Law* in 1999 prior to water conflicts in Cochabamba, Bolivia. Jona Razzaque, 'Trading water: the human factor', RECIEL, 13/1 (2004): 15–26.

20 For examples from South Asia, see: 'Participatory rights in natural resource management: role of communities in South Asia' in Jonas Ebbesson and Phoebe Okowa (eds.) *Environmental Law and Justice in Context* (Cambridge: Cambridge University Press, 2009) 117–138.

21 Costa v ENEL (case 6/64), 1964, ECR 585.

22 Ludwig Kramer, 'The EU: a Regional Model?' in Gerd Winter (ed.), *Multilevel Governance of Global Environmental Change* (Cambridge: Cambridge University Press, 2006) 333.

23 Article 5(3) of the Treaty of the European Union. Official Journal of EU, C83/13, 30 March 2010.

24 Article 191 and 192 of the Treaty on the Functioning of the European Union, Official Journal of the European Union, C115/49 (9.5.2008). Wouter P.J. Wils, 'Subsidiarity and EC Environmental Policy: Taking People's Concerns Seriously', Journal of Environmental Law, 6 (1994): 88–89.

25 The EU signed the Aarhus Convention in 1998 and approved it in early 2005.

26 Regulation (EC) No 1367/2006 on the application of the provisions of the Aarhus Convention on Access to Information, Public Participation in Decision-making and Access to Justice in Environmental Matters to Community institutions and bodies.

Directives concerning public access to environmental information and public participation reflecting the provisions of the Aarhus Convention.[27]

Second, the transformation of sovereignty (thus, prioritising the rule of law) is apparent when a state allows human rights bodies to determine the quality of life of citizens and to ascertain the property and ownership rights of indigenous people. It is possible for individuals, communities, NGOs or groups of individuals to come to the European Court of Human Rights,[28] Inter-American Commission on Human Rights[29] and African Commission on Human Rights[30] if they are victims of any violation. In addition, these regional courts allow NGOs to submit *amicus curiae* briefs during the written procedure and, in some cases, take part in oral hearings.[31] Unfortunately, access for individuals and communities to the Court of Justice of the EU (CJEU) is still quite restricted.[32] Noting these practices in other regional courts along with the access to justice provision of the Aarhus Convention, it is time to rethink about the standing of individuals and communities at the CJEU.

Third, the recognition of the rights of indigenous peoples over their resources affirms their cultural rights and rights to lands, waters, territories and natural resources, genetic resources and traditional knowledge. The UN Declaration on indigenous peoples' right acknowledges the collective right of the indigenous peoples to genetic resources and associated traditional knowledge as well as a right to participate in the development of national laws on access and benefit-sharing and traditional knowledge.[33] They have the right to redress or compensation if there is no free,

---

[27] Council Directive 2003/4/EC, Council Directive 85/337/EEC (EIA Directive), Council Directive 96/61/EC, Directive 2003/35/EC.

[28] However, the application of margin of appreciation gives the Court the flexibility needed to avoid damaging confrontations between the Court and the member states and enables it to balance the sovereignty of Member States with their obligations under the Convention. For example, *Hatton v. The UK*, judgment of 08 July 2003, § 122. See also, Guerra and Others v. Italy, 1998-I ECHR, Judgment of 19 February 1998. *Lopez-Ostra v. Spain*, ECHR (1994), Series A, No. 303C.

[29] Article 44, American Convention on Human Rights. OASTreaty Series No. 36, 1144 UNTS 123.

[30] Decision regarding Communication 155/96 (Social and Economic Rights Action Center/Center for Economic and Social Rights v. Nigeria), Case No. ACHPR/COMM/A044/1, 27 May 2002.

[31] Article 36 of the European Convention on Human Rights, as amended by Protocol 11. Article 44(2), Rule of the European Court of Human Rights (June 2009). Articles 2(3) and 44 of the Rules of Procedure (November 2009).

[32] Article 19, Treaty of the EU, op. cit. Article 263, Treaty on the Functioning of the EU, Official Journal of EU, C 83/47, 30 March 2010.

[33] Article 27, UN Declaration (2007), op. cit.

prior informed consent.[34] Although the Declaration is by nature aspirational and is not legally binding, the significance of its full and unqualified recognition of the sovereign rights of indigenous peoples to natural resources has far-reaching implications.[35]

Communities (including indigenous people) and NGOs at the national level can access to courts if there is a violation of constitutional or other rights. Nature, scope and strength of these rights depend on the legal systems, democratic traditions and legal cultures of states. In Europe, e.g. right to access the court of law can be protected by the Constitution.[36] Judicial review is one procedural technique by which decisions of public bodies exercising environmental responsibilities can be challenged in court and a means by which the courts supervise public bodies in the exercise of their powers or carrying out their duties.[37] Another option for people to go to court is through civil suits. A class action may be used in all tort based claims that have an impact on a large number of people (e.g. climate litigation in the USA).[38]

The above discussion shows that the sovereign powers of states over their natural resources are no longer absolute and the limitations pertaining to resource sovereignty include a number of internationally imposed rules that reflect global concerns.[39] While the international institutions play a role in reshaping the scope of resource sovereignty in the interest of present and future generations, issues such as ownership of resources at the national level and the extraterritorial effects of some domestic environmental laws remain crucial in exploring the changing face of resource sovereignty.

---

34 Article 2, ibid.

35 Economic and Social Council, Prevention of discrimination and protection of indigenous peoples and minorities, E/CN.4/Sub.2/2001/21, 11 June 2001. Report on Indigenous peoples' permanent sovereignty over natural resources, Special Rapporteur of the Commission on Human Rights, E/CN.4/Sub.2/2004/30 and Add.1, 2004.

36 Economic Commission for Europe (2008), op. cit.

37 Jeffrey Jowell, Andrew Le Sueur, SA de Smith, Lord Woolf, *De Smith, Woolf and Jowell's Principles of Judicial Review* (London: Sweet and Maxwell, 1999).

38 *Connecticut v. American Electric Power Company, Inc.; Comer v. Murphy Oil Co.; California v. General Motors Corp.* David Grossman, 'Tort based climate litigation' in William CG Burns and Harry Osofsky (eds.) *Adjudicating climate change: state, national and international approaches* (Cambridge: Cambridge University Press, 2009) 193–229.

39 Excellent discussion on the changing concept of territorial sovereignty can be found in: Alexander Kiss and Dinah Shelton, *International Environmental Law,* 2nd edn. (New York: Transnational Publishers, 2004); Edith Brown Weiss, 'International Environmental Law: Contemporary Issues and the Emergence of a New World Order', Georgetown Law Journal, 81(1993): 675-710. Klaus Bosselmann, *The Principle of Sustainability: Transforming Law and Governance* (Aldershot: Ashgate, 2008) 145–174.

2.1. *Ownership and Resource Sovereignty*

While the limits of sovereignty are still being debated at the academic level,[40] it is difficult to find a balance between the sovereignty of state and the ownership[41] of natural resources. The discussion on ownership of natural resources shows that the government, as custodian or trustee of the natural resources, should manage natural resources. The UN Resolution 1803 shows that internal sovereignty is shared between peoples and the state, and implies that peoples have some control over the management and development of natural resources and have a right to be consulted. The common Article 1 of the International Covenant on Civil and Political Rights and the International Covenant on Economic, Social and Cultural Rights provides:

> 2. All peoples may, for their own ends, freely dispose of their natural wealth and resources *without prejudice to* any obligations arising out of international economic co-operation, based upon the principle of mutual benefit, and international law. In no case may a people be deprived of its own means of subsistence.

These Covenants further add:

> Nothing in the present Covenant shall be interpreted as impairing the inherent right of all peoples to enjoy and utilize fully and freely their natural wealth and resources.[42]

The UN Resolutions and Human Rights Covenants emphasise that peoples[43] are free to consider how they want to utilise their natural resources. They proclaim peoples' sovereignty over their natural resources, and include people who are not independent to protect their resources[44]

---

[40] Anthony Anghie, *Imperialism, Sovereignty and the Making of International Law,* (Cambridge: Cambridge University Press, 2004). Robert Jackson (ed.) *Sovereignty at the Millennium* (Oxford: Blackwell, 1999).

[41] Ownership provides exclusive right and control over property. It gives the right to possess, use and enjoy the benefits and dispose of the natural resource to the exclusion of others. Natural resources which are considered as public properties do not fall under this definition. This chapter does not deal with ownership of the global commons.

[42] Article 47 of the Covenant on Civil and Political Rights and Article 25 of the Covenant on Economic, Social and Cultural Rights. Also, article 21 of the African Charter on Human and Peoples' Rights.

[43] 'Peoples' may include those who are under colonial occupation, indigenous people, or the whole of the population. Emeka Duruigbo, 'Permanent sovereignty and peoples' ownership of natural resources in international law', George Washington International Law Review 38 (2006): 52.

[44] Anghie (2004), *supra*, 217. Anghie discusses the issue of people who are under colonial rule.

as well as the entire population of a state.[45] These international documents do not make any clear distinction between the territorial sovereignty and ownership of natural resources. At the domestic level, the issue of ownership is largely guided by the constitutional right to natural resources, and is a combination of private, community and state ownership often requiring balancing of competing claims.[46] States may hold ownership of many resources important to the national economy in the name of 'people'. Natural resource can be privately owned by individuals or companies, or it may be part of community ownership whereby people have the collective right to enjoy and utilise the natural resources.[47] Even where the natural resources are under private or community ownership, the state by virtue of territorial sovereignty retains the right to regulate the way individuals or community exercise their property rights and people will have the right to be compensated if the resources are expropriated.[48]

As for the indigenous peoples, the right to own their property and natural resources is acknowledged in UN Declarations,[49] Conventions,[50] regional human rights instruments[51] and case laws.[52] These documents recognise a broad range of human rights held by indigenous peoples, most notably the right to own property, the right of ownership of the lands they historically or traditionally use and occupy, the rights to self-determination and autonomy, the right to development, the right to be

---

[45] Duruigbo, *supra*, 52.

[46] Nicholas Haysom and Sean Kane, Negotiating natural resources for peace: Ownership, control and wealth-sharing, Briefing Paper 2009, Geneva: Henry Durant Centre for Humanitarian Dialogue, 8–12.

[47] Jan Hancock, *Environmental Human Rights: Power, Ethics, and Law* (Aldershot: Ashgate, 2003) 138–139.

[48] Johan G. Lammers, *Pollution of International Watercourses* (The Hague: Martinus Nijhoff, 1984) 390–392.

[49] Article 3, 4, 26-28, 32 of the UN Declaration on the Rights of Indigenous Peoples (2007), adopted by GA Resolution 61/295 (13 September 2007).

[50] Article 7, 15, International Labour Organisation Indigenous and Tribal Peoples Convention No. 169/1989.

[51] 1969 American Convention on Human Rights; African Charter on Human and Peoples' Rights, adopted June 27, 1981, OAU Doc. CAB/LEG/67/3 rev. 5, 21 ILM 58 (1982).

[52] *Awas Tingni Mayagna (Sumo) Indigenous Community v. Nicaragua,* Judgement of 31 August 2001, Inter-Am Ct H.R. (Ser. C) No 79 (2001). Maya indigenous community of the Toledo District v. Belize, Case 12.053, Report No. 40/04, Inter-Am. C.H.R., OEA/Ser.L/V/II.122 Doc. 5 rev. 1 at 727 (2004). Decision regarding Communication 155/96 (*Social and Economic Rights Action Center/Center for Economic and Social Rights v. Nigeria*), Communication No. ACHPR/COMM/A044/1 (African Commission on Human and Peoples' Rights, May 27, 2002).

free from discrimination, and a host of other human rights. However, Article 46 (1) of the UN Declaration states:[53]

> Nothing in this Declaration may be interpreted as implying for any State, people, group or person any right to engage in any activity or to perform any act contrary to the Charter of the United Nations or construed as authorizing or encouraging any action which would dismember or impair, totally or in part, the territorial integrity or political unity of sovereign and independent States.

According to Schrijver,

> States are under an obligation to exercise permanent sovereignty on behalf of and in the interests of their (indigenous) peoples. This implies that States are increasingly accountable, also at an international level, for the way they manage their natural wealth and resources, but also that for the time being (indigenous) peoples ...are objects rather than subjects of international law.[54]

This leads to the conclusion that indigenous peoples will continue to be deprived of their resources through mineral extraction, environmental contamination, expropriation of land, bio-prospecting, patents and other intellectual property rights. While it can be argued that governments are the custodian or trustee of the natural resources for the benefit of present and future generations, it is difficult to ensure that the governments are discharging their responsibilities in good faith.[55] Similar arguments can be applied to water resource management where multinational corporations (MNCs) are investing a large sum in water infrastructure projects, and depriving the people of water by hiking the price of water (e.g. in Bolivia, Ghana, India).[56]

2.2. *Domestic Law with Exterritorial Effects*

When a state applies its sovereign rights, these rights oblige states to preserve the environment irrespective of the effects that their action

[53] 2007 UN Declaration on the Rights of Indigenous Peoples, UN Doc A/Res/61/295 (2 October 2007).

[54] Schrijver (1997), *supra*, 390.

[55] Duruigbo (2006), *supra*, 67.

[56] Jernej Letnar Cernic, 'Corporate obligations under the human right to water', Denver Journal of International Law and Policy, 39 (2010) 303. Gordon McGranahan and Jessica Budds, 'Privatization and the Provision of Urban Water and Sanitation in Africa, Asia and Latin America' (London, UK: IIED, 2003).

might have on neighbouring states or on regions beyond.[57] Environmental problems are not always contained within a state and states do apply their environmental law extraterritorially.[58] Under Principle 21 of the Stockholm Declaration, states have recognized that they should strive to ensure that activities within their respective jurisdictions do not cause extraterritorial environmental harm.[59] While it is unlikely that domestic environmental law will have direct assertion of extraterritorial effect, there are some examples[60] where states can assert direct extraterritorial jurisdiction.

There are examples where domestic environmental law have extraterritorial implications allowed by international treaties or national case laws.[61] First, states may have domestic laws that impose reporting or disclosure requirements on foreign companies. Second, for the protection of global environmental concerns, states are allowed to have domestic measures with extraterritorial implications. States frequently impose requirements on actors operating within their territories in an attempt to reduce transboundary environmental risks (i.e. risks emanating from within their territorial boundaries with the potential to cause environmental damage abroad),[62] to control the export of environmental hazards to other states,[63]

---

57 Johan D. van der Vyver, *State Sovereignty and the Environment in International Law*, South African Law Journal, 109 (1992) 472–76. Duncan A French, 'A reappraisal of sovereignty in the light of global environmental concerns', Legal Studies, 21/3 (2001) 376–399.

58 Patricia Birnie, Alan Boyle and Catherine Redgwell, *International Law and the Environment* (Oxford: Oxford University Press, 2009) 143.

59 Declaration of the United Nations Conference on the Human Environment (Stockholm Declaration), Stockholm, 16 June 1972; UN Doc. A/Conf.48/14, 11 ILM 1461 (1972), Chapter I. See also: Principle 211 of Stockholm Declaration. Principle 2 and 13 of Rio Declaration. Rio Declaration on Environment and Development, Rio De Janeiro, 13 June 1992, UN Doc. A/Conf. 151/26 (vol. I), 31 ILM 874 (1992). Trail Smelter Arbitration (1941) American Journal on International Law, 35, 684-734. Legality of the Threat or Use of Nuclear Weapons, ICJ Report 1996, 226.

60 For example, the flag state's jurisdiction over ships or jurisdiction over a foreign polluter in a private tort-based claim.

61 For example, *Environmental Defense Fund v Massey* 986 F 2d 538 (DC Cir. 1993) US National Environmental Policy Act could be applied to the activities of the National Science Foundation in Antarctica on the basis that the decision to incinerate waste was taken in the US, and also that the US scientific mission was within US control, in an area not subject to the jurisdiction of another state. Jennifer A. Zerk, Extraterritorial Jurisdiction: Lessons for the Business and Human Rights Sphere from Six Regulatory Areas, Corporate Social Responsibility Initiative, Working Paper No. 59, June 2010.

62 1979 Geneva Convention on Long Range Transboundary Air Pollution; the 1985 Vienna Convention for the Protection of the Ozone Layer; 1991 Espoo Convention, 1998 Aarhus Convention.

63 1989 Convention on the Control of Transboundary Movements of Hazardous Wastes and Their Disposal; 1998 Convention on the Prior Informed Consent Procedure for Certain Hazardous Chemicals and Pesticides in International Trade.

or impose ban on imports of products derived in an environmentally harmful way,[64] or generally to discourage poor environmental practices beyond their own jurisdictions.[65] The 1991 Espoo Convention is a good example of extraterritorial jurisdiction over actors and activities abroad in the environmental field. The Espoo Convention requires state parties to give early notice to other states of domestic projects that may have environmental implications beyond their own borders, and to consult on areas of concern. It also requires state parties to ensure that potentially affected people in other states receive timely and adequate information about the project, and have the right to participate in environmental assessment procedures. This Convention suggests a number of different ways that domestic environmental legislation can potentially have extraterritorial implications, e.g. through measures designed to help identify and reduce the risks of transboundary harm and extending enforcement rights to people outside the jurisdiction.[66]

3. External Factors and Sustainable Resource Management

There are three main areas where resource management at the national level is influenced by external factors such as the export market requirements, social/environmental requirements and lending requirements of international financial agencies. These factors impact on how countries allow market access and investments in the country and highlight the obligations on states created by international law and institutions.

3.1. *Influence of Export Market Standards*

Product and quality requirements such as eco-labelling and packaging,[67] or various international standards[68] are examples of some of the external factors that influence natural resource management at the domestic level. Adoption of environmental standards for products by exporting countries

---

64 1973 Convention on International Trade in Endangered Species of Wild Fauna and Flora.

65 Birnie, Boyle and Redgwell, *Supra*.

66 Articles 2,3,5 and 6 and Appendix IV.

67 FIELD, Legal and Policy Issues in the Market Access Implications of Labelling for Environmental Purposes, (UNCTAD, 2003), available at: http://www.unctad.org/trade_env/test1/meetings/bangkok4/ecolabelling%20briefing%20paper.pdf (accessed 29 February 2012).

68 For example, ISO 26000 on Social responsibility. Available at: http://www.iisd.org/standards/csr.asp (accessed 28 February 2012).

means developing countries are, in many instances, unable to meet the standards face the prospect of losing their exports. There are examples where EU fish import ban caused an adverse impact on the small fishermen, e.g., in Bangladesh and Tanzania.[69] In 1997, the ban in Bangladesh was imposed on the ground that exports of this commodity did not meet the provisions of EU's HACCP (Hazard Analysis Critical Contact Point)[70] regulations. It put the country's shrimp export industry under severe strain and led to serious market disruptions. About a million people related to shrimp culture in different stages of the production process were affected and the cost was equivalent to US$ 65.1 million.[71] Similarly in Tanzania, two consecutive bans on the import of fist from the Lake Victoria into the EU market caused an adverse impact on the fist industry, in terms of foreign exchange earnings, income and employment generation. The first ban was imposed on fresh fish exports to the EU in 1998 because of a cholera epidemic and the second ban was imposed in 1999 for fish poisoning. Following the ban, about 4000 people (let alone small fishermen who could not find a market for their catch) were suspended from work.[72] Tanzania reported that 40% of its fisheries workforce had been laid off, and the country had lost US$ 46.9 million as a result of the ban.[73]

In order to access export markets, developing countries need to have regulatory and institutional mechanisms enabling them to comply with the export market requirements. There are often high costs associated with ensuring compliance with export market standards.[74] The fixed costs associated with technical compliance with EU standards are often very high, and in order to be economic, these fixed costs need to be carried across a large volume of production and exports. This can create problems for relatively small scale exporters, who can find the costs of compliance quite uneconomic. A study suggests that Bangladesh spent

---

69 Similar bans were imposed on Kenya and Uganda. Negotiating Agenda for Market Access: Cases of SPS and TBT (Geneva, April 2001), organised by CUTS International.

70 HACCP requires producers to identify food safety hazards that may arise, and establish adequate process controls to prevent or minimise their occurrence.

71 Mustafizur Rahman, EU ban on shrimp imports from Bangladesh: A case Study on Market Access Problems faced by the LDCs, available at: www.unctad.org/trade_env/test1/meetings/standards/mustafizur.doc (Accessed 28 February 2012).

72 Flora M. Musonda and W. Mbowe, The Impact of Implementing SPS and TBT Agreements: The case of Fish Export to European Union by Tanzania (April 2001), available at: http://www.cuts-international.org/sps-analysis-sps_case_tan.htm (Accessed 28 February 2012).

73 Ibid.

74 UNCTAD, Environmental requirements and market access for developing countries (2004), available at: www.unctad.org (Accessed 28 February 2012).

over US$ 17.6 million to upgrade plants alone in 1997–98 in an attempt to respond to the EU and US shrimp export requirements.[75] Affected by similar EU fish ban between 1997–98, Uganda drafted *Fish (Quality Assurance) Rules 1998* that sets out procedures regarding fish inspectors, fish sanitary certificates, the placing of the market, the approval of establishments and official landing sites, and quality test. The governments of Uganda (in 2004) and Bangladesh (in 1998) drafted National Fisheries Policy ensuring that all necessary quality and safety requirements are put in place for trade in national and international markets.[76]

The standards set at the regional level such as the EU do not allow any non-parties to be part of the standard setting processes. In the international standard setting bodies, such as ISO[77] or CODEX[78] do not have enough participation from developing countries and, in many instances, public interest groups do not have capacities to understand the issue under discussion.[79] Lack of full and effective participation from developing countries mean the standards created do not reflect the priorities of developing countries and, thus, these countries are either unable or unlikely to comply with such standards.[80]

3.2. *Social and Environmental Requirements*

Along with product quality requirements, exporters are being confronted with additional requirements, such as social (e.g. equal remuneration, labour standards) and environmental (e.g. labelling, sanitary and phytosanitary measures).[81] For many developing countries, issues of food safety,

---

[75] Boaz B. Keizire, Implications of liberalisation of fish trade for developing countries – a Case Study for Uganda (July 2004), available at: http://www.nri.org/projects/fishtrade/uganda.pdf (Accessed 28 February 2012).

[76] For case studies on Uganda and Bangladesh, see Natural Resources Institute, Policy Research Implications of Liberalisation of Fish Trade for Developing Countries (July 2004), available at: http://www.nri.org/projects/fishtrade/index.htm (Accessed on 28 February 2011).

[77] International Organisation for Standardisation. Available at: http://www.iso.org/iso/home.html.

[78] Codex Alimentarius. Available at: http://www.codexalimentarius.net/web/index _ en.jsp.

[79] Jona Razzaque, 'Transparency and participation of civil society in international institutions related to biotechnology' in Sophie Thoyer and Benoit Martimort-Asso (eds) *Participation for sustainability in trade* (Aldershot: Ashgate, 2007) 137–160.

[80] Ibid.

[81] There are several international guidelines for states and multinational corporations to protect human and environmental rights, e.g., Ruggie Guidelines on business and human rights, OECD Guidelines for multinational enterprises, UN Global Compact, Equator Principles.

product identification, traceability are becoming increasingly important in accessing export markets, for example, the EU. The European consumers are concerned about the quality (from both health and food safety points of view) of the food they eat and the conditions under which it is produced.

Similar concerns can be found in the renewable energy sector dealing with biofuels.[82] The objectives of the EU Renewables Directive (2009)[83] is to achieve a 20% share of energy from renewable sources in the Community's gross final consumption of energy and a 10% share of energy from renewable sources in each Member State's transport energy consumption by 2020.[84] The 2009 Directive establishes sustainability criteria for biofuels and bioliquids.[85] According to the Directive, biofuels produced from 'wastes, residues, non-food cellulosic material, and lignocellulosic material' shall count two times for national obligations and the 2020 transport target.[86] This provision encourages the use of second generation fuels i.e. those produced from non-food or waste products. The minimum GHG saving from the use of biofuels and bioliquids relative to fossil fuels should be 35%, this saving rises to 50% from 2017.[87] Biofuels and bioliquids must not be made from land:

- with high biodiversity value such as primary forest, highly-biodiverse natural grassland and other designated habitats,[88]
- that had high carbon stock but no longer has that status, e.g. wetlands, continuously forested areas, peatland.[89]

While the above sustainability criteria do not include any social aspects, the Commission will report, every two years, on social impacts of the EU's biofuel policy including food security (especially in developing countries), land use rights and wider development issues.[90]

There are, however, concerns about the use of biofuel as a sustainable form of renewable energy source. Verification will be fundamental to

---

[82] 'Biofuels' means liquid or gaseous fuel for transport produced from biomass (Article 2(i)). Article 2(e) defines biomass.
[83] Directive 2009/28/EC. The deadline for implementation was 5 December 2010.
[84] Article 1, 3, 5, Annex I.
[85] Article 1 and 17 of the Directive.
[86] Article 3. This only applies to transport biofuels and not bioliquids for heat or electricity (Article 21(2)).
[87] Article 17(2).
[88] Article 17(3).
[89] Article 17(4).
[90] Article 17(7).

ensure any standards to actually impact on the sustainability of the biofuels market place.[91] The verification requirements in the Directive are flexible and weak.[92] Whether or not the sustainability criteria are complied with will be assessed on the basis of company information, or through voluntary certification schemes, or through the existence of bilateral and multilateral agreements.[93] Economic operators will be responsible for ensuring adequate independent auditing of the information they submit and the evidence they provide.[94] For the sustainability criteria to be a success, the auditing process must ensure that systems used are 'accurate, reliable and protected against fraud'.[95]

3.3. *Influence of Multilateral Lending Agencies*

Donor communities including bilateral and multilateral development assistance and lending agencies have a huge influence on the national law and policy making in many developing countries. Multilateral lending agencies, such as the World Bank and the International Monetary Fund (IMF), occasionally use their influence over the development agenda and countries' access to external funds to advance their trade liberalisation. A common example of such influence is environmental impact assessments (EIA) in infrastructure projects. In many developing countries, EIAs are carried out to meet the demands/requirements of the donor/lending agencies and remain largely a 'top-down' requirement. The World Bank, for instance, requires the borrower to demonstrate that the project to be funded is environmentally sound.[96] Multilateral lending agencies also play a crucial role in creating legal and institutional frameworks in developing countries to administer EIAs.[97]

---

[91] Catherine Bowyer, Biofuels Provisions in the Renewable Energy Directive – A Summary, EU Environmental Policy Briefing, Brussels: IEEP (2008). See European Commission, Communication from the Commission on voluntary schemes and default values in the EU biofuels and bioliquids sustainability scheme (2010/C 160/01), 19.06.2010.

[92] Laura German and George Schoneveld, Social sustainability of EU-approved voluntary schemes for biofuels: Implications for rural livelihoods (2011). Working Paper 75. CIFOR, Bogor, Indonesia. Available at: http://www.cifor.org/publications/pdf_files/WPapers/WP75German.pdf (accessed on 12 March 2012).

[93] Article 18.

[94] Article 18(3).

[95] Article 18(3).

[96] World Bank Operational Policy 4.01 on Environmental Assessment (1999), revised in February 2011.

[97] Christopher Wood, Environmental Impact Assessment in Developing countries (2003) at 8. Jona Razzaque, 'Participatory rights in natural resource management: role

Multilateral lending agencies influence could be seen in the natural resource sector (e.g. water, mining, forestry) with a direct impact on the poor communities in law and middle- income countries. They can impose conditionality attached to a loan or to debt relief – which may include anti-corruption measures or privatisation of key public services. For instance, privatisation of water services has become a precondition for many developing countries who want to access IMF and World Bank funds for water and sanitation programmes.[98] The IMF demands water services in exchange for debt relief,[99] and the World Bank promotes commodification of water, cost recovery and private public partnership in this sector.[100] In countries where water industries are not making any profit, the World Bank is 'unlikely to approve a water sector loan without the explicit or implicit condition of water privatisation, as concessions, leases, or management and service contracts.'[101] According to a study, around 38 of the 42 Poverty Reduction Strategy Papers (PRSP) include privatisation and 27 of these specifically include water privatisation or greater private sector involvement in water supply services.[102] It is argued that the main consequence of water services privatisation is that water will become a privilege only for those who can pay high prices, by excluding the poor.[103]

The effect of privatisation of services without effective community participation can be seen in Bolivia – in the often cited case of Cochabamba.[104]

---

of communities in South Asia' in Jonas Ebbesson and Phoebe Okowa (eds.) *Environmental Law and Justice in Context* (Cambridge: Cambridge University Press, 2009) 117–138.

98 In May 2002, the World Bank Director for Water and Power declared that water and sanitation loans would not be awarded to African countries unless they allow for the participation of private companies. Also, during 2000, IMF's loan agreements with at least 12 developing countries included conditions imposing water privatisation or cost recovery requirements. See: CIEL, Briefing paper on 'Water Traded' (March 2003) 1.

99 Under the IMF Poverty Reduction and Growth Facility (PGRF), many developing countries governments have agreed to have their loan conditioned to the privatisation of their water sector. Multinational Monitor, Bearing the Burden of IMF and World Bank, vol 22 (9) September 2001. Available at: (cited by CIEL, Water Traded, 2003).

100 General encouragement towards privatisation can be found in World Bank, Private Sector Development Strategy – Directions for the World Bank Group (World Bank, 9 April 2002. Also see: World Bank, Water Sector Resource Strategy: Strategic Directions for World Bank Engagement (February 2003).

101 Steven Shrybman, 'Thirst for Control', *Blue Planet Project* (Council of Canadians, January 2002) 4. Available at http://www.blueplanetproject.net/cms_publications/TFC_E.pdf (accessed 12 March 2012).

102 World Development Movement, Denying Democracy: How the IMF and the World Bank take power from People (May 2005), 8–9.

103 Gunnar Aegisson, The Great Water Robbery, One World Action (August 2002).

104 There are many examples where different actors collaborate to ensure affordable water supply services: Ana Hardoy, Jorgelina Hardoy, Gustavo Pandiella and Gastón

In 1998, the IMF approved US$ 138 million loan for Bolivia and wanted structural reforms for the nation. The Bolivian Government agreed to sell various public enterprises including oil refineries and a local water agency in the province of Cochabamba. In 1999, the World Bank in its Bolivia Public Expenditure Review discouraged water subsidies.[105] In the same year, the Bolivian Government granted a contract to supply water to Cochabamba to Aguas del Tunari, subsidiary of a multinational water company (Bechtel corporation). Aguas gained the rights not only to supply water to the municipalities' network, but also for industrial, agricultural and residential uses throughout Cochambamba province. In effect, all the rights to access water in Cochabamba were transferred to Aguas.[106] To give effect to the contract, the Bolivian Government passed *Law 2029* (*the Drinking Water and Sanitation*) in 1999 that enables the privatisation of drinking water services and aims at full cost recovery of all water related services. Within the three months, Aguas increased water tariffs in different parts of the province. With this increase in price, the government gave in to the mass protest from the people of the community and terminated the contract with Aguas.[107] The management of the local water company was turned over to its employees and the citizens of Cochambamba as part of the community management of water supply services. The Cochabamba example also shows how the local community played a crucial role in persuading the governments to repeal the unpopular privatisation law.

Another example where lending agencies influence the national priorities is the PRSPs, initiated by the IMF and the World Bank in 1999. This country based strategy for poverty reduction provides the operational basis for IMF and the World Bank's concessional lending and for debt

Urquiza, 'Governance for water and sanitation services in low-income settlements experiences with partnership-based management in Moreno, Buenos Aires', Environment and Urbanization, 17/1 (2005), 183–200.

[105] In the Executive Summary of the report, the World Bank stated that 'No subsidies should be given to ameliorate the increase on water tariffs in Cochabamba', arguing that all water uses should have bills that reflect the full cost of proposed expansion of the local water system. World Bank, Report on *Bolivia Public Expenditure Review,* Green Cover No. 19232-BO (June 14, 1999).

[106] Kathleen Slattery, What went wrong? Lessons from Cochambamba, Manila, Buenos Aires and Atlanta (2003) Annual Privatization Report 2003, available at: www.rppi.org.

[107] Malgosia Fitzmaurice, 'The Human Right to Water', Fordham Environmental Law Review, 18 (2007) 537.

relief under the Heavily Indebted Poor Countries (HIPC) Initiative.[108] In order to access funds from the World Bank or the IMF, or to be eligible for debt relief under the HIPC Initiative, countries are required to draft a strategy that charts out their development priorities and describe the government's policies and programmes to promote growth and reduce poverty. This PRSP is imposed to guide all financing provided to the country by donor institutions. The PRSP encompasses poverty oriented extra-budgetary activities, and various non-financial considerations that may have an important bearing on poverty reduction. The World Bank 2002 Report mentions that, in PRSPs, the government has identified areas of legal reform, for example, water law in Bolivia, land law in Malawi and judicial reform in Mozambique and Burkina Faso. These PRSPs show that, in many countries, the government is proposing to streamline legal and institutional arrangements in natural resources and other sectors to achieve the poverty reduction strategies.[109] The PRSPs have been criticised on the ground that their content is heavily influenced by the existing IMF and World bank programme conditions, and by the representatives of these two lending agencies.[110] A Word Development Movement report cited examples from Gambia, Ghana, Guinea, Malawi, Mali and Mozambique where water privatisation was already a condition of a WB or IMF programme before being included in the PRSP.[111]

An important aspect of this type of 'conditionality' in the form of aid, loans, debt restructuring can lead many developing countries to encourage legal measures which are purely based on environmental concerns[112] rather than sustainable development policies that take economic and social development and equity goals into account.

---

108 The HIPC initiative aims to reduce external debt burdens of the most heavily indebted poor countries to sustainable levels. To be considered for HIPC initiative assistance, a country must face an unsustainable debt burden, beyond traditionally available debt-relief mechanisms, establish a track record of reform and sound policies through IMF and WB supported programmes, have developed a PRSP through a broad based participatory process. Available at: www.imf.org.

109 IMF and World Bank, Review of Poverty Reduction Strategy Paper (PRSP) Approach: Early Experience with Interim PRSPs and Full PRSPs (March 2002).

110 World Development Movement, *supra.*

111 Ibid.

112 For example, removal of indigenous communities from their land without rehabilitation to introduce wildlife or repossessing lands from small-farmers to plant biofuels crops.

4. International Agreements Influencing the Domestic Resource Sector

International agreements are known by a wide range of titles (e.g. treaty, convention, protocol, declaration, charter, action plan, programme of action) and may create binding as well as non-binding obligations. If the agreement is a 'declaration', it may not be legally binding[113] as the term generally indicates that the parties do not intend to create binding obligations but merely want to declare certain aspirations. Examples are the 1992 Rio Declaration on Environment and Development, the 2000 UN Millennium Declaration and the 2002 Johannesburg Declaration on Sustainable Development. There are examples of 'declarations' which were not originally intended to have binding force, but their provisions may have reflected customary international law or may have gained binding character as customary law at a later stage, as is the case with 1948 Universal Declaration of Human Rights. On the other hand, a 'treaty' creates a binding obligation and countries ratifying the agreement become bound to implement the obligations created under the treaty at the national level.[114] These declarations (and principles contained therein) have influenced a large number of binding agreements, national laws and judicial decisions.[115] In countries with 'monist' systems, the treaty has the force of law within the country, while countries with 'dualist' systems require implementing legislation for the treaty to have legal effect. In both cases, changes to national laws and institutions are often required to reflect the new commitments.

4.1. *Legislation to Protect the Environment*

In line with the trend in international law to adopt framework conventions (e.g. Biodiversity Convention, Climate Change Convention), low and middle income countries are adopting framework laws at the national

---

[113] However, the provisions of the 1948 Universal Declaration of Human Rights are accepted as customary international law. Jona Razzaque, 'Right to a healthy environment in Human Rights Law' in M. Baderin and M. Ssenyonjo (eds.) *International Human Rights Law: 60 Years after the UDHR* (Aldershot: Ashgate, 2011) 115–135.

[114] Malcolm Shaw, *International Law* (6th edn, Cambridge: Cambridge University Press, 2009).

[115] Patricia Birnie, Alan Boyle and Catherine Redgwell, International Law and the Environment (3rd edition, Oxford: Oxford University Press, 2009); Philippe Sands and Jacqueline Peel, Principles of International Environmental Law (3rd edition, Cambridge: Cambridge University Press, 2012).

level.[116] These instruments aim to achieve the objectives of sustainable development through a single fundamental and comprehensive framework law, often supported by other sectoral regulations (e.g., environmental law, trade and energy law). In most cases, these comprehensive laws introduce various legal principles, specify the administrative responsibilities of authorities at the national and local level and arrange financial mechanisms to support projects promoting sustainable development.[117] These laws also tend to promote the use of best available technologies, elaborate on procedures for EIA and establish the right to information. In the environmental field, examples of these framework laws can be found in Asia[118] and Africa,[119] aiming to protect the environment and human health. These environmental regulations often establish specific agencies or directorate with enforcement powers to deal with various types of environmental pollution. For example, Uganda national environmental statute provides that anyone charged with misusing natural resources or illegal traffic in hazardous waste will be liable to pay a hefty fine.[120] Similar enforcement provisions, *albeit* weak and somewhat ineffective, are found in the framework regulations of India, Pakistan and Bangladesh.[121]

Various environmental principles, such as the precautionary principle, polluter pays principle, sustainable development, are integrated in many of these regulations and various pollution standards and licenses have been set out by the agencies to implement the law. For example, the biosafety regulations in India follow precautionary principle. Precautionary approach can be taken regarding the facts, data and measurement issues surrounding the risk assessment procedures, and broader political, moral and economic questions about the technology being applied. The GM brinjal and GM cotton case in India highlight that any risk regulation needs to comply with international obligations and be fair, effective,

---

[116] National reports of member states of the climate change convention and biodiversity convention. Available from http://unfccc.int/national_reports/items/1408.php and http://www.cbd.int/reports/ (accessed 15 March 2012).

[117] UNEP, Environmental Law Training Manual (Nairobi, 1997), Part III (National Legal Regimes).

[118] 1986 Environment Protection Act (India), 1997 Environment Protection Act (Pakistan), 1995 Environment Conservation Act (Bangladesh).

[119] 1999 National Environment Management and Co-ordination Act (Kenya), 1989 Environment Conservation Act (South Africa), 1995 national Environment Statute (Uganda).

[120] Patricia Kameri-Mbote and P. Cullet, Biological Diversity Management in Africa: Policy Perspectives(1999) IELRC working Paper. Website: www.ielrc.org.

[121] Jona Razzaque, *Public Interest Environmental Litigation in India, Pakistan and Bangladesh* (The Hague: Kluwer, 2004), Chapter 3.

accountable and open.[122] Since the commercialisation of Bt Cotton in India, NGOs such as Gene Campaign have been voicing their concerns about the inadequacies of the existing laws to control the potential environmental and health hazards of GMOs. Despite two separate public interest litigation,[123] the government has still not revised its regulatory framework to comply with the Biosafety Protocol.[124] In 2006, the Supreme Court of India directed the Genetic Engineering Approval Committee of India not to approve any GM crop for fresh field trials. However, in 2008, the Supreme Court of India revoked the ban it had earlier placed on the approval of large scale field trials of transgenic crops. It took this decision after balancing the commercial interests, food security and environmental concerns. This example highlights that existing Indian laws dealing with GM crops are inadequate to protect human health and the environment and the weak legal provisions (e.g., Patent Act of India) have allowed multinational companies such as Monsanto to receive the patent to commercialise GM seed or plant (e.g., Bt. Cotton). [125]

4.2. *National Implementing Measures of MEAs*

A number of multilateral environmental agreements (MEAs) suggest mechanisms for the development of national level plans, programmes and strategies as well as their implementation. These plans set forth how a country could comply with its obligations under the MEA. For example, the biodiversity related conventions, the Basel Convention and the Stockholm Convention – all propose national level planning.[126] These plans provide for the establishment of a national focal point to work with

[122] India, a party to the Convention on Biodiversity and having ratified the Cartagena Protocol in 2003, is committed to the safe handling of GM organisms. Bt.Cotton was the first transgenic crop to be released in India. After its introduction in 2002, there has been a lot of controversy surrounding its performance and impact on the environment and biodiversity.

[123] Gene Campaign public interest litigation of 2004, another public interest litigation was filed in 2005.

[124] It challenged the constitutionality of the Rules for the Manufacture, Use, Import, Export and Storage of Hazardous Micro-organisms, Genetically Engineered Organisms or Cells, 1989 framed under the Environment (Protection) Act, 1986.

[125] The Patent (Second Amendment) Act 2002 deals with the GM seeds. Vandana Shiva et al, *Corporate hijack of biodiversity: How WTO-TRIPS Rule Promote Corporate Hijack of People's Biodiversity and Knowledge* (New Delhi: Navadanya, 2002).

[126] Basel Convention on the Control of Transboundary Movement of Hazardous Wastes and Their Disposal, Mar. 22, 1989, U.N. Doc. UNEP/WG.190/4, reprinted in 28 I.L.M. 657 (1989). Stockholm Convention on Persistent Organic Pollutants, May 22, 2001, 40 I.L.M. 532 (2001).

the relevant MEA Secretariat to promote implementation.[127] The MEA Secretariat or the Global Environment Facility (GEF) might provide guidelines to countries for the preparation of their plans.[128] These national plans can assist countries to assess their legal, policy and institutional strengths and weaknesses, prioritise needs and measures, and identify and evaluate the costs of implementation.[129] Each of these plans or programmes forms an integral part of the implementation of MEAs at the national level. When formulating these plans, national authorities need to recognise the potential for synergies with other international conventions and identify common themes.

Such national implementing measures include legislation, policies, and action plans. Examples can be found in Africa and Asia, where domestic legislation was passed in order to comply with obligations under international environmental agreements. In Africa, a large number of wildlife laws are influenced by international rules related to wildlife management and conservation. For example, *Kenya Wildlife (Conservation and Management) Act 1976* has adopted the provisions of the 1973 Convention on International Trade in Endangered Species of Wild Flora and Fauna (CITES) by banning all game animal hunting and revoking all licenses to trade in wildlife products. The influence of 1989 Basel Convention was evident in *Hazardous Wastes (Management and Handling) Rules 1989* in India. It may also be possible to amend existing legislation or adopt a regulation which implements a thematically related cluster of agreements, e.g. biodiversity or waste management.[130] In addition to regulations, a number of countries are preparing national strategies and plans to implement the 1992 Convention on Biological Diversity and the 1994 Convention to Combat Desertification.[131] National Implementation Plans can identify legal, policy and institutional strengths and weaknesses, and assist countries in evaluating the costs of implementation. Each of these

---

127 UNEP, Draft Manual on Compliance with and enforcement of multilateral environmental agreements (DEPI: Washington DC, 2004).

128 See: NAPA Guidelines by Climate Change Convention Secretariat for LDCs to prepare the NAPA. The GEF operational Guidelines for the National capacity Self Assessment (NCSA) helps countries to identify country level priorities and needs for capacity building to address global environmental issues.

129 UNEP Draft Manual on Compliance with and enforcement of Multilateral Environmental Agreements (2004), available at: http://www.unep.org/dec/docs/unep_manual.pdf (accessed 12 March 2012).

130 ibid.

131 A list of these countries which have prepared National Biodiversity Strategy and Action Plan (NBSAP), National Adaptation programme of Action (NAPA) and National Action Programme (NAP) are available in the convention website: www.biodiv.org.

national plans stresses the importance of consultation and participation of communities in its preparation and implementation.[132]

4.3. *Issue Based Model Law*[133]

Within environmental legal field, there are several issue based model laws.[134] Model laws can be a useful tool to control corporate actors while these companies are involved in, e.g., patenting seeds and traditional knowledge.[135] Under the Biodiversity Convention, providers of traditional knowledge are encouraged to make benefit sharing arrangements with users such as companies and governments.[136] These arrangements could open up new sources of income for local communities or other entities in developing countries. For example, the traditional healers of Samoa were acknowledged in a benefit-sharing agreement concerning the development of prostratin, an anti-AIDS compound derived from the Samoan native *mamala* tree (*homalanthus nutans*). It proposes that revenues from the development of prostratin will be shared with the village where the compound was found and with the families of the healers who helped discover it.[137]

However, many biodiversity rich countries are concerned about the inherent conflict between the two agreements: TRIPs Agreement[138] that accommodates private rights (e.g. patent) and can potentially overrule the sovereign rights of member states over genetic resources recognised by

132 UNEP Draft Manual (2004), *supra*.

133 Reference to Model Law can be found in commercial arbitration, e.g. UNCITRAL Model law on International Commercial Arbitration. UNCTAD Model Law on Competition.

134 OAU African Model Legislation for the Protection of the rights of local communities, farmers and breeders, and for the regulation of access to biological resources. OAU African Model Law on Biosafety; Model National Legislation on the Management of Hazardous Wastes and Other Wastes as well as on the Control of Transboundary Movements of Hazardous Wastes and Other Wastes and their Disposal, Basel Convention Secretariat, available at: archive.basel.int/pub/modlegis.pdf.

135 Jona Razzaque and Manisuli Ssenyonjo 'Protection of Traditional Knowledge and Human Rights Obligations: the Status of Discussion in International Organisations', Netherlands Quarterly of Human Rights, 25/3 (2007) 401-436.

136 For example, the Nagoya Protocol on Access to Genetic Resources and the Fair and Equitable Sharing of Benefits Arising from their Utilization to the Convention on Biological Diversity (2010). Available at: http://www.cbd.int/abs/ (accessed 28 February 2012).

137 WIPO, Intellectual Property and Traditional Knowledge, WIPO Publication 920(E), Geneva: WIPO, available at http://www.wipo.int/freepublications/en/tk/920/wipo_pub_920.pdf (accessed 15 January 2010).

138 Agreement on Trade-Related Aspects of Intellectual Property Rights, Apr. 15, 1994, Marrakesh Agreement Establishing the World Trade Organization, Annex 1C, The Legal Texts: The Results of the Uruguay Round of Multilateral Trade Negotiations 320 (1999), 1869 U.N.T.S. 299, 33 I.L.M. 1197 (1994).

the Biodiversity Convention.[139] The concerns of biodiversity rich countries are related to the impacts of patent protection on genetic resources and associated traditional knowledge.

First: patents over plant varieties require these to be genetically uniform, which favours the commercial production of seeds at a global scale rather than locally adapted varieties. The cultivation of uniform varieties is linked both to the loss of agro-biodiversity and to the increase of genetic erosion, making crops more vulnerable to diseases.

Second: the intellectual property right, as a private property right, does not adequately protect the rights of communities over their traditional knowledge.[140] The developing countries fear that arrangements under the intellectual property rights regime do not provide protection to the countries and communities that supply the genetic material and traditional knowledge.[141] However, it is possible for the developing countries to adopt higher standard of laws (e.g. *sui generis* laws) than required by TRIPs Agreement and include provisions on benefit sharing.[142]

Third: the level of access and benefit sharing of traditional knowledge depends on the model followed at the national level to protect traditional knowledge, culture and indigenous practice. The impacts of intellectual property rights laws in developing countries can be very negative for small farmers. For example, patents can make seeds more expensive for small farmers due to royalty payments, restrictive contracts and increased commercialisation. According to ActionAid,[143] only a handful of multinational corporations hold the vast majority of the 918 patents on rice, maize, wheat, soybean and sorghum, with 633 patents, or nearly 69 per cent, on the staples.

Fourth: there are problems of 'bio-piracy' in respect of genetic resources and traditional knowledge. Control and use of genetic resources remain a crucial issue both for the public and private industries and for communities dependent on these resources. Through patents, the biotechnology

---

139 Article 15 of 1992 Biodiversity Convention.

140 Martin Khor, *Intellectual property, Biodiversity and Sustainable Development: Resolving the Difficult Issues* (London UK: Zed Books and Penang, Malaysia: Third World Network, 2002) Chapter 2.

141 Council for Trade-Related Aspects of Intellectual Property Rights, The Relationship Between the TRIPs Agreement and the Convention on Biological Diversity: Summary of Issues Raised and Points Made, IP/C/W/368/Rev.1, 8 February 2006, 8.

142 UNEP/IISD, *Trade and Environment: a Handbook,* Canada: International Institute for Sustainable Development (2005), 73-74.

143 John Madeley, Crops and Robbers (London UK: Action Aid, 2001)Available at http://www.actionaid.org.uk/doc_lib/crops_robbers.pdf (accessed 15 January 2012).

industries can claim ownership of genetic resources and in effect, own the knowledge developed by indigenous farmers or resources which were developed by nature. Granting private property rights over the traditional knowledge raises serious questions in respect to 'prior art',[144] and can also viewed as 'bio-piracy.' Bio-piracy is defined as 'the illegal appropriation of life – micro-organisms, plants, and animals – and the traditional cultural knowledge that accompanies it.'[145] Many academics have termed this as 'biocolonialism' or 'bioprospecting' whereby companies or institutions from the industrialised countries appropriate the genetic resources and traditional knowledge in the biodiversity rich countries and become the new owner of these resources.[146]

These biopirates can be individuals or institutions who impose exclusive control over the resources or knowledge. There are a number of ways that biopiracy can take place: unauthorised use of traditional knowledge and technologies, unauthorised use of biological resources and lack of benefit sharing with the resource providers such as the community and tribes.[147] Biopiracy allegations arose in several cases:[148] a US patent granted for the healing properties of turmeric, known for centuries in India; a US patent on the 'ayahuasca' plant, considered sacred and used for medicinal purposes by Amazon's indigenous peoples.

---

144 The 'prior art' is the body of knowledge that exists prior to the invention. It helps to determine whether or not the invention is 'new' and 'non-obvious'.

145 Marcia E. DeGeer, 'Biopiracy: The Appropriation of Indigenous Peoples' *Cultural Knowledge', New England Journal of International & Comparative Law*, 9/1 (2002), 179.

146 Lakshmi Sarma, 'Biopiracy: Twentieth Century Imperialism in the Form of International Agreements', *Temple International and Comparative Law Journal*, 13 (1999) 107. Shiva (2002), *supra*. Rosemary J. Coombe, 'Intellectual Property, Human Rights and Sovereignty: New Dilemmas in International Law Posed by the Recognition of Indigenous Knowledge and the Conservation of Biodiversity', Indiana Journal of Global Legal Studies, 6 (1998) 59.

147 Graham Dutfield, 'Identification of Outstanding ABS Issues: Access to GR and IPR. What is biopiracy?', International Expert Workshop on Access to Genetic Resources and Benefit Sharing, 2005, available at: http://moderncms.ecosystemmarketplace.com/repository/moderncms_documents/I.3.pdf (accessed 10 January 2012).

148 Ashish Kothari and R V Anuradha, 'Biodiversity and Intellectual Property Rights: Can the Two Co-Exist?', Journal of International Wildlife Law and Policy, 2/2 (1999) 204–223. Commission on Intellectual Property Rights, *Integrating Intellectual Property Rights and Development Policy* (London: Commission on Intellectual Property Rights, 2002), Chapter 4 (Traditional knowledge and Geographical Indications). Available at http://www.iprcommission.org/papers/pdfs/final_report/Ch4final.pdf (accessed 15 January 2012).

In recent years, the African Union[149] has drafted the African Model Law for the *Protection of the Rights of Local Communities, Farmers and Breeders, and for the Regulation of Access to Biological Resources* (2000) to protect common resources with a common tool, while allowing for flexibility to adapt it to the priorities and needs of each African country.[150] This aims to help African countries fulfil their obligations to TRIPS Agreement and Biodiversity Convention. The ultimate aim of the Model Law is to ensure that the local communities, farmers and plant breeders can contribute to and benefit from the sustainable development of the region. It provides the necessary framework for member states of the African Union to design specific national legislation consistent with their political orientation, national objective and level of socio-economic development.[151] Some African countries have been looking into the provisions of Model Law while drafting their national legislation on relevant issues,[152] but it is too early to assess impact of Model Law on the poor communities of the region. Similar examples of Model Law can be found for the Pacific island states.[153]

4.4. *Incentive based Legislation*

A number of MEAs include economic instruments including market-based mechanisms as a way to implement the treaty at the national level. These instruments can generate financial resources, attract funds to environmentally friendly technologics, create employment opportunities

149 The African Union has 54 members and is based on the common vision of a united and strong Africa and on the need to build a partnership between governments and all segments of civil society, in order to strengthen solidarity and cohesion amongst the peoples of Africa. Available at: http://www.au.int/en/ (accessed on 12 March 2012).

150 Johnson A. Ekpere, The OAU Model Law and Africa's Common Position on the TRIPS review Process (2001), ICTSD Discussion paper, available at: http://www.iprsonline.org/ictsd/docs/IPR_collection.pdf (accessed 28 February 2012).

151 Caroline Lasen-Diaz, Regional Approaches to implementing the Convention on Biological Diversity: The Case of Access to Genetic Resources (2000). Available at: http://www.field.org.uk/files/access.pdf (accessed 28 February 2012).

152 Kent Nnadozie, Integrating African perspectives and Priorities into Genetic Resource Regulations: A Resource Guide for Policymakers (2004) IUCN Policy and Global Change Series: Trade and Biodiversity. Available at: http://www.iprsonline.org/ictsd/docs/KentNnadozieMarch04.pdf (accessed 28 February 2012).

153 Pacific Model Law for the protection of traditional knowledge and expressions of culture (2009). Available at: http://www.forumsec.org/resources/uploads/attachments/documents/PacificModelLaw,ProtectionofTKandExprssnsofCulture20021.pdf (accessed on 28 February 2012).

and encourage investments.[154] A number of countries are complementing incentive based regulations with existing 'command and control' based regulations. While effectiveness of a regulation is depended on how it matched the need of the particular country, the public and popular will, the 'command and control' approach follows a 'top-down' approach. The main criticism of this type of regulations is that it does not offer any incentive to the operator of a facility to reduce pollution below the mandated level.[155] Examples of this type of legislation can be found in Asia, Africa and Latin America.[156] On the other hand, incentive based mechanisms, such as tradable permits and pollution charges can provide a stimulus of technological change and innovation in pollution control. MEAs such as CITES, Climate Change Convention opt for incentive based regulatory approach.[157] Examples of economic incentives can be found in Philippines (efffluent charge), Thailand (leaded gas tax) and Chile (tradable emission permits).[158]

5. Concluding Comments

This chapter shows that the transformation of resource sovereignty is apparent in two ways. On the one hand, between two states, limitations on sovereign rights to exploit their own natural resources or to pollute their environment are based on the need to balance the interest of competing sovereigns. Accordingly, as stated in the 1992 Rio Declaration, a state's sovereign rights are limited only to the extent that exercising these rights caused *significant* environmental harm in the territory of another state. Domestic law with extraterritorial effect expands or reforms the

---

[154] United Nations Environment Programme, Creating pro-poor markets for ecosystem services (2005), concept note, *available at* http://www.unep.org/DEC/Support/Cross_Cutting/ProPoor.asp (accessed on 28 February 2012).

[155] Richard B. Stewart, 'Models for Environmental Regulation: Central Planning Versus Market based Approaches', B.C. Environmental Affairs Law Review, 19 (1992) 547.

[156] United Nations Environment Programme. Global Environment Outlook (2000). Available at: http://www.unep.org/Geo2000/ (accessed on 28 February 2012).

[157] Sujata Gupta and Dennis A Tirpak, Policies, Instruments and Co-operative Arrangements, Chapter 13, Working Group 4, 4th Assessment (IPCC, 2007). Available at http://www.ipcc.ch/pdf/assessment-report/ar4/wg3/ar4-wg3-chapter13.pdf (accessed on 12 March 2012). Erwin H. Bulte, G. Cornelis van Kooten and Timothy Swanson, Economic Incentives and Wildlife Conservation 2003. Available at http://www.cites.org/eng/prog/economics/CITES-draft6-final.pdf (accessed on 12 March 2012).

[158] Robert C. Anderson, Incentive based Policies for environmental management in developing countries (2002), Resources for the Future Issue Brief. Available at: http://www.rff.org/rff/Documents/RFF-IB-02-07.pdf (accessed 28 February 2012).

notion of territorial sovereignty. Indeed, these laws can be used by rich countries over poor countries for economic dominance and trade restrictions in the guise of environmental protection.[159]

On the other hand, it is in fact external market forces (in the form of standard, conditionality, export requirements) that are driving the sustainability agenda at the national level. In many instances, lack of appropriate balance between the role of the state, market and the private sector creates a conflict between access and sustainability. How to ensure that 'sustainability' agenda pushes market agenda and not the other way round? The usual suspects come in the form of inclusive policy making processes, regulation with effective monitoring, enforcement with adequate penalties, right based approach to resource management and access to cost effective remedies.

The above discussion shows, first, some developments in the field of extraterritorial control of the activities of other states (e.g. the Espoo Convention) or non-state actors (e.g. MNCs) by home state, for example, the EU Directive on renewable energy. Second, the development of the right based approach allowing people to go to court and bring a case against the state for failing to protect its people against the harmful acts of multinational corporations. Human rights treaties[160] have transformed the international legal field by allowing individuals to challenge the sovereign of states over their natural resources. With the progress of environmental law, it became apparent that human rights law and environmental law treat sovereignty differently.[161] Human rights law limits state's control over individuals within its territory and allows individuals to bring action against its own state. Environmental legal regime recognises the limits on national sovereignty and, at the same time, accepts that states have permanent sovereignty over natural resources unless they are damaging global commons or have adverse transboundary effect.

Third, the global dimension in environmental problems (e.g. issues of common concern such as the climate change, impossibility to divide the

---

159 Howard Mann and Yvonne Apea, 'Dispute Resolution' in Adil Najam, Mark Halle and Ricardo Meléndez-Ortiz, *Trade and Environment: A Resource Book* (Canada: ICTSD, 2007) 67–76.

160 For example, Universal Declaration of Human Rights, adopted 10 December 1948, UNGA Res. 217 (AIII), U.N. GAOR, 3rd Session, pt 1, at 71, U.N. Doc A/ 810 (1948). American Convention on Human Rights, O.A.S. Treaty Series No. 36, 1144 U.N.T.S. 123, *entered into force* July 18, 1978. African Charter on Human and Peoples' Rights, adopted 27 June 1981, 1520 UNTS 217, (1981) 21 I.L.M 59 (entered into force 21 October 1986).

161 Harry Osfosky, 'Learning from Environmental Justice: A New Model for International Environmental Rights', Stanford Environmental Law Journal, 24 (2005) 71.

environment as in the case of air pollution) and the fact that environmental issues do not respect territorial sovereignty (e.g. shared river, forests or habitat) make it vital that environmental issues need to be internalised in domestic law. However, these internalisation of environmental issues – be it in the form of model law, incentive based instruments – will not be sustainable if it is done as an 'eyewash' without any effective monitoring and enforcement mechanisms and any active involvement of the people.

To a large extent, a state-centred approach to international law-making has led to the adoption of solutions to environmental problems that cannot deliver the impetus for change for the peoples of the state. To push the sustainability agenda to lead to a transparent, inclusive and accountable system of governance at the national level, resource development decisions need to have support from most affected communities including resource right holders. To proactively include the poor and marginalised groups in resource decisions will require both the project proponent and the government to adapt their strategies of information dissemination and adopt methods of citizen participation that take into account the social, economic, cultural and geographic characteristics of the population in question. Greening of economy needs to promote transparency and accountability through access to information and stakeholder involvement in decision-making, open processes that engage citizens and ensure social inclusion supported by institutions and interest groups

THE RIGHT TO WATER IN SOUTH AFRICA: CONSTITUTIONAL MANAGERIALISM AND A CALL FOR PLURALISM

Nathan Cooper and Duncan French

1. Introduction

> The right to water and to pursue sustainable development goals, so fundamental to developing countries, should be understood to increase the standards of responsibilities of investors in the water sector. The provision of water services in developing countries is not, and cannot be understood as, just another business venture.[1]

The shift over the last two decades from primarily State-control to more mixed systems of public/private ownership and management of the domestic-supply of natural resources has unsurprisingly resulted in both political and normative debates on the efficacy, social desirability and fairness of permitting increased private-sector involvement in the provision of "public" responsibilities.[2] This debate, ideologically driven in part, has generated much consternation within various elements of civil society, which have often viewed such a trend as counter-intuitive to social development and poverty reduction.[3] Nowhere has the debate been more contested than in relation to the water sector, especially in developing or least developed countries. The purpose of this chapter is however not to engage with the debate at the macro-level, but rather to utilise this broad context to consider one particular example, namely the commercialisation of water services in South Africa, which is itself used to explore certain general themes surrounding the linkages – sometimes explicit, sometimes less so – between law and development. To this end, the South African constitutional right to water and its operation is considered within a

---

[1] Lawyers' Environmental Action Trust et al., Amicus Curiae Submission in *Biwater Gauff (Tanzania) Ltd. v. United Republic of Tanzania*, paragraph 11. See ICSID Case No. ARB/05/22, Procedural Order No. 5 (2 February 2007).

[2] Ann-Christin Sjolander, *The Water Business, Corporations Versus People* (London: Zed Books, 2005).

[3] Bethan Emmett, *In the Public Interest: Health, Education and Water and Sanitation for All* (Oxford, Oxfam, 2006).

broader discussion of relevant international development and human rights law as it is this international context which frames the domestic right, conferring explicit normative authority (as will be seen from the South African jurisprudence), as well as delimiting its current form (as an individual right subject to progressive realisation within the State's available resources).

Though the majority of private-sector involvement and investment funding of South African water provision is currently not "foreign" in nature or character,[4] and thus this chapter purposely does not consider international investment law,[5] many of the overarching issues are similar. In particular, the chapter seeks to consider the increasing influence of commercialisation in water supply and infrastructure (typified by, but not limited to, private sector involvement) and, importantly, the relevance of rules, human rights norms and legal processes within that economic transformation. As has occurred generally, this issue has resulted in disquiet in South Africa as to the appropriateness of private management and control of such a key resource. However, whilst there is a general debate to be had as to the balance between liberalisation and regulation in this sector (as in any other area of privatisation of supply), the chapter argues that the debate itself is fundamentally misaligned if it limits itself to this, rather abstract, dichotomy. In particular, such an approach will often fail to incorporate within its scope a more nuanced and critical understanding of the relevance of law. Law as a tool of development – as with foreign direct investment – is invariably a blunt instrument and its overall utility can rarely be measured effectively in abstract or theoretical terms but must always be placed within a much broader context of interplaying factors.[6]

---

[4] *Cascal*, formerly *Biwater*, a British/Dutch multinational owns a 90% interest in the Greater Nelspruit Utility Company (GNUC), which operates under the name *Silulumanzi*. Cascal has also acquired a 73.4% interest in *Siza Water*, the company that has responsibility for providing water and wastewater services to the Dolphin Coast region near Durban. Also, since 1999 *Durban Metro Water* (the municipal water services provider) has worked in partnerships with the French private sector firms *Lyonnaise des Eaux* and *Vivendi*. See: "Water and Sanitation Program" (WSP) last visited: October 2011 http://www.wsp.org/wsp/sites/wsp.org/files/publications/af_durban.pdf.

[5] See Owen McIntyre, 'Water Service Privatisation and Recognition of the Human Right to Water in International Investment Law: Finding Fertile Ground in Unlikely Places' in Duncan French (ed), *Global Justice and Sustainable Development* (Leiden/Boston: Martinus Nijhoff, 2010) 207, as well as generally Muthucumaraswamy Sornarajah, *The International Law on Foreign Investment* (Cambridge: Cambridge University Press, 2010, 3rd ed).

[6] See David M. Trubek, 'Toward a Social Theory of Law: An Essay on the Study of Law and Development' 82 *Yale Law Journal* (1972) 1–50, 1: 'Since the implicit, a priori

Thus, whilst consideration will be given to such broad themes as the right to water and sustainable development, the chapter largely eschews general principles in favour of the particularities of the immediate context of South Africa. And on this, two insights will be highlighted so as to understand better the growing commercialisation of water supply. First, while the existence of a constitutional right of access to water within South African law has been rightly heralded, of equal importance is the very apparent policy limitations placed upon such a right by the South African Constitutional Court. The *constrained expression* of the right thus becomes as important as its existence, which the chapter refers to as 'constitutional managerialism'. And secondly, the historical and popular context in which the right must be implemented. Namely, in a post-Apartheid South Africa, where disadvantage – but more than that inequality – remains rife, questions of access and price are not just abstract indices of effectiveness and fairness, but concurrently raise the issues of social equity and community empowerment.

These 'additional' themes of constitutional managerialism and the historical-popular context around the right to water are neither complementary nor necessarily mutually supportive. Indeed, they would seem to pull in very different, if not opposite, directions. However, that is paradoxically not of concern when what one is seeking to construct is a framework to reflect better the complex array – and interaction – of factors that reveal the impact of the *law-in-practice*. Such factors must include the constrained interpretation and practical application of the right to water, as well as recognising how social inequality and poverty frame the question of access to sufficient water as being both crucial and pressing. An analysis which begins and ends at the judicial interpretation of the right will invariably fail to reflect the wider socio-economic and political context.[7]

Thus, the chapter concludes that when considering the commercialisation of water supply (or any other developmental topic), issues such as these must be fully incorporated within the discourse if the analysis is to

conclusions about the role of law are no longer valid, we must turn to systematic efforts to understand the relationships among the legal, social, economic, and political orders. In any such effort, comparative research and cross-cultural generalizations will play a major role'.

[7] Despite this, one should not lose sight of the importance of principle and the extent to which constitutional principles should be both aspirational in tone as well as being normative forces for ongoing societal change. Nevertheless, as will be noted below, there is the risk of turning rights-based litigation into simply a matter of "resolving" a technical legal problem which is equally problematic.

even begin to reflect the untidy state of the actuality. In particular, such intended ambiguity adds a layer of social reality to increasingly sterile debates of public v. private, market v. State-control and commodification v. human right, which have for too long dominated legal understandings of both economic regulation and constitutional rights.[8] Throughout the chapter we suggest that the current right to water, as expressed individually, needs to be contextualised by environmental factors, a realism regarding domestic water use, the limits of litigation, and the need for greater community empowerment in allocation decisions. We do not argue against an individual right to water, but suggest variously that procedural alternatives (offering different routes by which to address problems of insufficient water – for instance, community participation rather than litigation) can more firmly connect the right to water to the complex social and economic realities of the particular domestic context.

2. International Development Law: Context and Overarching Themes

In studying how the right to water within a domestic jurisdiction is affected by the twin pressures of increased private sector ethos and the implementation of human rights norms, the first thing that is very noticeable is that it highlights the artificiality of the legal discipline. On a subject that crosses human rights, economic law, constitutional rights, public regulation of liberalised services, development, and (perhaps) international investment and environmental law, approaches that are limited in perspective will only ever be able to tell part of the overall story. More significantly, where one begins one's analysis will often be a strong determinant of where one's analysis will end. This is not a criticism of individual research, but reflects the traditional problems that legal analysis, especially in the development field, has faced.[9]

---

[8] Though in no way the exclusive response to these debates, one should also recognise the important role of customary norms within modern legal systems (P. Ørebech et al., *The Role of Customary Law in Sustainable Development* (Cambridge: Cambridge University Press, 2005) ix: 'Duncan A. French, in his book on the role of the state and sustainable development (2002) [sic], wrote "For many developed States a key challenge is how to achieve sustainable development without a return to centralized planning, an anathema to most States with developed market economies"...we propose that "bottom-up systems" like customary law play a role in the achievement of viable social systems').

[9] See generally, David M. Trubek & Alvaro. Santos (eds), *The New Law and Economic Development: A Critical Appraisal* (New York: Cambridge University Press, 2006).

Moreover, an approach that is principally focused domestically may have some recourse to, but will unlikely rely heavily on, international legal norms. Similarly, an international human rights (or investment law) perspective may utilise the national situation as a useful case-study or means of contextualisation, but its arguments will ultimately remain shaped by its own (sub-)discipline and its conclusions will invariably revert to the universal when making its concluding comment. In short, international development law, which for the present is used as a catch-all term to describe any aspect of international law touching upon development – human rights, trade, investment, environment, *et cetera* – must intrinsically be tied to the domestic experience of development. As Qureshi and Ziegler note, 'International development law (IDL) covers a number of spheres. Indeed, it covers as many spheres as there are ways of facilitating development...Further, the goal of development can be realised both at the domestic level, as well as through international efforts'.[10] Unfortunately, the relationship between the *global* and the *local* on this issue often only ever seems tangential at best. Moreover such an (admittedly neat) binary approach to understanding the relevance of law in development fails to grasp the inter-linkages and interfaces between jurisdictional levels. Though both the right to water and sustainable development – principles briefly reviewed below – have the conceptual capacity to cross jurisdictional divides, it is arguable that much of the literature remains fragmented and framed by traditional disciplinary parameters.

A. The Right to Water: The Universal Ideal?

Access to sufficient water is a basic requirement for life. Despite not being explicitly mentioned as a human right in the Universal Declaration of Human Rights[11] or the International Covenant on Economic Social and Cultural Rights (ICESCR),[12] access to sufficient water has been progressively recognised internationally as a human right since the 1977 UN

---

[10] Asif H. Qureshi and Andreas R. Ziegler, *International Economic Law* (London: Sweet & Maxwell, 2011, 3rd ed) 615–616.

[11] Universal Declaration of Human Rights, *adopted* 10 Dec. 1948, G.A. Res. 217A (III), 3 U.N. GAOR (Resolutions, part 1) at 71, U.N. Doc. A/810 (1948). *Hereafter* UDHR.

[12] International Covenant on Economic, Social and Cultural Rights, *adopted* 16 Dec 1966, 993 U.N.T.S. 3 (*entered into force* 3 Jan. 1976), G.A. Res. 2200 (XXI), 21 U.N. GAOR Supp. (No. 16) at 49, U.N. Doc. A/6316 (1966). *Hereafter* ICESCR.

Water Conference in Mar del Plata.[13] Since then, basic water provision has been described variously as a 'basic right'[14] and a 'basic human need'.[15] In General Comment No. 15 (2002), issued by the Committee on Economic, Social and Cultural Rights, interpreting Articles 11 and 12 of the ICESCR, water as a prerequisite for the realisation of other human rights is emphasised, as well as it being restated that access to water is itself a human right.[16] The International Law Association's 2004 Berlin rules on water resources[17] further reflects the development of an internationally acknowledged right of access to water within the customary international law applicable to water management.

The importance of acquiring adequate water and sanitation has also been recognised by the international community and articulated within the Millennium Development Goals (MDGs). Target Seven of the MDGs commits the international community to 'halve by 2015 the proportion of the population without sustainable access to safe drinking water'.[18] This goal looks unlikely to be achieved on time, and almost 900 million people continue to suffer from the effects of limited access to poor quality water.[19] Against this reality the formal endorsement by the UN General Assembly of the right to water, on 28 July 2010 may thus be of symbolic importance. Though it has undoubtedly brought the issue into the mainstream of

---

[13] United Nations General Assembly resolution 32/158 of 19 December 1977. Resolution II of the conference declared that 'All peoples, whatever their stage of development and their social and economic conditions, have the right to have access to drinking water in quantities and of a quality equal to their basic needs'.

[14] The Dublin Statement on Water and Sustainable Development Adopted January 31, 1992 in Dublin, Ireland International Conference on Water and the Environment, Principle 4. "Dublin Principle," last accessed: October 2011, http://www.un-documents.net/h2o-dub.htm.

[15] 1st World Water Forum, Marrakech 22 March 1997: "Marrakech Declaration," last accessed: October 2011, http://www.ielrc.org/content/e9712.pdf.

[16] UN Doc. E/C.12/2002/11 (20 January 2003) *Hereafter* GC15: 'The human right to water entitles everyone to sufficient, safe, acceptable, physically accessible and affordable water for personal and domestic uses' (paragraph 2). The Comment also exhorts the States Parties to 'adopt effective measures to realise, without discrimination' the human right to water (paragraph 1).

[17] The International Law Association Berlin Conference (2004) Water Resources Law, Chapter IV Rights of Persons: Article 17 *The Right of Access to Water*. "The Berlin Rules," last accessed: March 2012, www.internationalwaterlaw.org/documents/intldocs/ILA_Berlin_Rules-2004.pdf.

[18] "Target 7.C," last accessed: October 2011, www.un.org/millenniumgoals.

[19] "UN-Water Global Annual Assessment of Sanitation and Drinking-Water Report (GLAAS) 2010, UNICEF First Annual High-Level Meeting of Sanitation and Water for All 23.4.2010, Washington, DC," last accessed: October 2011, www.who.int/water_sanitation_health/glaas.

public debate,[20] it has also highlighted the lack of consensus still surrounding the content and provenance of the 'right to water'. Not only was there a high number of abstentions from the resolution, but the legal basis for the right to water has been contested, with even supporters of the right framing it quite differently. Whereas the primary sponsor, Bolivia, stated that 'the rights to safe drinking water and sanitation are independent rights, which must be recognised as such',[21] Germany and Spain, co-sponsors of a similar resolution before the Human Rights Council, rather considered access to safe drinking water and sanitation to be a component of the right to an adequate standard of living recognised in Article 11 of the International Covenant on Economic, Social and Cultural Rights.[22] On the other hand, the position of the United States was that the July 2010 General Assembly resolution was not reflective of existing international law 'as there is no right to water and sanitation in an international legal sense as described by the draft resolution'.[23] Clearly these divergent positions will also impact upon what States consider to be their responsibilities on this matter and whether they will accept legal consequences for violations thereof.

B. Sustainable Development: The Global Mantra?

As an over-arching goal of the international community and an increasingly recognised principle of international law, sustainable development nevertheless remains as nebulous as it ever did. Though it is increasingly finding judicial support, bringing together themes of environmental protection, economic growth and, more recently, social development, which has undoubtedly solidified its universal appeal amongst both States and civil society, sustainable development continues to defy precise analytical description.[24] Indeed, it is perhaps contrary to the very spirit of sustainable development to separate it from such ideas as the human right to water, international investment law and the like, as its very rationale is

[20] UN GA resolution 64/292 "The human right to water and sanitation", UN Doc. A/RES/64/292 (3 August 2010): 'recognizes the right to safe and clean drinking water and sanitation as a human right that is essential for the full enjoyment of life and all human rights' (paragraph 1).

[21] UN Doc. A/64/PV.108, 5b.

[22] Ibid. at 6a and 7a, respectively.

[23] Ibid. at 8a.

[24] Malgosia Fitzmaurice, *Contemporary Issues in International Environmental Law* (Cheltenham: Edward Elgar, 2009) 67: 'the true nature of which remains mysterious and elusive despite its wide use (or perhaps overuse)'.

the integration of such considerations.[25] Nevertheless, as a lens by which to understand the relationship between law and development, it remains distinctive. But this distinctiveness, though appealing, is inherently shallow if it fails to provide a substantive means by which to progress the reform agenda which surrounds it. As Fitzmaurice has surely rightly noted, '[t]he continuing reliance on clichéd and worn out definitions should be abandoned and the concept (or principle) of sustainable development must acquire a tangible and concrete content'.[26]

Such 'concrete[ness]' can however occur in numerous ways. First, reference has already been made to its inclusion in case-law, both in international and domestic courts. Of particular note was the recent judgment of the International Court of Justice in *Pulp Mills on the River Uruguay* (2010), in which it remarked upon the 'interconnectedness between equitable and reasonable utilization of a shared resource and the balance between economic development and environmental protection that is the essence of sustainable development'.[27] In a similar vein, the South African Constitutional Court, relying on specific textual reference to sustainable development within the Constitution had occasion to note in the *Fuel Retailers* Case (2007) that the Constitution

> recognises the interrelationship between the environment and development; indeed it recognises the need for the protection of the environment while at the same time it recognises the need for social and economic development. It contemplates the integration of environmental protection and socio-economic development. It envisages that environmental considerations will be balanced with socio-economic considerations through the ideal of sustainable development.[28]

---

[25] Duncan French, 'Sustainable Development and the Instinctive Imperative of the Justice in the Global Order' in French (ed), above note 5, 3: 'The promotion of and, equally significantly, the endorsement of synergies between the conservation and sustainable utilisation of natural resources, the protection of the natural environment and improvements in human development are goals that the international community continues to endorse…in seeking to cement further the connections between these goals, it remains the case that the notion, the principle – if not now – the mantra of sustainable development continues to best encapsulate why making, and then maintaining these linkages is considered of universal importance in maximising human well-being whilst also respecting ecological limitations'.

[26] Fitzmaurice, above note 24 at 108.

[27] Judgment of 20 April 2010, paragraph 177.

[28] *Fuel Retailers Association of Southern Africa v. Director-General Environmental Management, Department of Agriculture, Conservation and Environment, Mpumalanga Province and* Others 2007 6 SA 4 (CC) paragraph 45.

Secondly, the principle can be made more definite through amplification; perhaps the best example of this being the drafting of the non-binding International Law Association (ILA) 2002 New Delhi Declaration of Principles of International Law relating to Sustainable Development,[29] which brings together seven discrete, yet inter-related, established and emerging principles of international law. These are the duty of States to ensure the sustainable use of natural resources, the principle of equity and the eradication of poverty, the principle of common but differentiated responsibilities, the principle of the precautionary approach to human health, natural resources and ecosystems, the principle of public participation and access to information and justice, the principle of good governance, and the principle of integration and interrelationship, in particular in relation to human rights and social, economic and environmental objectives. Though some query the utility of such derivative principles,[30] they are increasingly impacting both the policy sphere and at the normative level, both globally and nationally.

Third, and building upon the principle of integration previously referenced, is to emphasise the process-based understanding of sustainable development, which underlines the importance of integrated decision-making.[31] Nevertheless, though techniques such as environmental/sustainability impact assessments and enhanced public participation provide a glimpse of how sustainable development might be operationalised, it is debatable whether without recourse to normative guiding principles – be they those identified by the ILA or others – sustainable development can substantively be achieved. In other words, it is a curious amalgam of process and substance that distinguishes sustainable development from the *status quo ante*, from which it is seeking to improve upon. But it is the very scope of the challenge that sustainable development is confronting which is its inherent weakness. In light of the

---

29 ILA resolution 3/2002, annex as published as UN Doc. A/57/329 (2002).

30 Vaughan Lowe, 'Sustainable Development and Unsustainable Arguments' in Alan Boyle and David Freestone (eds), *International Law and Sustainable Development: Past Achievements and Future Challenges* (Oxford: Oxford University Press, 1999) 26: '[t]he components themselves do not have the appearance of archetypal norms'.

31 Duncan French, *International Law and Policy of Sustainable Development* (Manchester: Manchester University Press, 2005) 72: 'A procedural approach does, however, have the advantage of respecting differences in socio-economic, cultural and political situations, while at the same time requiring integration of concerns – such as environmental considerations – into economic and political decision-making'. See below for discussion of the concept of Integrated Water Resource Management (IWRM) as an expression of sustainable development relevant to that particular sector.

continued aspirational nature of sustainable development, one must conclude, therefore, that though the principle has become a *sine qua non* of modern political society and thought, it has achieved less in terms of real change.

3. Water and the South African Constitutional Court: Managing Aspiration

The previous part has highlighted the limitations of a purely global understanding of the role of law as a tool for development. The remainder of the chapter will now highlight, through an analysis of the right to water in South Africa, how a national perspective may equally be insufficient if it is not broadly contextualised; in particular, how one can have a national perspective without truly appreciating the *impact* of the law within that jurisdiction. For that, one must delve deeper than domestic law to consider the social acceptance of the law, to find its true normative expression. This is uncomfortable territory for any lawyer, but especially an international lawyer.

As signatory to the ICESCR, South Africa is committed to the full realisation of the rights contained therein. While realisation of these rights may be achieved progressively, South Africa's commitment is to take steps that are 'deliberate, concrete and targeted as clearly as possible'[32] towards meeting the goal. Moreover, access to sufficient water is an explicit right in the South African Constitution.[33] Other constitutional rights are related, directly or indirectly to this right, namely the right to equality, right to human dignity, right to life, property rights,[34] right of access to housing, right to have access to courts, and the environmental right.[35] In short, access to sufficient water is an internationally acknowledged

[32] CESCR General Comment No. 3: The nature of States parties obligations (Art. 2, par.1) (UN Doc. E/1991/23 (14/12/1990)) paragraph 2.

[33] Section 27(1)(b) of the Constitution:
(1) Everyone has the right to have access to -
  (a) health care services, including reproductive health care;
  (b) *sufficient* food and *water*
  (c) social security, including, if they are unable to support themselves and their dependants, appropriate social assistance.

[34] Section 25(8) (regarding how far measures can be taken to achieve land, water and related reforms in order to redress the results of past racial discrimination).

[35] Section 24: Everyone has the right-
(a) to an environment that is not harmful to their health or well-being; and
(b) to have the environment protected, for the benefit of present and future generations, through reasonable legislative and other measures that-

(if not uniformly accepted) and nationally protected right for all people in South Africa. Despite this, access to sufficient water is not a reality for many in the country. Moreover, any discussion of the right to water must be framed within the reality that water in South Africa is a scarce resource.[36] Increasing demand from urban centres for water for domestic use jostle with demands from industry, mining and agricultural sectors.[37] These demands are made in an officially 'water stressed' country[38] that has rainfall less than the global average, falling unevenly across the country.[39]

With the advent of majority rule in 1994 it was clear that a significant change in approach to water supply and water rights was necessary, based on the acceptance of two fundamental factors; the extreme inequality of water distribution (pre-1994) and the overall scarcity of water in terms of the total available to the country. A brief overview of the General Household Survey (2010) gives the most recent picture of the nation's access to water for domestic use. Average access nationally to on-site or off-site piped or tap water is 89.3%,[40] leaving over 5 million people without such access.[41] Of those who received piped water from a municipality, almost 25% experienced interruptions in their piped water supply at least once a month.[42] Moreover, those with access to water do not necessarily have access to *sufficient* water as section 27 of the Constitution stipulates. This issue has significant bearing not only on people's general level of health and well-being[43] but also has been a key feature of the legal

---

(i) prevent pollution and ecological degradation
(ii) promote conservation; and
(iii) secure ecologically sustainable development and use of natural resources while promoting justifiable economic and social development.

36 Michael Kidd, *Environmental Law* (Cape Town: Juta & Co. Ltd., 2008) 64.

37 Ibid. at 65.

38 Department of Water Affairs and Forestry *White Paper on a National Water Policy for South Africa* (April 1997), paragraph 14.

39 Kidd, above note 36 at 64.

40 All percentages from the "General Household Survey (2010)" last accessed: July 2012, www.statssa.gov.za/publications/P0318/P0318June2010.pdf.

41 Calculation based on figure for total population of South Africa of 48,700,000 as stated in the GHS 2010.

42 (24.4%, GHS 2010). Fieldwork undertaken by Nathan Cooper in February 2010 in Winterton in rural Kwa-Zulu Natal concurred that interrupted water supply is regularly experienced, with significant associated consequences for health and education, as well as highlighting systemic discrimination as to how access to water is experienced.

43 Patrick Bond & Jackie Dugard, 'Water, Human Rights and Social Conflict: South African Experiences' 1 *Law, Social Justice & Global Development Journal* (2007) 8. The quality of water supply is also a crucial aspect of the definition of the human right to water as detailed by GC15.

disputes over constitutional provisions. Indeed, failure to access sufficient water remains a significant stumbling block to both socio-economic development and political stability.[44]

Sufficient water has been quantified variously between 20 and 50 cubic litres per person per day (lpd).[45] In South Africa, the ANC's Reconstruction and Development Programme (RDP) set sufficient water at a minimum quota of 25 lpd, accessed within 200 metres of a household. However, as the discussion of the recent case of *Mazibuko* will reveal, defining sufficient water is problematic. But even using the RDP quota of sufficient water (25 lpd), a significant proportion of South Africans still do not have access to even this, sixteen years into the democratic era. The recognition, promotion, protection and fulfilment of the goal of access to sufficient water therefore remain crucial aims.

The following discussion of legislation and case law will consider the imperatives and application of the constitutional right to water in South Africa. But it is important also to note the paradigm shift regarding water services that is emerging across the continent and which provides the context for the legislation and judicial decisions under consideration.[46] Previously, water had very much been seen as a public asset, acknowledging its necessity for life and informing allocation decisions accordingly. A distinctive shift has occurred within the past twenty years towards understanding water primarily as a commodity, introducing a rationale of commercialisation to water service delivery. Central to this rationale is the requirement that the costs of water services are recovered from users, and preferably, profit is generated beyond this.[47]

The commercialisation of a municipal service like water (and the corresponding commodification of water) does not necessarily require that water services be provided by the private sector. Indeed there need not be private sector involvement at all. What it does require however is that all actors involved in the service operate with a 'private-sector'

---

[44] See generally Alec Russell, *Bring Me My Machine Gun: The Battle for the Soul of South Africa, from Mandela to Zuma* (Jackson, TN: Perseus Books, 2009).

[45] Peter H. Gleick, 'The Human Right to Water' 1 *Water Policy* (1998) 496.

[46] See generally, Graham Harrison, *The World Bank and Africa: The Construction of Governance States* (London: Routledge, 2004); James Ferguson, *The Anti-Politics Machine: Development, Depoliticization, and Bureaucratic Power in Lesotho* (Minneapolis: University of Minnesota Press, 1994); World Bank Development Report 2004: "Making Services Work for Poor People," last accessed: October 2011, http://go.worldbank.org/ZPTUFPVPGO.

[47] Sean Flynn & Danwood Mzikenge Chirwa, 'The Constitutional Implications of Commercialising Water in South Africa' in D. McDonald and G. Ruiters (eds), *The Age of Commodity, Water Privatisation in Southern Africa* (London: Earthscan, 2005) 59.

(or 'market-oriented') logic. Therefore a collage of national and provincial legislation, municipalities, (domestic and international) private companies and public-private partnerships can all contribute to a commercialised water service. Just such a collage is the reality in South Africa.[48]

A. Constitutional Rights and Sustainable Development

A variety of promulgating legislation has been enacted in order to implement the constitutional right to water. Of particular importance are the Water Services Act 108 of 1997 (WSA) and the National Water Act 36 of 1998 (NWA). However, the aim of these pieces of legislation when taken together is wider than simply the achievement of the right to water. It aims also towards the realisation of the right to environment in section 24 of the Constitution, which requires legislative measures to 'secure ecologically sustainable development and use of natural resources while promoting justifiable economic and social development'. In order to combine the constitutional ambitions of realising the right to water and the right to environment, the WSA and NWA seek to incorporate the practice and rationale of Integrated Water Resource Management (IWRM). As a systematic process for sustainable development, IWRM considers questions of water allocation within the contexts of economic and social development and environmental protection. Such an interconnected approach to water allocation is aimed at encouraging long term sustainability. The emphasis on sustainability is balanced by an explicit recognition of the right of all people to clean water and sanitation at an affordable price.[49]

The WSA is the principal legislative mechanism to actualize the obligations of the state. The WSA aims to provide *inter alia* 'the right of access to basic water supply and the right to basic sanitation necessary to secure sufficient water and an environment not harmful to human health or well-being'.[50] The Act further addresses the social and ecological purposes of water respectively, setting 'national standards and norms and standards for tariffs in respect of water services' and aiming 'to promote effective water resource management and conservation'.[51] Basic water

[48] Sjolander, above note 2 at 65–93.
[49] Global Water Partnership Technical Committee Background Papers No.15. "Social Equity and Integrated Water Resources Management" last accessed October 2011, http://www.gwp.org/en/The-Challenge/What-is-IWRM/.
[50] WSA section 2(a).
[51] WSA sections 2(b) and 2(j).

supply is defined in the WSA as 'the prescribed minimum standard of water supply services necessary for the reliable supply of a sufficient quantity and quality of water to households including informal households, to support life and personal hygiene'.[52] The Act sets the minimum quantity for basic water supply as 25 litres of potable water per person per day (25 lpd), or 6 kilolitres per household per month.[53] This minimum quota is to be provided free of charge and is designated as Free Basic Water (FBW).[54] Water services authorities, including municipalities, are charged with a duty 'to consumers or potential consumers in its area of jurisdiction to progressively ensure efficient, affordable, economical and sustainable access to water services'.[55] But there are no explicit provisions within the Act on how 'access' is to be achieved.

The NWA is also important in implementing the constitutional right to water. The chief aim of the Act is the protection of South Africa's water resources and as such the NWA adds ecological aspects of the right to water to the primarily social aspects stressed in the WSA.[56] Yet, it is increasingly recognised that the differing emphases of these two Acts should not encourage incompatible agendas regarding water resources and water services. The WSA and the NWA are to be read in conjunction with the aim of facilitating access to sufficient water for all within the context of present and future ecological sustainability.[57] Whether this occurs in practice, however, remains debatable.

The right of access to sufficient water requires a definition of *sufficiency* and *access*. Neither terms are defined in the Constitution, but as already

---

[52] WSA section 1.

[53] WSA, Water Services Regulations, Regulation 3 (b) (GN R 509, Government Gazette of 8 June 2001). The figure of 6 kilolitres (6000 litres) is based on 200 litres per household for each 30-day month. This assumes no more than 8 people per household (200 litres divided by 8 people = 25 lpd). The adequacy of the 25 lpd minimum as well as the assumption of no more than 8 people per household were considered in the *Mazibuko* case discussed below.

[54] This commitment to free basic water was reiterated in the Free Basic Water Programme 2001. *See* www.dwaf.gov.za/dir_ws/fbw/ (last accessed: October 2011). As of 2009 the South African government was providing 36.5 million people with free basic water, out of a total population of 48.5 million. There remains an estimated 12 million without access to sufficient water, quantified in the WSA as 25 lpd of free basic water.

[55] WSA section 11(1). The application of this duty on municipalities can be considered within the broader context of the onus on municipalities to provide basic services and realise basic socio-economic rights. One might question however the ability of municipalities to provide such services in the face of severely limited resources and capacity.

[56] Louis Kotze, 'Access to Water in South Africa: Constitutional Perspectives from a Developing Country', 1 *Ymparistojuridiikka* (2009) s.70–106, 78.

[57] Ibid at 79.

discussed, *sufficient* water has been defined in the literature variously as between 20 and 50 lpd and has received legislative definition as 25 lpd. Sufficiency has been described as being dependent on three factors, accessibility, adequate quality and adequate quantity.[58] These factors encompass the five components of the human right to water as interpreted by the Committee on Economic, Social and Cultural Rights, namely that water must be sufficient, safe, acceptable, physically accessible and affordable.[59]

Together, the constitutional right of access to sufficient water and its promulgating legislation have framed the goal of realising access to sufficient water within a rights-based approach. Consequently, discussion of access to sufficient water has been conducted largely using 'rights-talk'; framing problems and obligations within the paradigm of individual rights. The following discussion of the recent case of *Mazibuko*[60] considers the limits of rights-talk in realising access to sufficient water. It illustrates the degree to which the courts are prepared to *manage* the constitutional right to sufficient water and, consequently, the limitations to using such a right as the primary vehicle for realizing sufficient water for the indigent and disenfranchised. The case also highlights the courts' lack of consideration of sustainability. Indeed the interconnectedness of social, economic and environmental factors that IWRM emphasises seems to be recast throughout the case as three mutually exclusive spheres.

B. *Mazibuko*: Constitutional Managerialism of the Right to Water

The case was brought on behalf of a group of residents from Phiri, an area of Soweto near Johannesburg, and it challenged the legality of installing pre-payment water meters, in light of the constitutional right to sufficient water.[61] Installation was undertaken by the City of Johannesburg and its

---

58 John Scanlon, Angela Cassar and Noemi Nemes, *Water as a Human Right?*, IUCN Environmental Policy and Law Paper No 51 (Switzerland and Cambridge UK: Gland 2004) 28.

59 *See* General Comment No 15, above note 16.

60 *Mazibuko and others v City of Johannesburg and others* (Centre on Housing Rights & Evictions as amicus curiae) [2008] JOL 21829 (W). Hereafter *Mazibuko* (W). For information, (W) indicates High Court, (SCA) indicates the Supreme Court of Appeal and (CC) indicates the Constitutional Court.

61 On appeal to the Constitutional Court, amicus curiae for *Mazibuko and others* was the Coalition Against Water Privatisation in South Africa (CAWP), a community-based

water company Johannesburg Water in response to acute water losses in Soweto as a result of corroded pipes, an inaccurate tariff system (that meant more water was used than was predicted to be necessary) and a 'culture of non-payment' for water services that had 'arisen originally as part of the resistance to apartheid local government'.[62]

The case examined the obligations of the City of Johannesburg and Johannesburg Water regarding access to water and the supply of free water for residents who cannot afford to pay. It was contended that since pre-payment water meters, by design, require users to pay for water in advance, access to sufficient water is curtailed if users cannot afford to pre-pay. Such a situation was commonplace for Phiri residents and was raised as incompatible with the Constitutional right to sufficient water. The WSA's quantification of sufficient water as a minimum standard of 25 lpd was directly challenged in this case on the basis that what is a *sufficient* quantity of water depends on the requirements of users in particular social circumstances. For instance, those growing their own food require more water than those who do not. Similarly, people using waterborne sanitation require a greater volume of water to support life and personal hygiene than those using pit latrines.[63]

Thus, the applicants challenged the legality and validity of Regulation 3(b) of the WSA (that set the minimum water supply at 25 lpd or 6 kilolitres per household[64]). They contended that the regulation was based on misconceptions about the amount of water necessary for residents in Phiri individually, but also about the number of people living in each

NGO that has been organizing and advocating for South Africans' right to access adequate and affordable water in Johannesburg and Cape Town since 2003. See: "program partners," last accessed October 2011, http://www.uusc.org/program_partners/CAWP. CAWP is part of the Anti-privatisation forum (see: http://apf.org.za/spip.php?article2 last accessed October 2011).

[62] *Mazibuko and others v City of Johannesburg and others* [2009] JOL 24351 (CC). Hereafter *Mazibuko* (CC) paragraph 166.

[63] This is particularly pertinent to the interpretation of sufficient water in the Constitution since section 27 links food and water: 'Everyone has the right to have access to- (b) sufficient food and water'. Also, since sanitation is not listed in section 27 of the Constitution, but is recognised as a right in the Water Services Act (section 3(1)), the volume of water that is sufficient must depend on the type of sanitation system being used.

[64] Not only does section 3 of WSA reiterate the Constitutional right of access to sufficient water, it expands it to include basic sanitation. The approach of including the right to basic sanitation within the right of access to sufficient water was upheld by the South African High Court in *Manqele v. Durban Transitional Metropolitan Council* 2002 (6) SA 423 (D&CLD).

household on average.[65] As a result it was contended that the regulation failed to provide 'sufficient water' as per the Constitution.

In determining the applicants' grounds, the High Court had regard to General Comment Number 15 of the United Nations Committee on Economic, Social and Cultural Rights. Applying the General Comment, the court's view was that 'The State is under an obligation to provide the poor with the necessary water and water facilities on a non-discriminatory basis'.[66] Moreover, the progressive realisation of the Constitutional right of access to sufficient water meant that:

> Retrogressive measures taken by the state are prohibited. If such retrogressive measures are taken, the onus is on the state to prove that such retrogressive measures are justified with reference to the totality of the rights provided for in the Covenant.[67] The state is obliged to respect, protect and fulfil the right to water.[68]

The installation of prepayment meters was held to be just such a retrogressive step, preventing residents from access to sufficient water that they had previously enjoyed (before the prepayment meters, Phiri residents had access to a constant supply of water – despite many accruing arrears as a result[69]). The High Court clearly felt such an approach was taken without adequate objective justification.

It was held that, given the particular needs of the Phiri community (including the need to use waterborne sewerage) a volume of 50 lpd would be a more appropriate quantification of sufficient water than the statutory 25 lpd limit. Satisfied that the respondent could provide this increased amount 'without restraining its capacity on water and its financial resources'[70] the High Court decided wholly in the applicants' favour, granting a declaratory order that Regulation 3(b) was unconstitutional and invalid and ordering that 50 lpd be provided to Phiri residents, free of charge for those without means to pay.

---

65 *Mazibuko,* (W) paragraph 166. The 6 kilolitres minimum is based on a household of eight people, while it was submitted that the actual average was more than 16 people.

66 *Mazibuko,* (W) paragraph 36.

67 ICESCR, above note 12.

68 *Mazibuko,* (W) paragraph 37.

69 *Mazibuko,* (W) paragraph 38. Note: prior to installation of pre-payment meters and the associated improvements made to water pipes as part of the City's water services improvement project in Soweto, 'Operation Gcin'amanzi', water services were poor, but the volume of water available was unlimited (except when affected by intermittent technical problems).

70 *Mazibuko,* (W) paragraph 181.

The City of Johannesburg and Johannesburg Water appealed to the South African Supreme Court of Appeal in February 2009.[71] The quantity amounting to sufficient water for Phiri residents was reduced on appeal to 42 lpd. But the High Court's approach was otherwise upheld. The Supreme Court of Appeal addressed the questions of whether the appellants must provide Phiri residents with access to that quantity of water and whether the appellants must provide such access or access to a lesser quantity of water free of charge.[72] The Supreme Court held that the constitutional right to sufficient water was not a right of immediate fulfilment. Rather, this right like those regarding housing, health care and food are rights to be progressively realised, their progression being limited by lack of resources. Consequently, the right to sufficient water is not an 'unqualified obligation'.[73] However, the appellant's concern was not the quantity of water it may be obliged to provide, (the appellant did not contest that a volume of 42 lpd was deliverable) but whether this quantity must be provided free of charge. Referring to General Comment 15 the court accepted that the accessibility of water 'must be affordable for all'.[74] Consequently not being able to pay for water meant no access to water. The constitutional right to sufficient water (revised to 42 lpd) must therefore be provided at an affordable price. Where residents cannot afford to pay for this sufficient water and can prove this to the satisfaction of the water services authority, the court held that the appellants have an obligation to provide it free of charge in so far as this can reasonably be done having regard to the appellant's available resources. The City of Johannesburg and Johannesburg Water were directed to formulate a revised water policy accordingly.[75]

Mazibuko in the High Court and the Supreme Court of Appeal was heralded as an important milestone in socio-economic jurisprudence in South Africa.[76] It showed the courts' willingness to push the legislature towards concrete manifestations of constitutional rights and not to allow the 'progressive realization' of these rights to result in unconstitutional

[71] *City of Johannesburg & others v Mazibuko & others* (Centre on Housing Rights & Evictions as *amicus curiae*) [2009] JOL 23337 (SCA). Hereafter *Mazibuko* (SCA).

[72] *Mazibuko* (SCA) Summary.

[73] *Mazibuko*, (SCA) paragraph 16. Quoting Chaskalson CJ in *Soobramoney v Minister of Health (KwaZulu-Natal)* 1998 (1) SA 765 (CC) paragraph 11.

[74] Ibid, paragraph 12(c)(ii).

[75] *Mazibuko*, (SCA). Summary.

[76] Linda Jansen van Rensberg, 'The Right of Access to Adequate Water [Discussion of Mazibuko v The City of Johannesburg Case No 13865/06]' 3 *Stellenbosch Law Review* (2008) 434.

policies. The impetus to promote and fulfil the right of access to sufficient water was clearly discernible (particularly in Tsoka J's High Court judgment[77]) in the acceptance of the need for sufficient water to be a quantity that promotes dignity and goes beyond the minimum of Free Basic Water already set.[78] The potential implications of *Mazibuko* for people living in similar situations to the Phiri residents were significant. Both judicial decisions appeared to demonstrate the courts' engagement with polycentric matters in order to help realize socio-economic constitutional rights more quickly and more explicitly than would otherwise be the case. But the environmental implications of *Mazibuko* may have been significant too, potentially doubling the demand for water from a significant portion of the population,[79] in a 'water-stressed' country.[80]

However, in September 2009 the Phiri residents appealed to the Constitutional Court (unhappy with the Supreme Court of Appeal's order to reduce the amount water deemed to be sufficient from 50 to 42 lpd). This was the first time the Constitutional Court had considered the proper interpretation of the right of access to sufficient water. The orders made by the High Court and Supreme Court of Appeal respectively were set aside. The Constitutional Court maintained that litigation regarding the positive obligations of socio-economic rights was an important element of government accountability.[81] However, it was held that

> The Constitution does not require government to be held to an impossible standard of perfection. Nor does it require courts to take over the tasks that in a democracy should properly be reserved for the democratic arms of government.[82]

In particular, the City's Free Basic Water policy was held not to be in conflict with section 27 of the Constitution and that the installation of prepaid water meters was declared lawful. The Court was satisfied that while the Free Basic Water Policy was flawed, it was consistent with the constitutional right of access to sufficient water.[83] This was particularly so since the City of Johannesburg had continued to amended its Free Basic Water Policy during the course of the litigation to reflect ongoing concerns.[84]

---

77 See generally *Mazibuko* (W).
78 *Mazibuko* (W) paragraph 1.
79 van Rensberg, above note 76 at 434.
80 Kidd, above note 36 at 64.
81 *Mazibuko* (CC) paragraph 160.
82 *Mazibuko* (CC) paragraph 161.
83 *Mazibuko* (CC) paragraph 163.
84 *Mazibuko* (CC) paragraph 163.

The Constitutional Court's decision reflects an impetus to maintain a clear separation of powers and for courts to refrain from encroaching on matters of resource allocation, which are principally under the purview of the legislature and executive.[85] The judgment imported a highly policy-orientated approach to the right of access to sufficient water. Here the right is contextualized within broader government policy and its progressive realization is accepted where there is evidence of improvement and a continually revised policy. Such an approach is perhaps understandable in a country with limited resources and manifold social and economic problems. But it emphasizes the tension at the heart of the justiciability of socio-economic rights; the pragmatism of progressive realization versus the necessity of immediate fulfillment. To those Phiri residents now denied a quantum of water commensurate with their needs and necessary for their dignity, their *right* to water would seem to ring hollow. Arguably the Constitutional Court's decision illustrates the limitations of using rights to achieve real access to sufficient water.

The social, economic and environmental considerations central to an IWRM approach to water allocation are visible to differing degrees in the courts' engagement with the *Mazibuko* case. But it is the social concerns of the Phiri residents pitched against the economic impetus of Johannesburg Water that are seen most clearly. The High Court and Supreme Court of Appeal afforded more weight to the social considerations of the individual necessity for water and dignity; the Constitutional Court emphasized the nature of water as an economic good and the pragmatic limitations of progressive realization. The question of sustainability was raised at the Constitutional Court in relation to the ability of Johannesburg Water to provide a particular quantity of sufficient water per person. But this was distinctly a question of *economic* sustainability linked to the assumption that the water provider must be able to operate competitively, and within a commercialized water service paradigm.

Moreover, concerns about environmental protection and the potential ecological implications of doubling the quantum of sufficient water were

[85] This reflects the approach of the High Court in *Manqele v. Durban Transitional Metropolitan Council* 2002 (6) SA 423 (D&CLD). The volume of water deemed sufficient for the purposes of the Constitution section 27 and the WSA section 3 had not yet been prescribed (The WSA had been enacted, but the associated regulations [GN R 509 of 8 June 2001] had not been promulgated). The court held that the minimum volume of water must be prescribed by regulation. In the absence of the regulation the applicant relied on an incomplete right, rendering it unenforceable. Determining sufficient water was 'a policy matter which falls outside the purview of the role and function of the court and is inextricably linked to the availability of resources' (paragraph 427).

conspicuous by their absence from the judgments, especially of the High Court and Supreme Court of Appeal. Neither court mentioned the environmental right (particularly the requirement for sustainable development) in section 24 of the Constitution. Despite environmental protection and sustainability featuring heavily in the legislation, these considerations appeared neither in the *ratio* nor *obiter* of the *Mazibuko* judgments. Indeed the absence of environmental considerations is common to rights-talk in general as individuals' rights claims are contested largely in isolation from the realities of resource scarcity.[86] Undeniably, the existence of a right of access to sufficient water has helped reduce the number of people living with insufficient water in South Africa. The right has had positive substantive and normative effects and has underpinned significant legal victories.[87] But as Pieterse[88] and Bond[89] assert, human rights generally and South African constitutional rights specifically concentrate on consciousness-raising and recognition of an individual's rights to necessities, rather than on redistribution and reparation. As already discussed, the unequal (and for many, inadequate) distribution of water resources in South Africa reflects more general problems of inequality and poverty, exacerbated by the legacy of apartheid. In this context, measures to address distributional inequity and to reverse and repair the effects of systemic discrimination would seem appropriate in effecting significant social transformation.[90] However, the lack of emphasis on redistributive justice within the rights discourse inevitably limits the transformational potential of these rights.

c. A Commons Approach: Community Empowerment and Sustainable Allocation?

Having recognized the (perhaps inevitable) divide between the concern given to social and environmental factors within constitutional and

[86] Karen Bakker, 'The 'Commons' Versus the 'Commodity': Alter-globalization, Anti-privatisation and the Human Right to Water in the Global South' 39(3) *Antipode* (2007) 436.

[87] See: *Residents of Bon Vista Mansions v Southern Metropolitan Local Council* [2002] JOL 9513 (W).

[88] Marius Pieterse, 'Eating Socio-economic Rights: The Usefulness of Rights Talk in Alleviating Social Hardship Revisited' 29 *Human Right Quarterly* (2007) 796–822.

[89] Patrick Bond, 'Fighting for the Right to the City: Discursive and Political Lessons from the Right to Water'. (paper presented to the Right to Water Conference 2010, Syracuse University, New York, 29 March 2010). http://ccs.ukzn.ac.za/files/bond%20syracuse%20 Fighting%20for%20the%20Right%20to%20the%20City.pdf (last accessed: October 2011).

[90] Richard G. Wilkinson and Kate Pickett, *The Spirit Level – Why More Equal Societies Almost Always Do Better,* (New York: Bloomsbury, 2009).

legislative documents whilst at the same time such factors failing to be adequately reflected within court decisions, two things become much clearer. First, that there is a long way to go before water access and allocation can be said to be underpinned by the mantra of sustainable development (as characterized by an IWRM approach). And secondly, that the human and constitutional right to water cannot be relied on to provide equitable and sustainable water allocation. To this end, the constitutional right to water must be considered a useful, but limited, approach to securing community access to a common resource.

A liberal analysis of rights tends to focus on flawed implementation;[91] sound ideas suffering from insufficient resources or poor application. But a radical critique highlights the limitations of using rights to achieve genuine socio-economic improvements, focusing on the way that rights – whether they are internationally accepted human rights or constitutional rights – give moral claims legal form.[92] In so doing the moral claim is diluted, turning it into a technical legal problem and bureaucratizing away the imperative to meet the claim.[93] When conceived as a legal problem, considerations like progressive realization, reasonableness and available resources become acceptable explanations for unmet claims. The moral claim that everyone should have access to the quantum of water required for dignified existence is immediately diminished. Similarly, the Constitution provides for the progressive realization of socio-economic rights generally, but only within available resources.

An alternative to the limitations of rights-talk, as well as a response to the current inchoate implementation of sustainable development as a State-centred policy objective, is the formation of a 'commons' strategy for water allocation.[94] The commons is a new way to express a very old idea,[95] that some forms of wealth belong to all of us, and that these community resources must be actively protected and managed for the good of all.[96] In contrast to individualised consumption within a rights-based paradigm, a commons strategy emphasises shared utilisation. It echoes the

---

91 Ibid. at 15.

92 Pieterse, above note 88 at 796–822.

93 Ibid.

94 "On the Commons," last accessed October 2011, www.onthecommons.org/content.php?id=1467. 'On the Commons' is an NGO that seeks to draw attention to the importance of the commons in the modern world, advance commons-based solutions that will help achieve environmental restoration, social justice and global cooperation.

95 See various contributions to Ørebech et al, above note 8.

96 Ibid.

emphasis on interconnectivity within IWRM. But unlike IWRM, a commons strategy avoids emphasising individual water rights, in favour of communal needs. This shift in focus may offer a more effective model of implementing sustainable water allocation, while avoiding the pitfalls of rights-talk inherent in debates on the right to water. A commons strategy would encourage decisions on water allocation to be made at the lowest appropriate level, involving all users to input into collective decisions that transcend a compromise of competing interests, in favour of corporately 'owned' allocation decisions that best serve each community.[97] Commodification of water is resisted.[98] Rather than emphasising the contrasting paradigm of water as necessity, conceived of in terms of individual imperatives, a commons approach emphasises that the necessity claim of the individual is moderated by the needs of the community within their economic, environmental and social realities and constraints.[99]

The form that commons strategies can take may vary and the degree to which commons strategies are process-oriented, rather than aimed towards substantive change, will depend on the context in which they emerge. It is not suggested that such strategies will replace the legally embedded and individually focused right to water. Therefore, the current obligations of the State regarding this right will remain. Following the experience of some countries, such State obligations could be expanded through common law, using something similar to the 'public trust doctrine'. Indeed, arguably, in drafting the 1996 Constitution, South Africa's legislators have already reintroduced the public trust doctrine as part of national law.[100] But while ultimate responsibility for protection and management of water resources will remain with the State, commons ideas offer an interface between the individual right and the experiences of communities hitherto disconnected from the fulfilment of the right and disenfranchised from associated decisions about allocation of the natural resource.

A commons strategy, if innovatively applied to water allocation, may be able to avoid the limitations of the right of access to sufficient water, and

---

[97] Jay Walljasper, *All that We Share: A Field Guide to the Commons* (New York: The New Press, 2010) 161. Note; here 'ownership' is not used in the legal sense. Proprietary rights are of course unaffected. Rather, it is decisions about allocation that are owned corporately; having been negotiated and agreed by and on behalf of the community.

[98] Ibid.

[99] Ibid at 160.

[100] David Takacs, 'The Public Trust Doctrine, Environmental Human Rights and the Future of Private Property'. 16 New York University Environmental Law Journal 711 (2008): 14–18.

allow sufficient water to be restated as a moral claim, made corporately by and for people within the community. Indeed, given the social, economic and environmental imperative for sustainability that any commons strategy must consider, an IWRM approach to water services could find its functional imperative of sustainability rejuvenated beyond the limitations of rights-talk. However, romanticizing community control of resources must be avoided. Local allocation decisions and policies are equally capable of being discriminatory since inequitable power relations exist at a small as well as a large scale. Given the embryonic expressions of currently existing commons strategies, it will be important to be mindful of such potential problems as these expressions evolve. But, driven in part by the failure of rights-talk to effectively incorporate environmental protection and even to deliver resources to all individuals effectively, commons ideas are on the increase.[101] At the very least, commons ideas offer a radically different alternative to the atomistic assumption inherent in the mechanisms of commodification, as well as the framework of individual human and constitutional rights.[102] Locally sensitive approaches to water service allocation that respond to the priorities of specific communities while emancipating users as decision-makers may offer the key to a more effective (if also invariably untidy) approach to managing South Africa's water resources.

One small example of such a commons approach to water resources can be seen in the Burlington informal settlement outside Durban. Although the municipality had provided piped water to a number of homes here, the cost of water from this source quickly proved prohibitive for residents. They became indebted and eventually the pipes were disconnected, leaving residents with only the pre-existing standpipes (each serving around 30 dwellings) through which to access water. In February 2010, Nathan Cooper visited this settlement as part of empirical research to talk to residents about *their* experiences of access to water. He saw and heard how the community, many of whom had had their water supply disconnected, had organised themselves into those who were able to collect water from the standpipe (both those physically able and those who had time) and those who could not. Those not able to use the standpipe (including older residents) were receiving a small amount of money from their younger neighbours in order to ensure that their water bills were paid and that they could continue to enjoy water piped to their

[101] Bakker above note at 86.
[102] Walljasper, above note 97 at 161.

homes; while able bodied residents relied again on the standpipe. Community leaders met to decide who to prioritise in this system, and to monitor how it worked. In the midst of poverty and hardship, and faced with a regression in their level of access to water, the Burlington residents were choosing to engage with the problem of water-poverty from the perspective of shared, community needs, rather than focusing on their individual rights. What can truly be described as a commons approach is thus beginning to take root.[103]

Though almost idealistic in its radical application, in contrast to the *status quo*, a community approach such as the one highlighted above may nevertheless prove more effective than a reliance on judicial decisions that are "far away" both geographically and experientially from the very communities that are most dependent upon the Constitution. Moreover, in giving effect to community priorities and considerations, this is again in sharp contrast to a constitutional provision which is managerially applied and artificially individual in focus.

4. A Concluding Thought

The right to water in South Africa is widely heralded as an exemplar of the incorporation of socio-economic rights in domestic constitutional law. This is undoubtedly true, but only up to a point. As this chapter has highlighted, seeking to achieve development through law often only goes to reveal its fragmentation, both within the discipline and across jurisdictional boundaries. Though international development law is broadly conceived and includes both the *mechanics* of development (trade, investment and finance) as well as increasingly seeking to instil an overarching *moral* framework (through the elaboration of relevant human rights norms) it remains decidedly remote from human experience. Indeed, though the right to water and sustainable development – both principles that originated in international law – have the conceptual potential to reach across such boundaries, the extent to which this has meaningfully occurred remains contentious. In contrast, domestic law is often considered as a more effective means of giving effect to developmental priorities, particularly in a context such as South Africa where constitutional rights arguably better represent on-the-ground social and economic needs. Nevertheless, as this chapter has argued, the formalism of law – be that

103 Taken from interview transcripts during fieldwork in South Africa (February 2010).

international law or domestic, constitutional law – can never ultimately reflect how the law is perceived and operationalised at the grass-roots level. Constitutional provisions have an important symbolic and catalytic role, but one should hesitate before forming the view that such codification will *per se* engender full and complete normative implementation. Clearly, it will not.

In the specific matter of giving effect to the right to water in South Africa, the constitutional right remains frustratingly inchoate, but more than that can raise (false) hope beyond what can realistically be achieved. Moreover, despite judicial differences between the lower and higher courts in *Mazibuko*, the final judgment – representing what is ultimately a constrained expression of a moral claim – signifies the inevitable limitation of achieving development through law. What actually occurs is that the Constitutional Court has filtered the moral claim through a legal lens, which invariably diminishes the significance of the overriding goal to be reached. Perhaps in a democratic society, this is as much as can be expected from a judicial forum;[104] any more is pure utopia. However, legitimate questions can be asked of the other pillars of government regarding resource allocation decisions at the macro level. The principle of 'progressive realisation within available resources' that frames the right to water both as a human right and constitutionally, cannot be separated from executive decisions about investment priorities. While constrained judicial decisions may reflect the realities of the limited resources made available in promulgation of the right to water, the question remains why more resources are not directed towards achieving this most basic of necessities.

But as the final part of the chapter notes, this need not be the end of the tale. There are other approaches, such as an emphasis upon collective rights and commons allocation, which might equally provide an alternative, and perhaps more effective, means to achieve developmental goals, even if they currently stray beyond the confines of what is considered generally appropriate. Moreover, such approaches also emphasise the significance, nay the necessity, of moving away from the traditional and sterile dichotomies in development discourse – public v. private,

[104] One should also not diminish the crucial role for a court in balancing not just the claims before it, but also the wider agendas on both sides of the issue to determine the wider public interest. For instance, as the *amicus curiae* in *Mazibuko* was part of an anti-privatisation forum (see the information at note 61), the rights-claims brought on behalf of the Phiri residents could not realistically be separated from the interests of those representing them. This may, in turn, diminish the moral claim underlying the substantive right.

market v. State-controlled, commodification v. human right, indeed international v. municipal – and towards more pluralist interpretations of the interlinkages between law and development. And though such interpretations may be less easy to categorise and rationalise from a formal legal perspective, they are as much part of the social reality as are keynote constitutional judgments which as lawyers, both international and domestic, we are inevitably, but perhaps falsely, drawn towards.

FOOD SECURITY, BIOFUELS AND CORPORATE SUSTAINABILITY

Thomas West

1. Introduction

It is well established that global warming is a consequence of humanity's own doing, its attitude to natural resources, and the excesses of industrialisation and economic development over many decades. It is also recognised that in order to reverse our excesses and the domination of economic demands, a balanced and integrated approach is required in environmental and development questions and this requires political commitment and cooperation.[1] Sustainable development principles provide the basis for the integration of environmental principles and policies into economic and development decision–making,[2] providing the solutions needed to make economic development more environmentally sustainable.[3] A continual adjustment is therefore required within policy that follows all three pillars of sustainable development to provide flexibility to country's needs. Once it is accepted that there is no 'one size fits all' solution to development, because of the complexities and breath of the sustainable development concept, the conflicting and ambiguous conceptual and ideological positions[4] can be seen in a complementary way that reflects the profound change in the way society views the relationship between economic activity and the environment.[5] A move towards establishing a global green economy should provide the framework to do just that where cooperation is based on fairness, justice, openness and where real and earnest consensus prevails rather than competitive exploitation.

---

[1] UN GAOR 46th Sess., Agenda Item 21, UN Doc A/Conf.151/26 (1992), c 1.2 and 1.4.

[2] Duncan French, International Law and Policy of Sustainable Development (Manchester: Manchester University Press, 2005), 11.

[3] John C. Dernbach, 'Creating the Law of Environmentally Sustainable Economic Development,' Pace Environmental Law Review 28, no. 3 (2011): 614, 641.

[4] Jude L. Fernando, 'The Power of Unsustainable Development: What is to be Done?,' The Annals of the American Academy of Political and Social Science 590, no. 1 (2003): 7. Wilfred Beckerman, 'Sustainable Development Is it a Useful Concept?,' Environmental Values 3, (1994): 205.

[5] Danial Barstow Magraw and Lisa D. Hawke, 'Sustainable Development' in The Oxford Handbook of International Environmental Law eds. Danial Bodansky, Jutta Brunnée, and Ellen Hey (Oxford: Oxford University Press, 2007) 614.

A significant obstacle to establishing the idea of a green economy is what lies behind the ideological motivations of significant political and economic powers and elites that have driven modern capitalism for decades. Ever since the 1970's, the global north has dominated the international institutions and the world trade system with neo-liberal ideology and policies of privatisation, deregulation and liberalisation giving entrepreneurs and multinational corporations (MNCs) the freedom to innovate and to take risks to pursue profit. In exercising this freedom, the boundaries between public domination of the state and citizenship and the private dominion of the markets, entrepreneurship and consumerism have been redrawn[6] to the point the state has increasingly little significance and control of economic power. This motivation towards profit with risk has largely been at the expense of social and environmental integrity on a global scale. Modernisation in the name of globalisation and the need to maintain international competitiveness provides the political and economic elites with justification for the dominance of economic competition and explanation for inaction in mitigating rising social and environmental inequity and injustice. As a consequence of this enormous power created by ideological motivations MNCs and business are permitted and continue to monetise or 'commodify' natural resources unsustainably on an industrial scale and exploit the global trade system for economic dominance.

Food security and the influence of biofuel production is a good example of how these unsustainable motivations cause social and environmental damage. This chapter will examine the level of corporate control over the rights to food security, the construction of the global food regime and the influence of biofuels to food insecurity. The discussion in parts 2 and 3, first explores how the right to food is ineffectual in controlling corporate behaviour and the obstacles to universal food security, and second shows that food security should be achieved at the community or local level and the role that government should play in achieving this. Parts 4.1, 4.2 and 4.3 then examine the political economic relationship within the corporate food regime and the political and institutional response to accommodating the increasing demand for food and energy. Part 4.4 examines the relationship with biofuels in particular.

---

[6] Simon Lee and Stephen McBride, 'Introduction: Neo-Liberalism, State Power and Global Governance in the Twenty-First Century' in Neo-Liberalism, State Power and Global Governance, eds. Simon Lee Stephen McBride (Dordrecht: Springer, 2007), 1–2.

2. A Rights based Approach to Food and Progressive Realisation

Poverty, gender inequality, racism and lack of corporate and political will are all some of the factors that prevent access to food and create the conditions for chronic hunger, malnutrition, under-nutrition and even obesity issues. Food may be simply not available or too expensive or contain too little nutrients to provide sufficient sustenance or contain unhealthy fats and other substances that endanger health. These examples of food insecurity can severely restrict the ability of individuals to satisfy their right to food established in international legal instruments.[7] The root drivers of food insecurity are largely political and economic in nature. There is enough food to compensate for natural disasters but the question is whether there is enough economic or political will to make it available.[8] The key to achieving universal food security[9] is a committed and coordinated approach by the international community towards achieving access to food[10] that recognises in its entirety the right to food as a concept with fundamental legal status and that can be accessible, enjoyed and relied upon by every person without discrimination.[11] It must form part of the package of reforms required in establishing an international sustainable green economy and part of the significant shift in economic and political will that is required to rebalance an overweight and dysfunctional global economic system.

---

[7] Universal Declaration on Human Rights (1948), art 25, GA res. 217 A (III), UN GAOR, 3d sess., Resolutions, pt. 1, U.N. Doc. A/810 (1948); International Covenant on Economic, Social and Cultural Rights (1966), art 11, GA Res. 2200A (XXI), 22rd Sess. UN GAOR Supp. (No 16), UN Doc. A6316 (1966); Convention on the Rights of the Child (1989), art. 24(2)(c) and art 27(3), GA Res 44/25, UN GAOR, 44thSess., Supp. (No.49), U.N. Doc. A/48/49 (1989); Convention on the Elimination of All Forms of Discrimination Against Women (1979), art 12(2), UN GA A/Res/ 34/180, UNTS 13 (1981); Convention on the Rights of Persons with Disabilities (2006), art 25(f) and art 28(1)1, GA A/RES/61/106, U.N. Doc A/RES/61/106.

[8] Eric Holt-Giménez, 'From Food Crisis to Food Sovereignty: The Challenge of Social Movements' Monthly review 61, No. 3 (2009): 154.

[9] By using the word 'universal' to describe food security the right to food is considered of the same status as civil and political rights, such as the right to life and the right to one's dignity.

[10] G8 Summit statement, 'L'Aquila' Joint Statement on Global Food Security: L'Aquila Food Security Initiative (AFSI), 35th G8 Summit 10th July 2009. Available at: http://www.g8italia2009.it/static/G8_Allegato/LAquila_Joint_Statement_on_Global_Food_Security%5B1%5D%2co.pdf [last accessed 12 February 2012].

[11] Committee on Economic, Social and Cultural Rights, Substantive Issues Arising in the Implementation of the International Covenant on Economic, Social and Cultural Rights: General Comment 12 (Twentieth session, 1999), The right to adequate food (Article. 11) Geneva: ECOSOC E/C.12/1999/5, ¶ 18.

An obvious obstacle to achieving realising a right to food is the ineffectual state of the law. The content of the right to food, having been neglected as part of political strategies to relate economic, social and cultural (ESC) rights to other rights, particularly the right to work and the workforce, has only relatively recently been clarified by General Comment 12[12] and standards developed.[13] The realisation of the right to adequate food is where every man, woman and child has physical and economic access to adequate food at all times or the means to procure it.[14] This requires both availability of food that is of adequate quality and quantity and the physical and economic accessibility to the means to procure it.[15] It is said that food security can be achieved when availability and accessibility are achieved by all people at all times.[16] This achievement is through the realisation of the right to food by providing access, and access to entitlements to natural resources.[17] With this aim, states are expected to take steps to respect, protect and fulfil their population's entitlements to access.[18] However the language of article 11 ICESCR[19] is for a 'progressive' realisation of the right to adequate food. The appropriateness of this type of right can be brought into question if the parties to the ICESCR and the other international instruments are not able or willing to advance real respect, protection and fulfilment of essential resources, such as food and water as individual rights. Rather, it is assumed that realisation needs to be taken over time or progressively as it is unable to be done in a short time.[20] The question arises whether this is appropriate regarding food where the political and economic interests stifle meaningful realisation particularly concerning access, and whether therefore, because food has become

[12] General Comment 12: The right to adequate food (Art. 11) (cited in note 11).

[13] Christian Courtis, 'The Rights to Food as a Justiciable Right: Challenges and Strategies,' Max Planck Yearbook of United Nations Law 11, (2007): 322–3.

[14] General Comment 12: The right to adequate food (Art. 11) (cited in note 11), ¶ 6.

[15] Id ¶ 8 and 13.

[16] World Food Summit 1996, Rome Declaration on World Food Security. Available at: http://www.fao.org/docrep/003/w3613e/w3613e00.htm [accessed on 11 February 2012].

[17] Jean Drèze and Amartya Sen, Hunger and Public Action, (Oxford: Oxford University Press, 1989) 22.

[18] States must respect the right to food by not arbitrarily undermining access. States must also provide protection from third parties such as MNCs from interfering with access, and measures must be taken to improve access and provide access free of discrimination. See Lorenzo Cotula, Moussa Djiré and Ringo W. Tenga, The Right to Food and Access to Natural Resources, (Rome: FAO, 2009) 35.

[19] General Comment 12: The right to adequate food (Art. 11) (cited in note 11), ¶14.

[20] Committee on Economic, Social and Cultural Rights, 'General Comment 3, The nature of state parties' Obligations', 5th session, 1990, Geneva: ECOSOC UN Doc. E/1991/23, annex III at 86, ¶ 9.

a global commodity, the right to it should have a more fundamental status with global attention. These rights need to be separated from a state's public policy goals and principles so they are rights that can be individually relied upon.

The disparities in constitutional recognition of ESC rights have meant the justiciability of the right to food has been approached in different ways. In Argentina, the local courts are able to recognise article 11 ICESCR directly.[21] The US Supreme Court however does not refer to international human rights but rather its own constitutional provisions.[22] These disparities do not show effort for progressive realisation of the right to food and a denial of the right outside of administrative convenience, particularly where there is no constitutional recognition. The ICESCR does respect the different types of legal systems but still expects some development of the concept to be made. One option the courts have explored is to class violations of the right to food as violations of the right to life and whether an action or omission can be deemed reasonably adequate, even though it is limited to specific cases in its application, such in instances of lack of access to food and starvation and interference with human dignity.[23] Decisions such as these shows the interrelatedness of the right to food to fundamental rights such as the right to life and that issues that involve access to food are capable of influencing other important fundamental

---

21 In Buenos Aires Administrative court Trial Court No. 3 C.M.D. y atros c. GCBA s/amparo, of 11 March 2003, the plaintiff and her family in a food program applying directly article 11 ICESCR and articles 24(2)(c) and 27(3) of the UN Convention on the Rights of the Child. In Buenos Aires Administrative court Trial Court No. 4 González Rayco, Artidoro c. GCBA s/amparo, of 19 May 2005 the court again provided a cancer patient with adequate food through a food plan.

22 In US Supreme Court, U.S. Department of Agriculture v Moreno, 413 U.S. 528, June 25, 1973 the US Supreme Court did not refer to a human or constitutional right to food but instead referred to the constitutionality of eligibility requirements of the food stamp programme. In U.S. District Court, 2nd District, Robidoux v Kitchel, 876 F. Sipp.575 (D. Vt. 1995) the court found the plaintiff ineligible for a food stamp programme due to missing federal processing deadlines and he would need to seek alternative resources.

23 In People's Union for Civil Liberties v Union of India & Others, in the Supreme Court of India, Civil Original Jurisdiction, Writ Petition (Civil) No.196 of 2001 the court held a failure to implement a food scheme even while there were ample food stocks was considered a violation of the right to life. Similarly in Inter-American Court of human Rights, Sawhoyamaxa Indigenous Community v Paraguay, of 29 March 2006,¶ 155 the court held that the right to life was violated because the state failed to ensure access to food, water and health services. The Inter-American Court of Human Rights determined that there was a positive obligation concerning the right to life which included providing access to food where there is an immediate risk to life of a determinate number of people, where the necessary measures were not taken and powers exercised that could be reasonably deemed adequate to prevent or avoid the risk.

rights. With this view progressive realisation is therefore likely to fall short of appropriate implementation. This is somewhat implied when a constitutional formula is used to make up for this deficiency, if a court is unable to refer to article 11 directly, to provide for social or welfare duties and in regarding the right to food as a notion of human dignity. By employing the minimum core approach[24] constitutional principles are positive state obligations imposing minimum essential levels of rights. In Einwohnergemeinde[25] the Swiss Federal Court applied this principle and considered that basic minimum conditions should guarantee all basic human needs such as food, clothing and shelter to prevent undocumented foreigners from being reduced to beggars. When constitutional and political requirements are given priority the shortfall of a progressive approach is illustrated. In Grootboom[26] the lower courts considered that South African law required the government only to take action concerning adequate housing within the resources available and to 'progressively implement' the right to adequate housing.[27] On appeal, the South African constitutional court set a reasonableness standard to establish a constitutional baseline for government policies on the basis that the limitation of rights must be reasonable.[28] In doing so it rejected the minimum core approach as being too inflexible and that rights and obligations can only be established in context allowing for a less content-focused approach. Legislation, policy and the implementation of that policy, although determined to be reasonable by the court on the day, allows the legislature flexibility to prioritise housing, education and health schemes according to its resources.[29] The decision distinguishes between minimum core rights relating to the primary right to housing, or other ESC rights such as food, and the reasonableness approach that relates delivering access to ESC right. Progressive realisation to bring about access to food within this

---

[24] Committee on Economic, Social and Cultural Rights, 'General Comment 3, The nature of state parties' Obligations', 5th session, 1990, Geneva: ECOSOC UN Doc. E/1991/23, annex III at 86, ¶ 10.

[25] V. v. Einwohnergemeinde X. und Regierungsrat des Kantons Bern (BGE/ATF 121 I 367) Swiss Federal Court of 27 October 1995.

[26] Government of the Republic of South Africa and Others v Grootboom and Others 2001(1) SA 46 (CC).

[27] The rights of children to shelter are unqualified according to section 26(2) of the constitution and therefore the state had to act regarding children.

[28] Grootboom, at ¶ 33 (cited in note 30).

[29] Elisabeth Wickeri, 'Grootboom's Legacy: Securing the Right to Access to Adequate Housing in South Africa?' Centre for Human Rights and Global Justice Working Paper No 5 (2004), 19.

interpretation is therefore dependent on a flexible determination of the reasonableness of government action rather than on requiring set standards that can be individually relied upon. [30]

The acceptance of economic and social rights is still disparate, arguably permitted because of the progressive realisation requirements. The UN Special Rapporteur on the right to food, for example, is tasked with the role to strengthen the protection and promotion of the right to food but is criticised by ideological objections critical to the emerging view that the economic, social and cultural human right should be justiciable and equal in status to civil and political rights.[31] Governments have thereby also criticised the Special Rapporteur positions as contrary to the current development ideological and neoliberal economic consensus, such as objection to the suggestion that free trade in agriculture may not benefit poor farmers who make up the majority to those in the state of food insecurity in the world. [32] State bureaucracies do not always behave rationally or in the interests of their peoples, even to the extent in committing violations. Equally the need for progressive realisation to be part of general public policy in order to be implemented can only thereby be determined by the willingness of states to recognise the right and also report adequately to the international institutions regarding on their implementation methods.[33] The predominance of economic ideology and perpetual limited resources has inevitably prioritised human rights problems according to those requiring attention. Food unfortunately is a complex issue involving interaction between many factors, which other issues such as clean water, sanitation, shelter and primary health care are cheaper to

---

[30] In Mazibuko and Others v City of Johannesburg and Others (CCT 39/09) [2009] ZACC 28; 2010 (3) BCLR 239 (CC); 2010 (4) SA 1 (CC) (8 October 2009) the applicants followed the Grootboom approach and asked the court to determine the reasonableness city water policy. The constitutional court again rejected the minimum core approach preferring, as a matter of democratic accountability, the legislative and executive institutions of governments to be best placed to investigate social condition in the light of available resources. In doing this the court has limited further its adjudicatory role in dealing with ESC rights by waiting for the executive and legislature to implement international human rights principles rather than applying them it access to food had fundamental legal status.

[31] Andrew Lang, World Trade Law after Neoliberalism: Re-imaging the Global Economic Order, (Oxford: Oxford University Press, 2011) 110–117.

[32] Sally-Anne Way, 'The Role of the UN Human Rights Bodies in Promoting and Protecting the Right to Food,' in Food and Human Rights in Development Volume I: Legal and Institutional Dimensions and Selected Topics, Wenche B Eide and Uwe Kracht eds. (Oxford: Hart Publishing, 2005) 224–5.

[33] Hans Morten Haugen, *The Right to Food and the TRIPS Agreement* (Leiden: Martinus Nijhoff Publishers, 2007) 109.

guarantee.[34] This complexity is amplified by the complexities of retrieval of monitoring data and statistical information required for implementing the progressive realisation approach.[35] Most states are not set up to accommodate these requirements.

Progressive development requires the willingness to move towards a legal status that can be relied upon. Instead, its language of article 11 ICESCR panders to economic and political power that for decades has only permitted economically or politically convenient solutions that continues to perpetuate food insecurity, and fail to address the root causes of lack of access to food. Governments and corporations continue to exploit weakness in the law in the race for economic competitiveness and will continue to do so as long as there is no absolute reason at the universal level to stop. Human rights principles after all are generally designed to provide basic standards where principles are classed as fundamental rights. The progressive rights fall short of this. If a continual upward pressure through political will or convention is not maintained, the provision loses any value, certainly to individuals wishing to rely upon it. Equally economic and political elites who tend to comply with the law to its minimum are not likely to act beyond what is commercially most profitable and conserves the most power and control in the market. Business survival in a competitive market depends on competitiveness and is a fundamental characteristic of a free market and this can only encourage minimalist compliance with international rights which is a regressive pressure rather than progressive pressure for change.

Without a solid legal acknowledgement of the fundamental status of right to food, food security will invariably get pulled down by the commercial interests seeking maximum competitive advantage. It is fair to say therefore that the 'progressive' tool used in international treaties and instruments as it is in article 11 ICESCR is not going to be an appropriate mechanism where the economic market and political interests are so intertwined. Constitutional courts also need to be able to apply in a uniform way the right to food that controls economic and political failings,

---

34 David Beetham, Democracy and human rights (Oxford: Blackwell Publisher, 1999) 130–131.

35 Audrey R. Chapman, 'A "Violations Approach" for Monitoring the International Covenant on Economic, Social and Cultural Rights Human Rights Quarterly', Human Rights Quarterly 18, No. 1 (1996): 30; As well as these ideological problems the progressive realisation approach itself is overused with the effect that many rights of this nature have to be realised at the same time.

particularly MNCs. If the international community is serious about tackling poverty and food insecurity, the bottom line must be firmly and conclusively drawn by the law and not determined by market competition. It is clear that the approach the courts have taken is driven by constitutional acceptance or lack of acceptance of the right to food and any willingness to apply ESC rights generally with the same status as civil and political rights. To ensure uniform constitutional acceptance the right to food needs to have the same status as civil and political rights. The position of the Swiss Federal court in Einwohnergemeinde is probably the most conducive to individual expectation of article 11 ICESCR and its interrelation to the right to life. The fundamental right to be free from hunger[36] obliges governments to step in to mitigate the harmful effects the MNCs have created. If however there is no uniform bottom line regarding the right to food, MNCs will continue to exploit their economic positions because of the disparities in effectively realising of the right to food.

Another considerable obstacle to universal food security is therefore a failure to acknowledge that the relationship between political systems and business needs to be rebalanced. Political players may have their own interests in the business and are pandered to by lobbyists and other economic interests from the few dominant major multinational players who inevitably exert their influence over political policy-making for their advantage.[37] In this capacity, because of the considerable economic benefits, corporate actors and politicians predominantly work the same vested interests that can only work against the move towards sustainability and undermine the good intentions behind a green economy. Rebalancing this relationship is fundamental and can only be carried out with sufficient integrated and coordinated reform at the international level and by way of a significantly determined shift in thinking that also rebalances economic power towards a global green economy. Poverty alleviation is one of the main themes of a green economy but without a qualifying standard driving the right to food, economic and political convenience will continue to interfere with the creation of mechanisms that deal with lack of access to food.

The lack of corporate responsibility for social and environmental damage is a direct obstacle to fulfilling a collectively global food security

36 International Covenant on Economic, Social and Cultural Rights 1966, art 11(2) (cited in note 7).

37 Naomi Hossain and Duncan Green, Living on a Spike: How is the 2011 food price crisis affecting poor people? Oxfam Research Report, June 2011, 43.

and a major contributor to food insecurity. There are too few MNCs who also control the commodity markets.[38] Not only is competition smothered by their sheer size but they have a huge commercial influence if not virtual control over quantity, nutritional quality, any adverse substances within food and arguably also its cultural acceptability within the regional food systems. These very attributes reflected in article 11 ICESCR are the responsibility of states not corporations. This responsibility however bears little influence on those beyond state jurisdictions. Host states do have responsibility to protect the food regime through effective national laws, but these legal protections are often influenced by multilateral and bilateral investment agreements and the control of economic interests of the stronger parties.[39] The weakness of the status of the right to food and the discretion states have in progressively implementing it acts as an incentive and encouragement to corporate business to act without economic, social and environmental responsibility to achieve their goals. Although states have a right to enjoy permanent sovereignty over their natural resources[40] they also have an equitable duty to sustainably utilise and manage for the long term the exploitation of its natural and cultural resources within the interests of the development and well-being of its citizens.[41] MNCs that do not act in the best interests of social and environmental well-being interfere with every human person's entitlement to participate, contribute and enjoy economic, social, cultural and political development[42] and ultimately also the development and environmental needs of future generations.[43] Corporate irresponsibility is therefore not only an obstacle to achieving food security but also an obstacle to developing the sustainable and equitable principles that will underpin a future green economy.

---

[38] Sophia Murphy, 'Globalization and Corporate Concentration in the Food and Agriculture Sector' Development 51 (2008) 527; Bill Vorley, 'Food, Inc.: Corporate concentration from farm to consumer,' UK Food Group (2003), Available at: http://www.iatp.org/files/UKFG-Foodinc-Nov03.pdf [last accessed 14 February 2012].

[39] Lorenzo Cotula, Moussa Djiré and Ringo W. Tenga, The Right to Food and Access to Natural Resources Using Human Rights: Arguments and Mechanisms to Improve Resource Access for the Rural Poor (FAO, Rome: 2009) 29, 40; Luke Eric Peterson, Human Rights and Bilateral Investment Treaties: Mapping the role of human rights law within investor-state arbitration, Rights & Democracy (International Centre for Human Rights and Democratic Development), 2009. Available at: http://www.dd-rd.ca/site/_PDF/publications/globalization/HIRA-volume3-ENG.pdf, [last accessed 14 February 2012] 12.

[40] UN General Assembly Declaration on Permanent Sovereignty of Natural Resources, G.A. res. 1803 (XVII), 17 U.N. GAOR Supp. (No.17) at 15, U.N. Doc. A/5217 (1962), ¶ 1.

[41] United Nations Rio Declaration on Environment and Development, A/CONF.151/26 (Vol. I) at 4 & 10.

[42] Declaration on the Right to Development, UNGA Res. 41/128, 4 December 1986.

[43] Rio Declaration at 3 (cited in note 46).

The earth is held on trust in an intergenerational equitable partnership entitling use of the earth's natural resources in a way that comparably provides quality, options and access to food by every individual.[44] Corporate responsibility needs to be an active part of this relationship supported by the political classes, which truly respects individual rights to access to life essentials such as food.

3. The Illusion of Global Food Security: Good Governance for Food Security

Global food security is actually an illusory concept that is in fact formed from the synthesis of many fully sustainable food security models. This collective achievement of food security should be capable, in principle, in achieving regional and then also global food security if every person gets between 2200-2800 calories per day.[45] The pursuit of global food security should not therefore be seen as achieving an all-encompassing 'one size fits all' model but rather creating a sustainable global system of trade and production that operates in a way that does not detrimentally conflict or interfere with regional food security models. It is worth noting that nature itself, as the source of our food, has its own parameters and processes of selection. It would be wise for mankind not to think that it can force nature out of its diversity and parameters of biological capabilities otherwise mankind will find itself subject to its own episode of natural selection as our own flawed expectations fail. In our pursuit of one global system we forget that it is our diversity and adaptability, as part of nature, which is our success. Engineering the global food system towards 'global food security' is therefore a fallacy. Problems maintaining food security in a number of regions may create a global food problem and fulfil the concept of global food insecurity. These drivers may be regional in character or the result of actions by global actors or trends. Taking this point of view exposes the failings and drivers of food insecurity more vividly and exemplifies the need to accept that agricultural production and trade should be treated differently than other forms of trade. Not only is it in the interests of achieving the idea of global food security but also in establishing agricultural sustainability as a constituent part of sustainable development at its foundation.

---

44 General Comment 12: The right to adequate food (Art. 11) (cited in note 11) ¶ 5–8.

45 2200–2800 calories per day is a well-established WHO guideline of nutrition.

The right to food is state centric and extends only as far as the relationship between governments and individuals within a state's jurisdiction. It is not designed to operate between global actors and individuals worldwide. The result is that various states and non-state actors can contribute to global food insecurity and world hunger if realisation of the right to food at national level is weak. Economic and political obligations from a variety of legal regimes outside the human rights regime, such as contractual conditions between MNCs and international financial institutions (IFI), can become more prominent than unrealised human rights obligations. In the interests of corporate responsibility these other legal regimes should develop compatibility[46] within an integrated international structure. Such a structure should accommodate a new economic approach, such as the emerging concepts of green economics, which would establish a sustainably balanced and equitable approach to food security.

The right to food is connected to the economic health of the country. Equitable distribution and local accessibility is needed but regional or global yields of food may not necessarily guarantee equity of access or distribution on the scale that is adequate for a whole society. Hunger is due to actual acute lack of food availability which is overwhelmingly linked to poverty, political or structural problems and exigencies.[47] The best way to combating hunger is therefore a matter of access to regional economic growth within the regional economic system first and then through it access to the global system. Bypassing the local and regional market will only undermine the foundation of food security regionally. Non-agricultural sectors can actually benefit where their agricultural productivity is improved[48] but economic growth cannot be allowed to bypass the poor and vulnerable groups. This growth will be lacking if the poor lack substantive freedom to establish their own ownership over adequate food resources, to grow it themselves or to purchase it. The fight against hunger must focus on the 'entitlement' of each person's consumption or enjoyment of food and not on the economic supply of food.[49] Starvation, hunger and malnutrition are not just about agricultural production and food production but the entire economy and society, the social and

[46] Smita Narula, 'The Right to Food: Holding Global Actors Accountable Under International Law', Columbia Journal of Transnational Law 44 (2006): 695.

[47] Amartya Sen, *Poverty and famines: An essay on entitlement and deprivation* (Oxford: OUP, 1984) 39.

[48] Wendy S. Ayres, Alex McCalla, 'Rural Development, Agriculture, and Food Security' Finance and Development 33 (1996): 8.

[49] Amartya Sen, *Development as Freedom* (Oxford: Oxford University Press, 1999), 162.

economic interdependencies. Acquiring food is an ability that must be earned to command and establish ownership over commodities and exercise entitlement to it. Instituted government obligations and constitutional traditions that follow a human rights approach can provide a foundation for individual power and food security. On the other hand, inefficient government policies and too much government control will have a negative impact on food security. As with other areas of the economy publicly provided services become inefficient without market competition. In the same way an inappropriate neoliberal economic approach that limits government spending, insists on privatisation, the removal of trade barriers and limitation of government interference in financial and capital markets may equally have a negative impact on individual power and food security if the poor and middle classes cannot benefit because the policies are global in their intention. Economic markets mechanisms should therefore provide enough services at the local level, the rights to which are guaranteed by government and the accountability of the market mechanisms enforced by government.

Governments that use subsidies are criticised because they can distort the market by changing prices and encouraging inefficient decision making thereby having a detrimental effect on consumer welfare and decreasing incentives to adopt new technologies.[50] Equally however economic policy that restricts government spending on food and welfare programmes has a negative effect on local economies resulting in a disproportionate suffering and largely on the most vulnerable. Economic growth takes time before income levels are raised sufficiently enough before government can disengage. Policy driving the right to be free from hunger and the right to adequate food will continue to favour the use of subsidies to agriculture and the provision of food to those that cannot afford to feed themselves[51] allowing the government to fill the gaps where the economic system either fails or is inappropriate. Governments should therefore not prematurely engage economic reform before it is socially and environmentally safe to do so and where local markets are not capable of responding to such reforms. Indigenous populations in particular may be subject to ethnic, racial, religious or caste discrimination which prevents opportunities to market access. Although economic policy will be opposed to such discrimination it has no way of preventing it and can inadvertently encourage it through the very nature of competition.

---

50 Narula, Columbia Journal of Transnational Law 44 (2006): 703 (cited at note 46).

51 *General Comment 12: The right to adequate food (Art. 11) (cited in note 11)* ¶ 1.

4. Corporate Food Regime and Sustainability

The present corporate food regime owes much of its substance to the development of capitalism which has little regard other than to its own motivations. Colonialism has brought with it into today's food regime the idea of nation centred division of labour between farms and manufacturing, separating the developed and developing world and maintaining that separation, and thereby also between the production of raw materials and the manufacture of products.[52] The deployment of monocultures, such as plantations, which has and continues to be ecologically destructive, has also been transferred. [53]

Examples can be brought from the US where inward orientated capitalism rules to control markets outside by intensive agricultural production and thereby establishing the practice of giving food aid.[54] Equally ecologically destructive was the introduction of agro-industrial farming across the US farm belt enabling the US to export to Europe through the Marshal plan and then the third world through the 'Green Revolution'.[55] The strategic selective industrialisation of the third world through green revolution technologies and the giving of food aid provided a way to align loyalties during the cold war and to internalise a national model of agro-industrialisation. Agriculture became transnational with linkages between national farm sectors specialising production for the global commodity markets and supply chains.[56] Intensive agricultural methods saw the injection of high yielding crops such as wheat, maize and rice and the dramatic increase in the use of subsidised agro-chemical non-organic nitrogen based fertilisers and pesticides displacing traditional organic fertilisers and displacing the natural nitrogen-fixing processes necessary for soil fertility. The result is food produced with lower nutrient value than before.[57] Agricultural industrialisation also dramatically increased the dependence of agriculture on the energy sector through oil derived products and

---

[52] Philip McMichael, 'Agrofuels in the food regime,' The Journal of Peasant Studies 37(2010): 610.

[53] Philip McMichael, 'A food regime genealogy', The Journal of Peasant Studies 36 (2009): 141.

[54] Philip McMichael, 'Global Development and the Corporate Food Regime' Rural Sociology and Development 11 (2005): 274.

[55] Philip McMichael, 'Agrofuels in the food regime,' 612 (cites in note 52).

[56] Philip McMichael, 'A food regime genealogy', 141 (cited in note 53).

[57] R.E. Evenson and D. Gollin, 'Assessing the Impact of the Green Revolution, 1960 to 2000,' Science 300 (2003): 760.

mechanisation.[58] It created more markets required to compensate for the damaging effects, particularly those connected with the health industry, pharmaceuticals and environmental solutions such as biofuel production. Industrial agriculture became orientated to the global market leading to the consolidation of power to large land owners. This not only put severe pressure on peasant agriculture but the green revolution also had the effect of deepening class, gender, and regional inequities.[59]

This global labour and capital orientated development has shaped political motivations not just to pacify farmers with subsidies, land reforms and technological development, or to bring agricultural assets under control, or to determine lands capital values. It has rather changed the neoliberal institutional setting from a state centric one to a global structure by way of privatisation and liberalisation at the bequest of transnational capital movement.[60] Bilateral and international free trade agreements have been heavily influenced by the aims of the structural adjustment programmes of the 1980's.[61] The WTO and its Agreement on Agriculture (AoA) has for example institutionalised and globalised this agricultural liberalisation within a vision for a globalised agricultural system, thereby transforming agriculture into a competitive market. While promoting free-market ideology however the agreement has enabled the developed countries to maintain trade-distorting subsidies and import restrictions.[62] This provides developed states with controlling advantages while the agreement requires all its members to surrender their right to pursue national food security measures and prohibits restrictive agricultural imports that would protect its population and livestock. [63] This undoubtedly restricts the sovereignty of developing nations to regulate food and agriculture particularly as those countries with debt and structural adjustment requirements are further disadvantaged as global governing

58 Philip McMichael, 'A food regime genealogy', 141 (cited in note 53).

59 Vandana Shiva, *The violence of the Green Revolution: Third World agriculture, ecology and Politics* (New York: Zed Books 1992) 52.

60 Philip McMichael, 'Agrofuels in the food regime,' 614 (cites in note 52).

61 Eric Holt Giménez & Annie Shattuck, 'Food crises, food regimes and food movements: rumblings of reform or tides of transformation?,' Journal of Peasant Studies 38 (2011): 111.

62 Carmen G Gonzalez, 'Institutionalizing Inequality: The WTO Agreement on Agriculture, Food Security, and Developing Countries', Columbia Journal of Environmental Law 27 (2002): 457.

63 Emelie Peine and Philip McMichael, Globalisation and global governance, in Vaughan Higgins and Geoffrey Lawrence eds, *Agricultural Governance: Globalisation and new politics of regulation* (Abingdon: Routledge, 2005) 22.

mechanisms are embedded in their state policy. There is a danger therefore that increasing global liberalisation will run parallel with increasing food insecurity if this imbalance in the global food regime is maintained by the dominant members of agricultural and food trade agreements. It will further enable agricultural corporations to have a monopolised power over the agricultural markets and the profits, over the growing links with food and fuel economies, and the supermarket revolution.[64] Land ownership is increasingly being concentrated because of the liberalised global trade in food and the declining availability of natural resources.[65] At the same time the levels of global hunger reached record levels while there was enough food to feed everyone.[66] Global food corporations also had record profits while food prices increased by 83% in three years.[67] The global south on the whole has become systemically vulnerable, from having yearly agricultural trade surpluses in the 1970's to becoming dependent on the global market for basic food and grains and having large trade deficits.[68]

4.1. *Sustainable Development and the Food Regime*

There is emerging consensus that institutional integration is integral to sustainable development, whether government or corporate.[69] Integration is not just between and within institutions but all influential actors. The food regime is already highly integrated between existing rules and practices of the international institutions through globalisation and the

64 Eric Holt Giménez & Annie Shattuck, 'Food crises,' 111 (cited in note 61).

65 Philip McMichael, 'A food regime genealogy', 143 (cited in note 53).

66 FAO. 2009. 1.02 billion hungry. Food and Agriculture Organization. Available from: http://www.fao.org/news/story/en/item/20568/icode/ (Accessed 12 January 2012).

67 World Bank, *Rising Food Prices: Policy Options and World Bank Response,* 2008. Available at: http://siteresources.worldbank.org/NEWS/Resources/risingfoodprices_backgroundnote_apr08.pdf (last accessed 12 January 2012).

68 FAO. 2004. The state of agricultural commodity markets 2004. Rome: Food and Agriculture Organization of the United Nations. Available at: ftp://ftp.fao.org/docrep/fao/007/y5419e/y5419e00.pdf, (last accessed 12 January 2012).

69 Sustainable development is the "development of the needs of the present without compromising the ability of future generations to meet their own needs" (World Commission on Environment and Development (WCED), Our Common Future (New York: Oxford University Press, 1987)). There is "a collective responsibility to advance and strengthen the interdependent and mutually reinforcing pillars of sustainable development—economic development, social development and environmental protection—at local, national, regional and global levels." (The Johannesburg Declaration on Sustainable Development, Adopted at the 17th plenary meeting of the World Summit on Sustainable Development, 4 September 2002, A/CONF.199/20, ¶ 5).

corporate entities ability to take advantage of the aims of globalisation. This integration however is not motivated to have effective regard for sustainable practices because of its motivation towards neo-liberal economics. For a food regime that is motivated by green economics however, sustainable development principles and aspirations need to be seen as central imperatives in the functioning of the bodies and corporations rather than optional add-ons to business strategies. The Draft International Covenant on Environment and Development, the New Delhi Declaration,[70] is designed to provide ecological and ethical guidance particularly on obligations on global issues and natural resources and issues of liability and compliance.[71] Companies could recognise this within their governance and accountability structures and that their operations and polices have an impact on human development, natural resources and the environment. Companies will have different business reasons to integrate sustainable principles and also different interpretations of what sustainable development means to their company. They may focus on managing risk to respond to changing business environments and stakeholder expectations or seek new business opportunities in new markets or seek to develop new business opportunities.[72] The overall rationality should therefore aim to reconcile any economic, social or environmental conflicts to the idea of balance and the legitimacy of the actions of all the actors involved in decisions that affect development. Principles 13 and 14 of the Stockholm Declaration[73] are broad to create non-binding obligations. However, States have the responsibility to set out those obligations,

---

70 ILA New Delhi Declaration of Principles of international law on sustainable development, Resolution 2002/3,2002,; The text of this Declaration also appeared as UN Doc. A/CONF.199/8, 9 August 2002, Available at: http://cisdl.org/tribunals/pdf/NewDelhi Declaration.pdf International Environmental Agreements: Politics, Law and Economics 2: 211–216, 2002.

71 Although not legally binding the declaration is the clearest guidance yet on drawing up a comprehensive list of rights and obligations to apply sustainable development principles. International law would thereby have a proactive role within the economic political system especially over social and economic inequalities and the ability of the less and least developed state to participate in the global economy. See Duncan French, 'Supporting the principle of integration in furtherance of SD: sideways glance', Environmental Law and Management 18 (2006).

72 Stratos, Sustainability Integration into Business Processes: A Study of Leading Canadian and International companies, July 2007, 2. Available at http://www.stratos sts .com/documents/SI_Report_%28full_74_pages%29.pdf (Last accessed 6 February 2010).

73 Stockholm Declaration of the UN Conference on the Human Environment, Stockholm, Sweden, 5–16 June 1972; UN Doc A/Conf 48/14/Rev.1, 11 ILM 1461. Principles 13 and 14, Available at: http://www.unep.org/Documents/Default.asp?DocumentID=97 &ArticleID=1503 (last accessed 12 February 2012).

through international agreement, international law and their domestic law, that enable and require all actors to achieve balanced and rational development decisions that are compatible with environmental needs.[74] This holistic integration at the domestic level and by international legal systems is therefore a prerequisite to applying international sustainability principles. The New Delhi Declaration has already initiated this and is capable of providing the legal structure.[75]

The current legal framework of domestic and international legal systems is in general not coherent and consists of only rudimentary rules on hierarchy, applicability and interpretation of sustainability development.[76] There is consequently a lack of clear understanding as to what the rules are supposed to achieve and this creates a system that integrates randomly and in an *ad hoc* manner. Coordinated and integrative approaches can be easily determined in principle but political interests among the developed states in particular still exert resistance where they conflict with interests of the international business community and the neoliberal economics. The attainment of sustainable development is about the process rather than the substance and the theoretical ideal. Equally, one does not have to define sustainable development definitively before integrative actions can be taken to incorporate what the central ideal of sustainable development is trying to achieve. For actors within the corporate food regime not to act sustainably on the basis that the principles are not fully defined is therefore not excusable. The solutions to unsustainable agricultural practices are on the whole quite obvious it is just the lack of desire and the decision to achieve them that presents the problem. An action orientated approach is required in international law by principle 4 of the Rio Declaration[77] and should influence composition and implementation of specific development measures in the creation and realisation of policy that can be legally interpreted and have practical application.[78] It provides a reference point for incorporating within treaties integrative decision-making and domestic adoption obligations.

---

74 'Agenda 21' at c 8.14 (cited at note 1).

75 'New Delhi Declaration' (cited in note 70).

76 Duncan French, 'Supporting the Principles of Integration in Furtherance of Sustainable Development: A Sideways Glance,' Environmental Law and Management 18 (2006): 112.

77 Jeffrey D. Kovar, 'A Short Guide to the Rio Declaration,' Colorado journal of international environmental law 4 (1993): 127.

78 Philippe Sands, 'International law in Field of Sustainable Development' British Yearbook of International Law 12 (1994): 338.

This ability to connect policy into practice is the most important connecting link to getting meaningful and effective application of integrative policy but it is severely restricted by weak and even corrupt practice at the political level. States may fail to integrate policy and decision-making that sufficiently controls the various actors and corporate interests for which the treaties were created.[79] This has happened at treaty level and at the inter-disciplinary level within national legal systems.[80] There are the usual explanations of food insecurity that economists and political leaders frequently use to neatly direct any contributing factors away from broader socio-economic explanations and the influence of global corporations and regulating bodies that shape the way foods are grown, how they are distributed and the ultimate consumer. There is little fundamental systemic or structural criticism. Only after decades of warning about climate change and the irrefutable evidence of damage to the environment have economists and political leaders, safeguarding neoliberal motivations, proliferated sympathetic policy for sustainability and the solutions to combat climate change, largely caused by systemic and structural policy in the first place.

4.2. *The Impossible Trinity*

The growing global population presents a dilemma of global proportions because it will eventually exceed the environments capacity to produce enough food. 40% of thc world's land is used for agriculture but up to 40% of that 40% is likely to be degraded.[81] It is urgent to find ways to feed properly the estimated 1 billion and rising malnourished people in the world,[82] the 2 billion people considered undernourished due to dietary imbalance or specific nutritional deficiencies. Food production must increase by an estimated 50 – 100% to feed everybody in the world in 2030 and meet FAO assurances there will be enough food to feed the world's population.[83] Unsurprisingly, the commitment to halve the number of malnourished

79 David M Ong, 'The Progressive Integration of Environmental Protection within Offshore Development Agreements', in Malgosia Fitzmaurice and Milena Szuniewicz, Exploitation of Natural Resources in the 21st Century, (The Hague: Kluwer Law International, 2003) 113.

80 Id.

81 FAO, The state of Agricultural Commodity Markets (Rome: FAO (2009) 6, 9.

82 Pedro Sanchez et al., Halving hunger: It can be done. London: UN Task force on Hunger, (London: Earthscan 2005) c 1, available at: http://www.unmillenniumproject.org/documents/Hunger-lowres-complete.pdf (accessed 14 January 2012).

83 FAO, The State of Agricultural Commodity Markets, 6 (cited in note 81).

people by 2015 is considered unachievable particularly as many developing countries have found themselves worse off than in the 1960's and 1970's[84] and unable to resolve the damage caused by failed international financial and green revolution initiatives. We have to stop going backwards before we can go forwards.

The rising global population and the increasing affluence of the emerging economies is increasing demand for food and energy. A rise in energy, primary commodities, and food prices has revealed the vulnerable weaknesses in many developed economies, such as those based primarily on knowledge-based services, while businesses from emerging economies, such as the BRIC (Brazil, Russia, India, and China) countries, have entered the primary commodity and agricultural markets.[85] The strategies to address economic vulnerabilities and the inevitable demand for new found affluence are radically altering world agriculture, food and energy. It is the perception and mitigation of risk of an ever increasing future demand for food and energy and the perception that biomass energy is a solution for climate change mitigation, in particular biofuels, that has upset food security requirements. This speculation relies on the volatility in the global commodity markets to replace working and established food systems. Established incentives set by States to reduce oil dependency are increasing the demand to convert food into biofuel.[86] Volatile oil prices are also attributed to the incentive to transfer to biofuel production and to rising cost of producing food particularly the costs of petro-chemical fertilizers and pesticides which are then passed on to the consumer. The increase in food prices can therefore be attributed to market volatility, rising fuel prices, and an increase in the demand for biofuel.[87]

The dilemma is how to accommodate this increase in global demand for energy and food while also complying with the global efforts to mitigate climate change and to find new sources of energy to replace non-renewable sources. Renewable energies are likely to contribute significantly towards a solution to the world's energy problems with the right types and

---

[84] UNDP, Human Development Report 2011, 'Sustainability and Equity: A Better Future for All' (New York: Palgrave Macmillan 2011) Ch1., Available at: http://hdr.undp.org/en/reports/global/hdr2011/download/ (accessed 12 January 2012).

[85] Bernadette Andréosso-O'Callaghan, and M. Bruna Zolin, 'Land, Biofuels and Food Security: Another 'Impossible Trinity Theorem'?' in Current Issues in Economic Integration: Can Asia Inspire the "West"?, eds. Andréosso-O'Callaghan, B., Zolin, M. (Farnham: Ashgate Publishing, 2010) 115.

[86] FAO, The state of agricultural commodity markets (cited in note 81) 9.

[87] FAO, The state of food insecurity in the world 2008: high food prices and food security—threats and opportunities (Rome: FAO 2008).

if exploited in a sustainable way. The growth in biomass and in particular biofuels, producing bioethanol and biodiesel, as a carbon natural fuel source has particularly been seen as an alternative to oil dependency. The demand for crops grown for biofuel requires land and this can directly affect the demands on the existing biological requirements, such food security requirements or the preservation of rain forests. This is inevitably overshadowed by the prospective commercial benefits of renewable energy. As the discussion in part 4.4 shows, biofuels have been enthusiastically embraced but their production is fraught with controversy because, if unchecked, it inevitably and significantly affects the availability of land. As the scramble for land to grow biofuels increase, an 'impossible trinity' seems to be emerging where three conflicting objectives (biofuels, food security and land-use efficiency/ biodiversity) that affect food security and energy security policies may not all be able to be reconciled at once, certainly in their present form. However problematic to food security governments, particularly the EU, have decided to use biofuels as a means to address energy shortages and meet their GHG emissions targets.[88] At the same time, governments are also requiring the means to feed the growing world population with its increasingly diversified consumption patterns. Finally, recognising the limited supply of available arable land governments objectives are demanding, also at the same time, maximum efficiency in the use of arable land,[89] home or abroad.

The loser in this impossible trinity of objectives is food security because growing too much biofuel inevitably interferes with the availability of food and with the competitiveness of food production within the markets. The problem is therefore not a compatibility problem between food security and energy security but rather at what scale, or quantity, biofuels can be grown before a balanced interaction between energy security, food security and sustainable development is unachievable. This presents the need for a threshold to be established that considers at the local and individual levels at what point the food and energy security of affected communities is compromised and a threshold of how it affects the region's regional food security requirements as a whole. Local or regional food security should be a primary concern of all governments who have the responsibility to ensure that the production of food and non-food crops

88 Bernadette Andréosso-O'Callaghan, and M. Bruna Zolin, 'Another 'Impossible Trinity Theorem'?' 114 (cited in note 85).

89 Id. See also David Tilman et al. 'Beneficial biofuels – the food, energy, and environment trilemma', Science, 325 (2009): 270–1.

have no effect on local and regional food security requirements. As a matter of priority therefore governments would do well to re-evaluate their policies, especially if they are genuine in the primacy of food security objectives, towards their own food and energy security needs before the energy needs of others.

4.3. *Corporate Food Regime and Institutional Response*

What has emerged however is a food regime that drives towards global agriculture and, if permitted to continue, is dominated by corporate farmers, mostly in the form of MNCs.[90] Motivated by a politics of neo-liberal capitalism it is displacing the local and regional agricultural systems with a strategy for 'accumulation by dispossession'.[91] Characteristics of this process include the commodification and privatisation of land and the displacement of indigenous populations, and the conversion of various property rights into the private sphere and in so doing the suppression and dispossession of rights to the commons.[92] The emerging economies are altering the relationship between state and industry and especially MNCs, affecting land tenure and the lives of rural groups and indigenous populations mimicking the destructive patterns of industrial agriculture and forestry.[93] The traditional North-South trading relationships rooted in colonialism are supplemented by new relationships between the countries of the global south, especially Brazil and Indonesia, which may be further supplemented by relationships for capital from the global North.[94] The particular surge in interest in biofuels has produced a proliferation of transnational partnerships among the developing countries and their firms, developing country investors and producers, MNC's from the North and the South.

Systemically contradictory policy, exiting and emergent, govern and determine the direction of new development projects associated with the corporate food regime.[95] This continues to be the primary engine of global

---

[90] Philip McMichael, 'A food regime analysis of the 'world food crisis" Agriculture and Human Values 26 (2009): 285; Philip McMichael, 'Agrofuels in the food regime,' 614 (cites in note 52).

[91] David Harvey, *The New Imperialism* (Oxford: Oxford University Press, 2003) 145.

[92] Id.

[93] Dauvergne, P., and Neville, K.J., 'Forests, food, and fuel in the tropics: the uneven social and ecological consequences of the emerging political economy of biofuels', The Journal of Peasant Studies 37 (2010): 633.

[94] Id. at 637.

[95] Bill Pritchard, 'The long hangover from the second food regime: a world-historical interpretation of the collapse of the WTO Doha Round,' Agriculture and Human Values 31 (2009): 298.

food insecurity from which the structural and systemic drivers of food insecurity operate and from which the consequential drivers largely manifest. The global institutions are to a large extent responsible because of their own systemic structures. The WTO for example was created as an attempt to solve the regime crisis between the motivations of colonialism and US capitalism while maintaining mercantilist relations.[96] The power of agribusiness has been deepened by the WTO in creating itself like a private corporate food regime behind a multinational façade.[97] This enables an export-orientated regime to be constructed towards global farming while also permitting the retention of protectionist agricultural subsidies as food security practices.

The World Bank Group (WBG) promotes its 'responsible agro-investment' (RAI)[98] land deals as a win-win situation for developing countries where host nations will benefit from economic development, improved employment opportunities and agricultural infrastructure and investors will be able to profit.[99] The rising food and energy prices and the drive towards low-carbon resources has made land investment very attractive to equity and pension funds, individual investors and sovereign wealth funds. Indebted countries in the global south are particularly targeted because of their weak regulation and governance allowing for conversion of their land and forests to export agricultural products.[100] Directly contradicting efforts to mitigate the effects on local food security, land rights,

---

96 Id.; Oren Perez, *Ecological Sensitivity and Global Legal Pluralism: Rethinking the Trade and Environment Conflict* (Portland: Hart Publishing, 2004) 54–58.

97 Philip McMichael, 'Agrofuels in the Food Regime,' The Journal of Peasant Studies 37(2010): 614.

98 In anticipation of political repercussions over the current land investment deals, concerned governments and agencies have brought together an initiative to make such deals acceptable. The World Bank-led 'Principles for Responsible Agricultural Investment that Respect Rights, Livelihoods and Resources' (RAI) created with the World Bank, the International Fund for Agricultural Development (IFAD), the UN Conference on Trade and Development (UNCTAD) and the UN Food and Agriculture Organisation (FAO). The seven principles it describes now form the basis of these organisations 'Win-Win' policy towards legitimising land investments under the banner of sustainability. WBG, FAO, IFAD, UNCTAD, 'Principles for Responsible Agricultural Investment that Respect Rights, Livelihoods and Resources', January 25, 2010, last accessed 12th February 2012, http://siteresources.worldbank.org/INTARD/214574-1111138388661/22453321/Principles_Extended.pdf.

99 Klaus Deininger et al, 'Raising Global Interest in Farmland: Can it Yield Sustainable Benefits?' (Washington DC: World Bank, 2011) 95 Available at: http://siteresources.worldbank.org/INTARD/Resources/ESW_Sept7_final_final.pdf and http://www.responsibleagroinvestment.org/rai/ [last accessed 12 February 2012].

100 Id 10, For further NGO response see also 'World Bank admits 'land grab' risks, proceeds anyway,' Bretton woods Project, last accessed 12 February 2012, http://www.brettonwoodsproject.org/art-566651.

and other social and environmental problems, the WBG has responded by massively increasing funds available for land investment deals and with the drive to facilitate the best business environments for land acquisitions making it a contributing driver of this explosion of land deals.[101] The local indigenous population inevitably suffer. Poverty alleviation and life improvement is not generally part of the motivation for large scale land deals and little attention is given to human rights, food security and human dignity for indigenous and local populations.[102] It is perhaps the non-lending products that are most contradictory. The WBG provides direct help to investors by direct private investor financing of agribusiness firms, such as through the International Finance Corporation (IFC),[103] its private arm, in partnership with the Foreign Investment Advisory Service (FIAS),[104] to promote private sector investment in developing countries. The WBG's non-lending activities extend to administering the Technical Assistance and Advisory Service (TAAS).[105] It advises member governments into creating the necessary conditions for foreign investment and the facilitation of investment processes so the best possible route for investor companies is created. It will, for instance, advise on necessary legislative reform, reduction of institutional and administrative barriers to investment, the construction and development of development agencies within these countries, and the assistance in the creation of policy regarding tax, customs and land laws. It is not really surprising that when institutions such as the WTO and the WBG talk about sustainability programmes

---

101 'World Bank report on land grabbing: beyond the smoke and mirrors,' GRAIN, Last accessed 12 February 2012, http://www.grain.org/article/entries/4021-world-bank-report-on-land-grabbing-beyond-the-smoke-and-mirrors. In Latin America for example, it is the big corporations and joint ventures, behind the governmental rhetoric, that invest enormous amounts of money in land acquisitions. Millions of hectares of land are taken over by foreign investors for food and biofuel production for export. Foreign and local companies set up farmland investments vehicles to receive money coming mostly from US and European Pension Funds banks, private equity groups and wealthy individuals such as Radar Propriedades (a fund set up by Brazil's largest sugar producer, COSAN) and Annuity Association–College Retirement Equities Fund of the US. Louis Dreyfus (one of the biggest grain trading multinationals which received US$65 million investment from American International Group (AIG)). 'Land grabbing in Latin America,' GRAIN, http://www.grain.org/article/entries/3995-land-grabbing-in-latin-america.(accessed 12 February 2012).

102 Olivier De Schutter, 'How not to think of land-grabbing: three critiques of large-scale investments in farmland,' Journal of Peasant Studies 38 (2011): 252.

103 See website at: http://www1.ifc.org/wps/wcm/connect/as_ext_content/what+we+do/advisory+services/about+us/about+advisory+services

104 See website at: http://www.ifc.org/ifcext/fias.nsf/Content/AdvisoryServicesProducts_General.

105 See website at: http://www.ifc.org/tatf.

and support for small farmers they receive ample scepticism about their sincerity and motivations. Supplementing the old economic system with new unsustainable practices and then adding sustainable policies to that system to make it environmental is a sticking plaster which is not going to provide sustainable solutions for climate change mitigation or an adequate foundation for a sustainable green economy. Fundamental change of their motivations will need to be proven before they can be taken seriously about agricultural sustainability.

As the global economy improves the demand for food and energy is likely to outstrip production capabilities. Accounting for issues such as water scarcity and soil depletion, there simply is not enough arable land already in production to satisfy every country's ever increasing demand without somehow acquiring more, such as through land conversion and nationalisation or direct investment or both.[106] Direct investment for land acquisitions, otherwise known as 'land grabbing', is an example and involves governments and MNCs in acquiring land to grow food or biofuel for export[107] effectively transporting food and energy insecurity implications to the host country. If the host country is not able to absorb this added demand on its arable land it can be devastating for the environment and also detrimental to that region's food security. It may significantly decrease the host's own perhaps limited supply of arable land and decrease its own ability to satisfy its own energy and food requirements. A major driver for investor countries to make government backed land acquisitions is food security, particularly countries in the Middle East, such as Saudi Arabia.[108] The supply of food in these countries is under pressure as home agricultural production decreases due to degradation or depletion of natural resources, largely caused by unsustainable practices. Over-extraction of non-renewable ground water in Saudi Arabia for example has led the government to completely phase out wheat production and go from self-sufficiency to being completely dependent on imported wheat by 2016 prompting Saudi Arabia to seek new land in food insecure countries such as Sudan.[109]

---

106 David Hallam, 'International Investment in Developing Country Agriculture—Issues and Challenges,' Food Security 3, Suppl 1 (2011): 92.

107 Klaus Deininger, 'Challenges posed by the new wave of farmland investment,' Journal of Peasant Studies 38 (2011): 219–223.

108 Lorenzo Cotula et al, Land Grab or Development Opportunity?: Agricultural Investments and International Land Deals in Africa (London/Rome: IIED/FAO/IFAD, 2008) 53.

109 Lorenzo Cotula et al., 'Agricultural Investment and International Land Deals: Evidence from a Multi-Country Study in Africa,' Food Security 3, Suppl 1 (2011): 101.

4.4. *Sustainable Biofuels: An Oxymoron*

Apart from taking recently cultivated agricultural land out of production for food, land conversion by farmers and biofuel producers can inflict significant environmental damage, particularly deforestation and increase use of pesticides. The process of conversion generally increases GHG emissions[110] defeating the whole purpose of climate change mitigation targets to which biofuels are supposed to be one of the solutions.[111] The inevitable pressures of globalisation to convert land have detrimental consequences on environmental sustainability, particularly by decreasing biodiversity, land degradation, the effects of mono-cropping and water pollution, and on the sustainability of local and regional interests, such as the social vulnerabilities of small farmers and the poor.[112]

Local small scale biofuel regions produce and consume biofuel within the same locality. The rapid expansion of oil palm and Jatropha in Asian countries such as Malaysia, Indonesia and India interfere with the local biofuel regions of other developed and developing countries.[113] It disrupts and transforms small scale biofuel regional production into the integrated national network. This idea of development is said to offer developing countries an export market providing export farmers with better income and opportunities and in so doing boost the national economy.[114] Pro-poor programmes can be established with careful management and governance of biofuel production and trading allowing for a win-win situation. The development of biofuels in Brazil since the 1970's shows however that to achieve this win-win situation the production and trade set up needs to be well established, something many developing countries do not have.[115] These countries will become biomass exporters creating regions of biofuel producing countries with large-scale mono-cropping production that is centralised and homogenous and the refining done somewhere else where

110 Mark W Rosegrant et al., Bioenergy and Global Food Situation until 2020/2050, (Berlin/ Washington DC: German Advisory Council on Global Change (WBGU), 2008) 41, Available at: http://www.globalbioenergy.org/uploads/media/0807_WBGU_-_Bioenergy_and_global_food_situation_until_2020-2050.pdf (accessed 15 December 2011).

111 For example the process of burning virgin forests in Indonesia for palm plantations leaves slow burning peat for months, even years.

112 Arthur PJ Mol, 'Boundless Biofuels?: Between Environmental Sustainability and Vulnerability' Sociologia Ruralis 47, No.4 (2007): 300, 304.

113 Id. at 305.

114 Asbjørn Eide, The Right to Food and the Impact of Liquid Biofuels (Agrofuels), (Rome: FAO, 2008) 21.

115 Ben White & Anirban Dasgupta, 'Agrofuels Capitalism: A view from Political Economy', Journal of Peasant Studies 37 (2010): 635.

there is better infrastructure.[116] The control of the global biofuels network is therefore increasingly integrated, often within the same structure as the food regime, and out of the control of states. Production, investment, consumption, and governance are no longer in the hands of the farmers, cooperatives and individual processors but in the hands of large corporate entities and conglomerates that are actively encouraged by state agencies, constructed with and represented by the same interested business interests.[117] The local economy receives little benefit, is undermined and is losing its relevance. In so doing the environmental degradation of the soil and water through large scale high-input mono-copping farming techniques endangers food availability and affordability for the rural inhabitants.

Despite these social and environmental dangers, economic and political elites are determined to continue domestic policy objectives for the globalisation of biofuels to significantly mitigate climate change and contribute to global energy security and rural development of the developing nations.[118] Ironically these are also the policy objectives used to explain government support, or market interventions, of domestic biofuel industries. It is clear that biofuels production is driven by government policy creating the market for it. Although there has been little consideration for sustainability, the 'win-win' arguments dominate the global biofuel debates, particularly in the Europe and the United States. They see biofuels as one of the routes to meeting environmental concerns and mitigation of GHG emissions without affecting economic growth.[119] By setting their government targets for biofuel consumption the US[120] and EU[121] member states especially have triggered the globalisation of biofuels production and thereby the influence on the markets of the unpredictability of feed stock and biofuel production.[122] Tropical countries are particularly economically very attractive targets because of their low land and labour costs and high crop yields.

---

116 United Nations Conference on Trade and Development, 'Making Certification Work for Sustainable Development: The Case of Biofuels', New York: (2008) 29.

117 Arthur P.J. Mola, 'Environmental authorities and biofuel controversies,' Environmental Politics 19 (2010) 66.

118 Deepak Rajagopal and David Zilberman, 'Review of Environmental, Economic and Policy Aspects of Biofuels' World Bank Policy Research Working Paper 4341 7 (2007).

119 Id.

120 The US has set a yearly target to produce 35 billion gallons of bioethanol a year.

121 EU has set a target for 10% biofuel share by 2020. RED Renewable energy directive

122 European Commission, 'An EU Strategy for Biofuels,' Communication from the European Commission, COM (2006) 34 final.

In protecting domestic economic growth market intervention continues to play an important role in government policy and the retention of influence and control in the markets. Government subsidies and tax rebates mainly in the United States, EU and Brazil, have encouraged biofuel production with a domestic strategy to reduce reliance of fossil fuels and satisfy GHG emission reduction targets, improve energy security and to promote employment within the energy and farming sector.[123] Heavy subsidisation can have contradictory consequences. Biofuel subsidies are an inefficient and an expensive way to meet GHG targets and can actually inhibit and divert governments support from developing more efficient new technology. The social benefits to employment and the farming and biofuel productions industries are increasingly cancelled out by the economic dominance of, in general, the large multinational agro-industrial companies which have enormous lobbying power to maintain the subsidies for their own benefit.[124] This has drastically reduced the number of small holders and farm workers in the industry reducing competition and increasing monopolistic market forces. Land is acquired for large scale biofuel production as an accumulation of production capacity by these large companies who dominate the market.[125] Biofuels are also not a stable provider of energy security because of the potential fluctuating volume of crop production. In parallel with food supply, energy security suffers with uncertainty of supply. This is costly to the tax payer having to compensate the vast differences in market prices and costly to those dependent on the global market prices who have to compete. Although the US Congress has allowed the corn-based biofuel tax credits and restriction on imported biofuel from Brazil to expire, it was done in response to deficit reduction rather than a change in policy. The policy for domestic support is therefore likely to continue as the need to protect domestic economic growth remains important and as technology finds more desirable types of biofuels to produce. The roles that biofuels play in diverting food to energy use provides a case for GHG targets, subsidies and tax tariffs on production and processing to be removed because they demonstrate the

---

123 Simonetta Zarrilli, 'Development of the Biofuel Markets in Global Energy Governance: The New Rules of the Game' in Eds. Andreas Goldthau and Jan Martin Witte (Washington DC, Brooking Institution Press: 2010) 78.

124 With acquisitions of innovating biofuel companies such as Verasum US oil refiner Valero Energy has become one of the largest ethanol refiners in the US, In Brazil, Shell and launched a joint venture with Cosan, producing electricity, ethanol, and advanced biofuels to become Brazil's largest ethanol producer.

125 Simonetta Zarrilli, 'Development of the Biofuel Markets'. 77 (cited in note 123).

tensions between virtual unlimited demand and the constraints of natural resources.[126] Proper use of biofuel mandates could reduce the effects of biofuel production on the markets and satisfy the economic growth requirements if they are able to remove the need for targets and excessive subsidies. The production of biofuels, and the promoting subsidies, to meet US and EU targets is generally recognised to have caused the sudden increase in food commodity prices.[127] Mandates for blending biofuels exist in 31 countries and 29 states and provinces to date and also use subsidies and tax exemption to promote biofuels.[128]

Biofuels are profitable and attractive as fuel for transport because they are able to use, to a significant extent, the same existing infrastructures as petroleum fuel and are therefore competitive against high oil prices and more competitive with other renewable energies. The transport sector is considered one of the main reasons the EU will fail to meet the Kyoto targets[129] and so the 'bioenergy revolution' could also be seen as largely a political response in also finding a solution to the rises in oil prices, the predicted increasing volumes in the transport sector,[130] the problem of peak oil[131] and an ensuing future energy crisis which will raise the costs of production, processing and especially transport. EU renewable energy strategy towards biofuels uses the same 'win-win' arguments for the reduction of GHG emissions, diversification and development of fuel supply resources and rural employment and development opportunities.[132] To comply with its GHG emissions reduction obligations the EU created reduction targets through the Renewable Energy Directive.[133] The targets are designed to encompass a transparent and unambiguous set of rules for

---

126 UN Committee on World Food Security, A Report by the High Level Panel of Experts on Food Security and Nutrition, 'Price volatility and food security,' Rome: (2011).

127 Mark W. Rosegrant, Biofuels and Grain Prices: Impacts and Policy Responses, International Food Policy Research Institute: 2008. http://www.ifpri.org/sites/default/files/publications/rosegrant20080507.pdf, (accesses on 14 February 2012); Donald Mitchell, A Note on Rising Food Prices, Policy Research Working Paper 4682, World Bank (2008), http://www-wds.worldbank.org/servlet/WDSContentServer/WDSP/IB/2008/07/28/000020439_20080728103002/Rendered/PDF/WP4682.pdf (accesses on 14 February 2012).

128 REN21, 'Renewables 2011: Global Status Report,' (2011), available at: http://www.ren21.net/Portals/97/documents/GSR/REN21_GSR2011.pdf, (last accessed 14 February 2011) 14.

129 Biofrac, 'Biofuels in the European Union: A vision for 2030 and beyond,' Final report of the Biofuels Research Advisory Council, (2006) 6.

130 Id.

131 Colin J Campbell, Jean H Laherrère, 'The End of Cheap Oil,' Scientific American 278 (No.3) 1998: 78–83.

132 European Commission, *'An EU Strategy for Biofuels,' Communication from the European Commission*, COM (2006) 34 final at 1.

133 Council Directive 2009/28/EC, (Renewable Energy Directive).

the sharing of energy from renewable sources at EU and Member State levels.[134] Mandatory national targets are set at 10% for renewable sources in transport energy consumption by 2020.[135] It recognises that these targets need to be met in a sustainable way, and recognises the negative effects of biofuel production[136]by introducing a binding sustainability scheme.[137] Industry, governments and NGOs are encouraged to set the certification schemes on all type of biofuels, whether imported or imported, to implement the directive. The certificates however are voluntary schemes certified by the companies themselves. It is still left to the economic market to be sustainable. The whole production chain is then checked by independent auditors to ensure sustainable practices from field to fuel pump. When the certificates work they are also designed to protect untouched nature, particularly virgin forest. Only fuels that have these certificates can be included in the national targets and must be approved by the European Commission. The main weakness in this scheme is that the sustainability of these certificates is still very energy security focused and may not consider food security with the same environmental consideration. It does not solve the impossible trinity dilemma explained in part 4.2 which will require food security considerations to be part of the evaluation.

5. Concluding Comments: Corporate Sustainability for a Green Economy

To a great extent, food security is a victim of the debate over the status of different human rights and when they apply. Food security and the right to food to the individual, whose life depends on it, is about access to adequate food and the right not to go hungry. The drivers of food insecurity are however political and economic in nature and to reverse food insecurity requires a committed and coordinated approach to realise

134 Id at 10–11.

135 Id at 13.

136 Id at 18.

137 Id art 16–18. The scheme has two pillars that should be kept separated. A GHG balance focuses on the methodology of used, the elements required to account usage and counting of emission values. The second pillar is a certification scheme that controls implementation and the control system implemented at the world level, European Renewable Energy Council, European Renewable Energy Council, Renewable Energy in Europe: Markets, Trends and Technologies, (London, Earthscan: 2010) 241.

access to food that recognises it as a right of no difference than the right to life. The construction of the right to food itself is an obstacle to realisation because of disparities in its recognition and the willingness of governments and the courts to prioritise it as either an element of the right to life or to employ a minimum standard. This weakness is to a great extent determined by predominant economic ideology. The right falls short of implementation because competitiveness of the economic markets encourages minimalist compliance and regressive pressures. The progressive tool is therefore an inappropriate mechanism to realise the right to food. The relationship between political systems and business needs to be rebalanced towards integrated and coordinated reform at the international level and a shift in thinking towards economic, social and environmental responsibility.

The pursuit of a 'one size fits all' model is not going to achieve global food security as it is an illusory concept. A sustainable global system of trade will however respect the regional food security models and acknowledge that agricultural production needs to be treated differently than other forms of trade because of its complexities. The right to food is not designed to operate between global actors and therefore economic and political obligations of MNCs and IFIs tend to have more prominence than unrealised human rights obligations. These other legal systems need to become compatible and integrated with a new green economic approach where governments are permitted to act appropriately to fulfil food security requirements.

The current corporate food regime owes much of its existence to colonialism and inward orientated capitalism and their inspiration for the 'green revolution.' Intensive agriculture and industrialisation increased the dependency of agriculture on energy, linking energy and food in an interrelated relationship, orientated to the global market of labour and capital and consolidated by the power of large land owners and corporations. International institutions inspired by neoliberalism became transformed into global structures within which developed states, with controlling advantage and assets, have been able to restrict the sovereignty of undeveloped states to regulate their food security requirements. A global market rather motivated towards integrating sustainable development within its principles and aspirations offers an alternative. An obstacle to such a system is lack of desire and decision to act by the political and economic elites to instigate policy and practice. The need to satisfy energy demand, adequately feed the world and manage the land has created an impossible trinity of government policy, one which the economic motivations of neoliberalism cannot resolve growing food insecurity and environmental degradation. The corporate food regime is motivated by neoliberal capitalism and supplemented by North-South relationships. This systemically contradictory regime is the primary engine of global food insecurity which the international financial and trade institutions encourage. Food insecurity is effectively exported through badly regulated land acquisitions by government and MNCs. Land grabs have food, energy and environmental consequences that are not sustainable. The rush by governments to solve their climate change obligations with renewable energy, and particularly the production of biofuels, has exacerbated food insecurity, particularly through unsustainable subsidies and tax incentives and the use of GHG reduction targets in the US and EU. Largely integrated with the corporate food regime, the biofuels network is no longer controlled by governments but by economic interests and MNCs and conglomerates. Social expectations have moved the EU to instigate a sustainability strategy focusing not only on methodology but also on a certification scheme to ensure the European public they are consuming biofuel from a sustainable source. The impossible trinity dilemma is still not able to be resolved as long as neoliberal economics dominates the motivations of political and economic policy.

As well as creating a balance between economic, social and environmental aspects the relationship between business, the State and civil society needs to be restored. As shown above, the responsibility of the State to legislate and control the excesses of corporate power should go beyond State jurisdiction in the global arena because of the globalised markets. The WTO therefore should have a part to play because of its established network of trade agreements and influence, but it in doing so will have to reform its neoliberal foundation and recognise positively corporate sustainability principles as accepted practice, particularly regarding agricultural subsidies. As the clear cut roles of business and State no longer exist, the complexity of globalisation has enabled business and state to become mutually dependent entities. Societal issues and expectations have been neglected by states and rather given to business to reform and adapt to. There is a case for binding rules and regulations to be put in place defining minimum standards of corporate behaviour. Business should however be able to determine how corporate sustainable principles relate to their business model. The EU directive on Renewable Energy does have the right approach except that MNCs should not be relied upon to only voluntarily to comply with certification. Certification should apply to all renewable energy imported products and be compulsory and independent of commercial interest. The global agricultural regime has neglected societal issues. Government and international institutions have also neglected to encourage sustainable corporate behaviour in establishing global food and energy regimes and have as a result lost control of the social and environmental consequences. In a balanced relationship business learns to operate within interfering mechanisms from the State rather than to try to take control of it. Corporate sustainability will therefore require governments to be more aggressive and courageous in controlling corporate power.

Business is primarily concerned with the long term success of a company and in integrating sustainable development principles by agreeing to a common approach that progresses towards a long-term sustainable path. Corporate sustainability transfers the overall idea of sustainable development onto the business level, defining it as meeting the needs of direct and indirect stakeholders without compromising the ability to meet needs of future stakeholders.[138] The success of a sustainable agricultural business, for example, is therefore due to meeting stakeholder needs. Short term gains at the expense of future resources will only have negative effects. A sustainable business will also acknowledge the role it has in creating human needs and influencing consumption. NGOs, such as WWF and Oxfam, play a vital role in identifying these human needs of particular social interest. The conflicts between economic, social and environmental objectives are viewed as conflicts between short or long term objectives. 'Goal conflicts' arise due to short term orientation but a win-win situation is possible when 'goal conflicts' are changed to 'goal congruities' and sustainability is realised.[139] Economic success will be built and measured from safeguarding all kinds of capital, whether economic, social or environmental rather than financial results.[140] Business is therefore orientated to whether the design of systems or processes has long-term impacts on our societal and environmental systems, hence a precautionary view and preventative measures in policy making. Corporations therefore have to consider economic, social and environmental impacts and interdependencies. This is the crucial aspect in creating strategies for sustainable

---

138 Thomas Dyllick and Kai Hockerts, Beyond the Business case for Corporate Sustainability, Business Strategy and the Environment 11, (2002): 131.

139 Klause J. Zink, Ulrich Steimle, Klaus Fischer, Human Factors, Business Excellence and Corporate sustainability: Differing Perspectives, Joint Objectives, in Klause J. Zink ed., Corporate Sustainability as a challenge for Comprehensive Management, (Germany: Springer, 2008) 8.

140 Id 4, 6.

development. It is imperative to overcome conflicts between economic, environmental and social goals in the long-term. It combines economic success with conservation of the environmental and social responsibility.

The Rio+20 United Nations Conference on Sustainable Development offers the opportunity to establish a green economy that offers an alternative to failing neoliberalism, and a model by which to construct a new form of sustainable capitalism that balances the economic, social and environmental impacts. It is clear that corporate sustainability needs to be part of that solution particularly if governments are serious about food security and finding a sustainable solution to how we exploit our resources, adequately feed the world and fulfil are transport needs. Especially since the financial crisis, corporate social responsibility initiatives are very popular but do not go far enough. The proposed convention on corporate responsibility and accountability has much support from governments and large corporate entities. It will need to address principles of accountability, transparency and responsibility. The conference can also accelerate progress towards poverty eradication and the establishment of sustainable development within the economic system. It should acknowledge that the institutional governance regarding food security, climate change and biodiversity loss is not currently adequate. The three pillars need to be implemented with binding obligations. It should for example review the progressive realisation of the right to food. Perhaps the greatest achievement of the conference would be to set the foundation for a sustainable world economy.

CORPORATE SOCIAL RESPONSIBILITY AND THE DEFENCE OF HUMAN RIGHTS

Shanta Martin

1. Introduction

Hundreds of individuals, companies and government representatives engaged in a process at the United Nations over the past 6 years seeking to advance means of addressing the issue of business and human rights. The former Special Representative of the Secretary General on human rights and transnational corporations and other business enterprises (SRSG), Professor John Ruggie, did a commendable job of garnering near-global consensus among business, governments and civil society in support of his "Protect, Respect, Remedy" framework for business and human rights. The framework postulates that States have a duty to protect human rights including against abuse by companies, that corporations have a responsibility to respect human rights, and that individuals whose rights are abused by business should be able to access remedies. The UN Human Rights Council welcomed the framework in 2008. The Guiding Principles for implementing the framework were also ultimately accepted by the Human Rights Council at the conclusion of Professor Ruggie's work in June 2011.

During the SRSG's mandate, respect for human rights was often discussed within the discourse of corporate social responsibility (CSR), almost to the point of being used interchangeably. Indeed, the SRSG founded the 'Respect' pillar of the Framework on societal expectation, not on law.[1] Society wants business to respect human rights and, we are told, business is responding. That response, more often than not, is through the adoption by companies of CSR initiatives, some of which specifically mention human rights. According to the SRSG, corporate responsibility is

[1] Report of the Special Representative of the Secretary-General on the issue of human rights and transnational corporations and other business enterprises, UN Human Rights Council, *Protect, Respect and Remedy: a Framework for Business and Human Rights*, April 2008, A/HRC/8/5, para 9.

now so accepted as a concept that no businessperson in their right mind would say or do otherwise.[2]

There is no doubt that the rise of CSR since the 1990s reflects the capacity of affected host communities to get their stories heard in home states. Whereas companies could once rely on the obscurity of their remote operations to prevent abuses coming to light, this is now far less probable. With the advent of the internet and the speed with which information now moves around the globe, examples of corporate abuse can rapidly lead to public approbation in companies' home states. The effect of negative publicity can be profound, with share prices responding accordingly. Demands for improved corporate social performance have therefore increasingly come not only from activists, but from shareholders and other investors. For some companies, such as Shell and BHP Billiton, negative public exposure, including from media associated with litigation for breaches of human rights, has been the driving force that led to commitments to CSR. For other companies mindful of the potential for such exposure, CSR has been adopted as a kind of shield against possible future complaint. In this sense, the increased adoption of CSR has come in response to societal expectations as to how companies ought to behave.

Many States have also officially adopted CSR plans and strategies when responding to the challenge of business abuses of human rights. In 2009, for example, Canada adopted a Corporate Social Responsibility Strategy for the Canadian International Extractive Sector and appointed a CSR Counsellor for the extractive industries.[3] Denmark adopted mandatory CSR reporting with effect from 1 January 2009.[4] The European Union also addresses business and human rights issues within an overarching CSR policy.[5]

---

[2] According to Professor Ruggie, "the theological question—should there be CSR?—is so irrelevant today. Companies are doing it. It's one of the social pressures they've absorbed," as reported in "The next question – Does CSR work?" *The Economist*, 17 Jan 2008, http://www.economist.com/node/10491055.

[3] Canada, *Building the Canadian Advantage: A Corporate Social Responsibility (CSR) Strategy for the Canadian International Extractive Sector* (2009), available at http://www.international.gc.ca/trade-agreements-accords-commerciaux/ds/csr-strategy-rse-stategie.aspx?view=d.

[4] The "Act Amending the Danish Financial Statements Act (Accounting for CSR in large businesses)" was adopted by the Danish Parliament on 16 December 2008.

[5] See, for example, European Commission website, *Sustainable and responsible business – Business and human rights,* available at http://ec.europa.eu/enterprise/policies/sustainable-business/corporate-social-responsibility/human-rights/index_en.htm, last accessed 7 March 2012.

Questions must be asked, however, as to whether this adoption by States and companies of CSR actually results in greater corporate respect for human rights, and whether it assists rights-holders to defend their rights. Despite the increasing commitment of companies and many states to CSR over the last few decades, non-governmental organizations (NGOs) continue to document a steady tide of corporate-related human rights abuses.[6] In most of these reports, the companies involved espoused a commitment to CSR. How such a commitment to CSR marries with the continuing occurrence in corporate human rights abuses is often explained away by lack of diligence to foresee and prevent such abuse. However, greater examination is warranted of the interplay between the rise in CSR and its role in preventing corporate human rights abuse. This paper aims to challenge the predominance of CSR in the business and human rights debate. It will examine the role of law in the ability of individuals and communities to defend their human rights, and in ensuring corporate respect for those rights.

2. The Rise of CSR

Particularly in the last few decades, CSR has been the business response to growing public recognition of the shortcomings of relying passively on beneficial impacts flowing from business activity.[7] No doubt, this public realisation has occurred in part as a result of infamous cases of gross corporate neglect, such as the Bhopal tragedy.[8] More subtly, experience has

[6] Numerous examples of such reports are available on the Business and Human Rights Resource Centre (www.business-humanrights.org) and include, Amnesty International, *Undermining Rights: Forced Evictions and Police Brutality Around the Porgera Gold Mine, Papua New Guinea* (2010); Amnesty International, *Don't Mine Us Out of Existence: Bauxite Mine and Refinery Devastate Lives in India* (2010); Amnesty International, *Nigeria: Petroleum, Pollution and Poverty in the Niger Delta* (2009); Human Rights Watch, *Gold's Costly Dividend: Human Rights Impacts of Papua New Guinea's Porgera Gold Mine* (2011); Human Rights Watch, *A Strange Case: Violation of Workers' Freedom of Association in the United States by European Multinational Corporations* (2010).

[7] It should be noted that the debate regarding whether companies have broader social duties than the pursuit of profits has been going on for many more decades. Indeed, even by the 1950's it was no longer "fashionable for the corporation to take gleeful pride in making money": Theodore Levitt, The Dangers of Social Responsibility, 36 Harvard Business Review, Sept-Oct 1958 at 42, quoted in C A Hartwell Wells, 'The Cycles of Corporate Social Responsibility: An Historical Retrospective for the Twenty-First Century' (2002) 51 *University of Kansas Law Review* 77, at 100.

[8] Due to lax safety standards, thousands of people died and hundreds of thousands were seriously injured when highly toxic gas exuded from a chemical plant in the city of Bhopal, India, owned and operated by an Indian subsidiary of Union Carbide Corporation:

also shown that even without such disastrous events too many factors can intervene to prevent broader social benefits of corporate activity from being realised. For example, whereas companies often refer to the positive contributions that their businesses make to society through the provision of jobs, these benefits may be limited and transient. In the extractive industries sector, for example, the availability of low-skilled jobs often quickly tapers off after the initial construction phase. The result is that, after an initial increase in wealth among some workers, local community members often find themselves struggling to gain employment.[9] Mining companies often point to the flow-on effects of their operations, with perhaps dozens of jobs created through the establishment of ancillary businesses. These benefits to local economies and to the capacity of individuals to earn an income should not be denied. However, it is also important to recognise that almost invariably among the ancillary businesses are bars and brothels that can dramatically change the social dynamic in small remote towns. Women from mining-affected communities often complain about an increase in violence, alcoholism and prostitution accompanying the increased population brought about by an influx of a mostly male workforce.[10]

Another obstacle to positive social contribution by business relates to the ability of foreign companies to obtain extraordinary tax concessions from governments that bend over backwards to facilitate foreign direct investment. This occurs even where the financial benefits to the State and the broader population represent a tiny proportion of the vast profits to be made by the companies involved. For example, one Australian mining company in the Philippines obtained a six-year tax holiday for a mine that only had an estimated mine-life of six years.[11] In another case, a metals smelter was exempt from all host-state taxes and other charges for a period of 50 years with an additional 50 years at the company's option, except for

see *In re Union Carbide Corp Gas Plant Disaster at Bhopal, India*, 634 F Supp 842 (SDNY, 1987). It took more than 26 years for criminal convictions to be secured, and UCC remains an 'absconder' from the Indian courts: Amnesty International press release, "First convictions for 1984 Union Carbide disaster in Bhopal too little, too late", 7 June 2010, available at http://www.amnesty.org/en/news-and-updates/first-convictions-1984-union-carbide-disaster-bhopal-too-little-too-late-2010-06-07 last accessed 10 March 2012.

[9] See for example, S Martin, K Newell, *Oxfam Mining Ombudsman Report: Rapu Rapu Polymetallic Mine* (2008); Amnesty International, *Don't Mine Us Out of Existence* (2010).

[10] See comments from women during, for example, the 2007 Pacific Women and Mining conference: http://www.oxfam.org.au/explore/mining/how-mining-affects-women.

[11] Martin, above n 9.

a 1 percent royalty.[12] Consequently, development from the revenues that should flow into the State coffers from such investments may be entirely unrealised.

At times, the failure of companies to take into account the potential repercussions of their decisions and actions has resulted in devastating consequences for local communities. In East Java, Indonesia, for example, the decision not to use safety equipment in a gas extraction joint venture involving Australian-based company, Santos, was fatal and led to the rights of tens of thousands of people being abused. The joint venture's Indonesian operating company, PT Lapindo Brantas, failed to use safety steel casing while undertaking drilling at depths of almost 3km below the earth's surface. Scientists believe that this failure led to an eruption of steam, water, and mud on 29 May 2006.[13] The hot sulphurous mud has been flowing ever since at rates as high as 150,000m^3 per day, pouring out enough mud to fill 53 Olympic swimming pools daily. It has completely submerged at least 6 villages and 25 factories, killed 13 people and displaced 30,000 people. It has forced the relocation of roads, bridges, a railroad line and a major gas pipeline. Surreal images of roofs poking through the sludge give an indication of just how much mud has flowed from the site. By 2010, the mud covered seven square kilometres and was 20 meters thick. It is expected to continue flowing for decades.[14]

Given the apparently tenuous basis for expecting broader social benefit from corporate activity, proactive measures are often needed to ensure positive social impacts. CSR has a role in this regard; enlivening companies to the need to put in place positive steps for social contribution and to prevent inadvertent oversight. For many company executives, the commitment to ensuring a positive social impact is not mere words. Many would express genuine disappointment that the positive impacts of their companies are often largely ignored. Beyond the benefits of jobs

[12] Andrea Shemberg, *Stabilization Clauses and Human Rights* (2008), p 21. Such tax concessions may be written into freezing clauses in agreements between the company and host State so as to prevent new laws from being applied to the firm. Stabilization clauses may also build in additional tax reductions or other compensation if there are attempts to change applicable laws. Although some resource-rich countries have recently been seeking to increase the public share of extractive industry profits, some states may find themselves being sued by companies for breach of stabilization agreements.

[13] Richard J. Davies, Richard E. Swarbrick, Robert J. Evans, Mads Huuse, "Birth of a mud volcano: East Java, 29 May 2006", *GSA Today*: v. 17, no. 2, (2007) doi: 10.1130/GSAT01702A.1.

[14] Mark Kinver, "Indonesian Mud Volcano Flow 'to Last 26 Years'", *BBC News*, 25 Feb 2011, http://www.bbc.co.uk/news/science-environment-12567163.

and income, they point to their companies' community relations programs. They establish projects such as scholarships, health clinics, and agricultural assistance programs. Company personnel often assert that these projects are demonstrative of the company going above and beyond what is required by regulation, thereby illustrating the company's benevolence and fulfilment of its responsibility to broader society. What must also be recognised is that CSR policies and programs have institutional benefits. They can, for example, contribute to improved corporate culture or "conscience", which may lessen the potential for actions that would inadvertently infringe human rights.[15] Further, CSR policies can be an important reference against which to measure company actions, providing both internal and external stakeholders a useful point of leverage for positive change.

While the ability of CSR to deliver these broader social contributions is welcome, there are several problems with relying on CSR as the means by which to achieve corporate respect for human rights. First, the ill-defined content of CSR and its voluntary basis do not sit comfortably with the rights and duties that are a necessary part of human rights. Second, caution must be exercised in assuming that CSR inevitably ensures a positive impact on human rights, particularly where companies may be well aware of the negative impacts that may be generated by extremely profitable decisions. Third, there is the all-too-common practice of CSR being used as a PR smokescreen. These issues will be considered in turn.

3. Talking CSR – Do We Know What We Mean?

There is no single accepted definition of CSR. Many companies and industry bodies refer variably and interchangeably to "CSR", "sustainable development", securing a "social licence to operate", "business sustainability", or "corporate giving". The World Business Council for Sustainable Development (WBCSD) defines CSR as "the commitment of business to contribute to sustainable economic development, working with employees, their families, the local community and society at large to improve their quality of life".[16] The European Commission defines CSR as "a

[15] See for example, David Birch and Mark Glazebrook, 'Doing Business – Doing Culture: Corporate Citizenship and Community' in S Rees and S Wright (eds), *Human Rights, Corporate Responsibility: A Dialogue* (2000) 41.

[16] World Business Council for Sustainable Development *Corporate Social Responsibility – The WBCSD's journey* (2002), 2.

concept whereby companies integrate social and environmental concerns in their business operations and in their interaction with their stakeholders on a voluntary basis."[17] Governments have defined CSR variably as "how companies address the social, environmental and economic impacts of their operations and so help to meet our sustainable development goals", "the voluntary actions that business can take, over and above compliance with minimum legal requirements, to address both its own competitive interests and the interests of wider society", and "as the voluntary activities undertaken by a company to operate in an economically, socially and environmentally sustainable manner."[18] These definitions contain two core themes that undermine confidence in the capacity of CSR to contribute to greater respect for, and the protection and enjoyment of, human rights: one is that CSR is a definitively voluntary pursuit; and the other is that it is up to business to determine the precise content of CSR.

The insistence that CSR is a voluntary pursuit means that companies can choose not to engage in CSR at all or only in a limited fashion. Despite the apparent groundswell of CSR, the overwhelming majority of companies have eschewed the adoption of CSR. Several factors will determine whether a company will adopt CSR. The choice as to whether to adopt a CSR policy appears to vary geographically. The WBCSD found that the concept of CSR had relatively little support among companies in Taiwan, Thailand and Ghana, but more support in the USA and the Philippines.[19] Similarly, a Harvard Law School study found a much smaller proportion of Asian companies compared with European companies adopted human rights policies applicable to their supply chains.[20] One important factor is

---

[17] European Commission, Communication from the Commission to the European Parliament, the Council, the European Economic and Social Committee and the Committee of the Regions: *A renewed EU Strategy 2011–14 for Corporate Social Responsibility*, Brussels, 25.10.2011 COM(2011) 681 final, available at http://ec.europa.eu/enterprise/policies/sustainable-business/corporate-social-responsibility/index_en.htm, last access 17 March 2012.

[18] Definitions used by the UK, Canadian and Danish governments: http://www.bis.gov.uk/policies/business-sectors/low-carbon-business-opportunities/sustainable-development/corporate-responsibility; http://www.international.gc.ca/trade-agreements-accords-commerciaux/ds/csr.aspx?view=d; http://www.international.gc.ca/trade-agreements-accords-commerciaux/ds/csr-strategy-rse-stategie.aspx?view=d; http://www.csrgov.dk/sw50970.asp.

[19] See for example, the comments recorded in response to CSR in different parts of the world in Richard Holme, Phil Watts, WBCSD, *Corporate social responsibility: making good business sense* (2002), pp 12–13.

[20] Aaron Bernstein and Christopher Greenwald, *Benchmarking Corporate Policies on Labor and Human Rights in Global Supply Chains* (2009).

the extent of external demand to commit to CSR. The WBCSD found that respondents in Ghana, for example, considered that CSR was not high on the corporate agenda because it was thought to be too expensive, there was little outside pressure on companies, and there was a lack of government control. It appears that companies generally only choose CSR when there is a confluence of factors that effectively compel them to do so – whether the imperative comes from consumer demand, bad publicity, NGO campaigns, or government intervention. While the adoption of CSR is influenced by cultural, geographical, and political factors, the responsibility of companies to respect human rights applies to all companies in all contexts. Respect for human rights should not, therefore, be left to a choice dependent on a multiplicity of factors.

Beyond the choice as to whether to commit to CSR, companies are left to determine the content of CSR. Each company can adopt its own version of what it thinks society is demanding of it and what it chooses to be responsible for. In other words, there is no guarantee that a company that adopts CSR will include in its CSR policy a commitment to respect all human rights. Whereas a body of international law – treaties, declarations, authoritative statements by official human rights bodies, and the considered opinions of national and international courts – defines human rights, there is no common understanding of the content and scope of CSR. On the one hand, the term can be used self-servingly to encompass almost any philanthropic activity. On the other hand, CSR can refer inclusively to a company's genuine commitment to respecting human rights. But therein lies the rub. The imprecision of the term means that while one commentator may use it to refer broadly to beneficial social contributions, another may assume it to incorporate the specific commitments of a company to upholding human rights. Each will communicate a very different understanding of the content of the term, potentially resulting in joint agreement of the general "good" to be derived from CSR without any common understanding of whether, and if so how, human rights are to be addressed by a company.

Ultimately, reliance on CSR as the means by which companies are expected to commit to respecting human rights allows companies to determine the content of that commitment. This means that companies can choose not to commit to human rights at all, or to pick and choose which human rights they want to respect. The Business and Human Rights Resource Centre keeps a running tally of corporate statements that explicitly refer to human rights. There are currently 292 listed on the website, a tiny proportion of the 80,000-plus transnational companies operating throughout the world. A recent Harvard Law School review of over 2500 global companies found that only 28% of their supply chain policies referred to human rights, and only 6% of statements endorsed the eight core conventions of the ILO.[21] A review by the OECD of more than 145 codes of conduct, found that ILO standards were mentioned in only 10%, while a study conducted by the ILO into 215 codes found that only 15% contained references to collective bargaining or freedom of association.[22] If respect for human rights is a minimum criterion for corporate responsibility, there is little room to assert that companies can choose whether or not to respect rights and if so, which ones.

4. CSR and Deliberate Corporate Decisions

A further reason why there is a need to move beyond CSR, is that there is little empirical evidence to support the presumption that CSR results in greater respect for human rights. There has been an increasing number of credible allegations of corporate human rights abuses over the past few decades, despite the simultaneous burgeoning of CSR initiatives. Clearly, some of this increase in reporting is due to greater attention being paid by NGOs and the media to business and human rights. Interestingly, however, there has been relatively little quantitative analysis of the concurrence of improved human rights "performance" and the adoption of CSR. One of the few studies on whether CSR contributes to curbing human rights abuses of the largest worldwide MNCs recently found that MNCs that have adopted CSR initiatives are actually more likely to be involved in alleged human rights abuses.[23] On the positive side, the study found that the probability of being accused of directly abusing human rights decreases over the length of time in which the MNC has been involved in the CSR initiative, presumably as the company accumulates experience and better integrates CSR into its practices to avoid human rights abuses. Worryingly however, the study found that there was no similar decrease over time in

---

[21] Aaron Bernstein and Christopher Greenwald, *Benchmarking Corporate Policies on Labor and Human Rights in Global Supply Chains* (2009).

[22] OECD Working Party of the Trade Committee, *Codes of Conduct – An Expanded Review of Their Contents*, TD/TC/WP(99)56?FINAL, Paris (2000); ILO Working Party on the Social Dimensions of the Liberalisation of International Trade, *Overview of Global Developments and Office Activities Concerning Codes of Conduct, Social Labelling and other Private Sector Initiatives Addressing Labour Issues*, GB.273/WP/SDL/1(rev1) ILO, Geneva, (1998). See also Rhys Jenkins, *Self-Regulation in a Global Economy* (2001), 22.

[23] Davide Fiaschi et al, *To Abuse or Not to Abuse: This is the Question* (2011).

relation to allegations of corporate complicity in abuses committed by third parties. The study's authors posit that while companies appear to learn from CSR over time to improve their own human rights performance, they may also learn over time to 'outsource' abusive behaviour to third parties. Such outsourcing externalizes the risk associated with being directly linked to the abuse, while allowing the company to still reap the perceived benefits of the abuse.

The study reflects the fact that companies will be tempted to knowingly and deliberately engage in activities that result in human rights abuses if there are sufficient profits and benefits for the company. The reality is that in many cases, corporate human rights abuses have not just been the result of unintentional impacts, but of deliberate corporate choices and actions. Royal Dutch Shell and its subsidiaries, for example, have been, and continue to be accused of complicity in human rights abuses in the Niger Delta.[24] Company documents recently revealed as a result of a court case brought in New York demonstrate that Shell paid Nigeria's military in the 1990s to suppress opposition to its oil activities.[25] Shell had previously stated that the company played no part in any military operations against the Ogoni people. However, one internal document reports that a military operation to retrieve a Shell vehicle led to the death of an Ogoni man and the injury of two others. Rather than condemn the loss of life, Shell's response was to financially reward the military personnel involved "as a show of gratitude and motivation for a sustained favourable disposition towards SPDC [Shell] in future assignments".[26] Shell continues to deny that such payments were routine.

In the context of employment, which many companies highlight as their greatest contribution to the communities in which they operate, companies sometimes spectacularly fail to respect workers' rights. Consider, for example, the thousands of workers whose lives have been put at risk by irresponsible corporate policies and practices in the mining industry in South Africa. Mine workers suffered debilitating asbestosis as a

---

24 A recent report by Platform alleges that Shell's operations remain "inextricably linked to human rights violations committed by government forces", and that the company pays feuding militant groups in the Niger Delta in the full knowledge that the money is used to sustain conflict: Platform, *Counting the Cost: corporations and human rights abuses in the Niger Delta*, (2011), available at http://blog.platformlondon.org/2011/10/03/counting-the-cost-corporations-and-human-rights-abuses-in-the-niger-delta/.

25 Documents available at http://www.shellguilty.com/evidence/; J Vidal, "Shell oil paid Nigerian military to put down protests, court documents show", *The Guardian*, 3 Oct 2011, available at http://www.guardian.co.uk/world/2011/oct/03/shell-oil-paid-nigerian-military?intcmp=239.

26 http://www.shellguilty.com/wp-content/uploads/2009/06/exhibit31.pdf.

result of their employment at mines operated by subsidiaries of Cape plc in South Africa, where even children as young as 12 were employed to stamp down "fluffy amosite asbestos, which all day long came cascading down on their heads ... [and who] were kept stepping down lively by a burly supervisor with a hefty whip".[27] The conditions in which South African gold miners worked may also have led to thousands suffering silicosis and silico-tuberculosis as a result of exposure to dangerous levels of dust on Anglo American South Africa Ltd mines.[28] Employees in other industries, including the garment and sportswear industries, have also notoriously been the subject of pervasive human rights abuses at work.[29]

There are also notorious cases of man-made environmental disasters, which can severely impact human rights, such as the rights to food, water and the highest attainable standard of health. In Papua New Guinea, for example, some of the world's largest and wealthiest mining companies, including BHP Billiton and Barrick Gold Corporation, have made enormous profits from the Ok Tedi and Porgera mines. These mines, as with the Tolukuma mine further south in Papua New Guinea, operate using the cheapest form of waste disposal available, dumping millions of tonnes of waste into the country's once-pristine river systems. Just across the border in West Papua, the enormous Freeport McMoRan Grasberg mine does likewise. The choice to use this waste disposal system contributes to the billions of dollars made by these companies. Meanwhile, villagers dependent upon these rivers have found their water contaminated, their fish killed, and their crops unable to grow.[30] Many community members have also complained of illness and deaths as a result of the contaminated

---

[27] According to Dr Gerrit Schepers, a former government health inspector who visited the mines 17 years after regulations had been passed in England to control asbestos exposure: as quoted in B Castleman, "Export of Hazards – The Double Standard in Industrial Hazards", *The Multinational Monitor*, (1984) Vol 5(9).

[28] Legal proceedings have been issued against AASA in both the English and South African courts on behalf of gold miners who claim they contracted silicosis or silico-tuberculosis as a result of excessive dust levels on AASA mines up to 1998.

[29] See, for example, allegations made about employment conditions in Nike factories before the California Supreme Court in *Kasky v Nike Inc*, 27 Cal 4th 939 (2002). See also a report about workers treatment in sportswear factories in Asia: Oxfam Australia, *Offside! Labour Rights and Sportswear Production in Asia* (2006).

[30] The impacts of the Ok Tedi mine were recently reviewed by an independent scientist who concluded that very little, if anything, can be done to mitigate the widespread environmental impacts of the mine. He advised the mine operators to mitigate the significant social implications, including as a result of severe impacts on food availability and nutrition: Dr Alan Tingay, *Letter of Endorsement of Dr Alan Tingay*, 16 April 2007, available at www.wanbelisao.com/downloads.

water.[31] The companies engaged in this form of disposal continue to do so with full knowledge of its impact on downstream communities. Clearly, heavy reliance on voluntary CSR initiatives as the means by which companies will respect human rights fails to acknowledge the reality that corporate human rights abuses are not just a matter of unintentional repercussions that might be avoided with sufficient due diligence, but also a result of active decision-making.

5. Is CSR Just PR?

Finally, one of the reasons that human rights should not be subsumed into debates about CSR is due to the real potential for CSR to be used as mere public relations. Companies often publicise their commitment to CSR by highlighting projects that may be genuinely "good" for some stakeholders, but without significantly adjusting the manner in which the company operates. Shell's CSR campaign following accusations of its involvement in the Ken Saro Wiwa execution is a prime example. Despite millions spent on improving its corporate image, including by the adoption of CSR commitments, Shell continued to fail to rapidly respond to the devastating impacts of massive oil spills from its operations in the Niger Delta. This included waiting weeks before stemming two massive oil leaks in 2008 and 2009 that led to an oil spill as large as the Exxon Valdez disaster in Alaska.[32]

Similarly, as with other companies involved in the cases referred to above, the corporate group that owns PT Lapindo Brantas, the Bakrie Group, declares its commitment to CSR.[33] But it is difficult to see what this commitment means when one reviews the decisions the company took in the immediate aftermath of the mud flow. The Bakrie Group is a family business belonging partly to Indonesia's richest man, the billionaire government minister, Aburizal Bakrie. In 2006, shortly after the mudflow commenced, the Bakrie Group attempted to sell PT Lapindo Brantas for $2 to an offshore company.[34] The move was a blatant attempt to shift the company out of the reach of potential claimants demanding compensation

[31] Oxfam Australia, *Mining Ombudsman Case Report: Tolukuma Gold Mine* (2004) available at http://www.oxfam.org.au/explore/mining/impacts-of-mining.

[32] Following the commencement of legal action in the UK on behalf of 69,000 Nigerians, Shell admitted liability: http://www.leighday.co.uk/News/2011/August-2011/Shell-accepts-responsibility-for-oil-spill-in-Nige.

[33] http://www.bakrie-brothers.com/aboutus/page/csr.

[34] Raymond Bonner and Muktita Suhartono, "Indonesia gas blast linked to volcanic mud", *New York Times International Herald Tribune*, 23 Oct 2006, available at

and clean-up, which has been estimated at over a billion dollars. Moreover, for years, the company has continued to claim that natural causes, not the company's activities, led to the eruption. The company blamed a distant earthquake, a theory which the world's leading geologists from Britain, the United States of America, Indonesia and Australia found was patently false.[35] The debate over the cause prevented liability being attributed and delayed compensation to the thousands of people affected. In circumstances such as these, CSR commitments become a fig-leaf for corporate abuse.

Unsurprisingly, cases like those cited above have led to calls for companies to be held to account, most commonly by demand for increased regulation of companies – both within the States where the activity occurs (the host State) and the State where the company is domiciled (the home State). The corporate response has been to counter these proposals with the suggestion that regulation may not only be counter-productive by stymieing business innovation, but unnecessary. Business often lobbies against further regulation on the basis that it is superfluous because companies are aware of the problems and are committed to having a beneficial impact. Companies have sought to demonstrate this by adopting CSR policies, which note the potential negative impacts of business activities while seeking to distinguish the company's own activities from such impacts. CSR commitments highlight the company's determination to avoid such negative connotations, and focus attention on the company's positive contributions. But when CSR is regularly used to veil truths and avoid responsibility, it can be seen as a cynical attempt to prevent regulation that might actually curb corporate misconduct.

6. What Role for Law?

In circumstances such as the many referred to above, self-regulation is not the key. Clearly a third party is needed, one which prioritises the rights and interests of people over corporate interests. This should be the role of the State, which has a duty to protect people's human rights from abuse.

---

http://www.nytimes.com/2006/11/23/world/asia/23iht-blast.3642098.html. Lapindo was later 'sold' to another Bakrie Group company based in Malaysia, Minarak Labuan Co: PT Energi Mega Persada Tbk, "Lapindo Brantas is no longer consolidated in ENRG's book", Press Release 12 Sept 2007. Santos also sold its shares to the Malaysian subsidiary in 2008.

35 'Scientists say human error behind monster mud flow', *PM*, 10 June 2008 http://www.abc.net.au/pm/content/2008/s2270531.htm; Carl Stiansen, Robert Sanders, "Strongest evidence to date links exploration well to Lusi mud volcano", UC Berkley News Centre, 11 Feb 2010, available at http://newscenter.berkeley.edu/2010/02/11/mudvolcano/.

Too often, however, corporate and political interests converge such that the interests and rights of local communities are subsumed. This convergence occurs both with host State governments and home State governments. As such, governments are often reluctant to act to regulate and restrain corporate abuse. In many countries, this union between corporate and government interests can occur as a result of corruption of key decision-makers, but commonly it is a result of a more subtle collusion between the economically and politically powerful against the weak and marginalised. Governments and companies often cite the macro-economic benefits of a company's activities as a means of justifying the prioritisation of corporate interests. In India, for example, a country going through unprecedented economic development, the investments of Vedanta in Orissa were touted by both the company and local Orissa State authorities as beneficial "sustainable development" for local communities and the entire nation. Vedanta is pursuing a massive expansion of an alumina refinery in remote Lanjigarh. Local people were promised the impossible by officials who said the company would provide jobs to every family who sold their land and that "the area will be transformed into a Bombay."[36] A related bauxite mine project was also being pursued in an area home to Indigenous peoples who were not consulted on the development, in breach of their right to free, prior and informed consent. Instead of consulting local communities, the companies and government representatives sought to meet behind closed doors and make decisions on behalf of those whose lives would be irredeemably changed.[37] The distortion in power that results from cosy corporate-government relationships means that citizens are denied equal access and influence over their political decision-makers, thereby undermining democratic governance.

The problem of host government collusion in prioritising corporate interests over human rights is not necessarily resolved by appealing to home state governments. Most governments provide active assistance to companies based in their territories when seeking to gain favour in developing countries. Documents revealed through Wikileaks demonstrate the

---

[36] Amnesty International (2010), above n4, p 38.

[37] In Vedanta's view, what was more important than respecting people's rights was that "as enlightened and privileged human beings, we should not try to keep the tribal and other backward people in a primitive, uncared-and-unprovided-for socio-economic environment": Vedanta Resources letter to Survival, 2008, available at http://assets.survivalinternational.org/static/files/behindthelies/Ved_letter_distance-0805.pdf. Such disdain for the capacity of individuals, particularly Indigenous peoples, to make decisions frequently allows governments and companies to ignore rights regarding involvement in decision making.

close relationships between companies and their home states embassies in-country. Chevron, for example, which was being sued in Ecuador for massive oil contamination, received support from the US embassy to lobby for fraud cases against two Texaco employees to be dropped.[38] Diplomatic cables reveal that Chevron often "suggested that the USG [US government] pressure the GOE [Government of Ecuador] to assume responsibility for the environmental damage in the areas once operated by Chevron".[39] The cables also reveal Chevron's offer to fund "social projects" in exchange for a government agreement to shut down the trial. Similarly, in Peru, shortly after protestors had been killed, detained and tortured at the Monterrico mine site in the north of the country, embassy officials from Australia, the US, Canada, the UK and Switzerland, invited mining companies to meet with them to examine means of assisting the companies. A representative of Antamina, which is part-owned by BHP Billiton and Xstrata, proposed that the ambassadors encourage the government and the Church to rotate teachers and bishops through mining areas to prevent them fomenting anti-mining attitudes. A representative of AngloAmerican's Minera Quellaveco blamed the opposition to mining expressed by affected communities on NGOs such as Oxfam and Friends of the Earth. The ambassadors requested the companies provide specific examples of NGOs advocating violence and about "anti-mining teachers and priests who engage in inappropriate activities" so that the embassies could take the proposals forward.[40]

Given the extent to which political and economic interests of host and home governments may favour the interests of TNCs, the rule of law becomes essential in the quest for human rights protection. The ability of individuals and communities to defend their human rights is greatly enhanced when they can use legal protections to counter discretionary favouritism doled out by politicians, or a company's unilateral renunciation of any commitment to human rights in voluntary standards. In India, for example, activists defending the rights of the Adivasi Indigenous peoples who would have had their entire way of life decimated by the Vedanta bauxite mine, have mounted numerous legal challenges in the local courts. These challenges provided the opportunity for greater scrutiny to be placed on decisions that would otherwise continue to be made in dubious circumstances. By spotlighting the situation, such legal challenges can

[38] http://wikileaks.org/cable/2008/04/08QUITO323.html.
[39] http://wikileaks.org/cable/2006/03/06QUITO705.html.
[40] http://www.guardian.co.uk/world/us-embassy-cables-documents/38881.

also provoke more responsible political decision-makers to take action consistent with the law. In the Vedanta case, an expert panel established by the Ministry of Environment found that Vedanta's subsidiary had violated forest conservation and environment protection laws, and the rights of the Indigenous community "in active collusion with [Orissa] state officials".[41] Jairam Ramesh, the Indian Minister for Environment and Forests, said the National Government's decision to stop the mine and take action against Vedanta was "purely based on a legal approach".[42] While the laws in India do not go far enough to fully protect the international human rights of Indigenous peoples, there were at least some laws in place. In the absence of those laws, which were relied upon by the expert panel, the human rights of the Indigenous communities would have been entirely trounced in favour of Vedanta's investment interests.

The rule of law in home states is also an important protective mechanism for victims of corporate human rights abuses. When local legal systems fail to provide sufficient protections, many victims of human rights abuses have looked to recourse in the company's home State. In the UK alone, claims have been made by tens of thousands of foreign claimants for compensation resulting from activities of British companies in Peru, South Africa, Nigeria, the Ivory Coast, and Colombia.[43] In the United States, claimants have pursued litigation arising from corporate activities occurring in India, Ecuador, Nigeria, Colombia, Burma and Papua New Guinea.[44] Courts in other jurisdictions, such as Australia and Canada, have also considered claims brought by foreign claimants for corporate abuses in Papua New Guinea and the Democratic Republic of the Congo.[45]

Such claims not only provide the victims of the abuses with the prospects of remedy, they also represent an important opportunity to ensure

---

41 http://moef.nic.in/downloads/public-information/Saxena_Vedanta.pdf.

42 "Vedanta mine plan halted by Indian government", *Guardian*, 24 Aug 2010, http://www.guardian.co.uk/business/2010/aug/24/vedanta-mine-plan-halted-indian-government.

43 See, for example, the cases brought by Leigh Day & Co on behalf of victims in cases against Anglo American South Africa Ltd, Trafigura, Monterrico, BP and others: http://www.leighday.co.uk/Our-expertise/international-claims, last accessed 17 March 2012. The firm also represented victims in cases brought against Rio Tinto, Cape plc and Thor Chemicals: *Connelly v RTZ Corporation plc* [1998] AC 854, *Lubbe v Cape plc* [2000] 4 All ER 268, *Ngcobo v. Thor Chemicals Holdings Ltd*, [1995] T.L.R. 10; *Sithole v. Thor Chemicals Holdings Ltd.* [1999] T.L.R. 110.

44 See for example, *Aguinda v. Texaco* 303 F 3d 470 (2d 2002), *Alomang v Freeport-McMoran* 811 So 2d 98 (La App 2002), *Bano v Union Carbide* 273 F 3d 120 (2d Cir 2001), *Doe v Exxon Mobil* Docket No 01-1357 CIV (DDC 2002), *Doe v. Unocal* 963 F Supp 880 (CD Cal 1997), *Sarei v Rio Tinto Plc* 221 F Supp 2d 1116 (CD Cal 2002).

45 *Dagi v BHP* [1995] 1 VR 428.

that accountability is attributed. The potential for corporate accountability is in turn essential for assisting to deter similar future behaviour. In many respects, therefore, the capacity to bring cases under home state legal systems assists to close the "governance gaps", which are the root cause of the problem of corporate abuse of human rights.[46]

The role of international law should also not be underestimated in ensuring respect by companies for human rights. There has been discussion for some time about the potential for an international treaty directly applicable to companies. While not predisposed to such a treaty throughout his mandate, the SRSG considered the need for such an instrument in relation to the most egregious corporate human rights abuses.[47] However, even without such a treaty, existing international human rights law can play a key role in holding companies accountable for human rights abuses. For example, while the cases that have been brought against companies in home states have largely been based on claims in tort, many have expressly drawn on international human rights law to found the claim.[48]

7. Conclusion

The increased awareness by companies of responsibilities that extend beyond the welfare of shareholders has no doubt resulted in many beneficial outcomes both for companies and the societies in which they operate. Such awareness cannot, however, be equated to respect for human rights. Whereas the former SRSG declared that the baseline responsibility of companies is to respect human rights, to date most State initiatives to implement the Protect, Respect, Remedy framework have been pursued under the rubric of CSR. The predominance of CSR discourse in the

[46] Ruggie, above n 1. According to the former SRSG, "The root cause of the business and human rights predicament today lies in the governance gaps created by globalization – between the scope and impact of economic forces and actors, and the capacity of societies to manage their adverse consequences. These governance gaps provide the permissive environment for wrongful acts by companies of all kinds without adequate sanctioning or reparation. How to narrow and ultimately bridge the gaps in relation to human rights is our fundamental challenge."

[47] See SRSG, *Recommendations on Follow-up to the Mandate*, 11 Feb 2011, p 4, available at http://www.business-humanrights.org/SpecialRepPortal/Home/UNactionfollowingendofmandate, last accessed 17 March 2012.

[48] This applies not only to those cases brought under the Alien Tort Claims Act in the United States, which allows claims for torts committed in violation of the law of nations or a treaty of the United States. In the UK litigation against Monterrico Metals, for example, the pleadings made reference to the UN Convention Against Torture or Other Cruel, Inhuman or Degrading Treatment or Punishment.

context of debates regarding business and human rights leads to the conflation of CSR and corporate responsibility for human rights. Yet, the content of CSR is too poorly established and the concept too firmly rooted in voluntarism for this to be an effective basis on which to protect human rights.

It has become fashionable to eschew the 'voluntarism vs regulation' debate when talking about corporate responsibility for human rights. Several commentators insist that a 'smart mix' of voluntary and regulatory approaches is already at hand to effectively urge companies to respect human rights.[49] This may seem compelling, but States relying on CSR as the sole or primary means within which to promote or "require" corporate responsibility for human rights, do not reflect this 'smart mix'. Definitions of CSR emphatically require they be voluntary. If CSR is voluntary, it is optional. If corporate responsibility for human rights is CSR, then it follows that respecting human rights is also optional. Yet, an optional approach to respecting human rights is at odds with the rights and duties of States that arise from international human rights law, including the right to remedy. An essential part of protecting rights should be to ensure that corporations respect those rights. If States leave respect for rights as a purely voluntary pursuit, rights holders are placed in a precarious and vulnerable position, contrary to the State duty to protect.

States ought to ensure that the content of initiatives designed to ensure companies respect human rights draw very clearly from international law and are not entrenched in voluntary notions. While CSR can no doubt result in positive social contributions, the protection of human rights requires legal foundations. In the absence of such legal protection, the capacity of victims of human rights abuses to defend their rights, including the right to remedy, is severely curtailed. A solid foundational legal and regulatory base must exist to underpin the circumstances in which companies operate. This should be clearly reflected in international law and implemented in national law, whether by statute, regulations or judicial decisions.

---

[49] John Ruggie proposed the need for a smart mix in both the draft and final Guiding Principles: Report of the Special Representative of the Secretary General on the issue of human rights and transnational corporations and other business enterprises, *Guiding Principles on Business and Human Rights: Implementing the United Nations "Protect, Respect and Remedy" Framework*, (2011), A/HRC/17/31, p8. This has been taken up enthusiastically by, for example, the Executive Director of the Institute for Human Rights and Business: see for example, International Business Leaders Forum, "Event Report: Countdown to 2011 – Business and Human Rights event series", (2011), available at http://www.iblf.org/en/~/link.aspx?_id=70B6A7B07E524F9287F7FBED3F6BA406&_z=z, last accessed 16 March 2012.

NATURAL RESOURCES MANAGEMENT: PROTECTING FISHERIES IN THE 21ST CENTURY

Malgosia Fitzmaurice

1. Introduction and the Global Regulation of Fisheries

The depressing state of world fisheries is well-known in the international community and acknowledged by marine biologists, lawyers and international organisations such as the Food and Agriculture Organisation ('FAO'). The subject of fisheries illustrates very starkly unresolved issues of growing economic inequalities between States; the conflicts between trade and environmental protection arising out of economic globalisation; and institutional responses (regulatory and in the form of settlement of disputes) to the rapid depletion of fish stocks. In the field of fisheries the conflict between developing and developed States (South and North) is less pronounced than in other areas of the global exploitation of natural resources. Similarly, the conflict between economic development and environmental protection, which (roughly speaking) divides the developed and developing world, is not so striking, as developed States in this particular area of natural resources management tend to pursue unsustainable policies to a greater extent than developing States, as will be shown in the part of this Chapter concerning illegal fishing and the role in this of the flag of convenience.

Marine fisheries face a major potential conflict between artisanal fisheries, which are coastal and inshore, and the commercial mechanised fleets exploiting the off shore resources.[1] The conflict is compounded, in the case of a developing country lacking resources to build its own commercial fleet, by selling the rights to a distant water fleet fishery (DTW) of another nation (frequently an industrial nation). However, often such decisions are not based on detailed knowledge of the sustainable quantities of fish to be taken, since this defines the economic scope for development. Many countries conclude fishing agreements with the DTWs of developed countries, either international (between States); on a company

[1] Ian Payne, "The Changing Role of Fisheries in Developments Policy", http://www.odi.org.uk/resources/docs/2837.pdf [accessed February 8, 2012].

to company basis or, and at the EU level. Conflicts with artisanal fisheries may arise directly out of competition for fish, but also may involve the price-reducing impact of fish landed locally by commercial boats.[2]

Figures and statistics are the best evidence of dwindling fish stocks. The world's marine catch increased more than fourfold in the period between 1950 and 1992, from 18.5 million tons to 80 1/2 million tons. Seven out of ten (67 percent) of the ocean's commercially targeted marine fish stocks are no longer within ecologically safe limits (they are either fully exploited, overexploited, depleted or slowly recovering from collapse). Commercial fishing is one of the worst biodiversity threats. Other species are victims of overfishing in the marine food web (marine mammals; sea birds; turtles, etc) There is also the danger of so-called by-catch, i.e. the threat to other than fish species of being killed by fishing gear. For various reasons, such as the catch quotas of the European Union, 27 million tonnes of fish are thrown back into the sea every year (about 25 percent). In the main they do not survive. This quantity of wasted fish represents more than half of all the sea fish caught annually for human consumption. There are more than three and a half million fishing vessels in the world competing with each other. Therefore the aggregate global fleet of over a million industrial and semi-industrial vessels operate at an annual loss of around fifty billion dollars a year, which was compensated for by Government subsidies at the expense of the taxpayer. Fish is a very important source of protein (e.g. in Asia over a billion people depend on fish and seafood as their major sources of protein). Worldwide around thirteen million people make their living from fishing. There are also little-known facts about fishing, such as that the nets of one of the world's biggest trawlers could encircle more than a dozen Boeing 747 (jumbo jet) aircraft. The nets' circumference measures 2,048 metres and they have a mouth opening of 22.900 square metres. Ships using such nets have a capture rate of about ten tonnes of fish per hour. Some super trawlers have the capacity to catch and process into various products up to 200 tonnes of fish a day. Eight percent of the world's catch is produced by just 20 fishing nations which land around 80 percent of the total marine catch world wide.[3] Molenaar summarised

[2] Id.

[3] China, Peru, Japan, Chile, the United States, the Russian Federation; Thailand, Indonesia, Republic of Korea, Norway, India, Iceland, the Philippines, Democratic Republic of Korea, Denmark, Spain, Taiwan, Canada, Mexico, Vietnam, all information from accessed March 10, 2011, http://archive.greenpeace.org/comms/cbio/global.html see also Accessed March 10, 2011, http://archive.greenpeace.org/comms/fish/amaze.html, accessed 2012, See also: BBC News: "World's Oceans in 'Shocking' Decline", accessed March 30 2011, http://www.bbc.co.uk/news/science-environment-13796479 The Special Panel convened by the

as follows the reasons for the present disastrous state of the fisheries: insufficiently broad management approaches; weak enforcement regimes; the lowest possible common denominator; decision-making procedures; and over capacity. [4]

This essay will discuss the following questions: the global regulation of fisheries; illegal, unreported and unregulated fishing; the blueprint for the future. Fish stocks are protected mainly through the marine conventions and soft-law instruments. However, the protection of fish can also be achieved through environmental law instruments and trade. In this section jurisdiction, enforcement, exchange of information and the underlying principles of global cooperation in fisheries will be discussed and global instruments regulating fisheries will be outlined. Within this context the global conventions and soft-law instruments will be discussed. They are as follows: the 1982 United National Law of the Sea Convention (UNCLOS);[5] the 1993 Agreement to Promote Compliance with International Conservation and Management Measures by Fishing Vessels on the High Seas (herein after the FAO Compliance Agreement);[6] the 1995 United Nations Agreement for the Implementation of the Provisions of the United Nations Convention on the Law of the Sea of 10 December 1982 Relating to the Conservation and Management of Straddling Fish Stocks and Highly Migratory Fish Stocks (hereinafter the Fish Stocks Agreement);[7] the 1995 FAO Code of Conduct for Responsible Fisheries (hereinafter the Code of Conduct);[8] and the 2008 United Nations General Assembly Fisheries Resolution.[9] Global environmental treaties such as the 1992

International Programme on the State of the Ocean (IPSO) issued a report which states that 'they warn that ocean life is "at high risk of entering a phase of extinction of marine species unprecedented in human history". They conclude that issues such as over-fishing, pollution and climate change are acting together in ways that have not previously been recognised'.

4 Erik-Jaap. Molenaar, "Addressing Regulatory gaps in High Seas Fisheries", *International Journal of Marine and Coastal Law* 20 (2005): 533.

5 Accessed March 30, 2011, http://www.un.org/Depts/los/convention_agreements/texts/unclos/unclos_e.pdf.

6 Accessed March 30, 2011, http://www.fao.org/Legal/treaties/012t-e.htm.

7 Accessed March 28, 2011, http://www.un.org/depts/los/convention_agreements/texts/fish_stocks_agreement/CONF164_37.htm (entered into force in 2001), Peter Örebechet al, "The 1995 United Nations Straddling and Highly Migratory Fish Stocks Agreement: Management, Enforcement and Dispute Settlement", *IJMCL* 13 (1998): 120.

8 Accessed March 28, 2011, ftp://ftp.fao.org/docrep/fao/005/v9878e/v9878e00.pdf.

9 Resolution adopted by the General Assembly, 63/112. Sustainable fisheries, including through the 1995.

Agreement for the Implementation of the Provisions of the United Nations Convention on the Law of the Sea of 10 December 1982 relating to the Conservation and Management of Straddling Fish Stocks and Highly Migratory Fish Stocks, and related instrument,

Convention on Biological Diversity (CBD)[10] and the 1979 Bonn Convention on Migratory Species of Wild Animals (CMS)[11] must be also mentioned. The 1973 Convention on Trade in Endangered Species of Wild Fauna and Flora (CITES)[12] protects fish stocks through certain trade restrictions. Also relevant are the World Trade Organisation (WTO) Agreements such as the 1994 General Agreement on Tariffs and Trade (GATT).[13] Decisions of the WTO dispute settlement bodies also contribute to the protection of the living resources of the sea.

The confines of this essay will not allow for extensive consideration of all these complex issues. However, most of the relevant questions will be discussed.[14]

2. The Law of the Sea and Fish Stocks Protection

2.1. *Underlying Principles*

It may be said that the main general principle underlying the exploitation of fish stocks is permanent sovereignty over natural resources (which is connected to the flag State jurisdiction on the high seas) in areas under the jurisdiction of the coastal State. As to the particular principles, mention must be made to the precautionary principle, which is the guiding principle of the FSA.

---

accessed March 30, 2011, http://daccess-dds-ny.un.org/doc/UNDOC/GEN/N08/477/45/PDF/N0847745.pdf?OpenElement. There are several GA Resolutions concerning fisheries. The one discussed is the last one and all-encompassing. However, mention must also made of UNGA Resolution 59/25 (2004) (adopted on 17 November 2005, text available at: accessed March 29, 2011, www.dfo-mpo.gc.ca/fgc-cgp/index_e.htm). This Resolution built on the previous Resolutions and UN meetings devoted to fisheries. It stresses the role of the regional fisheries organizations in the protection of fish stocks. It also adopted the precautionary approach. It suggested the interim prohibition on bottom trawling.

[10] United Nations Convention on Biological Diversity (1992), 31 *I.L.M.* 818 (in force 1993), 193 parties.

[11] Convention on the Conservation of Migratory Species of Wild Animals (1989) (in force 1983), 113 parties.

[12] Convention on International Trade in Endangered Species of Fauna and Flora (1973), in force 1975), 993 *UNTS* 242.175 parties.

[13] General Agreement on Tariffs and Trade, (1947 in WTO), accessed March 28, 2011 http://www.wto.org/english/docs_e/legal_e/gatt47_e.pdf.

[14] The most recent publication on these subjects engaged in in-depth discussion of this issue: Margaret A. Young, *Trading Fish, Saving Fish. Interaction Between Regimes in International Law* (Cambridge, Cambridge University Press 2011).

2.1.1. *The Principle of Permanent Sovereignty over Natural Resources*

The concept of sovereignty is a very complex question which has many elements. In this chapter the issue is permanent sovereignty over natural resources, i.e. in this case fish stocks.[15] These rights have to be distinguished according to the zones in which the fish stocks are found (the highs seas; the territorial sea; and the exclusive economic zone) and whether they are confined to one zone or are transboundary. The rights constituting sovereignty over natural resources comprise a nexus of rights to possess, to use and to manage. From these rights follows the right of a State to the exploration and exploitation of its natural resources and also the right to profits obtained from these resources.[16] As Blanco and Razzaque observe, permanent sovereignty over natural resources is not currently absolute, but limited by several legal and economic factors. These authors submit that these factors are: the principle that permanent sovereignty must be exercised for the benefit of national development as well as the wellbeing of people; that the State has a duty to compensate foreign investors whose property has been expropriated following legal proceedings; that the State has the duty to protect the interests of indigenous peoples; and lastly that the State has the duty to cooperate (by way of notification and consultation) as regards shared natural resources.[17]

Of particular importance for fisheries management is the limitation on absolute state sovereignty over natural resources by way of entering into agreements and consenting to abide by the rules of international institutions.[18] As will be discussed later in this Chapter, the changing global and regional management of fish stocks is due a multitude of international agreements, which, like the FSA, introduce revolutionary new regulations limiting absolute State sovereignty over natural resources (fish stocks). The same relates to the role of regional fisheries organisations, which by expanding regulatory power limit the sovereignty of States in this respect.

There are several limitations on State sovereignty in relation to shared resources deriving from customary international law and treaties, such as

---

15 On this issue see e.g. Nico Schrijver, *Permanent Sovereignty Over Natural Resources* (Cambridge: Cambridge University Press, 1987); Richard Barnes, *Property Rights and Natural Resources* (Oxford: Hart Publishing 2009), Elena Blanco and Jona Razzaque, *Globalisation and Natural Resources Law. Challenges, Key Issues and Perspectives* (Cheltenham: Edward Elgar Publisher, 2011).

16 Barnes n. 15, 228–230.

17 Blanco and Razzaque n. 15, 10.

18 Id. 10.

the prohibition on causing transboundary environmental damage, a rule of customary international law which has been enshrined in Principle 21 of the 1972 Stockholm Declaration on Human Environment and Principle 2 of the 1992 Rio Declaration on the Environment and Development. Cooperation between States regarding transboundary resources is very important in relation to fish stocks, which e.g. are found in different exclusive economic zones. UNLCOS has several provisions concerning such fishery resources.

2.1.2. *The Precautionary (Approach) Principle*

The precautionary approach (principle) deserves mention as one of the underlying principles of the conservation of fish stocks, as it was expressly introduced in the FSA, which is probably the most important global international instrument in achieving the sustainable use of fish stocks. It also features in some of the regional fisheries treaties.[19] It is widely known that the precautionary principle (approach) has attracted a very extensive body of literature and has been the subject of continuing discussion as to its legal nature, effectiveness and implementation.

This approach is listed as one of the general principles underlying the FSA in Article 5 (c) to be applied in order to achieve the sustainable management of fish stocks. It is defined in Article 6(2) and also contained in Annex II to the agreement. Article 6(1) states that the precautionary approach will be applied by States 'to [the] conservation, management and exploitation of straddling fish stocks and highly migratory fish stocks in order to protect the living marine resources and preserve the marine environment'. Article 6(2) defines this principle as follows: 'States shall be more cautious when information is uncertain, unreliable or inadequate. The absence of adequate scientific information shall not be used as a reason for postponing or failing to take conservation and management measures'. Some of the formulations contained in this definition are far from clear. These include the phrase 'more cautious', the scope of which is very vague.[20] Article 6 contains specific provisions relating to the implementation of the precautionary approach in Articles 6(3)(a)–(d) and (4)–(7). There are several requirements concerning the implementation of the

---

19 On this issue see e.g. Tore Henriksen, "The Precautionary Approach and Fisheries: A Nordic Perspective", in: *Implementation of the Precautionary Principle. Approaches from Nordic Countries, EU and USA*, ed. Nicolaas de Sadeleer, (London: Earthscan, 2007), 153–180.

20 Id. 157.

precautionary approach, such as the development of data collection (Article 6(3)(d)). According to Henriksen, the most important requirement for the implementation of the precautionary approach under the FSA is the obligation to adopt and use reference points for each harvested fish stock (Article 6(3)(b) and (4)).[21] The 'reference point' is the value derived through scientific analysis expressed, *inter alia,* in terms of mortality rates or biomass of the spawning part of a stock (Annex I, para.1). Since the task of reference points is to direct the management of fish stocks by maintaining a stock above a certain level of biomass, the reference points serve as quantitative conservation and management objectives. The FSA introduced a new element to the reference points: the binding effect of reference points is more pronounced and the reference points are identified as a tool in implementing the precautionary approach.[22]

Some of the regional organisations, e.g. Commission for the Conservation of Antarctic Marine Living Resources(CCAMLR), also apply such an approach. In order to achieve precautionary approach, data are collected, and the Commission attempts to weigh up and balance the uncertainties associated with such data in a manner consistent with the Convention's objectives.

Management decisions are adopted taking into account such uncertainties in order to minimise the risk of long-term adverse effects on the resources concerned rather than avoiding making decisions until all necessary data are available. A 'precautionary' approach has been implemented to minimise the risks associated with unsustainable practices where there is uncertainty.[23]

---

21 *Id.* 159.

22 *Id.* 159.

23 Accessed February 8, 2012, http://www.ccamlr.org/Pu/e/sc/prec-app-intro.htm and http://www.ccamlr.org/pu/e/gen-intro.htm, R.P Hewitt, R.P. et al., " Setting a Precautionary Catch Limit for Antarctic Krill", *Oceanography,* 15 (2002); ed. Karl-Hermann Kock, "Understanding CCAMLR's Approach to Management", 2000, accessed February 9, 2012, the Executive Summary: "The objectives of the Convention, as laid down in its Article II, were translated into scientific meaningful working hypotheses as a first step. The precautionary approach to management was found to be most appropriate to guide all CCAMLR activities towards the regulation of exploitable resources given the considerable uncertainty associated with data collected in vast and largely unknown regions, and the complexity of the underlying marine systems. In addition to the core problem of developing multispecies exploitation strategies for the marine resources, CCAMLR is currently faced with three other problems: the incidental mortality of seabirds in fisheries, particularly long line fisheries; the entanglement of animals in marine debris; and the impact of fishing on the seabed". May 2000.

2.2. *The Nature of Control and Jurisdiction of States in the Context of General Agreements, Regulatory Techniques and Fisheries Management*

2.2.1. *The 1982 United Nations Law of the Sea Convention*

The regime of fisheries under the Law of the Sea Convention has been the subject of many publications. Therefore in this essay an outline of its most important provisions will be presented.[24] The Law of the Sea Convention has a complex set of provisions regulating fisheries both on the high seas and in the Exclusive Fisheries Zones (extending to 200 nautical miles from baselines measuring territorial seas), where 90 percent of fish stocks are located. The nature and control of the jurisdiction of States depends on the zone in which the fish stock in question is found. In their EEZs coastal States determine allowable catches and promote optimal resource use. Article 61 uses the term maximum sustainable yield and Article 62 optimum utilization. It is argued that the Law of the Sea Convention's use of terms is intentionally ambiguous in an attempt to make the LOS Convention more acceptable and open to broad interpretation.[25] However, the ambiguity of terms is a contributory factor to the lack of uniform principles of exploitation and conservation of marine living resources worldwide. Part V of the Law of the Sea Convention regulates fishing in the EEZs. The Convention takes a holistic view on the conservation of species, and its regulation therein is based on their interdependence.[26] There is a host of provisions regulating the following issues: conservation (Article 61), exploitation (Article 62), transboundary and straddling stocks (Article 63); highly migratory stocks (Article 64); marine mammals (Article 65); anadromous stocks (Article 66); catadromous stocks (Article 67); sedentary species (Article 68 and the continental shelf regime (Article 77(4)). Living resources on the high seas are regulated in Articles 116–120 and marine habitat protectionis provided by Articles 192–196. With the exception of Article 65, the Convention exhibits a preference for optimal exploitation of resources. As noted, the relevant provisions of the Convention are rather vague in setting the standards of exploitation of natural resources.[27]

---

[24] See, e.g. David Freestone and Zen Makuch, "The New International Environmental Law of Fisheries: the 1995 United Nations Straddling Stocks Agreement", *Yearbook of International Environmental Law* 1 (1996): 3–51; Peter Davis and Catherine Redgwell, "The International Legal Regulation of Straddling Fish Stocks", 68 *British Yearbook of International Law* (1997): 199–273.

[25] *Id.* 2.

[26] E.H. Buck, "U.N. Convention on the Law of the Sea: Living Resources Provisions", accessed 30 March 2011, http://www.fas.org/sgp/crs/row/RL32185.pdf.

As regards jurisdiction over straddling, transboundary and highly migratory fish, they are to be managed cooperatively through bilateral or multilateral international agreements between coastal States through whose waters these fish stocks range, as well as any States which fish these stocks on the high seas. If a coastal State is unable to harvest its entire allowable catch, it has the obligation to grant an access to its resources to other nations, subject to appropriate terms and conditions. The Convention provides special rights of access to surpluses of living marine resources within coastal nation EEZs for nearby developing nations that are landlocked or geographically disadvantaged. Regional, subregional or bilateral agreements are negotiated to indicate the provision of an equitable allocation to any such disadvantaged nation. It is the right of the coastal State to determine whether any harvestable surplus exists within its EEZ. Articles 65 (EEZ) and 120 (the high seas) regulate the protection of marine mammals, which calls for international cooperation through 'appropriate international organizations' (by which is understood the International Whaling Commission). Anadromous species spend most of their lives in the ocean, but spawn in freshwater. The primary interest in and responsibility for anadromous fish stocks is given to the States in whose rivers the stocks originate. Fishing for anadromous stocks is prohibited on the high seas, except in cases where economic dislocation might result. Coastal States through whose waters anadromous fish migrate are required to cooperate with the nations in whose territory the anadromous stocks originated. Catadromous species spend most of their lives in freshwater, but enter the ocean to spawn. The coastal States where these species spend most of their lives have for managing them. International cooperation is required where these species migrate through more than one EEZ. Sedentary species on the continental shelf are not defined, and this leads to many international disputes.

[27] As Buck observes: 'Articles 61(2) and 61(3) do provide a mandatory obligation to ensure that living resources are not endangered by over-exploitation and that threatened species are restored to levels which can produce their maximum sustainable yield. In addition, the phrase "as qualified by relevant environmental and economic factors," appearing in Article 61(3), provides a basis for harvesting at rates both above or below the maximum sustainable yield. However, the subsequent examples of how this qualification is to be interpreted focus on ways to protect against overharvesting or other possible justifications for exceeding the maximum sustainable yield, rather than providing any explicit acknowledgment that valid reasons may exist for refraining altogether from harvesting to achieve non-consumptive goals (e.g., tourism in reef environments or biodiversity conservation) or to respond to moral/ethical concerns (e.g., beliefs that large sharks, dolphins, and whales should not be killed)/, id. 3.

2.2.2. *The Fish Stocks Agreement (FSA)*

The Fish Stocks Agreement (FSA) was finalised and signed in the same year as the Estai incident (see below) took place, highlighting the problems regarding straddling fish stocks. As was noted above, straddling fish stocks are regulated by Article 63 of UNCLOS, which imposes an obligation of cooperation on coastal States and States fishing on the high seas. However, as was noted, the formulation of this Article lacked precision. Therefore the aim of the FSA was to complement the Convention in this respect (and concerning highly migratory species).[28] Article 4 states that 'nothing in this Agreement shall prejudice the rights, jurisdiction and duties of States under the Convention. This Agreement shall be interpreted and applied in the context of and in a manner consistent with the Convention.' The jurisdictional issues under the FSA Agreement are very complex, as they deal with all types of jurisdiction over fisheries: flag State jurisdiction; coastal State jurisdiction and port State jurisdiction.

The FSA is a framework treaty. The implementation of the Convention is entrusted to regional fisheries management organisations at regional (and sub-regional) fisheries management fisheries organisations (RFMOs) which are pivotal to the FSA. It is also said that the FSA favours the interests of coastal States over those of high seas fishing States.[29] According to Article 7(1)(a) States engaged in the harvesting of straddling and highly migratory fish stocks are under a duty to cooperate, through the relevant RFMOs. However, even if a State is not a party to the FSA, nevertheless, it has the obligation to apply conservation measures prescribed by RFMOs (Article 8(3)). The FSA imposes an obligation on States to co-operate in the RFMO, and when such an organisation does not exist States must enter into appropriate agreements for the conservation and management of fish stocks (Article 8(5)). According to Article 8(3) of the FSA, only States with a 'real interest' may become members of the RFMO. The 'real interest' was not defined by the FSA (more on that below). It is up to each and every RFMO to define the 'real interest'. According to Article (3) and (4) only States which are members of an RFMO and States which accept the conservation and management measures prescribed by RFMOs can participate in the harvesting of fish stocks in a particular area. Article 11 states that new entrants must be offered a fair portion of the total allowable catch (TAC) available under the RMFO, a rule which frequently causes

[28] P Örebech et al, n. 7, (1998): 120.
[29] Id. 121.

problems (see below). The FSA contains several provisions which go beyond the principle of *pacta tertiis nec nocent nec prosunt* in the law of treaties, as they create obligations for third States (outside the treaty regime). Article 17(3) requires that States that are members of the RFMO request non-members to comply with conservation and management measures adopted by the RFMO (such co-operation will result in benefits for non-member States). Article 33(1) obliges the Parties to encourage non-parties to become parties. Articles 17(4) and 33(2) allow the Parties to adopt measures in accordance with international law to deter non-parties from undermining the effectiveness of the FSA and/or management measures under the RFMO. Article 17(2) obliges States not in compliance with RFMO directives not to authorise vessels to engage in the fishing of stocks subject to the competence of such organisation. Article 6 of the FSA introduces the precautionary principle to stocks regulated by it. Since Article 7 is based on the compatibility principle, all stocks (in the coastal areas and on high seas) must be under the same regime; this principle is also to be adopted in EEZs. Compatible measures are to ensure the 'conservation and management of the straddling fish stocks and highly migratory fish stocks in [their] entirety' (Article 7(2)). The FSA leaves it to the member States of RFMOs to establish the way in which compatibility is to be achieved. There are two kinds of approaches: the top-down and the bottom-up. The first is based on the primacy of an organisation which directs a State on the compatibility measures; the second is based on the premise that this is a State which bestows the rights to the regional organisation for such compliance. It appears that FSA in some of its provisions supports the bottom-up approach, as Article 7(1) stresses the coastal States' exclusive sovereign rights within the areas under national jurisdiction and indicates the autonomous status of national EEZ management to which high seas RFMOs' decisions relate. However, ultimately it is up to each and every RFMOs to devise its own system.[30] The FSA adheres to flag State jurisdiction, which is a norm of customary international law. The only departure from general norms in this respect is the widening of the scope of States' obligations regarding their vessels. The responsibilities of States involve the flag State; the coastal State and the port State. Articles 18 and 19 deal with obligations of the flag State. According to Article 128(1) the flag State 'shall take such measures as may be necessary to ensure that vessels flying its flag comply with subregional and regional conservation and management measures'. Article 18(2) requires a flag State to ensure

30 Id. 128.

that high sea fishermen have a licence, authorisation or permit from such a State to engage in high seas fishing. The flag State can only authorise or issue a permit to fishing vessels flying its flag where it is able effectively to discharge its responsibilities with respect to such vessels under UNCLOS and the FSA (Article 8(2)).[31] The most innovative and controversial provisions are contained in Articles 21 and 22 of the FSA. Article 18 (3)(g)(i) states that when a State becomes a party to the FSA it consents to implement sub-regional and regional schemes for co-operation in enforcement according to Articles 21 and 22, including permitting duly authorised inspectors from other States to board its ships (the concept of 'inspecting State'). Articles 21 and 22 spell out the conditions for such an inspection.[32] Article 21(5) and (6) provides that the inspecting State shall notify the flag State immediately and the flag State shall either take enforcement action or authorise further investigation by the inspecting State. According to Article 21(8), if a flag State neglects to respond to a notification or to take action on the notification and the ship is deemed to have committed a serious violation, the inspecting State may force the ship to port for further investigation. The flag State has three working days in which to respond (Article 21(6)). Article 21(11) defines as 'serious violation' fishing without a permit, in a closed sea and failure to keep fishing records. Article 23 deals with port control. Article 23(4) lists the rights enjoyed by the port State. It has complete jurisdiction over fishing vessels visiting its ports relating to its technical conditions and handling operations, as well as controlling shipments and transhipments (Article 23(3)). According to Article 23(1) the port State has to adopt 'measures to promote the effectiveness of subregional, regional and global conservation and management measures'. The FSA has a complex procedure for the settlement of disputes, which draws on that in UNCLOS but with certain deviations it.[33]

---

[31] See also Article 18(3), which gives examples of the measures that the flag State is requires to take (a duty to prohibit fishing in areas of the high seas falling under the SFA without a licence or authorisation; the right of interested States to have access to information on national records on ship fishing [what is this that just 'fishing' isn't?] on the high seas *etc*.

[32] Inspectors have to be duly authorised (Articles 21(1) and 22(1)(a)); the procedures have been accepted through the RFMO and are published (Articles 21(2) and 12(3)); inspecting States have informed of the form of identification of the inspectors [Eh?] (Article 21(4)); and the inspecting State makes the inspection known to the flag State (Article 22(1)(b)).

[33] See in detail Örebech, n.7: 133–140.

The FSA is not a global treaty in the way UNCLOS is. There are several reasons for this.[34] Molenaar gives the following reasons for this state of affairs: objections to substantive aspects, i.e. the relationship between UNCLOS and the FSA (Article 4); the compatibility requirement (Article 7) and the Articles on the powers of inspecting States (12 and 22); Article 23 on port State measures; Article 1(3) on fishing entities 3. ('this Agreement applies *mutatis mutandis* to other fishing entities whose vessels fish on the high seas'). The other reasons are: a lack of capacity or resources; certain misconceptions as to aspects of the FSA, such as its spatial scope; basic objectives; its role in the wider framework of international fisheries and the law of the sea; and its relationship with RFMOs; and lack of direct interest (e.g. States not engaged in fishing on the high seas; coastal States whose zones do not overlap with the fishstocksin question (highly migratory and straddling); the cost benefit analysis leading to the conclusion that non-participation trumps participation).

The freedom of fishing on the high seas is maintained but limited by other treaty obligations; the rights, duties, and interests of coastal nations and is based on the obligation to cooperate in conserving and managing the living resources of the high seas. Compulsory dispute settlement is provided should conflict arise. According to classical international law, on the high seas the flag State is responsible for breaches of international law by a ship under its jurisdiction. This rule is also applicable to breaches in the subject of fishing. It may be added that such a rule is limited by international treaties in certain regulatory areas (see further below). Finally, according to Article 297(3)(b) domestic EEZ fisheries matters cannot be subject to compulsory dispute settlement proceedings.[35]

---

[34] See an incisive article by Erik-JappMolenaar, "Non-Participation in the Fish Stock Agreements. Status and Reasons", *InternationalJournal of Marine and Coastal Law* 26 (2011): 195–211.

[35] The Agreement applies in general to all fishing vessels that are used or intended for fishing on the high seas (Article II(1)). Exemption can be made for vessels of less than 24 metres in length (except that the general obligation in Article III(1) still applies) (Article II(2)). The Agreement is open to acceptance by any Member or Associate Member of the FAO, and by any non-member State that is a member of the United Nations, or of any of the specialized agencies of the United Nations or of the International Atomic Energy Agency. Procedures are specified for a regional economic integration organization Article 297(3)(b) provides that disputes can be submitted to conciliation when (1) a coastal nation has failed properly to conserve and manage EEZ living resources such that they become seriously endangered; (2) a coastal nation has arbitrarily refused to determine allowable catches and the capacity to harvest species desired by a foreign nation; or (3) a coastal nation has arbitrarily refused to allocate a declared surplus in a living resource to any foreign nation. However, Article 297(3)(c) prohibits a conciliation commission from substituting its

2.2.3. *FAO Compliance Agreement*[36]

The Agreement's main purpose is to define the obligations (jurisdiction) of flag States. This is effected by authorizing fishing vessels to fish on the high seas, and establishing a system of information exchange on high seas fishing activities designed to improve compliance by high seas fishing vessels and to limit the freedom of vessels that have a bad compliance record to 'shop around' for new flags.[37] The general obligation on flag States under the Agreement is to take such measures as may be necessary to ensure that vessels flying their flag do not engage in any activity that undermines the effectiveness of international conservation and management measures (Article III(1)). In order to achieve it States have three fundamental obligations concerning authorization. First, according to Article III(2) the Agreement requires that a vessel should not be allowed to fish on the high seas unless it has been authorized to do so in accordance with appropriate authorization procedures established by the flag State. Secondly, according to Article III(3), a flag State is not to authorize a vessel to fish on the high seas unless it is able, taking into account the links that exist between it and the fishing vessel, effectively to exercise its responsibilities under the Agreement. Thirdly, the Agreement specifically discourages States from reflagging. To this effect States are not to authorize a fishing vessel to fish on the high seas where it is known to have engaged in activities that have undermined the effectiveness of international conservation and management measures while registered in another State (whether or not that State is a Party to the Compliance Agreement).[38] According to Article

discretion for that of the coastal nation. Article 7(2) of Annex V states that a conciliation commission's report, including its conclusions and recommendations, is not binding (which is in line with *general international law*).

[36] On this subject see: C. Hedley. "*FAO Compliance Agreement' in* International Fisheries Agreements" Vol. 1, section 1.3. (London: Ocean Law Publishing, 2008); D. Balton, "The Compliance Agreement" in *Developments in International Fisheries Law*, ed. Ellen Hey (The Hague, Dordrecht: Kluwer, 1999); Patricia Birnie, "New Approaches to Ensuring Compliance at Sea: The FAO Agreement to Promote Compliance with International Conservation and Management Measures by Fishing Vessels on the High Seas", *Review of European Community and International Environmental Law* 8 (2002)48; G. Moore, "The Food and Agriculture Organization of the United Nations Compliance Agreement". *International Journal of Marine and Coastal Law* 9 (1994)412; R. Grainger, "High Seas Fishing Vessel Database", in eds. M.H. Nordquist and J.N. Moore, *Current Fisheries Issues and the Food and Agriculture Organization of the United Nations* (The Hague: Kluwer, 2000); G. Moore, "The FAO Compliance Agreement" in *Current Fisheries Issues and the Food and Agriculture Organization of the United Nations.*

[37] Hedley, n. 36.

[38] The exceptions are: (i) any period of suspension by the other State of an authorisation for such fishing vessel to be used for fishing on the high seas has expired; or (ii) no

III(8) Flag State Parties are obliged to take enforcement measures in respect of vessels which act in contravention of the Agreement, including, where appropriate, the imposition of sanctions, such as refusal, suspension or withdrawal of an authorization to fish. Such sanctions must be 'of sufficient gravity' to be effective in securing compliance with the requirements of the Agreement and to deprive offenders of the benefits accruing from their illegal activities.[39] Article VII concerns the situation of developing States. The Agreement stipulates that Parties must cooperate, at a global, regional, subregional or bilateral level, and, as appropriate, with the support of the FAO and other international or regional organizations, to provide assistance, including technical assistance, to Parties that are developing countries in order to assist them in fulfilling their obligations under the Agreement. According to Article IX(1), disputes are to be settled in the first place by consultations, with a view to reaching a satisfactory solution as soon as possible. If an agreement cannot be reached, the Agreement recommends further consultation. Recourse to another means of dispute settlement is based on the consent of all parties to the dispute (Article IX(2) and (3)).

2.2.4. *Various Types of Fisheries Regulatory Techniques and Fisheries Management*

a. *The 1995 FAO Code of Conduct for Responsible Fisheries*[40]

This Code is voluntary. Its provisions on principles and standards applicable to the conservation, management and development of all fisheries are of fundamental importance.

Certain parts of it are based on relevant rules of international law, including those reflected in UNCLOS. The Code also contains provisions that may be or have already been given binding effect by means of other

---

authorisation for such fishing vessel to be used for fishing on the high seas has been withdrawn by the other State within the last three years (Article III(5)(a) and (b)). Exceptions are allowed for the legitimate change of a vessel's ownership and – more generally – if the flag State determines, after having taken into account all relevant facts, that to grant an authorisation to use the vessel for fishing on the high seas would not in any case undermine the object and purpose of the Agreement (Article III(5)(c) and (d)).

39 Hedely, n. 17.

40 See also "Evaluations of Compliance with the FAO (UN) Code of Conduct for Responsible Fisheries", Fisheries Centre Research Reports 14(2) published by The Fisheries Centre, University of British Columbia, Canada, (2006), eds. T.J. Pitcher, D. Kalikoski, G. Pramod, accessed March 30, 2011 http://www.illegal-fishing.info/uploads/Univ-BC-FAO-compliance-report-06.pdf.

See commentary FAO Code of Conduct for Responsible Fisheries Rome, FAO. 1995. Accessed March 28, 2011 ftp://ftp.fao.org/docrep/fao/005/v9878e/v9878e00.pdf.

obligatory legal instruments among the Parties, such as the Agreement to Promote Compliance with International Conservation and Management Measures by Fishing Vessels on the High Seas, 1993, which forms an integral part of the Code (Article 1(1)). The Code is global in scope, and is directed toward members and non-members of the FAO; fishing entities; subregional, regional and global organizations, whether governmental or non-governmental; and all those concerned with the conservation of fishery resources and management and development of fisheries, such as fishermen, those engaged in the processing and marketing of fish and fishery products and other users of the aquatic environment in relation to fisheries (Article 1(2)).

It also covers all processes relating to fisheries (such as capture, processing of and trade in fish and fishery products, fishing operations, aquaculture, fisheries research and the integration of fisheries into coastal area management (Article 2(2))). The objectives of the Code are as follows: (a) to establish principles, in accordance with the relevant rules of international law, for responsible fishing and fisheries activities taking into account all their relevant biological, technological, economic, social, environmental and commercial aspects; (b) to establish principles and criteria for the elaboration and implementation of national policies for the responsible conservation of fisheries resources and fisheries management and development; (c) to serve as an instrument of reference to help States to establish or to improve the legal and institutional framework required for the exercise of responsible fisheries and in the formulation and implementation of appropriate measures; (d) to provide guidance which may be used where appropriate in the formulation and implementation of international agreements and other legal instruments, both binding and voluntary; (e) to facilitate and promote technical, financial and other cooperation in the conservation of fisheries resources and fisheries management and development; (f) to promote the contribution of fisheries to food security and food quality, giving priority to the nutritional needs of local communities; (g) to promote the protection of living aquatic resources and their environments and coastal areas; (h) to promote the trade in fish and fishery products in conformity with relevant international rules and to avoid the use of measures that constitute hidden barriers to such; (i) to promote research on fisheries as well as on associated ecosystems and relevant environmental factors; and (j) to provide standards of conduct for all those involved in the fisheries sector (Article 2). The Code introduced the obligation of co-operating between all entities engaged in fishing (Article 4(1)). The FAO fulfils the monitoring role through its Committee on Fisheries (Article 4(2)). States and international organizations, whether governmental or non-governmental, should promote the understanding of the Code among those involved in fisheries (including, where practical, by the introduction of schemes which would promote voluntary acceptance of the Code and its effective application (Article 4(4))). Full recognition should be given to the special circumstances and requirements of developing countries (including in particular the least-developed among them, and small island developing countries). States, relevant intergovernmental and non-governmental organizations and financial institutions should work for the adoption of measures to address the needs of developing countries, especially in the areas of financial and technical assistance, technology transfer, training and scientific cooperation, and in enhancing their ability to develop their own fisheries as well as to participate in high seas fisheries, including access to such fisheries (Article 5(5)). The Code provides for several general principles of responsible fisheries regarding their conservation and management, based on the precautionary approach (Article 6(5)). The conservation and management of fish stocks are based on the ecosystem approach (Article 6(1)).

According to Article 6(2), '[f]isheries management should promote the maintenance of the quality, diversity and availability of fishery resources in sufficient quantities for present and future generations in the context of food security, poverty alleviation and sustainable development. Management measures should not only ensure the conservation of target species but also of species belonging to the same ecosystem or associated with or dependent upon the target species'. The Code also stresses co-operation through relevant RFMOs. The Code defines the duties of all States engaged in fishing operations which are based on co-operation and exchange of information (Article 8(1) (1.10)); the duties of the flag State (Article 8(2)–(10), which are formulated like those of the FSA and emphasise the obligation to keep records and the enforcement of conservation measures; and port State duties (Articles 8(3) to 3(3.2)).

b. *The 2008 United Nations General Assembly Fisheries Resolution*

The Resolution is an all-encompassing instrument which deals with all possible aspects of fisheries, including their management. It call on States to enhance their co-operation through RFMOs; it urges the wider implementation of FSA and other FAO instruments; it deals with the special position of developing States and their capacity building; it calls for the elimination of IUU (see below).

The Resolution reaffirmed 'the importance it attaches to the long-term conservation, management and sustainable use of the marine living resources of the world's oceans and seas and the obligations of States to cooperate to this end, in accordance with international law…' (section I(1)) and referred to the relevant provisions of the Convention, in particular the provisions on cooperation set out in Parts V and VII, section 2, of the Convention and, where applicable, the Agreement. It also urged States, either directly or through global organizations (sub-regional, regional and global) or arrangements, to intensify their efforts to assess and address, as appropriate, the impacts of global climate change on the sustainability of fish stocks and the habitats that support them (section I(3)). It called on States to act in accordance with the Compliance Agreement and FSA (section I(4)), and relied in all aspects of fisheries operations on the precautionary and the eco-system approaches (e.g. section I (6, 7, 9)).

2.3. *The Exchange of Information*

One of the most important elements of rational fisheries management is the exchange of information Articles IV-VI constitute a second pillar of the Agreement, i.e. the exchange and free flow of information (the first being the management of global fisheries).[41] According to Article flag States are to make the information detailed in their vessel records available to the FAO and, in turn, the FAO is to make this information available to other contracting States and to fisheries management organizations (Article VI(4)). According to Article VI(8)(a), flag States are also obliged to inform the FAO promptly concerning violations by their fishing vessels, including giving information on action taken against those vessels that undermine the effectiveness of international conservation and management measures. According to Article VI(8)(b), other States may also draw a flag State's attention to violations by its vessels and may also provide a report to the FAO, which can then circulate this information to other contracting States, provided that the flag State concerned has an opportunity to comment on the allegations. The FAO developed the High Seas Vessel

[41] First, States Parties are required to exchange information on fishing vessels' activities, in order to help identify fishing vessels flying their flags that are reported to have engaged in activities undermining international conservation and management measures (Article V(1)). Second, where a (non-flag State) Party has reasonable grounds for believing that a fishing vessel voluntarily in its port has been used for an activity that undermines the effectiveness of international conservation and management measures, that party is required to notify the relevant flag State accordingly (Article V(2)). Third, the Agreement

Authorization Record (HSVAR), an online database, which proved to be not a very successful operation, partly because the very few relevant States had developed comprehensive national records.

2.4. *Enforcement and Compliance*

As regards the enforcement of the laws concerning the exploitation of natural resources the global instruments appear to follow the traditional law of the sea.

2.4.1. *The 1982 Law of the Sea Convention*

The above – described Articles referred to jurisdiction regarding natural resources on the high seas and in coastal waters (the Exclusive Economic Zone). According to the classical law of the sea the main responsibility for enforcement on the high seas rests with the flag State. However, different rules are applicable in the EEZs. According to Article 62(4) of UNCLOS the coastal State has the right to enforce its rights and regulations, which have a broad scope.[42] It may also be noted that as regards fish stocks which are of a shared or migratory nature, UNCLOS obliges States to cooperate in their conservation though regional fisheries organisations. The legal regime of RFMOs provides for flag State jurisdiction to enforce violations of the relevant regulations.

2.4.2. *The 1995 FSA*

Under this Agreement the flag State has the duty to investigate all alleged violations of a RFMO's conservation and management measures without delay and to take all necessary measures and, if sufficient evidence is available, to take legal action. Article 19(1) imposes on the flag State a duty to adopt all necessary steps to ensure compliance with all measures and

---

urges States, when and as appropriate, to enter into cooperative agreements or arrangements of mutual assistance on a global, regional, subregional or bilateral basis (Article V(3)). Fourth, the Agreement provides for the FAO to have a central role in receiving, organizing and distributing information.

[42] They concern, *inter alia,* "licensing of fishermen, fishing vessels and equipment, including payment of fees and other forms of remuneration, which, in the case of developing coastal States, may consist of adequate compensation in the field of financing, equipment and technology relating to the fishing industry; determining the species which may be caught, and fixing quotas of catch, whether in relation to particular stocks or groups of stocks or catch per vessel over a period of time or to the catch by nationals of any State during a specified period; regulating seasons and areas of fishing, the types, sizes and

enforce them, notwithstanding the place of the occurrence of the violation.

2.4.3. *Special Case of the Enforcement of and Compliance with Fisheries Law: Fish Piracy; Illegal, Unreported and Unregulated Fishing ('IUU'), the Control of States over Companies*

One of the greatest threats to fish stocks is so-called illegal, unreported and unregulated fishing,[43] which is closely related to the questions of enforcement and compliance.

It may be said, as the practice of the International Tribunal for the Law of the Sea indicates, there are so many cases which are related to this questions (also connected to the flag of convenience issues: see this chapter, further below).

This is a very widespread practice, which has resulted in the adoption by the FAO of the International Plan of Action to Deter, Prevent and Eliminate Illegal, Unreported and Unregulated Fishing (IPOA-IUU),[44] which is a non-binding document forming part of the FAO's fisheries policy, contained in the Code of Conduct for Responsible Fisheries. This organisation explains that IUU means the breaching of several rules, such as fishing without a permit; non-observance of fishing seasons; fishing for prohibited species; using illegal fishing gear; exceeding the allowable

---

amount of gear, and the types, sizes and number of fishing vessels that may be used; fixing the age and size of fish and other species that may be caught; specifying information required of fishing vessels, including catch and effort statistics and vessel position reports; requiring, under the authorization and control of the coastal State, the conduct of specified fisheries research programmes and regulating the conduct of such research, including the sampling of catches, disposition of samples and reporting of associated scientific data; the placing of observers or trainees on board such vessels by the coastal State; the landing of all or any part of the catch by such vessels in the ports of the coastal State; terms and conditions relating to joint ventures or other co-operative arrangements; requirements for the training of personnel and the transfer of fisheries technology, including enhancement of the coastal State's capability of undertaking fisheries research; enforcement procedures".

43 See K.W. Riddle, "Illegal, Unreported and Unregulated Fishing: is International Cooperation Contagious?", *Ocean Development and International Law* 37 (2006) 265; E. Hey, "Global Fisheries Regulation in the First Half of the 1990s," *International Journal of Maritime and Coastal Law* 17 (1997) 459; E. Franckx and C van Assche, "Contemporary High Seas Fisheries Law" in: *Contemporary Regulation of Marine Living Resources and Pollution. Essays Written by and in Honour of the International Francqui Chair Holder, Professor Dermontt Devine*, eds. E. Franckx et al. (Antwerp-Apeldoorn: Maklu Publishers, 2007) 29–69; in the same book see also Dermont Devine, "International Regulation of Marine Living resources and Pollution: Contemporary Issues", in *Contemporary Regulation...* 3.

44 IPOA-IUU adopted in June 2001 at the 120th Session of the FAO Council. Accessed March 30, 2011, www.fao.org/DOCREP/003/y1224e/y1224e00.htm. The following definitions are given in this document: "[*i*]*llegal fishing* refers to activities: conducted by national or

quota; lack of proper reporting. According to the FAO IUU fishing amounts to 30 percent of all catches.[45] It may also be mentioned that IUU is not confined only to the high seas but also exist in the exclusive economic zones (the EEZs). The annual value of IUU fishing on the high seas could be estimated at around one billion two hundred thousand US dollars.[46]

Riddle offered a very useful explanation of the core provisions of the IPOA-IUU. This author identified five all-encompassing themes: national legislation and plans of action; cooperation among States; coastal State measures; port State measures; and internationally agreed market-related measures. Riddle provided a table in which he listed all measures which were contained in over 75 recommendations to be adopted by States to eliminate IUU. All States should become parties to all relevant international fisheries instruments, including UNCLOS, the Fish Stocks Agreement (see above) and follow the FAO Code of Conduct for Responsible Fisheries. National legislation should address all elements of IUU fishing, including, *inter alia,* measures ensuring that nationals do not support IUU and measures to be taken against vessels without nationality engaged in

---

foreign vessels in waters under the jurisdiction of a State, without the permission of that State, or in contravention of its laws and regulations; conducted by vessels flying the flag of States that are parties to a relevant regional fisheries management organization but operate in contravention of the conservation and management measures adopted by that organization and by which the States are bound, or relevant provisions of the applicable international law; or in violation of national laws or international obligations, including those undertaken by cooperating States to a relevant regional fisheries management organization'; *Unreported fishing* is 'which have not been reported, or have been misreported, to the relevant national authority, in contravention of national laws and regulations; or undertaken in the area of competence of a relevant regional fisheries management organization which have not been reported or have been misreported, in contravention of the reporting procedures of that organization"]; *Unregulated fishing* is "in the area of application of a relevant regional fisheries management organization…conducted by vessels without nationality, or by those flying the flag of a State not party to that organization, or by a fishing entity, in a manner that is not consistent with or contravenes the conservation and management measures of that organization; or in areas or for fish stocks in relation to which there are no applicable conservation or management measures and where such fishing activities are conducted in a manner inconsistent with State responsibilities for the conservation of living marine resources under international law". Article 3.1–3.3.

45 "Excess Capacity and Illegal Fishing: Challenges to Sustainable Fisheries" (FAO, Rome, 2004), Accessed March 29, 2011, www.fao.org/newsroom/en/focus/2004/47127/undex.htm.

46 Mathew Gianni and Walt Simpson, "The Changing Nature of High Seas Fishing: how Flags of Convenience Provide Cover for Illegal, Unreported and Unregulated Fishing", Australian Department of Agriculture, Fisheries and Forestry, International Transport Workers' Federation, and WWF International (2005), Accessed March 27 2011, http://www.wwf.org.uk/filelibrary/pdf/flagsofconvenience.pdf.

IUU fishing on the high seas. IPOA-IUU recommendations also include sanctions against IUU vessels; and the prohibition of economic incentives for entities (private and public) engaged in IUU. States should also develop plans of actions to achieve the objectives of IPOA-IUU and establish effective monitoring, control and surveillance. The FAO also recommended cooperation between States within the framework of the regional fishery management organisations (RFMO). Recommendations also list the flag State's responsibilities regarding fishing vessel registration (most importantly to avoid registering vessels with a record of IUU). States should take all steps necessary to prevent IUU caught fish from being traded into their territories and to ensure transparency (internationally agreed market-related-measures).[47]

Mention must also be made of the 2005 FAO Model Scheme on Port State Measures to Combat Illegal, Unreported and Unregulated Fishing (hereinafter the Port State Model Scheme).[48] It is a soft-law document setting out minimum port State measures to be applied by responsible port States and RFMOs individually or through the adoption of regional MOUs.[49] According to the Model Scheme, port States should refuse the landing, transhipping or processing of fish caught byvessels flagged to a non-party of an RFMO, unless it can be established that the catch was taken in accordance with relevant conservation measures. The same recommendation applies to vessels that have been sighted engaging in IUU fishing activities in waters within national jurisdiction or in the area of an RFMO. The Scheme also includes the denial of access to port to vessels listed as IUU vessels by relevant fisheries bodies.[50]

The last needing to be mentioned is the 2009 Agreement on Port State Measures to Prevent, Deter and Eliminate Illegal, Unreported and Unregulated Fishing (the Agreement), approved by the FAO as an Article XIV instrument under the FAO Constitution.[51] The aim of this Agreement is to prevent, deter and eliminate IUU fishing through the implementation

---

47 See in depth, Riddle, n. 44, 270–276.

48 Council FAO, Hundred and Twenty-Eighth Session, Rome, 20–25 June 2005, Report of the Twenty-sixth Session of the FAO Committee on Fisheries, Rome, 7–11 March 2005, Doc. CL128/7, para. 25.

49 Adriana Fabra, Virginia Gascón and Rodolfo Werner, "The Use of Port State measures to Improve Fisheries Compliance. Issues and Instruments", Accessed 5 March 2011, http://www.illegal-fishing.info/uploads/Fabra-use-of-port-state-measures.pdf.

50 Id.

51 The World State of Fisheries and Aquaculture, accessed March 30, 2011, http://www.scribd.com/doc/52471585/41/FAO-Agreement-on-port-state-measures-to-combat-IUU-fishing.

of port state measures as a means of ensuring the long-term conservation and sustainable use of living marine resources and marine ecosystems. The Agreement will be applied by parties, in their capacity as port states, to vessels not entitled to fly their flags when seeking entry to parties' ports or while they are in port (with certain exemptions). The most important feature of this Agreement is the exchange of information relating to vessels suspected of engaging, or found to have engaged, in IUU fishing. The annexes, forming an integral part of the Agreement, specify the information to be provided in advance by vessels seeking entry to parties' ports and guidelines or inspection procedures, the handling of inspection results, information systems and training requirements. Central to the Agreement is the article concerning the requirement of developing states' position. A lack of capacity among port states parties could seriously impact on the effectiveness of the Agreement in meeting its objectives. Blocking the movement of IUU-caught fish into ports and onto national and international markets, together with making the operations of vessels engaged in IUU fishing more difficult, should affect cost-effectiveness i.e. reducing the incentives for IUU fishing.[52]

The best-known example of IUU fishing is the Patagonian tooth fish (*Dissostichuseleginoides*) and the Antarctic tooth fish (*Dissostichus-mawsoni*), which belong to the cod family. They are fished in the Southern Ocean and are sold commercially mostly as Chilean sea bass. As Riddle explains, this kind of fish proved to be most attractive for IUU fishing, as it inhabits a very remote part of the world (which makes enforcement and monitoring very expensive) and is very sought after, averaging four US dollars fifty five cents per pound on landing. According to the records of the Commission for the Conservation of Antarctic Marine Resources (the CCAMLR), some 120 tons of unreported tooth fish were caught in the 1996-1997 season. It is estimated that the trade had increased by 7,815 tons by 1999–2000, while reported catches decreased by 12,077 tons. As Riddle says, based on these data it appears that the IUU catch went up as the reported catches declined.[53] The same author notes that such a situation also indicates a 'blatant disregard for the conservation of fishery resources not only threatened the existence of the tooth fish stock, but also the legitimacy of CCAMLR's management and enforcement responsibilities'.[54]

52 Id.
53 Riddle n. 44, 268 (also 267).
54 Id.267,

Vessels engaged in IUU fishing for tooth fish tend to re – flag in order to conceal their identity, minimize costs and avoid any restrictions on their fishing activities (the latest FOC country open for re-flagging is Togo).[55]

2.4.5. *Enforcement and Flags of Convenience (the FOC) and IUU*

One of the main contributory elements of IUU is the existence of flags of convenience. As of 2005 over 1,000 large-scale fishing vessels continued to fly Flags of Convenience (FOCs).[56] Taiwan, Honduras, Panama, Spain, and Belize are the top five countries where companies that own or operate fishing vessels flagged to one of the top FOC fishing countries are based. The European Union countries as a whole top the list of countries of residence of FOC fishing vessels (Spain/Canary Islands amounting to approximately one-half of the EU total).[57] Georgia, Cambodia, Vanuatu and Bolivia appear to be new FOCs for fishing vessels. There are also a number of large-scale fishing vessels listed as flag 'unknown' on the Lloyd's Register of Ships amounting to 8.5 percent of the total number of large-scale fishing vessels on the database.[58] There is evidence of insufficient national legislation.[59] The burden of improving the situation regarding IUU rests on States (within whose jurisdiction the owners or managers of at-sea resupply ships and tankers reside) and RFMOs (within whose areas these vessels operate), which should aim to deter and eliminate IUU fishing, whether through observer programmes, in line with RFMO recommendations, and/or by other means.[60]

FOC account for a disproportionate share of vessels and tonnage losses; labour violations; oil spills; pollution violations; instances of inadequate communication and equipment; deliberate mislabelling of vessels to disguise their true identity; falsified certificates of competence and documentation of engine power output; unauthorised modifications of vessels structures (such as hull to conceal catch); discarded illegal fishing gear upon the sighting of protection vessels; altered satellite communications systems; falsified fisheries information; and piracy and overfishing in contravention of and without regard to international, national and regional regulations.[61]

[55] Gianni and Simpson, n. 47, 6, 26.
[56] Id. 3.
[57] Id. 15.
[58] Id. 18.
[59] Id. 18.
[60] Id. 68.
[61] Jessica K. Ferell, "Controlling Flags of Convenience: One Measure to Stop Overfishing of Collapsing Fish Stocks", *Environmental Law* 35 (2005): 332–333.

2.4.6. *Enforcement against IUU and the European Union (the EU)*

The European Union also took measures to eliminate IUU. In general, questions regarding fisheries within the EU such as management and the protection and allocation of quotas are regulated by the Common Fisheries Policy (the CFP), which takes a holistic approach to fisheries, based on the precautionary principle.[62] Since 1993 the EU has enacted several regulations implementing the CFP.[63] The enforcement of all aspects of the CFP is within the jurisdiction of individual EU member States regarding vessels carrying their flag. In 2002, the EU adopted the Action Plan on Illegal, Unreported and Unregulated Fishing.[64] The EU Action Plan is part of the 2002 Common Fisheries Policy reforms and sets out the necessary measures for the EU to comply with the IPOA-IUU. The Community action plan identifies 15 new measures or initiatives to be undertaken by: the Community itself, or through regional fisheries organisations and/or international organisations in order to implement the IPOA-IUU.[65] In

62 See EC No. 2371/2002, OJ L358/59, "On the Conservation and Sustainable Exploitation of Fisheries Resources under the Common Fisheries Policy", *Official Journal of the European Communities* L 358/59. Accessed March 2, 2011, http://eur-lex.europa.eu/LexUriServ/LexUriServ.do?uri=OJ:L:2002:358:0059:0080:EN:PDF.

63 Regulation EC No. 2847/93 establishing a control system applicable to the Common Fisheries Policy; Council Regulation (EC) No. 1093/94 of 6 May 1994 setting the terms under which fishing vessels of a third country may land directly and market their catch at Community ports [1994] OJ L121/3; Council Regulation (EC) No. 1447/1999 of 24 June 1999 establishing a list of types of behaviour which seriously infringe the rules of the common fisheries policy [1999] OJ L167/5; Council Regulation (EC) No. 2371/2002 of 20 December 2002 on the conservation and sustainable exploitation of fisheries resources under the Common Fisheries Policy [2002] OJ L358/59 (establishing conditions for the marketing of fish products and requiring Member States to cooperate with third countries and provide necessary assistance to ensure compliance with rules of the Common Fisheries Policy); and Council Regulation (EC) No. 768/2005 of 26 April 2005 establishing a Community Fisheries Control Agency and amending Regulation (EEC) No. 2847/93 establishing a control system applicable to the common fisheries policy [2005] OJ L128/1. All regulations are listed in Matthew Tsamenyi et al., "The European Council Regulation on Illegal, Unreported and Unregulated Fishing: An International Fisheries Perspective", *IJMCL* 25(2009): 12.

64 The Action Plan on Illegal, Unreported and Unregulated Fishing. Accessed March 3, 2011, http://www.ieep.eu/assets/81/CFP5.pdf.

65 According to this Action Plan the following key actions are promised, although without specifying a timeframe for delivery: at Community level · Controlling nationals – ensuring Member States take control over their nationals, discouraging them from flagging vessels under the jurisdiction of a state that is failing to meet its flag State responsibilities, and from committing infringements; · Trade measures to implement international rules - adopting rules banning the trade in fishery products taken in breach of international fisheries agreements, and making business in IUU derived products illegal; · Information and awareness raising – the public, consumers and the industry are to be alerted to the issue of

2007 the EU adopted a new strategy to prevent and eliminate IUU.[66] This policy adopted several measures: by integrating the trade dimension; finding more effective ways to persuade flag states unwilling or unable to exert adequate control over their fishing vessels to ensure compliance with the rules; through reaching a higher degree of compliance with international and EU standards by EU vessels and operators, generally in Community waters; through better cooperation in the investigation of IUU activities; and intensifying EU policy against IUU fishing on the high seas and in relation to developing countries.[67] In 2008 the European Parliament adopted a legislative resolution approving an amended version of the Commission's proposal. The amended proposal was adopted by the Council of the European Union on 29 September 2009 (in force as of 1 January 2010).[68]

IUU fishing and the EU action plan, based on a combination of printed, audiovisual and electronic media exercises; Within regional fisheries organisations (RFOs) · RFO plans for control and inspection - Initiate conservation and management measures to limit unregulated fishing, with priority to be placed on areas where Community rules are stricter; Regulation fishing activities - work towards establishing objective and transparent criteria for identifying IUU fishing activities, while supporting action of RFOs to invite flag States to take action against IUU fishing, and to exchange information on IUU vessels; · Identifying and monitoring IUU vessels - call upon RFOs to adopt action plans, with a priority to be given for high value fish; · Identifying and quantifying IUU catches - encourage RFOs to develop data collection procedures, covering quantities taken illegally and identifying the origin of these catches; · Certification and documentation - encourage the reform of certification/documentation schemes and the preparation of a prototype document for discussion in the FAO; At the international level · Improved information – transmitting information on the Community fleet to the FAO; · Strengthening international cooperation – participation in the network of monitoring agencies proposed by Chile and the USA; · Defining 'substantial link' – a Community initiative will aim to convene an international conference to negotiate an international agreement to determine the existence of a substantial link between a flag State and a vessel flying that flag; · Defining port State rights and responsibilities – to convene an international conference to negotiate an agreement defining the rights and responsibilities of port States concerning access by fishing vessels to port facilities; and In partnership with developing countries · Assistance to control unlawful fishing – technical and financial assistance for monitoring, control and surveillance activities, to be put in place in partnership with developing countries. Source: accessed March 24 2011 http://www.ieep.eu/assets/81/CFP5.pdf.

[66] Communication from the Commission to the European Parliament, the Council, the European Economic and Social Committee and the Committee of the Regions on a New Strategy for the Community to Prevent, Deter and Eliminate Illegal, Unreported and Unregulated Fishing, Commission document COM(2007) 601 final, Accessed March 25, 2011, http://register.consilium.europa.eu/pdf/en/07/st14/st14237.en07.pdf.

[67] Ibid.

[68] Council Regulation (EC) No 1005/2008 of 29 September 2008 establishing a Community System to Prevent, Deter and Eliminate Illegal, Unreported and Unregulated Fishing, amending Regulations (EEC) No 2847/93, (EC) No 1936/2001 and (EC) No 601/2004 and repealing Regulations (EC) No 1093/94 and (EC) No 1447/1999, Accessed March 27 2011, http://eur lex.europa.eu/LexUriServ/LexUriServ.do?uri=CELEX:32008R1005:EN:NOT; Commission Regulation (EC) No 1010/2009 of 22 October 2009 Laying down Detailed Rules

There are three pillars of the new control system for fisheries in the European Community. The first is the EU IUU Regulation; the second pillar is Council Regulation (EC) No. 1006/2008 of 29 September 2008 concerning authorisations for the fishing activities of Community fishing vessels outside Community waters and access by third-country vessels to Community waters; the third pillar concerns the control of compliance with the Common Fisheries Policy rules by EC vessels and by third country vessels fishing in Community waters. For this purpose, the European Commission on 14 November 2008 adopted a proposal for a Council Regulation establishing a Community control system ensuring compliance with the rules of the Common Fisheries Policy, which entered into force at the same time as the IUU Regulation, on 1 January 2010.[69] The EU IUU Regulation applies to IUU fishing and related activities effected within the jurisdiction of the EU member States, in addition to activities carried out by Community and non-Community vessels on the high seas or in waters under the jurisdiction of a third State. IUU within the maritime waters of overseas territories of the EU member States is treated as being carried out in the waters of third States. The definition of the IUU resembles that of the IPOA-IUU and the definition of the fishing vessel adopted therein is very broad.[70]

In general the Regulation grants very extensive rights to the members of the EU, and in particular to the port State in the area of the validation and verification of the necessary certificates.[71] EU member States are obliged every year to carry out inspections in their ports of at least 5 percent of landings and transhipment operations by third-country fishing vessels. The most fundamental feature of the EU IUU regulation is the establishing of the EU list of vessels identified by the EU and the Member States (also

---

for the Implementation of Council Regulation (EC) No 1005/2008 Establishing a Community System to Prevent, Deter and Eliminate Illegal, Unreported and Unregulated Fishing. Accessed March 26, 2011, http://eur-lex.europa.eu/LexUriServ/LexUriServ.do?uri=CELEX:32009R1010:EN:NOT Commission Regulation (EU) No 395/2010 of 7 May 2010 Amending Commission Regulation (EC) No 1010/2009 as Regards Administrative Arrangements on Catch Certificates, Accessed 24 March 2011, http://eur-lex.europa.eu/LexUriServ/LexUriServ.do?uri=CELEX:32010R0395:EN:NOT Commission Regulation (EU) No 468/2010 of 28 May 2010 Establishing the EU List of Vessels Engaged in Illegal, Unreported and Unregulated Fishing. Accessed March 25, 2011, http://eur-lex.europa.eu/LexUriServ/LexUriServ.do?uri=CELEX:32010R0468:EN:NOT.

69 European Commission, DG Maritime Affairs and Fisheries, Brussels, Belgium (2009), Handbook on the practical application of Council Regulation (EC) No. 1005/2008 of 29 September 2008 establishing a Community system to prevent, deter and eliminate illegal, unreported and unregulated fishing (the IUU Regulation).

70 Tsamenyi n 64, 14–15.

71 Id.

including vessels identified by RFMOs) as pursuing IUU fishing. In general it may be said that the EU IUU Regulation is in broad brushstrokes consistent with the provisions made under international fisheries instruments and adopted by RFMOs. The regulation goes further in listing non-cooperating States and permitting the unilateral imposition of trade restrictions and other economic sanction on those States.[72]

2.5. *Conclusions on this Part*

It may be said that combating IUU is a very daunting task. Due to the lack of strict international regulations, IUU is very difficult to eliminate. There is a notable lack of control over companies engaged in IUU. Due to the fact that the costs of fishing illegally are lower, illegal operators further contribute to the decline in stocks.[73] It was suggested that if economics is a key driving force behind IUU fishing, economic principles should be used to make the practice less attractive by making it more costly to mount and conduct IUU operations and by reducing the revenue from fish piracy.[74] The costs of IUU fishing can be increased by making illegal fishing riskier through the likelihood of getting caught and raising the penalties placed on IUU fishermen if caught. To act as a deterrent, the penalties for IUU should be sufficiently high and uniform in scope and applicability. Another deterrent would be a harmonised and co-ordinated approach to port controls which can also increase costs by forcing IUU vessels to take action to avoid detection and prosecution, thereby increasing steaming time (the travelling time to and from fishing grounds) as well as re-provisioning and refuelling costs. This approach means more extensive reliance on monitoring, control and surveillance (MCS) measures, both on vessels and in ports.[75] Such measures in ports include port inspections and the use of Catch Documentation Schemes (CDS). Regular port inspections can ensure that fish have been caught in accordance with relevant conservation and management measures. The most important factor for achieving a reduction in IUU is putting in place domestic legislation well as co-operation mechanisms to enable the country concerned to co-ordinate action with other countries operating ports, registering vessels under their flag or buying or selling fish.[76] OECD countries already

---

[72] Id. 30–31.
[73] OECD, 2006, Policy Brief: Making Sure Fish Piracy Doesn't Pay. Accessed March 26, 2011, http://www.oecd.org/dataoecd/26/37/35985301.pdf.
[74] Ibid.
[75] Ibid.
[76] Ibid.

have proper systems in place which allow for capturing IUU catch and they make better use of existing systems (increased use of on-board observers on fishing vessels, coupled with more frequent random searches, could improve reporting).[77] The role of the private sector cannot be underestimated. Close co-operation between private operators such as processing plants, wholesalers and supermarkets could help facilitate an accurate and verifiable chain of information. This would reduce the market for IUU caught fish. The legal fishing industry can also lend support through both co-operating and reinforcing monitoring and enforcement schemes, if consulted by governments on the design and implementation of enforcement approaches. Governments should make IUU less financially attractive by reducing fisheries subsidies and removing excess capacity. This is because subsidies have generated overcapacity in fleets, which means that there is a large pool of idle vessels. Government scrapping policies, if properly implemented, will also help to reduce overcapacity in the fleet.[78]

3. Settlement of Fisheries Disputes

The extent of the problem concerning IUU is also obvious in the number of cases before the International Tribunal for the Law of the Sea ('ITLOS') relating to this very issue.[79] The *Saiga,*[80] *Camouco,*[81] *Monte Confurco,*[82] *Grand Prince,*[83] *Volga*[84] and the *Juno Trader*[85] cases all concerned ships which had been re-flagged, in some instances several times, and ships with a tenuous link with their flag States.[86] The above-mentioned cases do not conform to the criteria prescribed for ship registration under the 1986 United Nations Convention on the Registration of Ships, set out in its Articles 7-9, in particular the provision that requires

---

[77] Ibid.

[78] Ibid.

[79] See on this topic: Tullio Treves, "Flags of Convenience Before the Law of the Sea Tribunal", *San Diego Int'L LJ*, 6 (2004) 179–189.

[80] M/V "Saiga" (*no.1*) (*St Vincent and the Grenadines v Guinea*), 110 *I.L.R.* 273 (ITLOS 1997); M/V "Saiga" (no.2) (*St Vincent and the Grenadines v Guinea*), 120 *I.L.R.* 144 (ITLOS 1999).

[81] "*Camouco"* (*Panama v. France*), 125 *I.L.R.* 164 (ITLOS 2000).

[82] "M*onte Confurco"*(*Seychelles v. France*), 125 *I.L.R.* 220 (ITLOS 2000).

[83] *"The Grand Prince"*(*Belize v. France*), 15 *I.L.R.* 273 (ITLOS 2001).

[84] *"Volga"* (*Russia v. Australia*), ITLOS Case No. 11, (ITLOS 2002) Accessed March 23, 2011, http://www.itlos.org/cgi-bin/cases/case_detail.pl?id=11&lang=en.

[85] *The Juno Trader* (*St. Vincent and the Grenadines*) Case N. 14, (ITLOS 2004), Accessed March 23, 2011, http://www.worldcourts.com/itlos/eng/decisions/2004.12.18_Saint_Vincent_v_Guinea_Bissau.pdf.

[86] Accessed March, 2011, *"Hoshinmaru"* (*Japan v, Russian Federation*) Case No.14 http://www.worldcourts.com/itlos/eng/decisions/2007.08.06_Japan_v_Russian_Federation1.pdf (ITLOS 2007); *"The Tomimaru"* (*Japan v. Russian Federation,* Case No. 15, (ITLOS 2007).

that the flag State or its national participate as owners or in the ownership of the ship and that officers and crew constituting a satisfactory part of the complement be nationals of or domiciled or lawfully in permanent residence in the flag State.[87] As Judge of the ITLOS, Professor Treves explained that even a flexible application of these standards clearly indicates that they were not complied with in the majority of the above-mentioned cases.[88] There were issues concerning the criteria on national ownership and national manning of the ship (e.g. in the *Saiga* case, the flag State was allegedly Saint Vincent, re-flagged from Malta), as to the beneficial owners (in the *Saiga* case, unknown), the crew being unconnected with nationality of the ship (in the case of the *Saiga* mostly of Ukrainian nationality, including the Master of the Ship).[89]

All these cases related to the 'prompt release' of vessels. This procedure is provided for in Article 292 of the 1982 UNCLOS, analysis of which exceeds the framework of this essay.[90] With the exception of the *Saiga, Juno, Hoshinmaru* and *Tomimaru*, all these cases were tooth fish prompt release cases. In the *Saiga* and *Grand Prince*, the ITLOS dealt with the nationality of the ships. In the *Monte Confurco* case, the Agent of France, Mr Triniquier, emphasised the ecological aspect of illegal fishing for tooth

---

Accessed March 25, 2011, http://www.worldcourts.com/itlos/eng/decisions/2007.08.06_Japan_v_Russian_Federation2.pdf. In these two cases the issue was illegal fishing but not the question of FOC.

[87] United Nations Convention on the Registration of Ships, signed 7 February 1986 (not yet in force), text on accessed March 21, 2011, http://www.admiraltylawguide.com/conven/registration1986.html.

[88] Treves, n.79, 180.

[89] In the *Camouco*, the flag State was Panama; the owner was a company in Panama with Spanish companies as beneficial companies. The master and most of the crew were Spanish. The ship after its release was re-flagged twice before its forfeiture by the French authorities. The *Monte Confurco* had the Seychelles as the flag State, with the owner as a company registered in Seychelles. There was no clear indication who were beneficiaries (presumably Spanish). The Master was Spanish and the crew was from various countries. In the *Grand Prince* case the indication was that the flag State was Belize. The owner of the company had a seat in Belize. The beneficial owners were Spanish, and the crew consisted of Spanish and Chilean nationals. In the *Volga* case, the flag State was the Russian Federation and the owner a Russian company. There was no indication as the beneficial owners. The Master was of Russian nationality; however, the chief mate, the fishing master and the fishing pilot were Spaniards; the rest of the crew consisted mostly of Chinese and Indonesian nationals, Treves, n.16, 180–181, In the *Juno Trader* the flag State was Saint Vincent and the Grenadines. Its owner was Juno Reefers Limited, a company incorporated in the British Virgin Islands and a branch of the South African seafood company Irvin and Johnson Limited, based in Cape Town. The Master of the *Juno Trader* was a Russian national, n. 22 (para. 33). n, 81.

[90] Article 292: Prompt release of vessels and crews: "1. Where the authorities of a State Party have detained a vessel flying the flag of another State Party and it is alleged that the detaining State has not complied with the provisions of this Convention for the prompt

fish. He stressed environmental danger to the stock of tooth fish in the waters of the Southern Indian Ocean. The Agent also noted great financial gains deriving from trade in this fish stock. He also observed the measures adopted by certain ships in order to avoid identification and that they are organized in some kind of network to assist each other. France called an expert, Professor Duhamel, to testify as to the fish stock in the area. The expert said that over-exploitation of the species could have serious consequences for the stock, especially as it reaches maturity late.[91]

Professor Crawford, representing Australia in the *Volga* case, also made several observations concerning the importance of the protection of tooth fish stocks:

> '...Australia seeks from you, this time as Respondent, another robust and precautionary step in the interests of the conservation of an endangered fish stock. This time it is Patagonian tooth fish, not southern blue fin tuna, a smaller fish but also long-lived and one again about which we do not know much. This time, however, the step we seek from you is not intervention; it is non-intervention – or rather the indication that in the context of the conservation and management of this species within the EEZ, strong enforcement measures and high bonds can be justified to prevent the repetition of flagrantly unlawful fishing. So we ask not for intervention but for non-intervention. We hope the result will be equally beneficial. There is no doubt the need is just as great... Commercial exploitation of Patagonian tooth fish is a recent phenomenon; it has only been commercially exploited for about a decade. If IUU fishing – illegal, unreported and unregulated fishing – is

---

release of the vessel or its crew upon the posting of a reasonable bond or other financial security, the question of release from detention may be submitted to any court or tribunal agreed upon by the parties or, failing such agreement within 10 days from the time of detention, to a court or tribunal accepted by the detaining State under article 287 or to the International Tribunal for the Law of the Sea, unless the parties otherwise agree. 2. The application for release may be made only by or on behalf of the flag State of the vessel. 3. The court or tribunal shall deal without delay with the application for release and shall deal only with the question of release, without prejudice to the merits of any case before the appropriate domestic forum against the vessel, its owner or its crew. The authorities of the detaining State remain competent to release the vessel or its crew at any time.

4. Upon the posting of the bond or other financial security determined by the court or tribunal, the authorities of the detaining State shall comply promptly with the decision of the court or tribunal concerning the release of the vessel or its crew."

On this subject see G.J. Gao, "Reasonableness of the Bond under Ar*ticle 292 of the LOS Convention: Practice of the ITLOS*", *Chinese Journal of International Law* 7 (2008) 115; Philippe Gaultier, "Urgent Proceedings before the International Tribunal for the Law of the Sea", *Issues in Legal Scholarship,* The Berkeley Electronic Press, (2011) 1, Accessed March 26, 2011, http://www.bepress.com/cgi/viewcontent.cgi?article=1105&context=ils.

[91] Statement of Mr. Trniquier, Oral Proceedings, Verbatim Records, ITLOS/PV 00/ 6/ Rev.1, 7 December, 2000, accessed 20 March 2011, http://www.itlos.org/start2_en.html.

permitted to continue, the stock will reach a crisis level within the next few years.[92]

The issue of fishing and the flag of convenience was noted in the *Saiga* case, where the ITLOS observed the evolution in the concept of the 'genuine link', especially concerning the obligations of States regarding compliance with international standards of fishing.[93]

4. Other Examples of Disputes Concerning Fish Stocks

4.1. *The International Court of Justice*

The case which concerned the powers of one of the RFMOs, i.e. the North West Fisheries Organisation (NAFO), was a dispute between Spain and Canada.[94] This RFMO was established on the basis of the Northwest Atlantic Fisheries Convention (both Canada and the EU are Parties). According to Article XI(1) of the Convention NAFO is 'responsible for management and conservation of the resources of the Regulatory Area', i.e. Grand Banks' Nose and Tail (the remaining Grand Banks are within the Canadian EFZ). There is a synergy between national and international measures and NAFO's task is to coordinate them.[95] According to Article XI(4) of the Convention Canada is granted 'special consideration' in allocating catches from Grand Banks in the light of their coastal communities relying on fishing such stocks. One of the important legal features of the NAFO is that the enforcement of its measures is the responsibility of its members States (under the 1988 Scheme of Joint International Inspection). Such enforcement is carried out by inspectors from Special Inspection Vessels. Inspectors may be placed on board the inspection vessels of another part only by agreement. It is the sole prerogative of the flag State to take a decision on possible prosecution in the event of an alleged infringement of NAFO conservation and management measures.

Although the case was dismissed on the basis of jurisdiction, the subject-matter of the case is a good example of the complexity of issues involved in fishing, especially regarding the jurisdiction of the coastal

92 Minutes f Public Sittings, held on 12,13 and 23 December 2002.
Held on 12, 13 AND 23 December 2002, the *Volga* case (*Russian Federation v. Australia*), Prompt Release, 12 December, 10 am, accessed 20 www.itlos.org/case_documents/2002/document_en_215.pdf.

93 Treves, n. 79, 187. See also Ferell, n. 61, 323–391.

94 *Fisheries Jurisdiction Case*(*Jurisdiction*) (*Spain v. Canada*), 1998, accessed March 19, 2011, http://www.icj-cij.org/docket/index.php?p1=3&p2=3&k=ac&case=96&code=ec&p3=4.

95 Davis and Redgwell, n.24, 206.

State; the powers stemming from the RFMO's membership and the freedom to fish on the high seas.[96] The case concerns straddling stocks which straddled the Canadian 200-mile limit and had been depleted so gravely that NAFO imposed moratoria on fishing them, with the exception of halibut (stocks were within the Canadian 200-mile zone and in the high seas area, beyond the Canadian Exclusive Fishery Zone (EFZ)). Until 1995 Halibut was not managed by NAFO but only by Canada. Other fish stocks in the high seas area were in the regulatory area of NAFO, an organisation with a wide membership, including the EU and Canada. NAFO resumed the regulation of halibut (in the danger of overfishing) in 1995 and set quotas which were objected to by the EU. In 1995 Canada seized a Spanish fishing vessel, the *Estai*, which was fishing over the quota set by NAFO, pursuant to the provisions of the Coastal Fisheries Protection Act (CFPA) and its implementing regulations, as amended in 1994. The amended Act permitted the boarding, inspection and seizure of foreign fishing vessels suspected of violating fisheries conservation and management measures for straddling stocks in the NAFO regulatory area. This Act was adopted as a consequence of the lack of enforcement powers by NAFO. Its objective was to subject any vessel which did not comply with good conservation rules to action by Canada.[97] The classes of vessel and the species of fish are listed in Regulations, and, following CFPA, were all straddling (including halibut), and the list included Spanish and Portuguese vessels as under special conservation measures, including the prohibition of fishing for Greenland halibut. Spain initiated the proceedings before the ICJ. In 1995 Canada and the EU signed an agreement settling the questions of conservation and enforcement measures and the dispute concerning the seizing of the *Estai*. The vessel and its captain had been released. In 1995 NAFO adopted the conservation and enforcement measures agreed to by Canada and the EU as regulations binding on all NAFO members. Spain argued that the dispute related to Canada's lack of 'title' to exercise jurisdiction on the high seas, the non-opposability of the Canadian legislation to Spain, the violation of Spain's rights by the seizure of the *Estai*, and Spain's entitlement to reparation. On the other hand, Canada asserted that the dispute concerned the adoption of measures for the conservation and management of fish stocks with respect to vessels fishing in the NAFO jurisdiction area and the enforcement of those measures.[98]

---

[96] Louise de la Fayette, "The Fisheries Jurisdiction Case. *Spain v. Canada* (Judgment of 9 December 1998)", *International and Comparative Law Quarterly* 48 (1999) 664.

[97] Davis and Redgwell, n.24, 211.

[98] Id. 667.

4.2. *The International Tribunal for the Law of the Sea*[99]

The cases in question were the *Bluefin Tuna* cases.[100] Bluefin Tuna is a commercially very valuable fish, with a primary market in Japan which, together with Australia, was taking the largest catches.[101] These cases have a plethora of legal issues; however, of interest to this essay is the subject-matter of the case and the role of the Commission for Conservation of Southern Bluefin Tuna. This Commission is an RMFO, established on the basis of the 1993 Convention on the Conservation of Southern Bluefin Tuna (the CSBT) concluded between Japan, New Zealand and Australia. The CSBT was preceeded by informal agreements between New Zealand, Japan and Australia allocating the total allowable catch (TAC). It may be noted that Korea and Indonesia and Taiwan at the time of the dispute also fished for bluefin tuna in this region, were not Parties to the CSBT, but had since joined the Convention.[102] This Commission is responsible for allocating the total allowable catch. The Commission's objective was to rebuild stocks of tuna to their 1980 level by 2010. Due to a disagreement between the parties as to the state of stocks, they decided to conduct the Experimental Fishing Programme (EFP). Since 1996 one of the tasks of the

---

[99] In 2007, the former President of the ITLOS, Professor Wolfrum, made a presentation on the Potential of the International Tribunal for the Law of the Sea in the Management and Conservation of Marine Living Resources. He was of the view that the ITLOS has several ways to prevent the further depletion of fish stocks. It can prescribe provisional measures (which are binding). They may be prescribed not only to protect rights but also to prevent serious harm to the marine environment. Therefore, the protection of stocks from total depletion would meet this criterion. Judge Wolfrum mentioned that the protection of living marine resourses can be the duty of the coastal State, flag State and port State. The ITLOS is also a forum for settling disputes concerning the interpretation and application of the Fish Stocks Agreement. The President mentioned other relevant Articles of UNCLOS which may be applied by the ITLOS in order to protect fisheries, such Articles 73 (relating the obligations of the coastal State), 64 obligation to cooperate); and 116–119 (relating to the conservation of marine resources on the high seas), 'The Potential of the International Tribunal for Law of the Sea in the Management and Conservation of Marine Living Resources' www.itlos.org/.../Speech%20Friends%20of%20the%20Tribunal%20ae%2011%2009.

[100] *Southern Blue Finn Tuna Cases* (*New Zealand v. Japan; Australia v. Japan*), *Provisional Measures*, Order of 22 August 1999, ITLOS, accessed March 30, 2011, http://www.un.org/Deps/los/ITLOS/Order-tuna34htm; S. Marr, 'The Southern Bluefin Tuna Cases-the Precautionary Approach and Conservation and Management of Fish Resources', *European Journal International Law* 11 (2000) 815; C.F Foster, " 'The Real Dispute' in the Southern Bluefin Tuna Case: a Scientific Dispute?", *International Journal of Marine and Coastal Law* 16 (2001) 571; Barbara Kwiatkowska, "The Southern Bluefin Tuna (New Zealand v. Japan; Australia v. Japan) Cases," *International Journal of Marine and Coastal Law* 15 (2000) 1.

[101] Foster, n. 101, 576.

[102] South Korea (as of 2001), Taiwan (Fishing Entity of Taiwan's membership of the Extended Commission) (as of 2002) and Indonesia (as of 2008) are also Parties now. Accessed March 30, 2011, http://www.ccsbt.org/docs/about.html.

Commission has also been the responsibility for implementing an experimental fishing programme (the EFP). Disagreement as to the scope of the EFP led to Japan commencing experimental fihseries on its own terms.[103] Both Claimants alleged that Japan had exceeded the quotas of the EFP. In 1998 Japan took one million four hundred thousand tonnes of this fish. In 1999, both New Zealand and Australia, in separate submissions, requested the ILTOS to prescribe provisional measures on the basis of Article 290(5) of UNCLOS, to order Japan to cease its EEP immediately and limit itself to its allocated national quotas. The Tribunal prescribed four provisional measures, recommended two other measures; and made two decisions on implementation. Japan pleaded that the dispute was not legal but scientific, and that the existence of the CSBT precluded reliance by the Claimants on the relevant provisions of UNCLOS (Articles 64; 116–119 and 300) and customary international law (the precautionary principle). It also submitted that provisional measures should not be prescribed due to a lack of urgency and the risk of irreparable damage. These arguments were rejected by the Tribunal. Despite the fact that the Tribunal could not conclusively assess scientific evidence submitted by the Parties, it prescribed provisional measures, as a matter of urgency, 'to preserve the rights of the parties and to avert further deterioration of the southern Bluefin Tuna stocks' (paras, 56-61 of the Order). Japan pledged to end the EFP on 31 August 1999 (a few days after the Order), thus putting in doubt the element of urgency connected to the prescription of provisional measures.[104] Unfortunately this case was not decided on the merits.

The above cases clearly indicate the complex character of all questions relating to fish management and the frequent inability of the RFMO to solve the problems. Despite the strict and far-reaching requirements of the Fish stocks Agreement regarding fishing, it is in fact for individual States to enforce fishing regulations, as is exemplified by the CCAMLR. It must be noted as well that as the Fisheries *Jurisdiction* case evidenced the tension between the freedom to fish and the growing jurisdiction of the coastal State, and exacerbates the inability of RFMOs to act efficiently. As was observed, the complicated and lengthy process of bringing new entrants into RFMOs is also one of the contributory factors to dissatisfaction with the role of RFMOs. It must be said that without these organisations all fish stocks would have been completely depleted by now. RFMOs keep them under review; initiate recovery programmes and present an

103 Foster, n. 101, 577.
104 See on this Dissenting Opinion of Judge Vukas, *SoutherenBluefinn Tuna* n.100.

objective view on their state. Therefore, in respect to many aspects of fish stocks management they play a beneficial role. In the area of the allocation of the TAC within the RFMOs' activities there always will be disagreements.

5. Fisheries and Regional Fisheries Management Organisations (the RFMOs)

5.1. *RFMOs: General Framework*

The RFMOs belong to a larger group of Regional Fisheries Organisations (RFOs).[105] RFOs are fundamental for the good governance of regional fisheries. It is generally accepted that organisations at the regional level are appropriate *fora* to perform specific functions regarding fisheries. However, as Sydness argues, they are not a homogenous group, and apart from different functions they also vary greatly in their structure.[106] Their membership is also regulated in a different way. Some of them are open; others require the fulfilling of certain conditions for membership.

It must also be noted that they respond to the evolution of the law of the sea, changing their scope of jurisdiction and functions to accommodate new developments. The RFOs are mostly established in response to a particular need at the regional level, and when the States of the region can identify common objectives relating to shared resources.[107] Sydness identifies three main categories of RFOs: scientific research organisations, regional cooperation and development organisations, and the regional fisheries management organisations.[108] The last type of organisation – the RFMO – is of interest in the present study. Its functions may comprise the collection and analysis of scientific information, the setting of regulatory measures (such as the determination of quotas) and the adoption of enforcement mechanisms.[109]

The fundamental role of the RFMOs regarding the protection of fish stocks was emphasised during the proceedings in the *Volga* case by counsel for Australia, Professor Crawford, who urged the ITLOS to act always in aid of regional fisheries agreements 'which are the only way, now and in

---

[105] A.K. Sydnes, "Regional Fishery Oganisations: How and Why Organisational Diversity Matters", *Ocean Development and International Law*, 32 (2001) 349.

[106] Id. 350–351.

[107] Id. 351.

[108] Id. 354.

[109] Id. 354.

the long term, of preserving the world's fish stocks. The relevant regional organisation here is that established by CCAMLR'.[110] However, membership of such organisations is not without certain difficulties.[111] One of the most important questions (which is still not satisfactorily resolved) is the meaning and the application of the concept of 'real interest' contained in Article 8(3) of the Fish stocks Convention, which states as follows: 'States having a real interest in the fisheries concerned may become members' of RFMOs. Molenaar construes a possible meaning of 'interest' from the structure of Article 8(3) and argues that it can be deduced that States fishing for stocks on the high seas (flag States which are actually fishing for the stocks concerned at the time of their application) and relevant coastal States (whose maritime zones are included in or adjacent to the RFMO's regulatory area) have a 'real' interest.[112] However, the same author states that the precise definition of what constitutes a 'real interest' is still unclear. For example 'real interest' may be only protecting of biodiversity, not fishing, and new entrants would aim at stopping fishing altogether. Such a situation may not be regarded as a 'real interest'.[113]

In practical terms, as was noted above, the system of joining RFMOs for new entrants is very varied. For example for the requirement of membership of other organisations (such as the FAO, UN or any other of its specialised agencies) as typical for FAO bodies, CCAMLR has a different condition, i.e. scientific interests.[114] The different type of entry is based on a so-called 'approval' procedure by other members, which can be very slow.[115] However, in general it can be said that the system of acceptance of new applicants is open and not unduly restrictive. The main problem is not the restrictive character of RFMOs but the dwindling fish stocks, and therefore new entrants are granted very few fishing opportunities.[116] For

---

110 *Volga* case, Statement of response by Australia, accessed on March 12, 2011, http://www.itlos.org/start2_en.html.

111 Erik -.Jaap.Molenaar, "Participation, Allocation and Unregulated Fishing: The Practice of Regional Fisheries Management Organisations", *International Journal of Marine and Coastal Law* 18 (2003) 457; id. "The Concept of 'Real Interest' and Other Aspects of Co-operation through Regional Fisheries Management Mechanisms", *International Journal of Marine and Coastal Law* 15 (2000) 475; Rosemary .Rayfuse, "Regional Allocation Issues or Zen and the Art of Pie Cutting", Berkeley Electronic Press (bepress)m, accessed March 2011, 23 http://law.bepress.comunswwps/flrps/art10.

112 Molenaar (2003) n.112, 462.

113 Id.

114 Id. 463, Arts VII92) and XXIX of the 1980 CCAMLR Convention for Conservation of Antarctic Living resources, in force 1982, 19 *I.L.M.* 837.

115 Id. 465.

116 Mollenar (2003), n. 112, 479.

example the Commission on the Conservation of Southern Bluefin Tuna refused to allocate fish quota to South Africa before it had become a member (although Korea and Taiwan were successful).[117]

It is also worth noting that the increasing number of RFMOs follows the procedure of cooperating with non-members, who can take part in the meetings, can receive allocating opportunities and are exempt from the measures aimed at IUU.[118] The allocation of fisheries opportunities is the most fundamental task of RMFOs. This can also deal with many complex issues, such as the reconciling of the sovereignty of the coastal States with the interests of the other member States in the RFMOs regarding the allocation of fishing activities and the lack of legally binding rules on the allocation of fisheries[119] RFMOs follow very complex and varied allocation criteria and it is therefore very difficult to draw any general conclusions.

5.2. *RFMOs and the Questions of Jurisdiction and Enforcement*

As Rayfuse observes, traditional concepts of international law such as the freedom to fish on the high seas (although restricted to some extent, by e.g. due regard, peaceful purposes, and the interests of coastal States) means that the vessels of any State (not a member of the RFMO or a party to the Fish Stock Agreement) may fish on the high seas within the regulatory area of an RFMO. The restrictions imposed by the Fish Stocks Agreement (i.e. freedom to fish is granted only to the parties to that Agreement or to those who agree to abide by the measures set by RFMO), are not yet a part of customary international law, and therefore on the basis of the *pacta tertiis nec nocent nec prosunt* principle non-parties (or non-members) are exempt from the obligations under the Agreement or the RFMO. Further, the principle of the exclusivity of flag State jurisdiction also limits the effectiveness of RFMO allocation. Therefore RFMOs have no legal standing to enforce their own allocation regimes against non-members, and are thus powerless against IUU. Rayfuse also argues that IUU is carried out by nationals of member States and RFMOs cannot prevent it. The main problem according to this author is the lack of a comprehensive compliance mechanism for RFMOs in respect of their members, who may have little interest (e.g. commercial) in complying with

[117] Rayfuse, n.111.
[118] Molenaar (2003) n. 111, 466.
[119] Id. 468. The same author also mentions Art. 7 (2)(d) and (e), ensuring compatibility, and Art. 24(a) on special requirements of developing States.

limitations on their fishing efforts when non-members are not so required to comply.[120]

As regards IUU, the RFMOs were granted unprecedented powers under the Fish Stock Agreement, in contrast to UNCLOS, which merely obliges States engaged in fishing on the high seas for transboundary stocks to co-operate with each other, at their discretion.[121] Several Articles of the Fish Stocks Agreement deal with the matter of IUU and grant very far-reaching powers to RFMO members in relation to non-members. Of particular interest are the following: Articles 8(4),[122] 17(4),[123] 21,[124] 22,[125] and 33(2).[126]

---

120 Rayfuse, n. 111, see also id. To Our Children's Children 's Children: From Promoting to Achieving Compliance in High Seas Fisheries, *International Journal of Marine and Coastal Law* 20 (2005), 509.

121 Arts.63, 64 (1), 66 (5) and 118 of the 1982 LOS Convention.

122 Art. 8(4): "Only those States which are members of such an organization or participants in such an arrangement, or which agree to apply the conservation and management measures established by such organization or arrangement, shall have access to the fishery resources to which those measures apply".

123 Art. 7(4): "States which are members of such organization or participants in such arrangement shall exchange information with respect to the activities of fishing vessels flying the flags of States which are neither members of the organization nor participants in the arrangement and which are engaged in fishing operations for the relevant stocks. They shall take measures consistent with this Agreement and international law to deter activities of such vessels which undermine the effectiveness of subregional or regional conservation and management measures".

124 Art. 21(1): "In any high seas area covered by a subregional or regional fisheries management organization or arrangement, a State Party which is a member of such organization or a participant in such arrangement may, through its duly authorized inspectors, board and inspect, in accordance with paragraph 2, fishing vessels flying the flag of another State Party to this Agreement, whether or not such State Party is also a member of the organization or a participant in the arrangement, for the purpose of ensuring compliance with conservation and management measures for straddling fish stocks and highly migratory fish stocks established by that organization or arrangement".

125 Art. 22(1): "The inspecting State shall ensure that its duly authorized inspectors
(a) present credentials to the master of the vessel and produce a copy of the text of the relevant conservation and management measures or rules and regulations in force in the high seas area in question pursuant to those measures; (b) initiate notice to the flag State at the time of the boarding and inspection; (c) do not interfere with the master's ability to communicate with the authorities of the flag State during the boarding and inspection; (d) provide a copy of a report on the boarding and inspection to the master and to the authorities of the flag State, noting therein any objection or statement which the master wishes to have included in the report; (e) promptly leave the vessel following completion of the inspection if they find no evidence of a serious violation; and (f) avoid the use of force except when and to the degree necessary to ensure the safety of the inspectors and where the inspectors are obstructed in the execution of their duties. The degree of force used shall not exceed that reasonably required in the circumstances."

126 Art. 33(2): "States Parties shall take measures consistent with this Agreement and international law to deter the activities of vessels flying the flag of non-parties which undermine the effective implementation of this Agreement".

These Articles protect the interests of member States of the RFMOs against the activities of non-members which are detrimental to them (allowing the adoption of measures in accordance with international law and that Agreement), and introduce extensive powers enshrined in Articles 21 and 22 which do not reflect present customary international law, granting to non-flag States powers of enforcement which, according to classical international law, belong to flag States. Article 23 is also given as an example of such far-reaching powers.[127] However, a view may also be expressed that such powers already exist under general international law[128] (the Agreement is innovative in the sense that it obliges States parties to the Fish Stock Agreement to expand port State powers).

Many of the RFMOs incorporate the provisions of Article 33(2) and introduce a two-tiered procedure. The first tier is based on the need for cooperation between all States engaged in fishing for the regulated species; the second involves specific measures to deter IUU by forcing non-cooperating non-members to co-operate or join an RFMO. Such procedure can be exemplified by CCAMLR.[129]

However, there is a lot of criticism concerning the powers of RFMOs (also CCAMLR). It is alleged that many of the vessels engaged in IUU belong in fact to flag States members of CCAMLR. Therefore law-abiding RFMOs must rely on flag States to provide accurate catch data for their vessels operating in fisheries.[130] CCAMLR was also derided for its inability to control the IUU of Patagonian tooth fish, because of CCAMLR members' vested interest in IUU fishing.[131] Many of the proposed changes within RFMOs are resented by States whose economies depend on fish as their main source of revenue, as they fear that the decision-making process in such bodies will switch from science-based to conservationist (as with the International Whaling Commission), which rules out exploitation.[132]

[127] Art. 23(1): "1. A port State has the right and the duty to take measures, in accordance with international law, to promote the effectiveness of subregional, regional and global conservation and management measures. When taking such measures a port State shall not discriminate in form or in fact against the vessels of any State".

[128] Molenaar, (2003) n. 112, 473.

[129] *Id.* 473–474.

[130] Article 2, See also COP5 Decision 'Ecosystem Approach', Nairobi, 15–26 May 2000 (Decision V/6; COP 7 'Ecosystem Approach', Kuala Lumpur, 9–20 February 2004 (Decision VII/11).

[131] Ferrell, n. 61, 360–361.

[132] Molenaar, note 4, 555.

6. International Environmental Law and Fish Stocks Protection

6.1. *The CBD*

Article 1 of the CBD states its objectives: 'the conservation of biological diversity; the sustainable use of its components and fair and equitable sharing of the benefits arising from the utilisation of genetic resources'. Article 2 of the CBD also includes marine areas under its jurisdiction.[133] The Convention is based on the ecosystem approach. "Ecosystem" means a dynamic complex of plant, animal and micro-organism communities and their non-living environment interacting as a functional unit'. As Young observes, such an approach conforms to a view expressed by an increasing number of fisheries scientists and conservation biologists that the large-scale protection of the marine environment is preferable to traditional exploitation rates that achieve maximum sustainable yields.[134] *In situ*[135] and *ex situ*[136] conservation also constitute its founding principles. The Conference of Parties is the main organ of the CBD the task of which is to review the Convention.

6.2. *The CMS*

Article II sets out the fundamental principles of the Convention: '1. The Parties acknowledge the importance of migratory species being conserved and of Range States agreeing to take action to this end whenever possible and appropriate, paying special attention to migratory species the conservation status of which is unfavourable, and taking individually or in co-operation appropriate and necessary steps to conserve such species and their habitat. 2. The Parties acknowledge the need to take action to avoid any migratory species becoming endangered 3. In particular, the Parties a) should promote, co-operate in and support research relating to migratory species; b) shall endeavour to provide immediate protection for

133 '"Biological diversity" means the variability among living organisms from all sources including, *inter alia*, terrestrial, marine and other aquatic ecosystems and the ecological complexes of which they are part: this includes diversity within species, between species and of ecosystems'.

134 Young, n. 14, 65.

135 " '*In-situ* conditions' means conditions where genetic resources exist within ecosystems and natural habitats, and. in the case of domesticated or cultivated species, in the surroundings where they have developed their distinctive properties": Article 2.

136 " 'x-situ conservation' means the conservation of components of biological diversity outside their natural habitats": Article 2.

migratory species included in Appendix I; and c) shall endeavour to conclude Agreements covering the conservation and management of migratory species included in Appendix II'.

Essentially the CMS is a framework Convention on the basis of which the Parties enter into agreements. The Convention has two Appendices. Appendix I lists endangered migratory species, the taking of which by any of the range countries is prohibited (Article III). Appendix II covers migratory species that have a poor conservation status, or that have a conservation status 'which would significantly benefit from international cooperation that could be achieved by an international agreement' (Article IV). The range parties can enter into conservation agreements (Article IV (3) and (4)) or less formal Memoranda of Understanding. The CMS covers all types of migratory species: terrestrial, avian and marine.

7. Trade Law and Fish Stocks Protection

7.1. *CITES*

CITES is essentially a trade Convention. However, due to trade restrictions imposed on trade in certain species it plays a role in the protection of biological diversity. It has to be said, as well that CITES has adopted the precautionary approach, so 'scientific uncertainty should not be used as a reason for falling to act in the best interest of conservation of species'.[137] Therefore, in this respect CITES has the same approach as biodiversity treaties. Its structure and working are very complicated and developed through the decisions of the Conference of the Parties (COP). The detailed description of this Convention exceeds the framework of this study, so only the most fundamental principles of its functioning will be given. This Convention is of relevance as it also regulates, *inter alia,* the trade in endangered marine species (Article 1). The trade includes export, re-export, import and introduction from the sea (i.e. 'transportation into a State of specimens of any species which were taken in marine environment not under the jurisdiction of any States': Article 1). This definition is not, however, without controversy. CITES is based on three Appendices. In broad brushstrokes Appendix I relates to species in danger of extinction, and in principle the trade in such species is essentially prohibited. Trade in specimens of these species is permitted only in exceptional circumstances. Appendix II includes species not necessarily threatened with

[137] CITES Resolution Conf. 924 (Rev. COP14) (CITES listing criteria 2007).

extinction, but in which trade must be controlled in order to avoid utilization incompatible with their survival. The COP has adopted in Resolution Conf. 9.24 (Rev. COP14) a set of biological and trade criteria in order to assist in determining whether a species should be included in Appendix I or II. Appendix III contains species that are protected in at least one country, which requires the cooperation of other CITES Parties in controlling trade. Regarding Appendix I specimens CITES an import permit issued by the Management Authority of the State of import is required. This may be issued only if the specimen is not to be used for primarily commercial purposes and if the import will be for purposes that are not detrimental to the survival of the species. The Annex II species require export permits, and the exporting country must prove that the commercial trade is not detrimental to the wild population and that the specimen was legally obtained. In the case of Appendix III and trade from a State that included the species in that Appendix, an export permit issued by the Management Authority of that State is required. There are approximately ten fish species in Appendix I and ten in Appendix II. However CITES is weakened by several exceptions.[138] The specimens are subject to up-listing and down-listing between Appendices I and II, and this is done on the basis of so-called amendments adopted by a two-thirds majority vote. Appendix III species may be moved between the Appendices at any time by any party. A notable weakness of CITES is also the possibility of reservations being entered by a party not in agreement with the listing of species. The application of CITES to marine species is not without its problems, such as claims by certain States that the listing in CITES and the law of sea conflict with each other.[139] Also some procedures adopted by CITES (such a 'look-alike') were also considered inappropriate for marine species.

7.2. *The WTO*

The detailed analysis of the WTO is beyond the framework of this article.[140] It may be said that there are several factors which are related to

---

[138] Article VII: # or specimens in transit or being transhipped [see Resolution Conf. 9.7 (Rev. CoP13)]; for specimens that were acquired before CITES provisions applied to them (known as pre-Convention specimens, see Resolution Conf. 13.6); for specimens that are personal or household effects [see Resolution Conf. 13.7 (Rev. CoP14)]; for animals that were "bred in captivity" [see also Resolution Conf. 10.16 (Rev.)]; for plants that were "artificially propagated" [see also Resolution Conf. 11.11 (Rev. CoP14)]; for specimens that are destined for scientific research; for animals or plants forming part of a travelling collection or exhibition, such as a circus [see also Resolution Conf. 12.3 (Rev. CoP14)].

[139] For a detailed overview see Young, n. 14 134–188.

[140] See Young, n. 14, 85–133; 189–240.

international trade which influence fishing activities. One such factor is State subsidies, which, it is argued, promote overfishing.[141] The SCM Agreement's purpose is to control the use by the WTO members of subsidies. As Young states, thus far the WTO members have been unwilling to challenge the fisheries subsidies of another WTO member, and perhaps the suitability of the SCM Agreement for the purposes of dealing with subsides in fisheries can also be doubted.[142] Also of importance is the 1994 GATT,[143] especially due to its Article XX.[144] However, the interpretation by WTO dispute settlement bodies of Article XX of the 1947 and 1994 GATT has been subject to many critical comments.[145] The WTO has hitherto decided no cases on fish stocks. However, there were cases such as the 1991/1992 *Tuna /Dolphin* cases[146] and the 1998 *Shrimp/Turtle*[147] cases in which the WTO took decisions on marine living recourses. The first of these cases originated from the 1972 US Marine Mammal Protection Act, which banned imports of tuna from countries that did not have a conservation programme designed to protect dolphins in the tuna-fishing process. Tuna frequently swim in schools underneath dolphins. In order to catch the tuna, fishermen used to drag large nets through the water and then pull them up under the tuna. Dolphins swimming above the tuna would be caught at the same time and die in the nets along with the tuna. According to the MMPA American tuna fishermen adjusted their fishing

141 Agreement on Subsidies and Countervailing Measures (1994), ('SCM Agreement). Accessed March 23 2011, http://www.wto.org/english/docs_e/legal_e/24-scm.pdf.

142 Young, n. 14, 91.

143 Accessed March 18, 2011, http://www.wto.org/english/docs_e/legal_e/gatt47_e.pdf.

144 Relevant parts of Article XX of the 1994 GATTT: 'Subject to the requirement that such measures are not applied in a manner which would constitute a means of arbitrary or unjustifiable discrimination between countries where the same conditions prevail, or a disguised restriction on international trade, nothing in this Agreement shall be construed to prevent the adoption or enforcement by any contracting party of measures…(b) necessary to protect human, animal or plant life or health…' and (g) 'relating to the conservation of exhaustible natural resources if such measures are made effective in conjunction with restrictions on domestic production or consumption'.

145 See indepth, Malgosia Fitzmaurice and Panos Merkouris, "Canons of Treaty Interpretation; Selected Case Studies From the World Trade Organisation and the North American Free Trade Agreement", in: eds. Malgosia Fitzmaurice, Olufemi Elias and Panos Merkouris, *Treaty Interpretation and the Vienna Convention on the Law of Treaties: 30 Years On* (Leiden: Martinus Nijhoff Publishers, 2010), 153.

146

147 Accessed February 7, 2012 http://www.wto.org/english/tratop_e/envir_e/edis08_e .htm, See Robert Howse, 'The Appellate Body Rulings in the Shrimp/Turtle Case: A New Legal Baseline for the Trade and Environment Debate', 27 *Colum. J. Envtl.* L. 491. Accessed 6 February 2012, http://www.worldtradelaw.net/articles/howseshrimp.pdf, Globalization 101 The Levin Institute, The State University of New York, Accessed February 8, 2012, http://www.globalization101.org/index.php?file=issue&pass1=subs&id=151.

practices to avoid such deaths and the US banned tuna from countries in which dolphin deaths from tuna fishing exceeded the deaths from US tuna fishing by more than 25 percent. As a result, tuna from Mexico, Venezuela, Panama, Ecuador, and the tiny Pacific island of Vanuatu were banned in 1990.[148] The embargo also applied to 'intermediary' countries handling the tuna en route from Mexico to the United States. Often the tuna is processed and canned in one of these countries (Costa Rica, Italy, Japan, and Spain, and earlier France, the Netherlands Antilles, and the United Kingdom. Others, including Canada, Colombia, the Republic of Korea, and members of the Association of Southeast Asian Nations, were also named as 'intermediaries'). The dispute resolution panel decided that the United States could not justify the MMPA's ban on Mexican tuna imports for several reasons.[149]

The United States had implemented a ban on shrimp from countries whose fishing fleets did not have special 'turtle excluder devices', to prevent endangered sea turtles from being killed in the shrimping process. India, Malaysia, Thailand, and Pakistan claimed that the law was a disguised restriction on free trade and challenged the measure in the WTO's dispute resolution process.

The Shrimp/Turtle case was based on the US Endangered Species Act of 1973 which listed as endangered or threatened the five species of sea turtles that occur in US waters, and prohibited their 'take' within the US, in its

---

[148] Under the regime of 1947 GATT the adoption of a dispute panel report by the GATT could be blocked by the country found to be in violation of GATT rules. Therefore the tuna-dolphin panel decision never took effect. The Uruguay Round reforms reversed this rule. All panel reports are binding unless a consensus of all WTO members blocks adoption. Globalization 101, The Levin Institute, The State University of New York, Accessed March 30, 2011, http://www.globalization101.org/index.php?file=issue&pass1=subs&id=149; see also accessed 30 March 2011, http://www.wto.org/english/tratop_e/envir_e/edis04_e.htm.

[149] The Panel interpreted the exceptions of Article XX narrowly so that any one country cannot undermine the multilateral trade rules. The US could not place an embargo on imports of tuna products from Mexico simply because Mexican regulations on the way tuna was produced did not satisfy US regulations. However, the US could apply its regulations on the quality or content of the tuna imported (a 'product' versus 'process' issue). The panel did not accept extra-territoriality (i.e. that GATT rules did not allow one country to attempt to enforce its own domestic laws in another country—even to protect animal health or exhaustible natural resources). The GATT panel protected the multilateral trading system. In 1992, the EU lodged its own complaint, which resulted in a second panel report circulated to GATT members in mid-1994. The report upheld some of the findings of the first panel and modified others. There was no consensus to adopt the report, a requirement under the old GATT system. Accessed March 30, 2011.http://www.wto.org/english/tratop_e/envir_e/edis04_e.htm. After the GATT decision, the tuna-dolphin agreements were negotiated between the United States [and whom?], The International Dolphin

territorial sea and on the high seas. This Act required that US shrimp trawlers use 'turtle excluder devices' (TEDs) in their nets when fishing in areas where there was a significant likelihood of encountering sea turtles. Section 609 of US Public Law 101–102 of 1989 stated that shrimp harvested with technology that might adversely affect certain sea turtles could not in principle be imported into the US.[150] Therefore, fishermen of countries that had any of the five species of sea turtles and harvested shrimp with mechanical means had in practice to fulfil requirements comparable to those implemented by US shrimpers (i.e. use the TEDs) if they wanted to be certified to export shrimp products to the US. The Panel decided against the US ban as inconsistent with GATT Article XI limiting the use of import prohibitions or restrictions, and GATT Article XX which dealt with general exceptions to the rules, including for certain environmental reasons. The US appealed and the Appellate Body found that the measure did qualify for provisional justification under Article XX(g), but did not fulfil the requirements of the chapeau of Article XX defining when the general exceptions can be relied on. The Appellate Body ('AP') said that under WTO rules countries have the right to take trade action to protect the environment, without WTO permission. It also said that measures to protect sea turtles would be legitimate under GATT Article XX provided the non-discrimination criterion was met.[151] The US lost the case because it discriminated between WTO members. It provided some countries, mainly in the Caribbean, with technical and financial assistance and longer transition periods for their fishermen to start using turtle-excluder devices. The AB decided that the US had to enter into agreements with the States which brought the dispute (following the practice of the countries in the Caribbean).[152]

Conservation Programme was established. According to the Levin Institute there are sceptical views by certain environmentalists about whether this programme will succeed. Accessed March 30 2011, http://www.globalization101.org/index.php?file=issue&pass1=subs&id=149.

[150] Accessed March 30, 2011, http://www.wto.org/english/tratop_e/envir_e/ediso8_e.htm.

[151] "This measure has been applied by the United States in a manner which constitutes arbitrary and unjustifiable discrimination between Members of the WTO, contrary to the requirements of the chapeau of Article XX" (para. 186).

[152] The dispute was further followed under Article 21(5) of the Dispute Settlement Understanding (DSU) (Implementation Dispute). Malaysia argued] that the US had not properly implemented the findings of the Appellate Body (i.e. Malaysia argued that a proper implementation of the findings would be a complete lifting of the US ban on shrimps. The US argued that it had been requested only to review its application of the ban). To this effect, the US had issued Revised Guidelines for the Implementation of Section 609 of Public Law 101–162 Relating to the Protection of Sea Turtles in Shrimp Trawl

In conclusion, the answer to the question whether trade (WTO) is good or bad for the fisheries sector is very difficult. It may be noted, however, that until the 1990s conflicts between trade disputes and the environment were rare and changed dramatically after the *Tuna/Dolphin* case.[153]

The main goal of the WTO has been the pursuit of the policy of free trade.[154] Article XX, which is the exception to this policy for resource conservation and environmental protection, has so far been interpreted in a narrow and capricious manner. The WTO tends to treat 'green protectionism' with a degree of scepticism as a way to use trade barriers to protect domestic industry from competition, under the excuse of environmental regulation. The WTO adheres to the view that the responsibility for environmental policy should be carried out at the national level and that general decisions on international trade policy should not be clouded by environmental issues. Therefore environmental policy goals should not be implemented through international trade which results in the reduction of gains from trade. However, the argument that responsibility for environmental policies should be shouldered by national governments has

Fishing Operations (the 'Revised Guidelines') which replaced those which were the basis of the dispute. They introduced new criteria for the certification of shrimp exporters. However, Malaysia argued that Section 609, as applied, still breached Article XI: 1 and that the US could not impose any prohibition unless an international agreement allowed it to do so. The US did not contest that the implementing measure was incompatible with Article XI: 1, but argued that it was justified under Article XX(g) and that new Revised Guidelines remedied all the inconsistencies that had been identified by the Appellate Body under the chapeau of Article XX. The implementation panel was formed in order to examine the compatibility of the implementing measure with Article XX(g). Its conclusion was that the protection of migratory species was best achieved through international cooperation. Contrary, however to the Appellate Body's decision that had instructed the US to negotiate an international agreement for the protection of sea turtles with the parties to the dispute, the implementation Panel stated that the obligation was only an obligation to negotiate (not to conclude). It ruled in favour of the US as it found that the US had indeed made serious 'good faith' efforts to negotiate such an agreement. Malaysia appealed against the findings of the implementation Panel, as it submitted that the Panel had erred in concluding that the measure no longer constituted a means of 'arbitrary or unjustifiable discrimination' under Article XX. Malaysia was of the view that the US should have negotiated and concluded an international agreement on the protection and conservation of sea turtles before imposing the import prohibition. The Appellate Body upheld the implementation panel's findings and rejected Malaysia's contention that avoiding "arbitrary and unjustifiable discrimination" under the chapeau of Article XX required the conclusion of an international agreement. All information from accessed March 30, 2011 http://www.wto.org/english/tratop_e/envir_e/ediso8_e.htm.

153 Environment and Globalisation, The Levin Institute, Accessed February 6, 2012, http://www.globalization101.org.

154 J.M. Harris, "Trade and Environment", 2008, *The Encyclopaedia of Earth*, accessed 7 February 2012, http://www.eoearth.org/article/Trade_and_the_environment.

been subject to severe criticism, which was based on the arguments that competitive pressures may result in trading nations reducing environmental protection, that such an approach fails to take into consideration the inadequate institutional structures in many developing countries; and finally that it is unsuitable for dealing with environmental problems which are transboundary or global.[155]

8. Conclusions: the Blueprint for the Future?

The above considerations clearly indicate that there is no regime in international law which would be fully successful in fighting the decline in fish and combating IUU. The existence of numerous international law instruments (both binding and of soft-law character) is no doubt helpful, but cannot be said fully to remedy the situation. Therefore it was suggested that the international regulatory framework for the high seas needs comprehensive implementation and development in order to provide an adequate and comprehensive governance structure if fish piracy is to be tackled effectively.[156] The establishment of RFMOs can be said to be beneficial for maintaining fish stocks, as they are competent to regulate some areas that are outside national jurisdictions. It is argued that their role could be greatly enhanced to combat IUU fishing. For example, non-members should be encouraged to join the relevant RFMO in order to ensure that sound practices are adopted for fishing in these areas, or, at the very least, that vessels follow the rules of the RFMO (they may publish lists of vessels that fail to abide by RFMO regulations or lists of vessels authorised to fish in an area) to exert pressure on countries more tightly to regulate fisheries. It is also submitted that RFMOs may also require legislative strengthening in order to act efficiently.[157] The role of RFMOs varies very greatly, and as was observed in relation to CCAMLR, they are not entirely successful. In fact, the flag State remains the main entity in fisheries management. The FSA has many controversial provisions (mostly pertaining to the enforcement of the law on the high seas), and, as was noted above, there are numerous reasons why it is not (and unlikely to become) a global agreement. It may also be observed that prevalent in fisheries commission opting out system, whereby a State can lawfully opt out of a recommendation of the Commission (as Norway opted out of the moratorium on

---

155 Id.

156 Accessed February 6, 2012, http://www.oecd.org/dataoecd/26/37/35985301.pdf.

157 Ibid.

commercial whaling imposed by the International Whaling Commission) further weakens the legal regime under RFMOs. In order to reduce IUU cost increases for IUU can also come from government-sponsored actions (e.g. the elimination of tax havens, the more effective identification of beneficial owners of vessels, and laws to combat bribery). There are 'softer' options, such as education to highlight the harmful effects of IUU fishing and corporate governance initiatives.[158]

From the ecological point of view scholars and practitioners agree that possibly the best approach is the so-called ecosystem approach to fisheries (although this is also not without its difficulties).[159] There are several definitions of what constitutes an ecosystem.[160] Tansley captures the gist of the ecosystem approach as an ecological community, together with its environment, considered as a unit, which is characterised by a constant interchange 'within each system, not only between the organisms but between organic and the inorganic'.[161] Wang identified the key features of an ecosystem: an ecosystem exists in space with boundaries that may not be explicitly set. Ecosystems are distinguishable from each other based on their biophysical attributes and their location; an ecosystem includes both living organisms and their abiotic environment, including pools of organic and inorganic materials; the organism interact with each other and interact with the physical environment through fluxes of energy, organic and inorganic materials among the pools. These fluxes are mediated and functionally controlled by species behaviour and environmental forces. An ecosystem is dynamic and its structure and functions change with time. An ecosystem exhibits emergent properties that are characteristic of this type and are invariant within the domain of science.[162] Humans are also the elements of ecosystems.

158 Ibid.

159 Erik-Jaap. Molenaar, "Ecosystem –Based Fisheries Management, Commercial Fisheries, Marine Mammals and the 2001 Reykjavik Declaration in the Context of International Law", *International Journal of Marin and Coastal Law* 17 (2002) 561; "Fisheries Management FAO, 2003" S. Parsons, "Ecosystem Considerations in Fisheries Management: Theory and Practice" *International Journal of Marine and Coastal Law* 20 (2005) 381. It is worth noting that the EBFM is based on the precautionary approach (see e.g. Reykjavik Declaration).

160 E.g. H. Wang, 'Ecosystem Management and its Application in Large Marine Ecosystems: Science, Law, and Politics', 35 *ODILA* (2004); A.G. Tanley, 'The Use and Abuse of Vegetiational Concepts and Terms', *Ecology* 16(1935) 284.

161 Tansley, n. 71, 299.

162 Wang, n. 161, 136.

Certain international environmental law regimes provide for the ecosystem approach, such as the 1992 Convention on Biological Diversity (the CBD). The Fifth Conference of the parties in 2000 defined this approach.[163] The CBD applies the ecosystem approach to both terrestrial and marine species.[164] The FSA does not explicitly incorporate the ecosystem approach. However, its Preamble[165] and the application of the precautionary principle indicate that the CBD departed from the single-species-based approach in fisheries management.[166] Parsons is of the view that the FAO Code of Conduct for Responsible Fisheries also has implications for applying the ecosystem approach in fisheries management. It has similar provisions on fisheries to the FSA, in that it suggests that the measures adopted in fisheries management should ensure the protection not only of the target species, but also non-target, i.e. species which are associated with or dependent on it.[167]

Another question is so-called 'ecosystem management'. As Parsons explains, the definition which gained much support is that proposed by the Committee on the Scientific Basis for Ecosystem Management of the Ecological Society of America. It defines ecosystem management as 'the best understanding of the ecological interactions and processes necessary to sustain ecosystem structure and function'. This Society identified the most important elements of management: long-term sustainability as a

[163] CBD, "Ecosystem Approach", Fifth Conference of the Parties of the Convention on Biodiversity, Nairobi, Kenya, may 2000. It was defined as follows: "[t]he ecosystem approach is a strategy for the integrated management of land, water and living resources that promotes conservation and sustainable use in an equitable way. The application of the Ecosystem Approach will help to reach a balance of the three objectives of the convention: conservation; sustainable use; and the fair and equitable sharing of the benefits arising out the utilisation of genetic resources".

[164] During the second of the Conferences of the parties in Jakarta ("Jakarta Ministerial Statement on Implementation of the Convention on Biodiversity (Jakarta Mandate on Coastal and Marine Biodiversity"). This mandate specifically linked conservation, the issue of biodiversity and fishing activities and identified the following areas of importance: integrated management of marine and coastal areas; marine and coastal protected areas; the ecologically sustainable use of marine and coastal living resources; mariculture; alien species.

[165] The Preamble notes that States parties to this agreement are "conscious of the need to avoid adverse impacts on the marine environment, preserve biodiversity, maintain the integrity of marine ecosystems and minimize the risk of long-term or irreversible effects of fishing operations". The wording of Article 5 (Part II) also hints at the possible ecosystem approach as it states: that States and States fishing on the high seas shall "[a]ssess the impacts of fishing, other human activities and environmental factors on target stocks and species belonging to the same ecosystem or associated with or dependent upon the target stock". See also Article 5(e), (f) and (g).

[166] Parsons, n. 159, 387–388.

[167] Id. 388.

fundamental value; clear operational goals; sound, more ecological models and understanding; understanding complexity and interconnectedness; recognition of the dynamic character of ecosystems; attention to context and scale; acknowledgment of humans as ecosystem components; and commitment to adaptability and accountability.[168]

In relation to fisheries mention must be made of the FAO Guidelines on the Ecosystem Approach to Fisheries. The FAO Guidelines define the purpose of ecosystem approach to fisheries as to 'plan, develop and manage fisheries in a manner that addresses the multiple needs and desires of societies without jeopardising the options for future generations to benefit from the full range of goods and services provided by maritime ecosystems'. According to these Guidelines the Ecosystem Approach to Fisheries is as follows: '[a]n ecosystem approach to fisheries strives to balance diverse societal objectives, by taking into account the knowledge and uncertainties about biotic, abiotic and human components of ecosystems and their interaction and applying integrated approach to fisheries within ecologically meaningful boundaries'.

The ecosystem approach, however, has to be viewed against the background of global issues such as inequalities in economic development; the conflicts between North and South; and the role of fisheries in combating poverty. Such a view was considered by Molenaar who very persuasively describes the complexity of the ecosystem approach and the plethora of elements which have to be taken into consideration, such as the interrelationship between marine mammals and commercial fisheries. First of all this author argues that a distinction has to be drawn between ecosystem management and ecosystem-based fisheries management (the EBFM). The first involves the balancing of social, economic, environmental, political and other interests, while EBFM deals with a sectoral approach which 'conforms to broader societal choices'.[169] However, there is no broadly accepted definition of EBFM. The contrasting approaches to EBFM are a single-or multi-species approach which does not capture the holistic picture, including humans, as EBFM does.[170] However, as the same author argues, there are several factors which make the application of EBFM problematic; thus States' choice is to incorporate less troublesome ecosystem considerations instead of ambitious but complex EBFM. First of all there is a spatial issue about aligning EBFM with Large Marine Ecosystems

168 Cited in Parsons, n. 160.
169 Molenaar, n. 160, 573.
170 *Id* 574.

(LMEs) which do not coincide with the partition of oceans into maritime zones. The determination of which functional relationships exist between ecosystems is a very complex matter, such as cause and effect relationships, which can be very chaotic. Therefore, there is limitation imposed by science.

Finally, the use of EBFM can be very costly, so that 'it may be sounder not to engage in fishing at all'.[171] Taking all this into account, Molenaar is of the view that EBFM in the future will be used as a complement to single- or multi-species management.[172]

In fact the only known commission to apply the ecosystem approach is the CCAMLR in the Southern Ocean. It was also the first body to apply the precautionary principle. The CCAMLR approach to the conservation of the marine living resources of Antarctica is defined in Article II. Harvesting in this area and associated activities are to follow these principles:

(a) the prevention of a reduction in the size of any harvested population to levels below those which ensure its stable recruitment. The size should not be allowed to fall below the level close to that which ensures the greatest net annul increment; (b) the maintenance of the ecological relationship between harvested, dependent and related populations of Antarctic marine living resources and the restoration of depleted populations to the level defined above; (c) the prevention of change(s) or minimisation of the risk of change(s) in the marine ecosystem which are not potentially reversible over two or three decades. CCAMLR takes into account all the delicate and complex relationships between organisms and the physical processes that constitute the Antarctic ecosystem and the interdependence between species (e.g. the relationship between fish and krill). To this effect CCAMLR closely monitors the effect which krill harvesting may have on krill-eating species and which in turn are eaten by krill predators.[173]

The issue which is beyond the framework of this essay is the question of cooperation between various legal regimes. As was explained in this study, fish stocks are subject to different legal regimes (such the rules of the law of sea and environmental law, in which can be singled out the regimes of the WTO and CITES). This question was investigated in detail by Young, who addresses the interaction between these different regimes which can

---

171 *Id* 585.
172 Id.
173 Parsons, n. 160, 409. See also D. Miller et al, " Managing Antarctic Living Resources: the CCMLR Approach", *International Journal and of Marine and Coastal Law* 19 (2004): 317.

broadly be categorised as deriving from parallel State membership of those regimes, mutual agreement by States or autonomous institutional arrangements.[174]

Young suggests that regime interaction should be constrained by procedural safeguards in order to ensure openness, transparency, participation and ongoing scrutiny and review.[175]

---

174 Young, n. 14, 243–287.
175 Id. 287.

EXTRACTIVE INDUSTRIES, CORRUPTION AND TRANSPARENCY

Indira Carr and Elina Konstantinidou***

Introduction

It is a truism to say that the primary aim of businesses is to seek and follow profitable industries. In this process there is always the danger that they may lose sight of integrity. Much ink has been spilt on the role of businesses as suppliers of bribes in business transactions, be they foreign direct investment (FDI), public procurement or sale and supply of goods and services. These bribes are paid for a variety of reasons from obtaining contracts, licenses and leases to beneficial tax deals. In recent times we have seen a number of multinational companies (MNCs) under the lens for alleged bribery. The dropping of its investigation of BAE by the UK Serious Fraud Office (SFO) on grounds of national interest was a high profile event that focused the attention of the public on the prevalence of corruption in the business sector and that of the international community on the lack of enforcement by the UK of its anti-corruption laws.[1] The high incidence of corruption is not unique to the defence sector. The "cancer of corruption"[2] touches other sectors

---

* I would like to thank both the Arts & Humanities Research Council (AHRC) and the British Academy for funding projects on corruption in international business, use of conditionalities to combat corruption and use of corporate social responsibility (CSR) as a tool to increase business integrity. I also wish to thank Elina Konstantinidou for her contribution of the section on Azerbaijan.

** Doctoral student, University of Surrey.

[1] See Indira Carr and Opi Outhwaite, 'The OECD Anti-Bribery Convention ten Years On', *Manchester Journal of International Economic Law* 5(1) (2008): 3. The SFO increasingly uses plea bargaining in corruption cases. For more on this see Indira Carr, 'Use of Plea Bargaining in Corruption Cases – A Desirable Development?' (forthcoming). See also Andre Lotz (2011) 'BAE Systems & Tanzania: Investigating 1999s Suspect Radar Deal', *Consultancy Africa Intelligence* 17 January 2011. Available at http://www.consultancyafrica.com/index.php?option=com_content&view=article&id=642:bae-systems-and-tanzania-investigating-1999s-suspect-radar-deal&catid=60:conflict-terrorism-discussion-papers&Itemid=265 (accessed 1 February 2011).

[2] This phrase was coined by James D Wolfensohn, President of the World Bank (WB). While the WB had been aware of corruption in its funded projects it had not addressed the issue on the grounds it was a political matter. Wolfensohn however brought about a change in the WB's thinking towards corruption by stating that "the 'C' word [being corruption] was not [to be defined] as a political issue but as something social and economic."

including the extractive industries sector. For instance, in 2008, BP was named in a lawsuit filed by the Chairman of Grynberg Production Corporation for alleged bribery involving public officials from Kazakhstan.[3] It is no exaggeration that even a cursory trawl through newspapers and journals in the English language reveals at least one or two reports of corruption on a daily basis with businesses as suppliers of bribes to the public sector. The high prevalence of business corruption related news in the media indeed endorses the findings of a World Bank (WB) survey measuring bribery from the private sector to the public sector worldwide conducted in 2000. This survey estimated bribery at US$ 1 trillion per annum.[4] According to Daniel Kaufmann "the main point is that [bribery] is not a relatively small phenomenon of a few billion dollars – far from it".[5]

This paper, in Part I, examines in general terms the measures taken at the international level to combat corruption both through regulatory and self-regulatory mechanisms to provide a broad understanding of the framework which has influenced or seeks to influence both policy-makers and businesses. Part II, in brief, provides an account of the link between poor economic growth and corruption in resource rich developing states to give the context for the recently adopted Extractive Industries Transparency Initiative (EITI) aimed at reducing corruption through the promotion of transparency both by companies and the state. Part III focuses on two states – Azerbaijan (a pioneer state of the EITI process) and Nigeria – with a view to highlighting the merits and demerits of incorporating the EITI as a voluntary process or within a statutory framework, as is the case in Nigeria with its the Extractive Industries Transparency Act, 2007 (NEITI Act).

JD Wolfensohn, 'Remarks at a Global Forum on Fighting Corruption', 24 February 1999 available at http://www.worldbank.org. (Accessed 1 March 2010.) On corruption in WB funded projects see for instance 'Dams On Trial The World Bank and the '"Cancer Of Corruption"' available at http://www.odiousdebts.org/odiousdebts/publications/Dams On Trial.pdf (accessed 1 March 2010) which describes the bribing of officials by major companies in the Lesotho Highland Dam project.

[3] 'BP named in Kazakhstan bribery lawsuit', available at http://www.mallenbaker.net/csr/page.php?Story_ID=2056 (accessed 1 January 2012).

[4] http://web.worldbank.org/WBSITE/EXTERNAL/NEWS/0,,contentMDK:20190295~menuPK:34457~pagePK:34370~piPK:34424~theSitePK:4607,00.html (undated interview with Daniel Kaufmann); see also 'Costs of Corruption' 8 April 2004 available at http://web.worldbank.org/WBSITE/EXTERNAL/NEWS/0,,contentMDK:20190187~menuPK:34457~pagePK:64003015~piPK:64003012~theSitePK:4607,00.html. (Both accessed 1 March 2010.).

[5] Ibid.

I. The International Anti-Corruption Framework

Since the mid to late 1990s there has been intense activity on the international scene to deal with corruption. The inter-governmental organisations such as the Organisation for Economic Cooperation and Development (OECD) and the United Nations (UN) promoted the combating and prevention of corruption through conventions aimed at bringing about harmonisation of anti-corruption laws across jurisdiction through ratification and effective implementation. Soft law instruments such as guidelines and principles were also devised for business to adopt and follow. In this part both regulation and self-regulation are explored in brief.

Before proceeding to the section on conventions a few words need to be said about the Principal-Agent-Client Model (PAC Model) since it has greatly influenced the anti-corruption framework. It has resulted in various changes to public administration systems such as transparency in public procurement processes[6] and declaration of public officials' assets. This model was put forward by Klitgaard and Rose-Ackerman[7] in response to the functionalist theorists[8] who saw corruption as playing an important function in the economic growth of developing countries. Some support can be garnered using illustrations such as India where the only way round the Licence Raj[9] was through bribes and kickbacks. However payment of bribes and kickbacks for circumventing the bureaucratic machinery of a state, if unchecked, poses the danger of entrenching corruption in the cultural, business and political ethos of a state. Corruption also creates an elite class, largely consisting of politicians, civil servants and businessmen and contributes to creating a huge gap between the haves and have-nots. This leaves scope for civil unrest and loss of legitimacy of the government

---

[6] On how corruption enters the public procurement process see for instance OECD *Bribery in Public Procurement: Methods Actors and Counter-Measures* Paris: OECD, 2007.

[7] Robert Klitgaard *Controlling Corruption* Berkeley: University of California Press, 1988; Susan Rose Ackermann *Corruption & Government* Cambridge: CUP, 1999.

[8] Among these theorists are Leys, Leff and Nye. See Colin Leys, 'What is the Problem about Corruption?' *Journal of Modern African Studies* 3 (1965): 215; N H Leff, 'Economic Development through Bureaucratic Corruption' *American Behavioural Scientist* 8(3) (1964): 8; and Joseph S Nye, 'Corruption and Political Development: A Cost-Benefit Analysis' in A Heidenheimer (ed) *Political Corruption: Readings in Comparative Analysis* New York: Holt, Reinhart & Wilson, 1970.

[9] Phillipe Aghion, Robert Burgess et al 'The Unequal Effects of Liberalization: Evidence from Dismantling the License Raj in India' December 2005, available at http://www.cepr.org/meets/wkcn/2/2360/papers/Burgess.pdf (accessed 12 December 2011).

in the eyes of the citizens. The recent Arab Spring provides a good illustration.[10] Bureaucratic systems within a state, from a governance perspective, are also likely to increase since corruption is likely to be seen as a lucrative and convenient source of wealth. And in extreme circumstances the state itself can become a financial predator[11] so that at every stage of daily existence the citizen is harassed into paying bribes.

According to the PAC model corruption is the betrayal of the principal's (P) interest by the agent (A) in pursuit of his own by accepting or seeking a benefit from the client (C) who is the service seeker. However for corruption the following conditions need to be present: (1) P should be in a powerful position; (2) A should have some discretion in administering the services, and (3) there is a lack or near lack of accountability.[12] So, where a state (P) has natural resources and the decision of to whom to give exploratory and extraction rights is left to the judgment of the public official (A) with no transparent processes and procedures on decision-making, the situation has the obvious potential to lead to corruption. The solution to reducing corruption is through greater competition, improving the environment within which discretion is allowed and exercised so that it imparts confidence in the way the discretion is exercised, and introducing greater accountability and transparency.[13] It could be said that accountability and transparency are two sides of the same coin. While

---

[10] See Lisa Anderson, 'Demystifying the Arab Spring' in *The New Arab Revolt* Foreign Affairs/CFR eBook, May/June 2011. Summary available at http://www.foreignaffairs.com/articles/67693/lisa-anderson/demystifying-the-arab-spring (accessed 15 January 2012).

[11] Michael Bratton and Eldred Masunungre, 'The Anatomy of Political Predation: Leaders, Elites and Coalitions in Zimbabwe, 1980–2010' Research Paper 09 (2011), Developmental Leadership Program.

[12] This is also often called the Weberian rational-legal model of administration. According to this model the public and private sphere of officials are separate and this separation has to be maintained (Max Weber, *The Theory of Social and Economic Organization* New York: Free Press, 1947). Until recently (the nineteenth century) in much of Europe the rule was of a patrimonial type and did not follow the Weberian rational-legal model. The transition to the Weberian model was a gradual one. For more on this gradual evolution from patrimony where all assets, personal and public, are owned by the leader to the modern Weberian model, see Douglass North and Robert Thomas *Rise of the Western World: A New Economic History* Cambridge: Cambridge University Press, 1996.

[13] For more on this see Indira Carr, 'Corruption, the Southern African Development Community Anti-corruption Protocol and the Principal—Agent—Client Model' *International Journal of Law in Context* 5(2) (2009): 147. While this model is used by both Klitgaard and Rose Ackerman to explain corruption in the public-private interface

accountability is normally construed as a counting exercise, in governance speak it is understood to include responsibility, answerability and responsiveness.[14] Providing explanations and justifications for behaving in a certain manner are central to the notion of accountability alongside any sanctions for behaving irresponsibly. Accountability implies both internal and external engagement in that being accountable extends to those within an institution and those outside of it such as the citizens. To make an institution answerable for its behaviour it is also important that there is transparency, access to information, which makes public scrutiny possible thus enabling exposure of institutional incompetence and corrupt behaviour. As Florini says "increased levels of transparency ... serve[s] the public interest, necessary to both good governance and well-functioning markets. It is a general principle of good governance that decision makers should be held accountable for their decision. Otherwise, error breeds upon error, and corruption breeds unchecked".[15]

Regional and International Conventions

Currently there are six regional and international conventions in force.[16] These are:

(1) Organisation of American States Inter-American Convention against Corruption 1996 (OAS Convention);[17]
(2) OECD Convention on Combating Bribery of Public Officials in International Business Transactions, 1997 (Anti-Bribery Convention);[18]

it could be easily adapted to explain corruption in the private sector which has also caught the attention more recently of policymakers.

14 For a variety of definitions of accountability see Andre Schedler, Larry Diamond and Marc Plattner *The Self-Restraining State: Power and Accountability in New Democracies* Bould: Lynne Reinner, 1999; Richard Mulgan, 'Accountability: An Ever-Expanding Concept?' *Public Administration* 78(3) (2002): 555–573; Robert Behn, *Rethinking Democratic Accountability* Washington DC: Brookings Institution, 2001; John Ackerman, 'State-Society Synergy for Accountability: Beyond 'Exit' and 'Voice'' *World Development* 32(3) (2003): 447–463.

15 Ann M Florini, 'Does the Invisible Hand Need a Transparent Glove? The Politics of Transparency' Paper prepared for the Annual World Bank Conference on Development Economics, Washington DC, 28–30 April 1999, 3.

16 There is also an EU Convention (but I have not listed this since it is devoted to fighting corruption involving community officials).

17 In force since 6 March 1997.

18 In force since 15 February 1999.

(3) Council of Europe Criminal Law Convention on Corruption 1999 (COE Convention)[19] and additional protocol to the Criminal Law Convention on Corruption 2003 (COE Protocol);[20]
(4) Council of Europe Civil Law Convention on Corruption 1999 (COE Civil Convention);[21]
(5) African Union Convention on Preventing and Combating Corruption 2003 (AU Convention);[22] and
(6) United Nations Convention against Corruption, 2003 (UNCAC).[23]

Of these, the most influential are the Anti-Bribery Convention and the UNCAC. The former focuses on the corporate sector as supplier of bribes to foreign public officials whilst engaging in international business transactions overseas. The latter comprehensive in scope has attracted more than 150 ratifications on the basis of which it could be said to be a near-global anti-corruption convention. For these reasons the discussion in this section is restricted to these conventions. This is not however to say that the other conventions are not at all influential. The OAS Convention is influential in the Americas, the AU Convention in Africa and the COE Convention within Europe. It should also be said that despite differences in some of the wording between the conventions there is a great deal of convergence in the substantive provisions. It could therfore be asked why have so many different conventions? No single reason is identifiable though there are a number of possible explanations. Firstly, region-specific conventions are likely to reflect the social and political issues and ethos specific to that region or part of that region. For instance, the AU Convention has a provision on funding of political parties (Article 10) which for instance is not found in the OAS Convention or the Anti-Bribery Convention. Second, regional conventions have the potential to impart ownership of the convention. This sense of ownership is particularly relevant for states with a colonial past. There is a tendency to see transplants of a legal framework devised by the developed world with suspicion and as a manifestation of neo-colonialism. Third, since regional conventions are likely to have a limited number of ratifications being restricted to members of the regional organisation, the monitoring of the implementation can be carried out with rigour. For example, the UNCAC

19 In force since 1 July 2002.
20 In force since 1 February 2005.
21 In force since 1 November 2003.
22 In force since 5 August 2006.
23 In force since 14 December 2005.

implementation review process is far behind those processes that are in place for the OAS Convention, the COE Convention and the Anti-Bribery Convention.

We will restrict ourselves, for the purposes of this paper, to the Anti-Bribery Convention and the UNCAC. The Anti-Bribery Convention was the result of a lengthy process of diplomatic pressure from the US which had passed its Foreign Corrupt Practices Act in 1977 (FCPA) when revelations surfaced that the payment of bribes to public officials, politicians and donations to political parties by US business whilst engaging in business abroad was commonplace.[24] The impetus for this Act also came at a time when the US was gripped with the Watergate scandal.[25] It took nearly twenty years to convince the economically developed countries that they needed legislation similar to the FCPA in place.[26] The end result was the Anti-Bribery Convention. Given the historical antecedents its scope is limited. It focuses on the bribe giver and requires contracting states to make active bribery of a foriegn public official an offence. A promise given directly or indirectly, a pecuniary or other advantage to a foreign public official in order to obtain business or other improper advantage in the context of an international business context is an offence (Article 1(1)). "Foreign public official" is defined widely to include civil servants, Members of Parliament, the judiciary and those working in public undertakings (Article 1(4)). The provision on sanctions expects that the states will adopt those that are effective and proportionate (Article 3). And since the aim of

24 A survey by the Security Exchange Commission found that "[m]ore than 400 corporations have admitted making questionable or illegal payments. The companies, most of them voluntarily, have reported paying out well in excess of $300 million in corporate funds to foreign government officials, politicians, and political parties. These corporations have included some of the largest and most widely held public companies and over 117 of them rank in the top Fortune 500 industries. The abuses disclosed run the gamut from bribery of high foreign officials in order to secure some type of favorable action by a foreign government to so-called facilitating payments that allegedly were made to ensure that government functionaries discharge certain ministrial [sic] or clerical duties. Sectors of industry typically involved are: drugs and health care; oil and gas production and services; food products; aerospace, airlines and air services, and chemicals." The House Report 95–640, 95th Congress, 1st Session, US House of Representatives. Available at http://10.173.2.10/criminal/fraud/fcpa/history/1977/houseprt.html (accessed 1 March 2010).

25 For more on the Watergate scandal see Keith Olson *Watergate: The Presidential Scandal that Shook America*. Lawrence, Kansas: Kansas University Press, 2003; Barry Sussman *The Great Coverup: Nixon and the Scandal of Watergate* Catapulter Books, 2010.

26 The response on the part of the UK, to suggestions that they adopt FCPA-like legislation is quite illuminating. It felt that the importance of the export market for the economy meant that they could not take the moral tone adopted by the US. See http://image.guardian.co.uk/sys-files/Guardian/documents/2007/05/29/ch06doc1.pdf (accessed 12 December 2011).

this Convention is to fight bribery from the supply side states are required to put in place measures regarding liability of legal persons, in accordance with their legal principles (Article 2).

The UNCAC by contrast is more ambitious not only in trying to fight corruption through the creation of a range of criminal offences by the States Parties (SPs) but also in recommending measures for preventing it. Unlike the Anti-Bribery Convention, the language of the UNCAC varies from the mandatory to the discretionary, from "shall adopt" to "shall consider adopting". The SPs therefore in some cases have a degree of flexibility in the adoption of the various offences. Amongst the offences listed by the UNCAC are both active and passive bribery (that is bribery from the supply side and the demand side) of national public officials (Article 15) and active bribery of foreign public officials (Article 16). The definitions of "public official" and "foreign public official" is wide to include persons holding a legislative, executive, administrative or judicial office as well as civil servants of an international organisation (Articles 2 (a), (b) and (c)). The other offences created by the UNCAC are bribery in the private sector (Article 21), embezzlement of property both in the public and private sector (Articles 17 and 22), trading in influence (Art 18), illicit enrichment (Article 20) and abuse of function (Art 19) and laundering and concealing the proceeds of corruption (Articles 23 and 24).

The UNCAC like the Anti-Bribery Convention also includes the liability of legal persons within its ambit and in Article 26(1) requires the SPs to establish the liability of legal persons in participation of the offences that have been established in accordance with the Convention. However states have the freedom to make legal persons subject to civil, criminal or administrative liability depending on their legal principles. Other areas addressed by the UNCAC are improvements based on transparency to the public procurement systems (Article 9), and enhancement of the accounting and auditing standards so that corruption-related payments are not hidden in financial statements (Article 12(1) and 15(3)).

Prevention is an important focus of the UNCAC and Article 5 sets out the preventive anti-corruption policies and practices that are to be followed by SPs. The SPs are expected to collaborate with each other and other relevant international and regional organizations in the pursuit of the anti-corruption goals (Article 5(4)). These goals include developing and implementing or maintaining effective co-ordinated anti-corruption policies that promote the participation of society and reflect the principles of the rule of law, proper management of public affairs and public integrity, transparency and accountability (Article 5(1)). Since participation of civil society, NGOs and community-based organizations are seen as essential elements in fighting and preventing corruption the SPs are required to promote their active participation (Article 13(1)). As part of enhancing public sector integrity states are expected to have mechanisms for asset declaration by public officials in place and also introduce codes of conduct. In order to improve detection protection of whistleblowers is also promoted (Article 33).

The establishment of specialized agencies and preventive anti-corruption bodies that disseminate knowledge about the prevention of corruption and implement preventive anti-corruption policies and practices is outlined in Article 5 (Articles 36, 6). The UNCAC also contains provisions on enabling co-operation between national authorities (Article 38), and international co-operation (Article 43), mutual legal assistance (Article 46) and extradition (Article 44). The issue of sanctions is addressed in Article 30 and depending on the gravity of the offence, states are free to use fines, imprisonment or a combination of both.

A unique feature of the UNCAC is the extensive provisions on asset recovery. Recovery of assets once they have flown out of the state into bank accounts in foreign jurisdictions can indeed prove to be difficult. The inclusion of these provisions is an innovative development and should work in favour of developing countries who are the victims of the flight of capital illegally obtained by their politicians and civil servants.[27]

As apparent from the brief description of the two conventions above the aim is to induce integrity both in the private and public sector and the UNCAC goes beyond creating criminal offences to also address important issues such as prevention and detection through the involvement of multiple stakeholders such as citizens, civil society and organisations. However the issue of whether regulation will of itself achieve the desired ends of fighting and preventing corruption is debatable. Regulation is prescriptive by nature and by giving rules and directions it moulds behaviour to achieve certain goals that are normally seen as necessary for the public good by

[27] For instance, during General Sani Abacha's term as President of Nigeria, he and his family are reported to have obtained through embezzlement and corruption around US$ 4 billion. Some of the funds were deposited in bank accounts in foreign jurisdictions. For more on this and recovery of these assets see 'Sani Abacha' available at http://www.assetrecovery.org/kc/node/5 (accessed 1 February 2011); Auszug aus dem Urteil der 1. öffentlichrechtlichen Abteilung des schweizerischen Bundesgerichtes im Fall Sani Abacha und weitere Beteiligte gegen das Bundesgericht (Verwaltungsgerichtsbeschwerde), vom 7. February 2005. See also Jena-Pierre Brun, Larissa Gray, Clive Scott and Kevin M Stephenson *Asset Recovery Handbook* Washington DC: The World Bank, 2011.

the policy-makers. The policy-makers in making rules expect them to be followed but this may not always be the case. So in order to ensure that rules are followed the policy-maker has a number of available tools ranging from heavy penalties (to act as a deterrent) to enforcement systems. While in theoretical terms (and in an ideal world) this sounds a workable system reality is always a few steps removed from the ideal conditions framing the policy-maker's thinking. In practice enforcement may not be and is not always efficient. Certainly, when it comes to corruption enforcement is not as effective as it should be even in developed nations who see themselves as adhering to and as the guardians of the rule of law. For instance, the OECD's review of the implementation of the Anti-Bribery Convention has exposed the lack of enforcement of the anti-bribery laws in the contracting states. The UK has been criticised consistently by the OECD for its lack of enforcement.[28] Without doubt the dropping of the investigation by the SFO of allegations of bribery by BAE did not help in displacing this criticism. And where states do not respect the rule of law or the judiciary is weak regulation seems a futile attempt to bring about a change in the behaviour of businesses. Against this background infusing ethical behaviour or integrity into the dealings of business through self-regulatory mechanisms seems an attractive weapon to have in the anti-corruption armoury.

Self-Regulation

The commercial world is no stranger to self-regulation. The standardisation of banking and accounting norms traceable to the fourteenth century is one illustration.[29] Of relevance to business integrity is the recent development of the concept of "corporate social responsibility" or CSR which focuses on companies behaving responsibly towards the environment and society at large.[30] In doing so the expectation within the CSR dialogue is

---

[28] See for instance OECD 'United Kingdom : Phase 2 bis Report on the Application of the Convention on Combating Bribery of Foreign Public Officials in International Business Transactions and 1997 Recommendation on Combating Bribery in International Business Transactions', available at http://www.oecd.org/dataoecd/23/20/41515077.pdf (accessed 11 October 2011).

[29] John Dunning, *Multinational Enterprises and the Global Economy* London: Addison-Wesley, 1993.

[30] CSR took shape during the 1950s and 1960s even though some felt that businesses were not equipped to enter the general welfare arena which would be best left to the State (Theodore Levitt, 'The Dangers of Social Responsibility' *Harvard Business Review* September-October (1958): 41). A number of social movements ranging from women's rights, consumer rights and rights of the newly independent countries to a healthy

that the companies will look beyond shareholders' interest and profit-seeking. Research in this area indicates that there is a "business case" for CSR since participation by stakeholders, other than shareholders and creditors, such as local communities and consumers contributes to economic efficiency and profits.[31] The most common approach to advancing CSR has been through company codes of conduct and there is evidence from a survey that there is support for such codes. Also the view that emerges from this survey is that collective codes of conduct such as the UN Global Compact would have a far reaching influence on CSR policies adopted by companies.[32]

Before examining how the international community has promoted CSR a few words on what could be said to be the negative features. Its self-regulatory, hence voluntary, nature means that it is open to abuse. This vulnerability inherent in CSR leads to the view held by many that it is nothing but "window-dressing"[33] or "green-wash."[34] Some also see the CSR movement simply as a means of blocking mandatory regulation.[35] Given the widespread cynicism towards CSR, transparency may provide the answer to communicating a company's serious engagement with ethical issues. A company could reveal its compliance systems and the extent to which they have contributed to the company furthering their CSR agenda for external scrutiny.[36]

environment are supposed to have influenced the CSR movements. Also the growing might of Multinational Corporations (MNCs) contributed to growing demands for CSR from activists such as Pesticide Action Network and Corporate Watch. See Laura Albareda, Josep Lazano, Antonio Tencati, Atli Middtun and Francesco Perrini, 'The Changing Role of Governments in Corporate Social Responsibility: Drivers and Responses'. *Business Ethics: A European Review* 17(4) (2008): 347.

31 See Peter Yeoh, 'The Direction and Control of Corporations: Law or Strategy?' *Managerial Law* 49(1/2)2007: 37. Fred Robbins, 'Why Corporate Social Responsibility should be Popularised but not Imposed' *Corporate Governance* 8(3)(2008): 330 and Charles Holliday, Stephan Schmidheiny and Philip Watts, *Walking the Talk: The Business Case for Sustainable Development* Sheffield, Greenleaf Publishing, 2002.

32 McKinsey and Company, 'Shaping the New Roles of Competition: UN Global Compact Participant Mirror' (2007) available at http://www.unglobalcompact.org/docs/news_events/8.1/McKinsey.pdf. Accessed 1 March 2010.

33 Mollie Painter-Morland, 'Triple Bottom-Line Reporting as Social Grammar: Integrating Corporate Social Responsibility' Business Ethics: A European Review 15(4) (2000): 352; EVK Fitzgerald, *Regulating Large International Forms* (UNRISD Technology, Business and Society Programme, Paper 5, Geneva, UNRISD, 2002).

34 Jedrzej Frynas, 'Corporate Social Responsibility and International Development: Critical Assessment' *Corporate Governance: An International Review* 16(4)(2008): 274.

35 Christian Aid, *Behind the Mask: The Face of Corporate Social Responsibility* (London, Christian Aid, 2004).

36 According to John Ruggie, less than one in four share such information with the public.

Many companies draft bespoke codes of conduct[37] to suit their needs (such as sector, geographical reach) but the international community has provided guidelines and rules for dealing with corruption. These standards are useful since they provide a common framework of reference thus bringing about greater impact through a harmonised approach. Of the corporate citizenship initiatives, the most widely known are those drafted by the OECD, the International Chamber of Commerce (ICC) and the UN.

The OECD Guidelines for Multinational Enterprises (Guidelines) aims to promote responsible behaviour on the part of companies located in the OECD states and includes the measures required for combating corruption. These range from greater transparency within organisations to adopting anti-corruption policies and securing compliance with these policies to prevention of slush funds and illegal contributions to political parties. States that adhere to the Guidelines have a national contact point (NCP) to whom instances of bribery can be reported. There is some indication that these NCPs have taken effective measures.[38]

The United Nations Global Compact (UNGC), a corporate citizenship initiative that has received global attention, provides a platform for companies to commit to its ten universal principles. Its tenth principle requires business to work against corruption in all its forms, including bribery. Launched across the five continents well over 2000 companies are reported as having signed up to the UNGC.[39] Upon signature the company is free to display the UNGC mark thus assuring that it subscribes to the its principles. Active engagement with different stakeholders is encouraged and to enable this, the Global Compact Office provides facilitation and support to all stakeholders. There is evidence of companies collaborating with local CSOs to set up ethical codes. For instance, Total South Africa[40] is reported as having set up an ethics management programme, a result of

[37] It is also not unknown for companies to adopt a bespoke code of conduct as a result of external pressures from activists and NGOs. Rio Tinto in Namibia is an instance of this which resulted in their adoption of Rossing Communities Policy for its mine in Rossing which includes with it corporate-community partnership and community health. John Ruggie, 'Managing Corporate Social Responsibility' *The Financial Times* 25 October 2002.

[38] For list of cases visit www.oecdwatch.org (an international network of CSOs that promote corporate accountability and responsibility). Accessed 1 June 2009.

[39] Further information on the progress made by these networks and list of participants (which include small and medium sized enterprises and large enterprises) are available at www.unglobalcompact.org (accessed 1 March 2010).

[40] A subsidiary of Total Société Anonyme.

collaboration with the Ethics Institute of South Africa[41] and the adopted code of ethics is intolerant of corruption and fraud.[42]

A downside of this initiative is that the UNGC does not include within it any processes for actively engaging in the auditing, implementation of the UNGC principles or sanctions for breaches though it does require companies to submit a progress report in respect of implementing the principles. The failure to report is de-listing. This is to ensure "some solid protection against free-riding, promote ownership by participants, and offer incentives for quality improvements over time".[43] Providing implementation guidance in the form of tools and activities related to performance models is also another activity provided by the UNGC. However, the lack of policing by the UNGC has been criticized widely since it is seen as enabling companies to "bluewash" their shortcomings with the UN's name.[44] If, in order to meet these criticisms, greater policing and penalties other than de-listing are introduced then it moves from being a voluntary scheme to a more regulated (voluntary) scheme, thus inching closer towards regulation. While there are strong arguments for such an approach the arguments made for the futility of regulation remains. Ensuring compliance through policing of voluntary schemes can be expensive in financial and effort terms and hence unlikely to be followed through satisfactorily.

Another initiative is from the International Chamber of Commerce (ICC). The ICC was the first organisation, in response to developments in the US in the 1970s, to formulate good commercial practice in relation to bribery in 1977 with its Rules on Extortion and Bribery. These Rules were amended in 2005 and then in 2011 when they were published as the Rules on Combating Corruption.[45] In brief, they prohibit bribery and extortion,

---

41 This is an independent not-for-profit organization initiated by South Africa to facilitate the development and implementation of ethics codes and assist in ethics code training. See www.ethicsa.org (accessed 1 June 2009).

42 See The Global Compact Regional Learning Forum, 'Creating a Culture Intolerant of Fraud and Corruption in Total South Africa (PTY Ltd)' in *Businesses Fighting Corruption: Experiences from Africa* (2007) available at http://www.unglobalcompact.org/docs/news_events/8.1/bfc_web.pdf (accessed 1 March 2010).

43 United Nations Global Compact 'Global Compact Governance' 19 February 2008, available at http://www.unglobalcompact.org/docs/about_the_gc/governance_update2008.pdf (accessed 1 March 2010).

44 Guy Standing, 'Decent Workplaces, Self-Regulation and CSR: From Puff to Stuff', DESA Working Paper No. 62 ST/ESA/2007/DWP/62 (2007), available at http://www.un.org/esa/desa/papers/2007/wp62_2007.pdf (accessed on 1 March 2010).

45 Text available at http://www.iccwbo.org/uploadedFiles/ICC/policy/business_in_society/Statements/ICC_Rules_on_Combating_Corruption_2011edition.pdf (accessed 1 November 2011).

be they direct or indirect, and the indirect acts of bribery and extortion cover not only the acts of agents (the usual indirect means of engaging in bribery) but other intermediaries who may act as a conduit such as consultants, lawyers and accountants. Facilitation payments are permitted only if a managerial review indicates that they cannot be eliminated.[46] If facilitation payments are to be made they should be small and paid to low level officials for actions that are routinely undertaken. Businesses are also expected not to cloak bribery as charitable payments.[47] The importance of training employees and the extension of the code to subsidiaries besides appropriate accounting and auditing standards are also advocated by these Rules. They also promote in Part III the implementation of "an efficient Corporate Compliance Programme (i) reflecting these Rules, (ii) based on the results of a periodically conducted assessment of the risks faced in the Enterprise's business environment, (iii) adapted to the Enterprise's particular circumstances and (iv) with the aim of preventing and detecting Corruption and of promoting a culture of integrity in the Enterprise".[48] The ICC also strengthens the business integrity of companies by promoting the protection of whistleblowers through its Guidelines on Whistleblowing.[49]

Besides the above there are a number of other initiatives such as those from Transparency International (TI).[50] In partnership with other

---

[46] This is in response to the Anti-Bribery Convention which does not requiring member states to criminalise facilitation payments. This means that bribes can be passed off as facilitation payments. Subsequent pressure from various quarters including the ICC resulted in a change. The OECD in its Recommendations of the Council for Further Combating Bribery adopted in 2009 now states in paragraph VI:

> "[I]n view of the corrosive effect of small facilitation payments, particularly on sustainable economic development and the rule of law that member countries should:
> (i) undertake to periodically review their policies and approach on small facilitation payments in order to effectively combat the phenomenon;
> ii) encourage companies to prohibit or discourage the use of small facilitation payments in internal company controls, ethics and compliance programmes or measures, recognising that such payments are generally illegal in the countries where they are made, and must in all cases be accurately accounted for in such companies' books and financial records."

[47] Most countries have special tax rules when it comes to charitable payments. If bribes are cloaked as charitable payments this means that businesses are getting a tax advantage for paying bribes!

[48] Article 10.

[49] Text available at http://www.iccwbo.org/uploadedFiles/ICC%20Guidelines%20 Whistleblowing%20%20as%20adopted%204_08(2).pdf (accessed 1 March 2010).

[50] Transparency International is a civil society organisation devoted to corruption issues. For further information visit http://www.transparency.org (accessed 1 March 2010).

stakeholders including MNCs, TI developed the Business Principles for Countering Bribery (BPCB) which was adopted in 2002. Its aim is to promote the adoption of values and practices to counter corruption in its diverse manifestations.[51] A special edition devoted to small and medium enterprises was also adopted in 2008. Socially responsible behaviour is at the core of all these initiatives.

However the above initiatives, being of a general nature, may not always be adaptable to the needs of ensuring transparency and accountability of particular sectors such as the extractive industry sector with its peculiar systems of bonus payments and royalties. In these circumstances sector specific initiatives seem a better option to provide frameworks to combat corruption. As stated earlier, transparency is seen as an important ingredient in fighting corruption and it is this feature that is promoted by the EITI. It expects transparency both on the part of the companies operating in the extractive industries sector and governments. The following section firstly examines corruption in this sector and the way the EITI has been received in Azerbaijan and Nigeria.

II. Extractive Industries, the Resource Curse and Corruption

In recent times the extractive industries[52] such as oil and gas have seen growing demands driven by globalization and the needs of emerging economies such as China and India.[53] A Report, published by PricewaterhouseCoopers in 2006, highlights investor confidence in the mining sector fuelled by "sustained raise in the commodity prices".[54] During the 1950s and 1960s it was widely believed by economists that abundance of natural resources would help third world countries.[55] The story however is very different to the expectations that the presence and exploitation of natural

[51] Available at http://www.transparency.org/global_priorities/private_sector/business_principles (accessed 1 March 2010).

[52] Extractive industries is commonly understood to be related to mineral and hydrocarbon products – e.g. oil, gas, gold. The NEITI Act, for instance, in s.21 defines "extractive industry company" as "any company in Nigeria that is engaged in the business of prospecting, mining, extracting, processing and distributing minerals and gas, including oil, gold, coal, tin, bitumen, diamonds, precious stones and such like …".

[53] Harry Broadman *Africa's Silk Road: China and India's New Economic Frontier*. Washington DC, World Bank, 2007.

[54] PricewaterhouseCoopers *Mine: Let the Good Times Roll* available at http://www.pwc.com/en_UA/ua/press-room/assets/pwc_mine_2006.pdf.

[55] Joseph Spengler (ed) *Natural Resources and Growth* Washington DC: Resources for the Future, 1961.

resources create. To illustrate, the abundance of oil in Nigeria with it estimated reserves of 37,200,000,000 barrels of crude oil[56] should in theory lift it comfortably out of the poverty trap. Given the global demand for oil coupled with shortages due to civil conflict in some of the other oil producing states, the expectation for rapid growth and better standards of living for the common man in Nigeria would not be an unreasonable one. Studies however indicate that over time Nigeria has witnessed an enormous increase rather than a decrease in poverty.[57] And, Nigeria is not alone in this. There are other natural resource rich countries that have been unable to lift themselves out of poverty such as Angola.[58] It is almost as if the natural resources of a country create economic stagnation and this inverse relationship between natural resources wealth and poverty levels is often termed the "resource curse". This resource curse phenomenon has been widely studied by economists since the 1970s. A number of explanations are offered for the low economic growth in resource rich developing countries. These range from the unpredictability of commodity prices[59] to the dominance of the extractive industries by foreign entities (MNCs) which would see a flight of capital rather than reinvestment in the local economy.[60] While there is some truth in both of these assertions, the stand taken in the 1970s by the Organisation of the Petroleum Exporting Countries (OPEC) in raising prices and lowering oil production indicated that trading terms for natural resources such as oil and gas might improve.[61] The 1980s and 1990s saw new developments with structural adjustment programmes to fuel economic growth and liberalization in the extractive sector. However, this period also saw the end of the Cold War and the Asian financial crisis which resulted in commodity prices

---

[56] https://www.cia.gov/library/publications/the-world-factbook/rankorder/2178rank.html (accessed 10 January 2012).

[57] See I.J. Okpe. and G.A. Abu, G.A. 'Foreign Private Investment and Poverty Reduction in Nigeria (1975–2003)' *Journal of Social Sciences* 19(3) 2009: 205–211; J.S Omotola. Combating Poverty for Sustainable Human Development in Nigeria: The Continuing Struggle. *Journal of Poverty*, 12(4) (2008): 496–517.

[58] See for example on Angola Theodore Hodges *Angola from Afro-Stalinism to Petro-Diamond Capitalism* Bloomington and Indianapolis: Indiana University Press, 2011.

[59] According to Ragner Nurske, 'Trade Measures and Buffer Policies of Low Income Countries' *Kyklos* 11(2) (1958); 141 the price fluctuations in the commodity markets would affect domestic economic policies.

[60] Albert O Hirschman *The Strategy of Economic Development* New Haven: Yale University Press, 1958.

[61] See Daniel Yergin *The Prize: The Epic Quest for Oil, Money, & Power* New York: Free Press, 1991.

falling sharply. Until this period the low economic growth in resource rich countries was explained on the basis of external events over which these states had no control. However since the Asian financial crisis international trade has boomed with economies such as China and India seeing a growth both in their import and export market, and the emergence of a middle class consumer base within the countries resulting in production of luxury goods such as fridges, washing machines and cars and other consumable for the domestic market. This has resulted in greater demand for fuel as well as metals such as iron ore and copper. The money being spent on exploration as indicated by the Metals Economic Groups[62] analyses also shows that the demand for commodities will grow and may indeed be difficult to sustain. Against this context why then is the resource curse still plaguing developing countries? One possible explanation to this inability to climb out of poverty seems to stem from weak state institutions and lack of public governance systems that result in corruption on the part of the political elite and officials within the public sector. The windfall from natural resources it seems almost contributes to the weakening of the existing state systems to such an extent that it operates in favour of the ruling elite and the public officials. The rentier state theory[63] is often put forward to explain the weak governance systems in a state dependent on natural resources. According to this theory where the major source of revenue for the state is from the export of natural resources members of the ruling elite do not to relate to their citizens or work towards the greater good. The political elite work towards maintaining their power through patronage and by weakening institutions that may pose a threat to their power. As Standing succinctly observes it will result in a "form of centralized government that is secretive, aggressive, paranoid and uninterested in public welfare. Such governments will plunder resource wealth for their own ends, and not use for the public good".[64] The long term consequence of relying on natural resource is that other areas of the economy such as

[62] Further details on exploration strategies and trends are available at http://metalseconomics.com (accessed 1 January 2012).

[63] This theory was put forward by Hossein Mahdavy 'The Patterns and Problems of Economic Development in Rentier States: The Case of Iran' in M.A.Cook (ed) *Studies in Economic History: The Middle East* Oxford: OUP, 1970; Douglas A Yates *The Rentier State in Africa: Oil Rent Dependency and Neocolonialism in the Republic of Gabon* Trenton, NJ: Africa World Press, 1996.

[64] André Standing *Corruption and the Extractive Industries in Africa* ISS Paper 153, October 2007, 4.

manufacturing or agriculture are likely to remain under developed and may also result in a negative impact on the social status of women.[65]

Opportunities for corrupt payments in extractive industries start from the exploration stage and continue through production and refinement stages. The practice in extractive industries of payments, for instance, through bonuses (payments to the government of the state for signing contracts for exploration and production, attainment of production levels) and royalties (payments which are levied as a percentage of production of oil or gas) provides ample scope opportunities for illegal payments and embezzlement of funds especially where the payments are not transparent and normally subject to confidentiality clauses. Against this background it make sense to infuse transparency to prevent corruption and expose it where it is present. This is the aim of the EITI.

III. Extractive Industries Transparency Initiative (EITI)

The EITI was adopted in 2003[66] and endorsed by the World Bank and the International Monetary Fund. It is a global coalition of companies, civil

---

[65] According to Michael Ross

> "Many of the predictions of modernization theory were accurate: for the last five decades, increases in income have been strongly correlated with improvements in female welfare ...Yet this pattern fails to hold for states whose economies are based on the extraction of oil and gas – not only in much of the Middle East, but in mineral-rich countries like Azerbaijan, Botswana, Chile, Gabon, Mauritania, Nigeria, and Russia, where female labor force participation and female political representation are lower than we would expect simply based on their income levels.
>
> I suggest this is because economic growth only triggers the social and political transformations we call "modernization" when large numbers of women move out of household work and into the formal market for nonagricultural wage labor – a process that typically occurs through the development of export-oriented manufacturing industries. Oil and gas production tends to crowd out these industries, shutting women out of the labor force. Economic growth that is propelled by oil and gas extraction hence tends to retard social, cultural, and political modernization. [o]il and gas production tends to crowd out these industries, shutting women out of the labor force. Economic growth that is propelled by oil and gas extraction hence tends to retard social, cultural, and political modernization. See 'Oil and Patriarchy' 2006, UCLA Paper, 3 available at http://www.international.ucla.edu/cms/files/ross.pdf (accessed 1 January 2012).

[66] For more information on EITI visit http://www.eiti.org (accessed 1 Mach 2010). The EITI's international secretariat is based in Oslo. The text of the EITI Principles and Criteria are available at http://eiti.org/eiti/principles (accessed 1 March 2010). The EITI was preceded by a movement involving a coalition of around 190 non-governmental organisations calling for transparency in payments made by corporations to host states called Publish What You Pay (http://www.publishwhatyoupay.org, accessed 1 March 2010). It was Tony Blair, the British Prime Minister, who is credited with the establishment of the EITI aimed at transparency relating to financial payment by both companies and host states.

society, donor agencies, investors and developing countries who are resource rich. Under this initiative all payments made by the oil, gas and mining companies to the government have to be published. The government is also to publish the revenues received. To become an EITI candidate a state has to provide detailed work plans together with relevant documentation to indicate how it is going to become EITI compliant. The validation process is a necessary step in achieving EITI compliant status which indicates achievement of a global standard. This process of validation is conducted by an independent validator chosen by the multi-stakeholders.

Azerbaijan

The Government of Azerbaijan has supported the EITI right from its launch and in 2003 indicated its readiness to participate in the initiative.[67] Its implementation is overseen by the National Committee on EITI.[68] With the launch, a Memorandum of Understanding (MOU)[69] was prepared and signed by the country's government, the extractive companies operating in the country[70] and the civil society representatives. The MOU sets down the rules to be followed by the signatories when conducting an audit for the purposes of disclosure of revenues.[71] The disclosure, made through a report,[72] is publically available.[73]

---

[67] http://www.eiti-az.org/ts_gen/eng/eiti/eng_eiti1.htm (accessed 1 January 2012).

[68] This body was established by Cabinet of Ministers Decision No. 224, headed by the chair of the State Oil Fund of the Republic of Azerbaijan (SOFAZ). For more information on SOFAZ and its objectives visit http://www.oilfund.az/en_US (accessed 20 December 2011).

[69] Memorandum of Understanding on Extractive Industries Transparency Initiative Implementation in Azerbaijan, available at http://www.eiti.az/en/doc/1 (accessed 11 February 2012).

[70] The participating companies are BP Exploration (Caspian Sea) Limited, State Oil Company of the Azerbaijan Republic, Total E&P Azerbaijan B.V, ITOCHU Oil Exploration (Azerbaijan) Inc., Statoil, TPAO, Commonwealth Oil and Gas, Exxon Azerbaijan Limited, ConocoPhillips, Amerada Hess (ACG) Limited, Energy Caspian Corporation, Lukoil Overseas, Chevron, Petro-HongKong-Pirsaat Oil Limited, Salyan Oil, Karasu Operating Company, Shell Azerbaijan Exploration and Production, Middle East Petroleum, Anshad Petrol JV, Shirvan Oil JV, Azgerneft JV, Inpex, Binagadi Oil Company, Rafi Oil F.Z.E, Naftiran Intertrade Co. (NICO) Limited, and Apsheron Investments Ltd.

[71] A copy of the Memorandum of Understanding can be obtained from the EITI at http://eitransparency.org/UserFiles/File/azerbaijanreports/azerbaijanmou.pdf (accessed 15 December 2011).

[72] Ibid p 2.

[73] Available on SOFAZ http://www.oilfund.az/index.php?page=hesabat-arxivi&hl=en _US and on EITI http://www.eiti.az/en/account/ (both accessed 11 February 2012).

The validation process took place in 2009 in two stages. The preparatory phase involved consultation of the documentation[74] for the EITI process,[75] discussion about methodology with EITI, collection of confidential submissions from all stakeholders and self assessment forms from companies.[76] The second phase involved meetings with the Azerbaijani Working Group[77] where views and feedback were collected from each stakeholder group. Based on these a Report[78] was published which on subsequent approval by the EITI gave Azerbaijan compliant status.[79]

It seems that the process of achieving compliant status may be flexible based on the Azerbaijan validation report. For instance, at the time of the validation, Azerbaijan did not have a Work Plan,[80] one of the requirements in the implementation and validation process.[81] The absence of this document is crucial since the validator has nothing against which the achievements can be reviewed. The EITI seems to have accepted the argument put forward by Azerbaijan that the MOU was a document similar to the Work Plan since it presented the key stages. It must however be said that despite the similarities the MOU omits some vital components. One of these elements is the timetable for implementation. Admittedly, while Azerbaijan did manage to fulfil the implementation requirements within the two year phase the MOU made no mention of the timetable.

---

[74] The documents included the MOU and the revenue reports that had been published by the EITI Azerbaijan. A full list of all reports published by Azerbaijan since the country published its first report in 2003 as a Candidate country in preparation for Validation process is available at http://www.eiti.az/en/account/ (accessed 11 February 2012).

[75] The Validation team was composed of a representative from Coffey International Development (international development consultants), a consultant from IPAN (International Petroleum Associates Norway) and a representative from PKF (a firm of accountants and business advisers).

[76] A copy of the Company forms can be found in Annex 2 of *Validation of the EITI in the Republic of Azerbaijan* at http://eiti.org/files/Azerbaijan%20EITI%20Validation%20 Report.pdf (accessed 24 December 2011).

[77] The Working Group consisted of representatives from the civil society (NGOs), government and company representatives. For a full list of those consulted see 'EITI Validation Report of the Republic of Azerbaijan', available http://eiti.org/document/Azerbaijan2009 Validation (accessed 11 February 2012).

[78] The Validator used the *EITI Validation Guide and Assessment Tools* http://eiti.org/ files/document/validationguide.pdf (accessed 12 February 2012) to compile the Report.

[79] Revalidation is scheduled to take place in 2014.

[80] A country work plan is a document which contains a public, financially sustainable work plan, including measurable targets, a timetable for implementation and an assessment of potential capacity constraints.

[81] The Indicator Assessment Tool for this indicator states that the Work Plan is the foundation of the country validation process. A key element of the country validation process is whether the timetable for implementation is being followed.

Neither was there any indication in the MOU of how the country planned to pay for the validation, an item which would have been addressed in the Work Plan. The need for a Work Plan cannot be overemphasised since it enables both the government and civil society to develop adequate plans and schemes for realisation of clearly structured aims. These include publication of reports, the time frame for publication and improvement in reporting styles.[82] Interestingly the Work Plan was finally agreed in 2010 which suggests that the argument that MOU was sufficient is a weak argument. Then why did the EITI approve the validation of Azerbaijan despite the absence of a Work Plan? The answer perhaps is simply a pragmatic one in that the EITI Secretariat wanted to get the EITI established by having its first compliant state. If this is a possible explanation then it does raise questions about the seriousness and weight of the EITI processes.

Besides the lack of the Work Plan, Azerbaijan delayed establishing the Multi-Stakeholder Group (MSG). It came into existence only after the Validation.[83] If participating governments are permitted deviation by the EITI Validation team the potential to undermine the entire purpose and effectiveness of the EITI is great. This is also not helped by the EITI's dependence on donations from the private sector.

Azerbaijan, so far, has disclosed 14 aggregated reports.[84] Being aggregated, information regarding the payments made by the companies operating within the country and the money received by the State is not broken down. This inevitably makes it impossible to trace any particular manipulations in revenues and payments.[85] Despite various suggestions by civil society, both the Government and certain companies remain adamantly opposed to switching to disaggregated reporting.

---

82 It should be mentioned that perhaps the main reason behind the waiver of the Work Plan was the fact that Azerbaijan started and developed the EITI process and published the reports prior to the EITI Validation guide being published. Taking into consideration the fact that Azerbaijan was one of the first countries to have the EITI implementation experience, it was agreed that certain allowances could be made.

83 Currently the MSG consists of 9 principal members and 3 substitutive members. The MSG comprises of representatives of the parties signatories to the MOU (civil society, government of Azerbaijan and extractive companies). Each group appoints 3 equal in rights principal members and 1 substitute member. Full text of the agreement on the establishment of the MSG in Azerbaijan can be found at www.oilfund.az/pub/tiny_upload/MSG_document_eng.pdf (accessed 10 February 2012).

84 Available at http://www.eiti.az/en/account/ (accessed 11 February 2012).

85 In government reporting, for example, when only the aggregated amount of revenue received from all companies operating in the country is shown, it is difficult to trace how much each participating company paid and for what. For the purposes of fighting corruption, it is important to identify whether an extra, unaccountable sum of money was paid by a company, for instance, to secure a certain contract.

The practice of contractual confidential clauses between the state and the extractive companies was expected to pose a problem for EITI implementation. There is however a communication from the State Oil Company of Azerbaijan (SOCAR),[86] stating that disclosure of the information about the payments does not contradict the confidentiality provisions of the agreements concluded between companies and the Republic of Azerbaijan.[87] This statement is of limited impact since it does not make the disclosure of information protected by confidentiality clauses immediately available. It merely makes it possible should the parties to the contract wish to disclose it.

The validation process in Azerbaijan has certainly exposed many theoretical[88] as well as practical issues. In so doing it leaves scope for improvements. However the EITI's voluntary nature does not make it easy to impose various conditions on the implementing Governments since it raises the spectre of non-participation by states. The EITI implementation process has also revealed that a lot of the work has been bestowed upon the MSG in Azerbaijan to regulate the implementation process and that at times too much time is spent on negotiations between the stakeholders, resulting in no substantial decision making.

The practical experience of Azerbaijan demonstrates that despite the fact that the country has been a compliant country for almost three years now, and has been publishing revenue reports on a regular basis, many questions still remain unanswered and the information provided by the reports is not sufficient enough to provide a clear picture of the revenues. Furthermore, some believe that after the validation, Azerbaijan has entered a period of stagnation in its implementation of EITI.[89]

---

[86] Communication No. 01-44/832 on 18 November 2004. The text of this document is taken from *EITI Validation Report of the Republic of Azerbaijan* available at http://eiti.org/document/Azerbaijan2009Validation (accessed 12 February 2012).

[87] The communication states that "Disclosure of the information about the payments constitutes a part of implementation of EITI…and it does not contradict the confidentiality provisions of the agreements concluded between your Company or Joint Company and the Republic of Azerbaijan".

[88] EITI does not provide any monitoring mechanism, thus leaving participants to their own devices. In most cases the civil society representatives try and persuade the government and the companies to formulate and follow strict rules of reporting. The EITI rules and criteria also do not provide concrete guidelines for reporting mechanisms, only templates that are selected randomly. The EITI rules and criteria therefore allow too much freedom of choice to implementing parties in terms of structure of their reports.

[89] Gubad Ibadoglu, 'Extractive Industries Transparency Initiative in Azerbaijan: Retrospective Review', available at http://www.azerbaijantoday.az/ARCHIVE/31/economics35.html (accessed 27 December 2011).

Nigeria

Nigeria achieved compliant status in 2011.[90] Interestingly Nigeria took the unusual step of implementing the EITI with a statute, the Nigeria Extractive Industries Transparency Initiative Act 2007 (NEITIA).[91] Nigeria is the first and only state to take such a step.

The Nigeria Extractive Industries Transparency Initiative (NEITI) is a self-accounting body under the Act with powers to sue and be sued which reports to the President and the National Assembly (section 1). Its objectives are to ensure due process and transparency in the payments made by extractive industries to government authorities, to monitor and ensure accountability in the revenue receipts of the Federal Government and to eliminate all forms of corruption in the "determination, payments, receipts and posting of revenue accruing to the Federal Government from extractive industries companies (section 2 (a) – (c)). Ensuring conformity with the principles of EITI is also a task of the NEITI (section 2(e)). The functions of the NEITI are set out in section 3 and these include (1) the development of a "framework for transparency and accountability" in the reporting and disclosure of revenues paid by the companies and (2) ensuring "transparency and accountability in the management of the investment of the Federal Government in all extractive industry companies". The NEITIA also has extensive provisions on the appointment of independent auditors and publication of reports (section 4) and the establishment of the National Stakeholders Working Group (NSWG) in section 5. The NSWG is a multi-stakeholder group that includes representative from civil society, labour unions and experts from the extractive industries (section 6(2)). The NSWG is imparted with a number of powers which include constituting special committees and engaging the services of consultants (sections 11 & 12). The publication of annual reports on the total revenue that has accrued to the Federal Government by independent auditors is a function expected of the EITI (section 14). An interesting aspect of the NEITIA is the creation of offences and penalties. These offences relate to giving of false information in respect of volume of production, sales and income (section 16(1)(a), rendering a false statement of account or failing to render a statement of account to the Federal Government (section 16(1)(b)) by an extractive industry company.

---

90 It is to be revalidated in 2016. Details of the two phases that Nigeria underwent are not given here since the section on Azerbaijan provides the details of the processes.

91 The NEITI Act is available at http://www.neiti.org.ng/files-pdf/neitiact.pdf (accessed 1 February 2012).

Penalties for these offences, on conviction, are N30,000,000. Failure or delay by an extractive industry to give information also attracts a penalty of N30,000,000. The Director and others associated with the management are also made personally liable where the extractive industry commits an offence and the penalty is a minimum of two years imprisonment or a fine of N50,000,000 (section 16(5)) unless he can show that the offence was committed without his consent or connivance, or he exercised such diligence expected of him taking into account the nature of his functions in the company and other relevant circumstances. Equally section 16(6) creates offences for a government (public) official who renders false statements or fails to render a statement of account. Again a defence is allowed which reflects the defence allowed to directors in section 16(5). Under the Act the President also has the power to revoke operational licences for failure to perform its obligations under the Act on the recommendation of the NSWG (section 16(4)).

The first set of audits for the period 1999–2004 published a number of flaws in the way the oil revenues in Nigeria were being managed. Areas identified for improvement included "revenue-flow interface between government agencies" and governance generally in the sector. A report released in 2009 for the year 2005 identified further weaknesses including financial discrepancies, and differences between what the companies said they had paid as taxes and what the state said they had received. Discrepancies were also identified in respect of bonuses and royalties paid. A third report covering the period 2006–2008 was published more recently in 2011 and a number of recommendations are made by this Report.[92] These include greater collection of relevant data on a regular basis by NEITI for facilitation of the audit process, better engagement with companies by NEITI in order to obtain an understanding of the way the companies operate so that the process of reconciliation[93] can take place sooner; and ensuring that all signature bonuses (bonus paid on signing) assessed and collected by the Department of Petroleum Resources are fully disclosed and confirmation by relevant appropriate agencies that these are received by the respective bank accounts.

---

92 *Nigeria Extractive Industries Transparency Initiative (NEITI) 2006–2008 Financial Report* available at http://www.neiti.org.ng/documents/neiti-2006-2008-reports-final-january-30-2012 (accessed 1 February 2012).

93 Reconciliation in auditing speak refers to a comparison of different sets of data in order to identify and investigate the differences and, if necessary, taking appropriate corrective action, to resolve the differences.

Even to the eyes of the non-experts like the authors of this paper a reading of the annual report makes the discrepancies in the figures as stated, for instance in relation to bonuses, by the companies and the government departments obvious.

Azerbaijan and Nigeria Compared

If Azerbaijan and Nigeria are compared what stands out is that by enveloping the EITI principles in a statute and creating offences and prescribing penalties for defaulting companies, their managers, and government officials Nigeria seems to have given EITI teeth. The question however is "are these the teeth of a real tiger or those of a paper tiger?". It is dependent on a number of factors: (1) willingness of the various stakeholders to follow the transparency principles with determination, (2) the availability of adequate resources to enable the NEITI to function efficiently; and (3) availability of experts who can meaningfully engage with the data and understand the causal links between the data provided by the companies and the state.

The next few years will be educative to assess the impact of the NEITIA and the NEITI in Nigeria. This depends on internal and external factors. Internally, will the NEITI see its role as a result-oriented one? Or, is it going to be driven by (negative) external conditions within the country? If it is the latter then intentions, however well-meant, will fizzle out such that it is yet another body lacking meaningful engagement. Its goal of achieving its objectives requires the necessary will and independence to follow the powers given to it under the Act. Given that the NEITI reports to the President it is left open to interference by the government of the day. The effectiveness of the NEITI is therefore strongly linked to how seriously Nigeria is willing to engage with combating corruption within the country.

As for Azerbaijan, it seems in the absence of the kind of structure provided by the NEITI the companies are still unwilling to engage in the process fully and the Multi Stakeholder Working Group (MSG) is not that effective in reaching decisions. This raises a number of questions, general and specific: "Do resource rich countries adopt these initiatives under pressure from the World Bank and developed nations since it may be tied in some way to aid or political backing from powerful Western countries?", "Can a culture of transparency emerge solely by relentless hectoring?" "Does the choice of the stakeholders in the MSG contribute to the success of the EITI?", "Do the auditors and the MSG have enough time and resources to delve deeply into the information and figures offered to them?" or "Is the success of any anti-corruption initiative closely linked to the presence of political will within a state to counter corruption?".

The experience in Azerbaijan suggests that the EITI processes are not that robust. There has been some attempt to study the effectiveness of the EITI with the recently published Evaluation Report by EITI.[94] It analyses the experiences of some of the countries that have been accepted either as candidate countries or have undergone the validation process. It has also set up a Strategy Working Group (SWG), where task is to look into the issues raised by the Report. There are however some issues both with the Report and the SWG. In methodological terms the Report is based on the country reports and documents provided by three countries', (Mongolia, Gabon and Nigeria) representatives. The Report however does not provide a list or copies of the reports which were analysed for the study. Neither are samples of questions asked of the interviewees provided. The structure and objectives of the newly initiated SWG are rather broad and unclear. There is no indication on what basis the current composition of the group was chosen.[95] The objectives of the SWG are to examine options and to make recommendations as to the EITI's future directions but it does not seem to have a clear methodology as to how this examination will take place apart from stating that it will be based on the abovementioned Report. There is insufficient material in the Report to also answer the questions that were posed in the previous paragraph.

Conclusion

This paper examined the developments in relation to corruption in general and in specific within the extractive industries sector. In general terms the fight against corruption through regulation and self-regulation is now fifteen years old. Of the self-regulatory measures, some are sector specific. The EITI is one of these. While it is felt we are making some progress due to high profile cases in the media it is misplaced. The progress is negligible since corruption continues to be a global problem.

---

94 'Evaluation of the EITI, 2011', (2011) Extractive Industries Transparency Initiative, http://eiti.org/document/2011-evaluation-report (accessed 10 February 2012).

95 For a list of SWG participants see 'EITI Board Paper 18–10'(18th EITI Board Meeting, Jakarta 2011) available at http://eiti.org/about/strategy-working-group (accessed 1 February 2012).

As to whether the EITI has the potential to put an end to the culture of corruption through transparency is highly debatable due to the voluntary nature of the initiative. The experience in Azerbaijan seems to indicate that the private sector and the government are still unwilling to provide certain types of information for there to be transparency in real terms. The Nigerian approach, with its regulatory flavour looks more promising but any fight against corruption requires political will. Where the ruling elite stand to gain it requires a fundamental value shift amongst them. Equally we need a sea change in core corporate values and a realisation on their part that their behaviour is causing untold misery to billions in the world. Obviously these victims are faceless but their facelessness does not make them less of a victim. All that the executive management of an oil company has to do is to walk in the countless slums in developing countries with a conscience and they will come face to face with the hitherto faceless victims. The countries where the multinationals are located also need to do more in enforcing their anti-corruption laws instead of turning a blind eye to the needs of the global poor through the provision of aid in the belief that they are contributing to relieving poverty.

INDEX